C0-AGW-704

STUDIES IN HISTORY, ECONOMICS AND PUBLIC LAW

Edited by the
FACULTY OF POLITICAL SCIENCE
OF COLUMBIA UNIVERSITY

NUMBER 455

THE RISE OF INTEGRAL NATIONALISM IN FRANCE

BY

WILLIAM CURT BUTHMAN

THE RISE OF INTEGRAL NATIONALISM IN FRANCE

With Special Reference to the Ideas and Activities of

CHARLES MAURRAS

BY

WILLIAM CURT BUTHMAN

1970

OCTAGON BOOKS

New York

Reprinted 1970
by special arrangement with Columbia University Press

OCTAGON BOOKS
A DIVISION OF FARRAR, STRAUS & GIROUX, INC.
19 Union Square West
New York, N. Y. 10003

LIBRARY OF CONGRESS CATALOG CARD NUMBER: 78-120239

To

My Wife
ERMA GUICE BUTHMAN

PREFACE

THIS study was undertaken to portray the rise of integral nationalism in France and to explain its nature. This dual purpose naturally necessitated the joining of analysis and historical narrative, a procedure that is beset with difficulties even for skilled and experienced writers, not to mention those who lack these attributes. In order to designate and clarify the elements that were brought together to form this nationalism, labels were used that may well be open to objection, as, for example, "Drumontism." These "isms" were used, not in the sense that they severally constituted complete systems of thought, nor in the sense that all of the thought of the person in question was taken over *in toto* by the nationalist theorists, but to suggest the borrowing of this or that point with which the name given is definitely associated or identified by the artificers of the nationalist theory. It was assumed that our objective did not require a full-dress criticism of the doctrines considered, since the purpose was to explain rather than to denounce. Occasionally questions are raised which will doubtless appear to the reader before he comes to them. Many doubts of the reader will perhaps not be mentioned at all, for, as has been stated, this was not conceived to be a criticism of integral nationalism.

If the given aim has been partially realized, if indeed this volume has any value at all, it should be ascribed to others. The author is particularly grateful to the General Education Board and to the Columbia University Council for Research in the Social Sciences for their generous material aid; to Madame Charlotte Muret of Barnard College for her helpful suggestions and letters of introduction; to Dr. Robert L. Campbell of Hendrix College for a critical reading of much of the manuscript; to President J. H. Reynolds of Hendrix College for encouragement and helpfulness in many ways; to Dr. Jacques Barzun of Columbia College for the prevention of many errors in both the French and English texts and for numerous helpful suggestions and criticisms; and, above all, to Professor Carlton

J. H. Hayes of Columbia University for his inspiring teaching, his encouragement, guidance, and genuine helpfulness, without which this particular study would never have been undertaken or completed. The writer is likewise grateful to the attendants of the Columbia University Library, of the New York City Library, and of the Bibliothèque Nationale for the unfailing efficiency and courtesy with which they met and filled his numerous demands.

For mistakes of fact, errors of judgment or interpretation, and other shortcomings of this work the author is, of course, solely responsible.

CONWAY, ARKANSAS,
JANUARY 1, 1939.

TABLE OF CONTENTS

PART I

FACTORS IN THE DEVELOPMENT OF FRENCH INTEGRAL NATIONALISM

"Comme eux [Montaigne, Pascal, le duc de Saint-Simon], il [Barrès] cultivait son moi dans le mystère, et cette culture précieuse lui révélait aussi la valeur du reste du monde. Il se sentait 'l'instant d'une chose immortelle.' Les sillons de Lorraine, les campagnes de France, les charniers de l'humanité tout entière se peuplaient de mânes et d'ombres qui lui révélaient ses devoirs.

Il était déjà dégoûté de l'anarchie.

Quelques opportunistes ou radicaux qu'il approcha ou fréquenta le dégoûtèrent tout autant des masques adaptés au visage de l'anarchie républicaine. Un nouveau parti se formait, national, militaire et autoritaire, le parti boulangiste. Barrès en fut et, lorsque ce premier parti fut dissous, il fonda le nationalisme.

Le *Figaro* de 1892 en conserve le souvenir. Depuis, il ne cessa de compléter et d'organiser sa pensée. Il faut à nos hommes de France quelque patrie particulière dans la patrie commune: c'est le thème des *Déracinés.* Il faut une 'raison qui commande dans l'Etat': c'est le thème de l'*Appel au Soldat.* Cette raison directrice doit être nationale et non cosmopolite: c'est le thème de *Leurs Figures.*

Mais comment s'y prendra Maurice Barrès pour constituer ce pouvoir central, pour le maintenir essentiellement et nécessairement dans le plan de l'utilité nationale? On le lui demandait l'été dernier [1900] dans l'*Enquête sur la Monarchie,* que publiait la *Gazette de France.*

Or, Barrès n'a pas répondu:—Par la royauté.

C'est mon scandale, Barrès n'est pas royaliste."

CHARLES MAURRAS, "Une campagne royaliste au 'Figaro'," l'*Enquête sur la monarchie* (Paris, 1925), 491-492.

"Les Lettres nous ont conduit à la Politique par des chemins que ce livre peut jalonner, mais notre nationalisme commença par être esthétique. Il tendait à restituer à la France des avantages contestés, ou méconnus, ou négligés. Sans perdre un seul instant de vue que la raison et l'art ont pour objet l'universel, nous remettions au jour les services et les hommages rendus à la beauté et à la vérité par les hommes de sang français. Nos déductions s'étaient nourries des caractères historiques et territoriaux de la France: le pays et les races, les provinces et l'État, les archives et les légendes, l'ample trésor des idées, de la poésie et des arts. Ce patriotisme d'origine immatérielle devait en devenir le plus réaliste de tous."

CHARLES MAURRAS, *Quand les Français ne s'aimaient pas* (Paris, 1926), xiii.

CHAPTER I

NATIONAL HUMILIATION AND THE "SACRED FLAME" OF REVENGE

"FRANCE is happy, Europe may live in peace," said Napoleon III shortly before the Second Empire was proclaimed.[1] These were disquieting words despite their peaceful intent, for, if France chose to consider herself unhappy, they suggested that Europe might well be on guard. They were also a proud reminder of the days of Louis XIV and of the warlike First Napoleon, when France was pitted against the greater part of Europe. While the Third Napoleon did not call upon the French to assume so heroic a rôle, their victories in the Crimean and Italian wars gave them a taste of glory which was the more pleasing for coming after the unheroic years of the July Monarchy. Most Frenchmen believed their armies to be the best in Europe. Furthermore, the rapidly increasing prosperity of the nation, the resulting brilliance of the exposition of 1867, the splendor of the court, and the beautification of Paris under the direction of Haussmann gave an impression of power and grandeur which was well-nigh convincing, even to Europe. Then, too, the supposedly disinterested and altruistic foreign policy of the "crowned dreamer," his apparent adherence to the principle of self-determination, enveloped the grandeur of the régime with a sort of moral halo.[2]

1 Quoted by Ernest Dimnet, *France Herself Again* (New York and London, 1914), 7; *cf.* J. H. Robinson and C. A. Beard, *Readings in Modern European History* (Boston, 1909), II, 91.

2 French nationalists of the "integral" school hold Napoleon III responsible for the unification of Italy and Germany. See Charles Maurras, *Gazette de France*, Jan. 15, 1900, found in *Dictionnaire politique et critique* (hereafter cited as D. P. & C.), articles of Maurras selected and assembled by Pierre Chardon in five volumes (Paris, 1932-1933), III, 150; also Ernest Dimnet, *op. cit.*, 10. Napoleon III's liberal nationalism, despite his interest in Poland and Rumania, was not free from the taint of opportunism. It was useful in the peaceful annexation of Nice and Savoy by plebiscite in 1860. In 1866 he instituted his *pourboire* policy. In 1870, in a letter to Rouher, he

The disenchantment caused by the humiliating defeat at the hands of *arriviste* Prussia and her German allies was the more complete, therefore, for having been administered by only a small and hitherto relatively unimportant part of Europe. How far France had fallen since the proud days of Louis XIV and Napoleon I! Instead of conquering or at least holding at bay the greater part of Europe, she had made a frantic, but fruitless, appeal for allies; she had made an abject and tearful plea for the retention of Belfort and had accepted its humiliating *quid pro quo,* the triumphal entry of the victor's soldiers into her capital city; she had likewise submitted to a " mutilation," if not a complete " polonisation," which was destined to keep the memory of these evil days alive. France was certainly not happy now; but the peace of Europe remained unbroken by a major war for forty-three years despite the proud dictum of Napoleon III noted above.

That this was so was not the fault of French patriots. The France that had suffered " diminution " now became the object of a fervent love and sympathetic devotion such as she had never been in happier days. *Revanche* became the " sovereign ideal " of many Frenchmen, even of some who had cherished the dream of a greater *patrie*. Renan back in the '50's had criticized French literature of the 17th century as being " too exclusively French " and as one that would suffer at the hands of a coming criticism whose *patrie* was the " human spirit "; [3] prior to the war he is quoted as having said, " If God and free will are empty words, patriotism is even more empty "; [4] and during the siege of Paris he is said to have scandalized a company of intellectuals by remarking that the sentiment of the *patrie* was natural in antiquity, that Catholicism had taken the place of the fatherland and that idealism had inherited the place

wrote these strange words: " Il faut se placer hardiment *sur le terrain des nationalités. Il importe d'établir à présent qu'il n'existe point de nationalité belge,* et de fixer ce point essentiel avec la Prusse" [Henri Hauser, *Le Principe des nationalités* (Paris, 1916) 26].

3 *Essais de morale et de critique,* 4th ed. (Paris, 1889), 34.

4 Ernest Dimnet, *op. cit.,* 18-19.

of Catholicism, that "idealists ought to disdain the miserable ethnographic ties that bind them to the soil of the fatherland," and that "he was unable to feel any of the moral indignation with which foreign domination filled patriotic hearts." [5] But in 1871 the same Renan admitted in his *La Réforme intellectuelle et morale* that his dream of an intellectual, moral, and political alliance between France and Germany had been smashed and that an abyss had been created that centuries would not fill.[6] "Those even," he now said, "who are philosophers before being patriots, cannot be insensible to the cry of two million men whom we were obliged to throw into the sea in order to save the rest from drowning, but who were bound to us for life and for death. France, therefore, has a point of steel embedded in her flesh which will no longer let her sleep." [7] Prussia had taken sixty-three years to get revenge for Jena; France, he counseled, should take at least twenty years to avenge Sedan.[8] Since the victory of the Germans had been one of science, reason, and of the old régime,[9] he suggested that France prepare for the day of vengeance by restoring the monarchy and to a certain extent the aristocracy, that she establish a national system of elementary and higher education, that she make this education more rugged and demand compulsory military service of all, that the French be more serious and submissive to regulation and discipline, and, above all, that they be more humble and distrustful of presumption.[10] Such was the reaction of one of the outstanding leaders of French

5 J. E. C. Bodley, *Cardinal Manning, The Decay of Idealism in France, The Institute of France* (London, 1912), 88; reported by Edmont de Goncourt in his journal of 1870 and published in 1890. Renan denied ever having made the statement. Bodley: "It is likely enough that he did say something about idealism being the successor of Catholicism, as this suggestion is found in his works."

6 (Paris, 1872), v.

7 *Ibid.*, 59.

8 *Ibid.*, 65.

9 *Ibid.*, 55.

10 *Ibid.*, 65.

thought, one who looked upon patriotism with contempt and who still regarded it as " contrary to the moral and philosophical influence " which he prized so highly.[11] He, too, shared the widespread passion for *revanche* even though he had perceived in German culture the future of civilization.[12]

Clericals, as well as philosophical freethinkers, were inspired by the " sacred flame." The war had been a two-fold defeat for them: a defeat of Catholicism as well as of France.[13] While they, no doubt, shared the general desire for peace in 1871 in opposition to the intransigent attitude of Gambetta and his friends, they also felt the sting of injured pride and were particularly angered by the early measures of Bismarck in Prussia that foreshadowed the coming *Kulturkampf*. When, after the fall of Thiers in May, 1873, they had considerable political power, the Ultramontanes gave to the " sacred flame " a mystic coloring by propagating the cult of the Sacred Heart. The impressive parade of the 20,000 devoted pilgrims on June 20, 1873, to the monastery of the Visitation at Paray-le-Monial, where Marie Alacoque is said to have had her visions in 1675, was a patriotic as well as a religious demonstration. " M. de Charette, late colonel of the Pontifical Zouaves," Hanotaux states, " laid on the tomb of the Saint the flag carried by his regiment at the bloody battle of Patay." [14] And the Bishop of Autun, who presided over the ceremony of the day, solemnly dedicated to the Sacred Heart of Jesus " France, our dearly loved country, with all its provinces. . . ." [15] This act of expiation was followed by another of possibly more lasting significance. Authorization of the Assembly was procured to build a temple on the heights of Montmartre which had been " watered by the blood of the first martyrs " and had been the starting point of the horrors of the Commune. This was consecrated to

11 *Ibid.*, viii.

12 *Ibid.*, vii.

13 Henri Galli, *Gambetta et l'Alsace-Lorraine* (Paris, 1911), 36.

14 *Contemporary France* (London, 1903), II, 82.

15 *Ibid.*, II, 83.

the Sacred Heart, to which, as has been noted, France had been dedicated. Begun in 1875 and completed only recently, it stands to-day in its Byzantine beauty and splendor as a memorial to the days of anguish and sorrow of the earlier post-war period: a votive offering of souls purified by national calamity.

Some there were, it is true, who for reasons of policy discouraged the ardent patriots in their hope of retribution. Paul Déroulède, who was seriously wounded by a Communard, visited as a convalescent the commander of the troops of Paris. The latter advised the fiery young patriot to leave the army and added, "You are wrong to believe in *revanche* and to imagine that some day you will fight to retake Metz and Strasbourg; our *bourgeois* conservatives and republicans will never risk that game."[16] General de Wimpffen, who had been forced to assume the inglorious rôle of accepting from the hands of von Moltke the terms of capitulation after Sedan, is said to have expressed the same opinion. Thiers, later proclaimed the "Liberator of the Country," said, "You may see the death of Herr von Bismarck, you will never see his abasement. . . ."[17] Men of affairs and men of finance opposed an adventurous policy. Few, however, would have taken the extreme position of Jules Grévy, who, in a conversation with Scheurer-Kestner, ex-representative of the Haut-Rhin, in 1871 emphatically declared that France should not think of war. "She must accept the *fait accompli*," he said. "She must renounce Alsace. Do not believe the fools who tell you the opposite and who are responsible for the fact that our misfortunes have been aggravated by a struggle without hope":[18] words that had a definitive ring "most distressing" to his visitor.

Clearly, the "fools" Grévy had in mind were Gambetta and his followers. Despite the charge of royalists and others that Gambetta "played the comedy" with revenge, that he used it simply as a means of consolidating the Republic,[19] he may be

16 Henri Galli, *op. cit.*, 29.

17 *Ibid.*, 29.

18 *Ibid.*, 28; *cf.* Charles Maurras, *Kiel et Tanger* (Paris, 1921), 268.

19 Charles Maurras, *op. cit.*, 286; *cf.* Henri Galli, *op. cit.*, i.

said to have personified it and to have been *the* "man of revenge." [20] He had been, in the second phase of the war, the "Carnot," [21] although an unsuccessful one, and the *"fou furieux,"* [22] as his royalist and moderate opponents described him; he had declared that so long as Prussia insisted upon the cession of Alsace, the war would never end; he had eloquently opposed the resolution favoring capitulation in the National Assembly at Bordeaux as a representative of the three departments that were to be surrendered and of the remaining department of Lorraine that was retained; he had also written and signed the protest of the representatives of Alsace-Lorraine. After retiring to San Sebastian for a time in a fit of disgust and discouragement, he returned to Paris and, in addition to resuming his political activities, founded the newspaper, the *République française,* with the aid of capital subscribed by friends in Alsace. Its program is not only a good definition of the idea and spirit of *revanche,* but is also a reminder of the proud statement of Napoleon III noted above. "We shall work," it says, "to put France back in a position to recover her rank, her safety, her provinces. . . . France is at the mercy of Germany. We are in a latent war; there is no more peace, neither liberty nor progress in Europe." [23] And true to its program, it became in part, at least, an organ of the annexed provinces; it published the correspondence of the con-

20 The wreath of flowers presented at his funeral by the *lycée,* Louis-le-Grand, bore the words, "A l'homme de la Revanche" (Henri Galli, *op. cit.,* 245). Mme. Juliette Adam, after noting his eclecticism in art and literature, says, "Mais en politique il n'a aucun éclectisme. Ce qu'il veut, c'est le relèvement de notre France. Nul n'a son accent, son émotion, lorsqu'il parle de nos provinces perdues. On se ferait alors hacher comme chair à pâté, petits et grands, humbles ou altiers, pour le suivre au moindre signe" [*Nos amitiés politiques avant l'abandon de la revanche* (Paris, 1908), 79].

21 Gabriel Hanotaux, *op. cit.,* II, 61: "Whatever may have been said to the contrary, Gambetta was the Carnot of this second part of the war."

22 Joachim Kühn, *Der Nationalismus im Leben der dritten Republik* (Berlin, 1920), 19; *cf.* Henri Galli, *op. cit.,* 14-15. His friends accepted the epithet with pride.

23 Henri Galli, *op. cit.,* 49.

quered cities; it featured all incidents of resistance to Germanization and applauded them.[24]

Gambetta did, apparently, permit himself to be drawn into an intrigue with Bismarck, or the " Monster," as he called him, in 1877 and 1878. He had been in Germany and had returned with the impression that the German military machine was invincible; immediate war, he thought, was therefore unwise. On the other hand, it was preëminently wise, politically, to quiet the fears of the moderates in France in the fall of 1877. He shared the " monster's " dislike of clericalism and had no love for Gontaut-Biron, French ambassador in Berlin and friend of his political foes. Bismarck, fearing the latter's influence at court, was likewise anxious to have him recalled. The Chancellor's flattering remarks concerning Gambetta personally and his seemingly veiled bid for an *entente* with France on the basis of an equilibrium and division of power on the Continent inspired in the French leader the hope of making a bargain that would restore the annexed provinces to France.[25] At any rate, he negotiated with Bismarck indirectly and very secretly through the wealthy sportsman, Henckel von Donnersmark, and to a less extent through the Italian statesman, Crispi, and von Blowitz, the *Times* correspondent at Paris. Mutual distrust prevented the meeting which both desired—at different times. The whole intrigue came to naught and was definitely over when in August, 1878, Gambetta rejected an invitation brought by von Blowitz because it was accompanied by the condition that Alsace-Lorraine be not mentioned.[26]

Gambetta had been both true and untrue to his idea of *revanche*. Hoping to restore the lost provinces to France as soon as possible, he was not averse to using peaceful means. This, however, was not in full accord with the hatred of Germany

24 Mme. Juliette Adam, *op. cit.*, 437-443: a letter from Gambetta to her, reviewing the foreign situation, dated Jan. 27, 1877.

25 Henri Galli, *op. cit.*, 157-162, 172: "Je ne serais pas revenu les mains vides," he told Joseph Reinach in 1881.

26 *Ibid.*, 179.

demanded by the idea and the spirit of *revanche*. But that the royalists should have criticized him for having made the effort was a case of the pot calling the kettle black, for they, too, had frequented the *salon* of Henckel von Donnersmark, and MacMahon had sent a special agent to Berlin in September, 1877, to assure the Chancellor that his government was one of peace and that a victory of the radicals in the approaching election would bring war.[27]

Having failed to get "*revanche*" by peaceful means, Gambetta now ignored his own famous *mot,* "always to think, but never to speak of it." [28] In 1879 he sketched a program that called for the quest of aid and allies, the perfecting of French armaments, the patriotic and civic education of the nation by emphasizing the virtue of sacrifice and adding oil to the "sacred flame" by such means as placing a heavy black border around Alsace-Lorraine on the French maps of Europe, and the continuance of an authoritative government.[29] He accordingly established friendly relations with all enemies of Pan-Germanism and encouraged French patriots confidently to expect the realization of their dream. That he was their "Star of the East" is seen in the great ovation given him on July 14, 1880, by the generals who were in Paris for a flag distribution ceremony, one year before the French began to observe the day as an official national holiday. Three days later, at a banquet given the generals, his political opponents and the weak-kneed were scandalized by the menu which bore the caption, "1880-18 . . *" [30] And several weeks later at the naval review at Cherbourg he reminded Europe "of what he constantly thought" and, after affirming his passionate interest in the army, added that French hearts were beating with the purpose of counting upon the future and of knowing "if there is an immanent justice here below." [31] This "immanent justice" was defined in

27 *Ibid.*, 149-150.

28 Victor Giraud, *Les Maîtres de l'heure: Maurice Barrès* (Paris, 1918), 78.

29 Joachim Kühn, *op. cit.*, 16; *cf.* Henri Galli, *op. cit.*, 192.

30 Henri Galli, *op. cit.*, 198.

31 *Ibid.*, 199.

the following manner by the poet and patriot, Paul Déroulède: "In truth, what is this immanent justice, if not a justice of Damocles made of iron and steel, and suspended not by a thread, but by the hand of all Frenchmen over the proud head of Germany." [32] Knowing the poet's sentiments, Gambetta gave him a place on the commission of civic and patriotic instruction.

As President of the Council (Nov. 10, 1881, to Jan. 26, 1882) Gambetta appointed to the ministry of public instruction Paul Bert, the inspirer of many patriotic text-books. He took special pains with the army and created consternation among his friends when he appointed erstwhile political foes to the general staff, among them General Miribel, who had worked out a plan of mobilization for the *Seize-mai* government which was to have been used for a *coup d'état.* This, coupled with his demand for constitutional change and the *scrutin de liste,* gave meaning to the cry of the royalists, "Gambetta, c'est la guerre!" and to that of the radicals that he was aiming at another dictatorship. The early defeat of his government was, therefore, almost a foregone conclusion. Despite his eloquent plea for unity defeat came on the question of constitutional change after he had been in office only two and a half months.[33]

Gambetta had opposed France's participation in the Congress of Berlin and the ensuing Tunis expedition until, at the last moment, it appeared that Italy might take Tunis. As Prime Minister he sought to appease Italy's ire and after his defeat, in the last speech that he made in the Chamber, he argued that France would do well to let England have her way in Egypt,

32 *Ibid.,* 200.

33 On the day after his defeat Gambetta took luncheon with his most faithful friends. Here Déroulède read a poem which the events of the day before had inspired him to write. One stanza (*ibid.,* 237):

Ils ne savent donc plus que sans ta voix ardente,
La France, sans lien pour grouper son effort,
Allait périr broyée ou rester dépendante
Et qu'elle a gagné là—sublime combattante—
Tout ce trésor d'honneur dont nous vivons encore!

that France could afford to make heavy sacrifices to keep her friendship. He thus opposed Bismarck's efforts to turn French aspirations from the Vosges and the Rhine to Africa. He wanted to save French blood for the former and, accordingly, encouraged the League of Teaching, the League of Patriots, and the gymnastic and rifle societies, in their work of preparing the French people for the eventual attack. Upon joining the League of Patriots in 1882, shortly after its formation, he wrote, " so long as I have only the little end of a finger, you will never be attacked . . . You will be welcomed everywhere. Proceed! " [34]

His sudden and premature death on the last day of the year 1882 was an occasion of national mourning in which the Alsatians and Lorrainers took a prominent part. This later fact, together with the general rise of stocks listed on the French stock exchange and the whole nature of his activities, just described, suggests that Jacques Bainville was a better royalist partisan than historian when he said that Gambetta's aim had been to establish a " Republic of Bismarck." [35] Far from wishing to establish a government that would be controlled in Berlin, he wanted it to be sufficiently authoritative to prevent such control. With his masterful character,[36] he could never have become a puppet of Bismarck. For a brief period, to be sure, he was carried away by the dream of a " peaceful *revanche* "; but, once disillusioned, his behavior was most gratifying to the integral *revanchards*. Déroulède, an outspoken leader of the latter, upon hearing of Gambetta's demise, said, " This death is a defeat." [37]

34 *Ibid.*, 239-240.

35 *Bismarck et la France* (Paris, 1918), 33.

36 Harold Stannard says, " In truth the republicans were afraid of their leader. For all the sincerity of his declarations that he sought but to interpret opinion, in his own favourite phrase, to serve democracy, he was a masterful, determined man—the most Napoleonic character France had known since Napoleon " [*Gambetta and the Foundation of the Third Republic* (London, 1921), 192].

37 Henri Galli, *op. cit.*, 246.

CHAPTER II

PAUL DEROULEDE, THE LEAGUE OF PATRIOTS, AND GENERAL BOULANGER

PAUL DÉROULÈDE became in many respects the successor of Gambetta.[1] He had less authority, it is true; but he continued the cry for vengeance and sought to establish an authoritarian government that would make its attainment more likely. In the last public address of his life, in December, 1913, he quite fittingly characterized himself as "the old crier of war." [2]

The story of Déroulède's life may be said to fall into two unequal parts: that prior to the war of 1870, and that after. In 1867, at the age of twenty-one, he attracted considerable attention as a poet, having had a play in verse presented at the Théâtre-Français. Being an ardent republican and hating the Imperial régime and the army that maintained it, he disliked and discounted the rumors of war that were floating about. And, when in July, 1870, these appeared to be only too well founded and the Parisian mob was in a rage for war, he fled the tumultuous streets of the capital and sought peace in the country. Here he was accosted by a peasant who wanted to know when the troops were leaving. His reply being one of indifference, the peasant gave him an "unforgettable look" that immediately roused him from his apathy and hostility. "At that moment," according to the brothers Tharaud, "the young man understood that he had wounded something human, something very noble, that mysterious kinship which unites, one to the other, all men of the same country." [3] This was the turning point of his life: he became a patriot.

He now lost no time acting upon his new discovery. He applied for military service and, being given a second-lieuten-

1 Joachim Kühn, *op. cit.*, 20.

2 M. le Bâtonnier Chenu, *La Ligue des patriotes* (Paris, 1916), 116.

3 Jérôme et Jean Tharaud, *La Vie et la mort de Déroulède* (Paris, 1914), 6-7.

ancy in a militia batallion, accompanied his unit to Châlons. When, however, it was almost immediately ordered back to Paris, he refused to go and was permitted to join the third regiment of the *zouaves*. He had been here only a few days when his mother brought his younger brother, André, to join him, saying to the officer in charge that she would have brought more sons had she had them. Several days later André was seriously wounded in battle. Paul took him up, and carrying him as best he could, sought to regain their regiment. But it was not to be: they were captured. Paul was permitted to look after his brother in a German ambulance for a week and to accompany him to a base hospital; then his prison career began. He was first sent to Berlin and then to Breslau, whence he made his hair-raising escape several weeks later. Upon his safe arrival in France, he reported for duty at Tours and was given a second-lieutenancy in General Bourbaki's army. Here he led a brilliant sortie, but the makeshift army was soon overwhelmed and retired across the border into Switzerland. Déroulède sorrowfully took leave of his comrades at the border and made his way to Bordeaux to report for duty again; but the war was now over. He, too, was something of a "*fou furieux.*"

When, a little later, the war of the Commune broke out, Déroulède joined the forces of the Thiers government. As he led a squadron into Paris, he was severely wounded, almost losing an arm. This from a French bullet, fired by a Frenchman! But he reserved his hatred for the Germans and was proud to say that he had never fired upon a Parisian.[4] During his convalescence he set about to inspire others with his feeling of hatred and desire for revenge; he wrote a collection of poems, his famous *Chants du soldat,* which immediately became a "best seller." It was so popular that he added a second book to it in 1875 and a third in 1882. Writing in 1871, in the last two stanzas of *Vive la France,* he said,

4 *Ibid.*, 20.

Oui, Français, c'est un sang vivace que le vôtre!
Les tombes de vos fils sont pleines de héros;
Mais, sur le sol sanglant oû le vainquer se vautre,
Tous vos fils, ô Français! ne sont pas aux tombeaux.

Et la revanche doit venir, lente peut-être,
Mais en tout cas fatale, et terrible à coup sûr;
La haine est déjà née, et la force va naître:
C'est au faucheur à voir si le champ n'est pas mûr.[5]

In the last verse of *Au docteur Bolbeau,* also in Book I, he was not so willing to concede delay.

La revanche est la loi des vaincus; nous le sommes.
Je la demande à Dieu, terrible et sans recours;
Prochaine et sans merci, je la demande aux hommes.
Les chemins les plus sûrs sont parfois les plus courts.[6]

And later, in the closing stanza of *A mes amis,* in Book III, he gave his readers his view as to how the end would be attained and an interesting description of his own rôle.

Je vis les yeux fixés sur la frontière
Et, front baissé, comme un boeuf au labour,
Je vais, rêvant à notre France entière,
Des murs de Metz au clocher de Strasbourg.
Depuis dix ans j'ai commencé ce rêve,
Tout le traverse et rien ne l'interrompt.
Dieu veuille un jour qu'un grand Français l'achève!
Je ne suis, moi, qu'un sonneur de clairon.[7]

When he wrote these last lines in 1882, the "great Frenchman" in whom he and many others placed their hopes was Léon Gambetta. We have seen how the latter had placed Déroulède on the commission of civic and patriotic instruction. After the fall of Gambetta the work of this commission was restricted by Ferry to the encouragement and supervision of

5 *Chants du soldat* (Paris, 1888), 6.

6 *Ibid.*, 76.

7 *Ibid.*, 317.

the " study " of gymnastics, which had been made compulsory by law.[8] Flags might be used at these exercises, he decreed, but not books, songs, or pictures. And although the gymnastic societies, so reminiscent of Father Jahn's *Turnvereine,* did an eminently patriotic service,[9] Déroulède was angered by the limitations that were imposed and resigned his place on the commission. Upon meeting Gambetta that same day, he confided to him that Ferry's great trouble was " atheism of the *patrie,*" to which the great tribune agreed.[10] Several days later Félix Faure, a member of the commission, proposed to Déroulède that they organize a free association to carry out the program that the ministry had rejected. And when, on the next day, M. d'Hurcourt, director of the newspaper, the *Drapeau,* and M. J. Sansboeuf, president of the *Association des sociétés de gymnastiques de la Seine* placed their organizations at his disposal and requested that he be present at a patriotic fête which they were arranging for May 12, 1882, under the patronage of Henri Martin, also a member of the above-mentioned commission, he agreed to come. On that day in the Heiser gymnasium, with Félix Faure presiding, was organized the *Ligue des Patriotes.* Henri Martin was elected president; the motto, " *Qui vive?—France,*" was adopted; and Déroulède, who was called upon to make a speech, gave them their program. " There are three things that I recommend very particularly," he said, " for the moral propaganda with which you have charged yourselves: develop everywhere, and in everyone, the patriotic spirit that will make them love the *Patrie* passionately; the military spirit,

8 *Mémoire du comité permanent de l'Union des Sociétés de Gymnastique de France sur la création d'une école nationale gymnastique à Reims* (Reims, 1882), 5.

9 *Ibid.,* 5: " Par la Gymnastique, l'adolescent se prépare aux marches longues, aux courses de résistance; elle lui apprend à ménager ses forces, à supporter la fatigue, à ignorer le danger; elle le façonne à la discipline, à la tenue, à l'esprit de corps, d'abnégation de solidarité; *elle lui inspire cette vertu suprême: le patriotisme!* Par elle, par ses enseignements, au jour de son arrivée au corps, il n'est pas conscrit, c'est un soldat! "

10 Jérôme and Jean Tharaud, *op. cit.,* 29.

which will make them serve it patiently and valiantly; the national spirit, which is the exact and reasoned knowledge of the interests and needs of the entire nation, and you should permit yourselves to be neither weakened internally by particularist enterprises nor dispersed externally by humanitarian undertakings. Let us concentrate, rally, love each other, aid each other, be Frenchmen, good Frenchmen, nothing but Frenchmen. As to the fraternity of peoples, we shall discuss it again on the day when Cain will have restored what he has taken from us." [11] Before France could liberate the conquered soil, she had first to liberate her own soul from foreign domination, he continued. This the League of Patriots must help bring about. It should do for Europe what the *Tugendbund* had done for Prussia.[12] To this end Déroulède went about the country encouraging the gymnastic societies, founding rifle societies, exhorting teachers to give their instruction a patriotic bent, dedicating monuments and speaking at cemeteries. Gambetta was so impressed by Déroulède's campaign that he told him, "Preach the sacred duty, the holy war, and in a year we shall see." [13] But the "great Frenchman" had gone to the great beyond before the year had passed.

Undaunted by this "defeat," he continued his "trumpet-blowing," hoping another "great Frenchman" would appear. Henri Martin died in December, 1883. His successor as president of the League was Anatole de la Forge, who soon gave way to Déroulède himself. This position he held until his own death in February, 1914. Under his direction the organization soon lost its nonpartisan character.[14] To the League's original

11 Chenu, *op. cit.*, 11-12; 39-40.

12 Joachim Kühn, *op. cit.*, 21.

13 Jérôme and Jean Tharaud, *op. cit.*, 36.

14 Henri Martin had insisted upon this point in his appeal of Aug. 4, 1882, to the members of the French legislature (Chenu, *op. cit.*, 123). The League had also added the following paragraph to one of its statutes: "Républicain, bonapartiste, légitimiste, orléaniste, ce ne sont là chez nous que des prénoms; c'est *Patriotes* qui est le nom de famille" (Chenu, *op. cit.*, 125).

aim, the "preparation of revenge," he now added another: revision of the constitution of 1875 by an appeal to the nation.[15] The constitution had already been a stumbling block to Gambetta; it should not be so again to the next "great Frenchman." Revenge could neither be prepared nor achieved under it, he felt. He had said France must first liberate her soul from foreign domination as a necessary prerequisite to freeing the conquered soil. A constitution that permitted a régime such as Ferry's, with its avowedly friendly policy toward Germany,[16] was obviously in need of mending. He remained a republican, it is true, but a conditional one.

Political events soon came to his aid. Ferry, whom the *revanchards* openly called "Bismarck" on the streets of Paris, was completely undone by the failure of the Tonkin expedition and the consequent fall of his ministry in 1885. He became the most hated man in France, though she owed him Tunis and Tonkin.[17] The Brisson government, however, continued his friendly attitude toward Germany until the French electorate expressed its discontent so clearly by increasing the monarchist representation in the Chamber from 98 to 204 that that policy no longer appeared feasible.[18] Another result of the election was that the Opportunists now needed the support of the Radicals whom they had hitherto bitterly opposed. This virtually enabled Clemenceau, the Radical leader, to dictate the appointment of General Boulanger to the ministry of war in the Freycinet government which was organized in January, 1886.[19] Clemenceau saw in him a general upon whose radicalism he could count, while Campenon, the outgoing minister of war,

15 Jérôme and Jean Tharaud, *op. cit.*, 38.

16 General Campenon, French minister of war, in 1884 told a group of foreign officers that united France and Germany would rule the world (Bruno Weil, *Grandeur et décadence du Général Boulanger*, translated by L. C. Herbert (Paris, 1931), 62).

17 *Ibid.*, 65.

18 *Ibid.*, 69.

19 *Ibid.*, 86; *cf.* Alexander Zévaès, *Au temps du Boulangisme* (Paris, 1930), 27-28.

liked his spirit. He first attracted general attention when, as leader of the French military deputation to the United States in 1881, he made a scene over the presence of a German flag on the boat by which he was being taken down the Potomac on the way to Yorktown. His ire was aroused at first by the fact that the German flag was larger than the French; then he decided that the German flag should not be displayed at all, since the Germans had done nothing to help win American independence. He, therefore, ordered that the "disagreeable emblem" he removed immediately. "But," to quote his biographer, Brantôme, "the confounded Yankee refused and assured him that there had been a certain number of German mercenaries in the French army sent by Louis XVI. Doubtless two dozen wretches. Boulanger declared that if the German flag were not hauled down at once, our delegation would embark for France immediately."[20] That brought the desired result; the flag was removed and Boulanger became the cynosure of French eyes.

His advance was now rapid. Upon his return he was appointed director of infantry in the ministry of war. It was while he was in this position that Déroulède had occasion to see him to obtain permission for the gymnastic societies to parade in the streets of Paris with rifles. The poet-patriot was so favorably impressed by the young general, who had told him that he, too, despised parliaments, that that same evening he enthusiastically announced to two of his friends, "I have found my man. His name is Boulanger."[21] This was in 1883. In 1884 he was appointed commander-in-chief of the expeditionary force in Tunis. Here he had a bitter quarrel with Jules Cambon, head of the civil government in Tunis, over the question of civil or military supremacy. By July, 1885, he was so exasperated that he offered to resign; then suddenly he returned to Paris without authorization. Less than six months later he was minister of war, and in another six months he was riding his

20 Quoted by Bruno Weil, *op. cit.*, 81.

21 Jérôme and Jean Tharaud, *op. cit.*, 42.

black charger, "Tunis," at the head of other officers in the military parade at Longchamp on July 14, on which occasion he was given an ovation such as few Frenchmen have been honored with.

That this extraordinary tribute to the young general on horseback was not entirely spontaneous, despite the great love of Frenchmen for military pomp and display,[22] is unquestionable. Many Parisians who had had a harsh experience with the army during the Commune still entertained a bitter dislike for it. The monarchists, moreover, while not sharing this dislike for the army in general, had no love for the war minister who had ordered the cavalry regiments, commanded by officers too openly royalist, away from the vicinity of Paris and who had but recently ordered the Duke of Aumale, fourth son of Louis Philippe (and his own former superior), to give up his commission in the army and leave French territory in accordance with the new exclusion act. His espionage law and measures to increase the size of the army had, it is true, been popular; also his celebrated decree regulating the beards worn by officers and men, though it caused much laughter and brought some ridicule.[23] But the great demonstration of July 14, 1886, was largely the work of Déroulède and his League.[24] He had visited "his man" on the day following his appointment to the ministry and in the interview informed him that he and his followers wanted a minister who would abolish the oppressive parliamentary system; he might reserve his decision until later, but the 300,000 members of the League of Patriots would support him; meanwhile he should encourage them in their work and participate in their fêtes;[25] he would do well to accept the tute-

22 On this trait Maurice Barrès says, "En face du terne Elysée, habité par un vieux légiste incapable d'un mouvement venu du coeur, qui seul toucherait les masses, le jeune ministre de la Guerre, chevauchant sur son cheval noir, dispose d'un éclat qui parle toujours à une nation guerrière..." [*L'Appel au soldat* (Paris, 1911), 54].

23 Bruno Weil, *op. cit.*, 92.

24 Jérôme and Jean Tharaud, *op. cit.*, 46.

25 *Ibid.*, 43-44. In their resolution bearing upon the Atchinoff incident of 1889 they claimed 240,000 members (Alexandre Zévaès, *op. cit.*, 157). See note 41, p. 37, below.

lage of Clemenceau for the time being, but he would soon be strong enough to impose his own will upon all. Although no formal agreement was made, the subsequent behavior of both parties betrayed a tacit understanding. The great ovation referred to shows how well Déroulède and his followers had been working for their "General *Revanche*." That the poet-patriot was pleased with the events of the day may well be imagined. Speaking to the members of the League, he said, "Some people have thought the wound in our side which the loss of Alsace-Lorraine has created has healed. You have continually reopened it. You have enlarged it. You have poured molten iron into it. You have let it bleed anew and have prevented the healing. The operation should not be without success. The result is surprising and has exceeded your fondest expectations." [26]

In order to make this intransigence seem less foolhardy and the realization of *revanche* more certain, Déroulède went to Russia in the late summer of 1886 to discuss with Katkoff, whom he greeted as the "minister of public opinion," [27] and with other Slavophile leaders, the mutual advantages of a Franco-Russian alliance. Cordially received by them, he was given a cold reception by Probêdonostsev, who thought that republicans must *ipso facto* be revolutionaries and atheists. From Tolstoy, the apostle of love and universal brotherhood, he also received little encouragement. Returning by way of Sweden, Denmark, Holland and Belgium, he asked that they, too, resist the influence of the Germans, promising that France would prevent their being "eaten up." [28]

Upon his return he found "his man" was more popular than ever, his praises being sung and spoken by thousands on the streets of Paris. Parliamentary opposition there was, however. Déroulède advised him to act while the army was still in his power; but Boulanger demurred, saying the people would

26 Joachim Kühn, *op. cit.*, 22.

27 Jérôme and Jean Tharaud, *op. cit.*, 50.

28 *Ibid.*, 61.

raise him higher if he fell. When the Goblet ministry was formed in December, 1886, he remained at the ministry of war. His position seemed secure and, to all appearances, was made more so by Bismarck, who, interested in securing the approval of the Reichstag for an increase of the German army, stressed the dangerous character of recent developments in France and thereby created a stormy reaction. All French eyes were now centered upon the "Minister of *Revanche*," who, true to his epithet, replied to the Iron Chancellor's expletives by rebuilding large barracks along the eastern frontier and provisioning Verdun, Toul, and Belfort for several years. When on February 8, 1887, Goblet and Boulanger asked the Chamber for additional credits to hasten the manufacture of the Lebel rifle, the response was unanimous. Albert de Mun, who was a deputy at this time and who later described the session in the *Gaulois* of September 21, 1905, said that even Bishop Freppel, who sat beside him, became excited and that "the fire of *Revanche* was in his eyes."[29] *Revanche* was indeed "sovereign" on that day, and its "minister" was unquestionably popular. Not again until after the Tangier and Agadir crises, a score of years later, was it to command the unity of support that it had at that time. For its culmination only a fitting occasion for war was needed. This the Schnaebele incident of the following April seemed to provide. So, at least, Goblet and Boulanger regarded it. They wanted to send an ultimatum which they had already drawn up and order mobilization immediately; but Grévy, who already in 1871 had given up the idea of revenge, suggested that they

29 After reading the first section of the bill, Goblet asked for a show of hands. De Mun described the reaction of the Chamber as follows: "Aussitôt, cinq cents bras se dressèrent ensemble avec un bruissement sourd: je vois encore Mgr. Freppel, à côté de moi, jetant en l'air, d'un élan saccadé, comme pour un mouvement du maniement d'armes, sa main largement ouverte: *le feu de la Revanche était dans ses yeux.* Ce fut ainsi avec une regularité toujours plus saisissante, après chacun des chapitres: *le geste banal avait pris l'apparence d'un rite sacré.* Au vote sur l'ensemble, il se prolongea comme une muette acclamation. Il sembla que l'âme de la patrie traversait la salle. Les spectateurs retenaient leur souffle. Les diplomates regardaient, serieux et surpris..." (Charles Maurras, *Kiel et Tanger*, 271).

could not well send an ultimatum before the German government had replied to their note. This reply was, however, conciliatory enough to satisfy the moderates in the Cabinet. Grévy now looked upon his president of the council and minister of war as dangerous men whom he should remove from power as soon as possible. Ferry, Freycinet, and other Opportunists shared this view, whether from jealousy,[30] fear for the republican form of government, or fear of defeat in another war. In any case, they brought about the overthrow of the Goblet ministry on May 17, 1887, and kept Boulanger out of the Rouvier ministry which was organized thirteen days later.

Now that Boulanger had fallen, would the people raise him higher, as he had confidently predicted to Déroulède? This proved to be a troublesome question during the ensuing nineteen months. His presence in Paris being a thorn in the flesh of the government because of popular demonstrations in his favor, Boulanger was exiled to Clermont-Ferrand as commander of the thirteenth army corps. The monster demonstration of his numerous friends and sympathizers at the railway station and their effort, though unsuccessful, to prevent his departure gave friends and foes alike the impression that he had won an important victory. But the Boulangists suffered a defeat in this curious warfare of demonstrations six days later when, with Déroulède leading, they greeted the July 14th procession of Grévy and the ministry with loud cries of "*Vive Boulanger!*" and jeers. For the friends of the government had prepared for just such an event and yelled "*Vive la France!*" and "*Vive le Président!*" so lustily that the cries of their opponents were pretty well drowned out. Efforts of the Boulangists to tamper with the soldiers and spread disorder in the ranks also failed. So the day marked the "first defeat" for Boulanger and enabled the Opportunists and their friends to "repair the damage" of July 8.[31]

30 Alexandre Zévaès, *op. cit.*, 53.

31 Bruno Weil, *op. cit.*, 212; Joseph Reinach, *La Foire boulangiste* (Paris, 1889), 78-79.

But the position of the Opportunists was not as secure as it seemed, for during the parliamentary vacation the Wilson scandal was brought to light. Monarchists and Radicals now tried to exploit it to their respective political advantage; also General Boulanger. After the Rouvier ministry had been defeated in November, after it had resigned and withdrawn its resignation, Boulanger came to Paris incognito and participated in the conferences of "the historical nights" of November 28-29 with a small group of Radicals and personal followers. Their purpose was to prevent the election of Ferry as Grévy's successor and to prepare a ministry of the extreme Left with Boulanger again at the ministry of war.[32] They were, however, unable to persuade anyone to agree to form a Radical ministry. It was while he was in the midst of the discussion on the second night that the General was called to the home of Comte de Martimprey, a royalist deputy. He went and spent more than an hour in conversation with Martimprey and Baron de Mackau, also a royalist deputy. They asked him to join the royalist cause and become the General Monk of France. Boulanger, doubtless hoping to unite the Right and Left against the Opportunists, accepted the proffered rôle, beginning his policy of lying duplicity which in the end ruined his cause and that of the royalists as well.[33] In accordance with this policy he again left his command at Clermont-Ferrand a month later and, well disguised except for his cane upon which his name was clearly engraved,[34] visited Jerome Bonaparte in Switzerland.

However, as he approached the Right he lost the support of the Left. The Radicals and the Opportunists had joined forces to elect Sadi Carnot to the presidency and to form a ministry headed by the Radical, Floquet, a ministry in which Boulanger had no place. The Radicals, while not in full control of the government, had an important share in its power and places,

32 Alexandre Zévaès, *op. cit.*, 75.

33 *Ibid.*, 79-80; *cf.* Bruno Weil, *op. cit.*, 437.

34 Bruno Weil, *op. cit.*, 263.

and for their share were willing to support the Opportunists against Boulanger and his new allies. The General was now a man with a grievance; and, as such, although he was still hailed as " General *Revanche* " by many admirers, became a sort of general of the discontented.[35] He would seek a vindication at the hands of the people; hence his approval of the " plebiscite " which Georges Thiébaud, one-time Bonapartist candidate, conceived and was authorized to direct. His name was placed in seven departments while he was still ineligible, being in active military service. This obstacle was removed, however, when in March the government ordered his retirement. His candidacy in the department of the Nord was now announced. The General himself made a campaign speech in which he denounced " the men who naively imagined they were suppressing war by suppressing the defense. . . ." [36] His press, the *Lanterne,* the *Intransigeant,* and the *Cocarde,* which was founded in 1888 to propagate Boulangism, took this up as a refrain and represented the legislature as " an association of eunuchs " and the ministers as traitors in Prussian pay.[37] His election on April 8 in the Dordogne department and his overwhelming victory in the election of the department of the Nord on April 15, a week later, were somewhat of a vindication, but not enough for one who wanted to be " raised higher " than the ministry of war.

35 Joseph Reinach in the *République française* of Mar. 11, 1888 (reprinted in *La Foire boulangiste,* 145-146) gave the following hostile, though doubtless in some respects true description of the Boulangist spirit: " L'état d'esprit boulangiste est celui des mécontents de tous les partis, de tous les fatigués, de tous les découragés, de toutes les ambitions déçues, des imbéciles qui rendent la République responsable des mauvaises récoltes, des niais qui ont gardé l'amour de panache, des malades qui, sans raison, se trouvant mal sur le côté gauche, se tournent sur le côté droit... C'est le sentiment d'inquiétude et de malaise qui fait préférer à ceux qui souffrent n'importe quoi, surtout un *n'importe quoi* qui paraît énergique, à ce qui existe . . . C'est la mauvaise humeur des anciens partis, impuissants à restaurer le prince de leur choix, mais prêts à acclamer toute solution qui ne sera pas la République... Sans l'état d'esprit boulangiste, qu'est le général Boulanger?—Rien."

36 *Ibid.,* 180.

37 *Ibid.,* 181-182.

In the course of the next nine months this desired elevation appeared on several occasions to be at the point of realization, despite the efforts of his political opponents. On the day of his entry into the Chamber in his new capacity as deputy he was escorted to the Palais Bourbon by a huge and enthusiastic crowd of admirers who would have taken the building by assault had he said the word. But the Moderates were now organizing counter demonstrations, and Joffrin, one of their leaders, joined Clemenceau, Ranc, and others in forming on May 25, 1888, the *Société des droits de l'homme*,[38] which drew up a program calling for war against Boulangism. His opponents also controlled the Chamber. When on June 4 he made his first speech (incidentally, it was written by Naquet), calling for the revision of the constitutional laws, the abolition of the party system, the grant to all Frenchmen of equal rights in the government, and the submission of the revised constitution to the people, his proposal was rejected by a big majority. Floquet remarked that his speech was as arrogant as any Napoleon had made after his many victories and, to the amusement of the deputies, added that at his age Napoleon was already dead.[39] But on July 12 the General with even greater arrogance demanded that the ministry dissolve the Chamber immediately. Floquet was now angry, and his caustic remarks elicited equally angry retorts from Boulanger who, among other things, called the president of the council a liar. Next day they fought their famous duel in the presence of the chief of police and several journalists, in which the General received a serious wound in the neck, while Floquet escaped with a light hand wound. Boulanger's popularity was apparently unaffected by the unhappy encounter (although his opponents wondered how he could expect to reconquer Alsace-Lorraine if beaten at foils by a sixty-year-old civilian), for in August he was re-elected to

38 Its proclamation stated that it would last as long as the peril it was designed to combat. During the Dreyfus affair the more famous league of the same name was founded.

39 Bruno Weil, *op. cit.*, 290.

the seat which he had resigned shortly after the duel and elected in two other departments as well. Boulangism was still strong and appeared to be growing more formidable, as its victory in the bitterly contested election of January 27, 1889, showed. That evening was one of golden opportunities; but Boulanger preferred simply to enjoy his victory rather than to improve upon it. He was deaf to the appeals for action of his political lieutenants in the café Durand and of the great mob outside in the Place de la Madeleine. Déroulède, who agreed that night actions were dangerous, did not insist; but he demanded that Boulanger present himself next day at the Chamber, where he would probably be hissed; then he should stalk out and call upon his followers to take it by storm.[40] This the General also vetoed. The crowd slowly dispersed and Boulanger spent the night in Marguerite de Bonnemain's apartment, though he could have slept at the Elysée.

This was the culmination of Boulangism; its disintegration came swiftly. While he who gave the movement its name went with Marguerite to Royat to relive the happy hours spent there before, the government took measures to defend itself. The *scrutin de liste,* which had been so skilfully exploited by their opponents in the interest of their "plebiscite," was abolished; the duc d'Aumale, now a personal enemy of Boulanger, was recalled from exile as a measure calculated to divide the monarchist and personal followers of the General, as it did at least for the moment; anti-parliamentary demonstrations were forbidden by Constans, the minister of the interior; and legal proceedings were instituted against the League of Patriots and its leaders. The League really had no legal status, never having secured the formal authorization required by law. So long as it remained nonpartisan its position was secure; but it had furnished Boulangism its best "soldiers" and had become one of the most powerful obstructionist forces in the country.[41] In

40 Jérôme and Jean Tharaud, *op. cit.*, 65.

41 Its last campaign against the government was characteristic. Atchinoff, a Russian religious fanatic, wanted to lead a group of followers into Abyssinia

the face of a government that was determined to crush the Boulangist movement, it could expect little mercy. In February the offices of its central committee were raided and its papers and documents confiscated and examined. From these it was learned that the League was organized as "an army of *coup d'état,* continually ready for mobilization,"[42] with its arrondissement, district, and street committees in Paris, in addition to the central committee and the departmental committees, and that every member of the League in Paris could be given any order of the central committee within two hours without using the postal, telegraph, or any other public service.[43] The government promptly dissolved so dangerous an organization and prosecuted its leaders for forming a secret society. Among them were three deputies, one of whom was Déroulède, and one senator, Naquet; but the ministry demanded and secured the suspension of their parliamentary immunity. The court, however, acquitted them of the charge of creating a secret society, though it fined each 100 francs for not having secured administrative authorization. What a sorry outcome for a movement that seven years earlier had begun with the blessings of Gambetta and for which the future seemed to hold so much promise!

The government, relentlessly pursuing its goal, also made it plain that the General was not to be spared. Moreover, there were rumors that action was to be taken against Rochefort and Dillon. Fearing arrest, they fled the country, much to the pleasure of Constans, who had advised that they be not

by way of French territory. Since Abyssinia opposed their coming and the Russian government was indifferent, the French governor of Obock territory was ordered not to let them land. Evading the French cruisers, they nevertheless disembarked at Sagallo and steadfastly refused to turn back until the French cruisers had bombarded the town, killed twelve of the group and wounded more (February, 1889). The directing committee of the League now opened a subscription for the "thousands" of dead and wounded, subscribing a thousand francs itself; it published resolutions denouncing the parliamentary government's lack of diplomacy in shedding Russian blood; and it sent regrets and words of fraternal devotion to Russia.

42 Alexander Zévaès, *op. cit.,* 155.

43 Bruno Weil, *op. cit.,* 326.

arrested at the frontier.[44] Their absence facilitated rather than hindered the plans of the government. Prosecuted and tried for conspiracy, to which they now added the crime of contempt of court for not appearing, they were condemned in August, 1889, to deportation to a fortified place.

But Boulanger, while carefully avoiding French territory, still had hopes. Deceiving his republican followers who had been pleased by his emphatic reaffirmation of his republicanism in his recent and last speech at Tours, he now drew up a list of candidates for the general election in September and October three-fourths of whom were royalists. Déroulède and Rochefort protested so vigorously against this "treachery" that the General consented to change the list, but the change came late and created confusion.[45] Monarchists and Boulangists together won but few more seats than the former had won alone in 1885. The vote of the new Chamber on the invalidation of the election of Boulanger himself in Paris was 350 to 217. The republicans were jubilant, their opponents discouraged. The municipal elections of 1890 were even more disappointing to the latter.

With his ambitions blasted, with the wholesale desertion of friends and the greatest blow of all, the death of Marguerite in July, 1891, he who had entertained dreams of regal power and the glory of reconquering the lost provinces now found reality and life itself unbearable. He sought release in self-inflicted death in the following September.

But the "sacred flame," though dimmed perhaps for having been put to partisan uses,[46] was not extinguished by the bullet that snuffed out the General's life. It inspired and in turn was fed by the Russian alliance. It likewise inspired and was similarly affected by Delcassé's policy later. Hanotaux's policy of *rapprochement* with Germany had in the meantime been more or less secret. The day of reckoning was merely postponed while

44 *Ibid.*, 341.

45 Jérôme and Jean Tharaud, *op. cit.*, 68-69.

46 Joseph Reinach, *Bruno-Le-Fileur* (Paris, 1889), 111.

alliances were made and while a nationalist doctrine was evolved which called for preparatory measures at home and the building up of the proper morale among Frenchmen against that day. When in 1905 Frenchmen were again in a receptive mood generally because of what Tardieu denominated the " unprecedented humiliation " of that year, this doctrine, cleverly propagated, intensified their resentment toward Germany and prevented the " sacred fire " from cooling.

Maurice Barrès, concerning whom we shall have more to say presently, declared that Boulangism failed for having lacked a doctrine.[47] An elaborated theory explaining why Frenchmen are French and therefore superior, and why they should be supremely patriotic, the adherents of Boulganism did not have. They were more concerned about the second-rate position of France as a nation, the causes of which they did not analyze deeply. If they can be said to have had a doctrine, it was one of action. It differed little from the program Gambetta had drawn up in 1879 and had followed until his death. They were interested in *revanche,* the recovery of the lost provinces and of French primacy in Europe. To achieve this France must have powerful armaments supported by a determined and warlike morale in the nation; hence their insistence upon increasing the strength of both in every conceivable way, by gymnastics, rifle practice, patriotic education, etc. France must also have allies—Russia, for example, or any enemy of Pan-Germanism; she must have an authoritarian government rather than a parliamentary one, one capable of pursuing a consistent policy and acting with force; and lastly, she must have one national party, not several quarreling for places and power. These were the principles of Déroulède and of Boulanger in his saner moments. Barrès retained them for the most part and may be said to have built up his doctrine around them.

47 Maurice Barrès, *Mes cahiers* (Paris, 1929), I, 250; *cf.* Charles Maurras, " Sur un mot de Barrès," *L'Action française,* Apr. 19, 1935: "Axiome, religion ou Prince des hommes!," he had said already in 1887, meaning a " certain doctrine," a " national and social sentiment " and a " personal power, a being of flesh and bone, a born chief."

CHAPTER III

DRUMONT AND NATIONALISTIC ANTI-SEMITISM

THE relation of the Boulangists with Drumont,[1] whose *France juive* appeared in 1886, was somewhat dubious. In this widely-read book Gambetta was pictured as not only having been in league with the Jewish bankers, but was denounced as a Jew himself.[2] Déroulède was not a true patriot; otherwise he would fight the Jews, Drumont said.[3] Anatole de la Forge as president of the League of Patriots had shamefully felicitated a Jew of Cologne who had regularly heaped injuries upon the French army. The League was therefore a far cry from the *Tugendbund* which had prepared the deliverance of Germany from the yoke of Napoleon.[4] These strictures were made to hurt, and probably did. Yet in 1888, despite this criticism of Boulanger's supporters and the fact that several of his ablest political henchmen — Naquet, Eugene Mayer, Arthur Meyer, etc. — were kinsmen of Abraham, the General is reported to have said, " It is particularly necessary to get rid of the Jews." [5] This was probably meant for the conservatives who, for the most part, had enjoyed and appreciated Drumont's book, for there is no record that the General applied this principle to his own organization. Drumont, possibly as a result of the alliance which Boulanger made with the conservatives, experienced a gradual change of heart toward the movement. He voted for the General on January 27, 1889, and was at the Place de

1 Henri d'Améras, in *Avant la gloire: leurs débuts* (Paris, 1903), gives an interesting account of Drumont's life before 1886 and of the preparation and publication of *La France juive.* His publisher, Marpon, was hopeful when he learned from the proofs that it might cause a scandal. The rumor that Drumont was a Jew himself originated at the publishing house.

2 I, 35; 530-541.

3 I, 487.

4 II, 212.

5 Joseph Reinach, *La Foire boulangiste* (Paris, 1889), 224.

la Madeleine that night.[6] In 1890 he described Déroulède as a disinterested devotee of the *Patrie* and, referring to his portrait of him in his book of 1886, he said, "I was unjust to him in those days, and I regret it." [7] Déroulède probably never liked certain passages in *La France juive*, but his rôle in the Panama and Dreyfus crises left little to be desired from the anti-Semitic viewpoint.[8]

Of the three general varieties of anti-Semitism, the religious, the economic, and the ethnic, Drumont's was primarily economic; [9] but his hatred for the Jews was so intense and his pen carried so much vitriol that he took his arguments where they could be found, and frequently they were in the other categories.

Taine had written the "Jacobin Conquest"; Drumont would write the "Jewish Conquest," he announced at the beginning of his famous book. The Jew alone profited from the Revolution. It was a veritable conquest, the enslavement of the whole nation by an "infamous but cohesive minority." [10] They have the cult of money; they are sordid, grasping, intriguing, subtle, deceitful. So equipped, they have continued the ancient struggle of the Carthaginians and Saracens against the hated Aryans, and have succeeded wonderfully. Having no inventive ability of their own,[11] they exploit the inventions of Aryan creators. They are parasites on a civilization they have not made. Of the estimated 150 billions of circulating wealth in France, they hold 80 billions.[12] Marx and Lassalle

6 Edouard Drumont, *De l'or, de la boue, du sang* (Paris, 1896), 281.

7 Edouard Drumont, *La Dernière bataille* (Paris, 1890), 138.

8 Jérôme and Jean Tharaud, *op. cit.*, 83-95; *cf.* Edouard Drumont, *De l'or, de la boue, du sang*, 68.

9 Edouard Drumont, *La Dernière bataille*, xi-xii; Bernard Lazare, *L'Antisémitisme* (Paris, 1894), 238.

10 *La France juive* (Paris, 1886), I, vi; confirmed partially by Bernard Lazare, *op. cit.*, 224-226.

11 A contention of Renan in his *Histoire générale des langues sémitiques*, quoted by Drumont in *La France juive*, I, 12.

12 *Ibid.*, I, 520-521.

were Jews; thus the Jews give the Socialist movement the direction they desire. They also control and inspire imperialism, for it is to enrich them that French soldiers succumb from typhoid fever in Tunis and from cholera in Tonkin.[13] Their display of their ill-gotten wealth is positively disgusting, particularly that of the American Jews who, coming from Germany originally and having amassed a few hundred thousand francs, come to Paris and ostentatiously spend them with a noise that is deafening. French noblemen, impressed by this orgy of spending and recalling that the castle needs repairs, marry into these families only to discover that the gold mine has been inundated. With few exceptions, these Americans are "very disagreeable creatures," with their loud talk, noisy laughter, and bad taste.[14]

Pursuing his economic argument in his later books, he found that the French Jews were also guilty of display, though not so crude and noisy. Frenchmen are gradually perceiving what the Revolution has brought them. "They discern some Jews vomited forth by all the ghettos, now installed as masters in the historic chateaux which evoke the most glorious memories of old France; they find the Rothschilds everywhere—at Ferrières and at Vaux-de-Cernay, in the abbey founded by Blanche of Castille; they find Hirsch at Marly, at the place of Louis XIV; Ephrussi at Fontainebleau, at the place of Francis I; the Dreyfus of the guanos at Pont-Chartrain. Walking along our avenues, they affirm that the most magnificent mansions are occupied by Jews, and that each of these homes recounts a theft, a bankruptcy, a throat-cutting, griefs and suicides." [15] Living in the sumptuous splendor of kings and lords, they unfortunately wield the power of kings and lords. The government intervenes to save the Comptoir d'Escompte, the

13 *Ibid.*, II, 227.

14 *Ibid.*, II, 252-254. He leaves his reader in doubt as to whether this is directed against American Jews only or against other Americans as well. He says, "L'Américanisme a envahi Paris presque autant que le Sémitisme."

15 *De l'or, de la boue, du sang*, vii.

Rothschild banking house, but not the Union Générale, a Christian concern. There is no equality. Rothschild is the "great Judge of France," as in the recent elections (1889) he has been its "great Elector." [16]

This Alphonse de Rothschild belongs to the order of rodents; he is a collossal white rat of the hamster variety, with his huge baggy cheeks in which he stores his provisions. His gnawing teeth are busy day and night in ships as well as houses, for the iron-plating of the former are no obstacle to his powerful incisors. To overpower them he makes one sink and the other crumble to the ground. He ruins whole fleets, making himself a water rat for the crossing from ship to ship, and he ruins whole cities. But he leaves no trace, except possibly a dusty debris or a parched dung, to mark his passage. There is also no noise: several rapid movements of the jaws followed by a vicious lunge, a muffled sigh and rattling of the throat of the victim, nothing more. He goes to his hole and watches for the next victim.[17]

But Rothschild is only the greatest in this order or race of rats, their rodential qualities having an ethnic character. They are cowardly, deceitful, and unsocial. They cannot live in an organized society, being still nomads and Bedouins. Their minds are not made "like ours," [18] for they have no consideration for the rights and interests of others. Once a desire possesses his mind, the Jew goes ahead undeterred by any scruplės of conscience. They look upon themselves as of "another essence" than gentiles.[19] There is no meeting them as equals: they are either above or below.[20] They may be recognized by "the famous crooked nose, the blinking eyes, the clinched teeth, the protruding ears, the square nails in place of the almond-round, the over-elongated torso, the flat feet, the

16 *La Dernière bataille,* 20-21.

17 *Ibid.,* 30-32.

18 *Ibid.,* 16.

19 *Ibid.,* 120.

20 *La France juive,* I, 22.

fleshy knees, the extraordinarily prominent ankle-bone, the soft and melting hand of the hypocrite and traitor. Often enough they have one arm shorter than the other." [21] While they pick up the Parisian jargon rapidly, their bad pronunciation is another sign by which they may be identified.[22]

Their religion also sets them apart. A religion that inspired the crucifixion of a child at Blois in 1071 and countless other crimes should not be tolerated. Moreover, they still hate the Christ as did their forbears when they cried at Jerusalem, "Tolle, et crucifige!" [23] They are therefore really more interested in the religious persecution that has been going on in France than their "valets," [24] the Protestants and the Free Masons.[25] The pact between the Jews and the Free Masons was definitely signed when Gambetta cried, "Le cléricalisme, voilà l'ennemi!" [26] Free Masonry is but a machine invented by the Jews to conquer the world; its calendar and ritual are Jewish.[27] Although Article XV of the constitution of the society forbids debates upon measures of the civil authorities and intervention in the struggles of political parties, it is mainly honored in the breach. This sect of 25,000 members has too much authority over the remaining 38,000,000 Frenchmen.[28] The Protestants have also been a powerful ally in this persecution, this attempt to suppress the religion of the majority of Frenchmen. While they are not inspired by the Jews' "special hatred of Him whom they have crucified," by a curious lack of logic they, too, bear a grudge against Him because they feel guilty towards Him.[29] Less greedy than the Jews, they

21 *Ibid.*, I, 34.

22 *Ibid.*, I, 30.

23 *Ibid.*, II, 382; also his *Sur le chemin de la vie* (Paris, 1914), 30.

24 *La Dernière bataille*, 26.

25 *La France juive*, II, 382.

26 *Ibid.*, I, 541.

27 *La Tyrannie maçonnique* (Paris, 1899), 14.

28 *Ibid.*, 43.

29 *La France juive*, II, 311.

have nevertheless abused the power which their alliance with the latter has given them.[30] Their great man, Coligny, was a false martyr, for documents prove that he was a rascal. One of their leading pastors, M. Monod of Marseilles, is a better English than French patriot; hence the pleasure he has evinced over the spread of English influence in Madagascar.[31] And the culmination of all of this will be the *grand soir* for which the Jews hope and pray so fervently, the time when France will be a solitude of ruins.[32] This will come to pass unless Frenchmen rise up and prevent it. Their slogan, their program, therefore, should be "France for the French." [33]

It was with ideas such as these, couched in a language that was deemed violent and extravagant even in France, where the absence of a rigorous libel law has made the use of such language almost a tradition, that Drumont attacked the Jews and their allies. But not satisfied with philippics only, he joined Jacques de Biez in 1890 in forming the *Ligue nationale antisémitique de France*, which described its work as one "of national awakening, of protection for the conscience of each, of mutual and fraternal assistance." [34] By means of enthusiastic meetings which it organized and sponsored, it was an effective agent in spreading Drumont's ideas; "it was," according to one of its supporters, "a fine movement of patriotic ardor." [35] But the most effective medium of anti-Semitic propaganda was the newspaper, *La Libre parole*, which Drumont founded in April, 1892, only a few months before the emergence of the Panama scandal.

Strange coincidences occur in this world of ours that often seem weird and uncanny. One of the most interesting of these is that precisely when Drumont was pouring his venomous

30 *Ibid.*, II, 353, 373.

31 *Ibid.*, II, 352-353.

32 *Ibid.*, II, 562.

33 *De l'or, de la boue, du sang*, 331.

34 Quoted by Albert Croquez, *Edouard Drumont* (Paris, 1909), 17.

35 *Ibid.*, 17.

hatred into *La France juive*, Cornelius Herz, a "hamster" and leech all in one, was preparing the stage for a play in which he was to show qualities that made Drumont's charges seem a tame, almost benign, statement of the case.[36] For it was in 1885 that Herz made his proposal to the Panama Canal Company that he secure the acceptance by the Chamber and Senate of a measure authorizing the Company to issue bonds. His fee was to be ten million francs, for which Baron Jacques de Reinach was to be guarantor.[37] The Company, being in a precarious position already, and fearing that a refusal would arouse the enmity of Herz and possibly also of Clemenceau who was in his debt, accepted the proposition. It was feared that they might make inconvenient exposures of corruption, maladministration, and waste, which would prevent the enactment of the measure desired, cause the failure of the Company, and bring in its train a financial panic. Herz, it seems, did but little bribing; his business was blackmail, for having secured 600,000 francs from the Company in 1886, he returned the contract. This was soon destroyed. Baron de Reinach now conducted the work of corrupting deputies, senators, ministers, and newspapers through agents whom he had used before in work of this nature. His gold proved irresistible to approximately a hundred deputies and senators,[38] several ministers, and several influential newspapers. The law was enacted. But despite this legislative aid, the Company, having lost the confidence of investors, crashed; it suspended payments on December 14, 1888.[39]

Although charges were made against Ferdinand de Lesseps and his son, the government did nothing; fearing a scandal and a possible political upheaval, and reluctant to drag into the

36 *De l'or, de la boue, du sang*, 68.

37 Bruno Weil, *Panama*, translated by Albert Lehman (Paris, 1934), 57.

38 *Ibid.*, 316. There were 104 names on the list of the investigating commission. *Cf.* Alexandre Zévaès, *Le Scandale du Panama* (Paris, 1930?), 231. George Adam in his *The Tiger: Georges Clemenceau* (New York, 1930), 98, gives 140 to 150 as the number of those guilty of accepting bribes.

39 Bruno Weil, *op. cit.*, 93.

criminal courts so distinguished a person as the elder de Lesseps, an Academician and member of the Legion of Honor, it preferred to let sleeping dogs lie. While there were many persons who for private as well as public reasons were interested in the dogs' continuing their sleep undisturbed, none was more concerned about it than Baron de Reinach.

One who troubled their sleep, and certainly the Baron's, was Cornelius Herz. Of German-Jewish extraction, he was born at Besançon. In his youth he accompanied his immigrant parents to the United States. He later became a naturalized citizen, received the degree of doctor of medicine in the city of Chicago, and, as a physician at San Francisco, specialized in electrical treatments which were frowned upon by most members of his profession. He soon returned to his native land, served in the medical corps of the army of the Loire, and, being appointed representative of the United States at an electrical congress that met in Paris, he came to be looked upon as an expert in electricity. He helped form electrical supply and telephone companies and, in addition to contributing capital and technical knowledge, served them by skillful lobbying and concession-hunting. He rose rapidly in the esteem of financial and political leaders; he visited Grévy and his family at the Elysée frequently; he consorted with Boulanger and Déroulède; he had a friend in Clemenceau whose newspaper, *La Justice*, he saved from bankruptcy by lending him the sum of four hundred thousand francs in 1883;[40] he was made a member of the Legion of Honor. He was honored, respected and, in some instances, feared.

Baron Jacques de Reinach, who learned to fear him, was also a German Jew; but he had no American passport. He was born at Frankfort-am-Main, the home of the Rothschilds. In 1863 he went to Paris, where he successfully applied the banking principles he had learned in his native city. He invested in big business projects such as the Southern Railway,

40 This is the figure that Déroulède gave in his famous denunciation of Clemenceau before the Chamber on Dec. 20, 1892 (*ibid.*, 235-245).

in the current construction projects in Paris growing out of the Haussmann program, and in war supplies for the government. To protect his operations and open the way for new ones he cultivated the friendship of successive ministers of finance and became a sort of unofficial financial advisor of the government; he hired agents to bring him accurate and frequently advance parliamentary information; he paid deputies to vote for measures he wanted passed and, if he had paid them once, they found it difficult not to do his bidding in other matters. Joseph Reinach, director of the *République française* and prominent Opportunist, was his nephew and son-in-law. The Baron received his title from the Italian government for secret services which his enemies described as treasonable. He was no angel, despite the sympathy he attracts because of his tragic death; [41] he was immensely wealthy, unscrupulous in attaining his ends and, to all appearances, more powerful than Herz. But the latter's power lay in his ruthlessness.

Why Herz blackmailed Reinach has never been revealed. Herz wisely left no written records. Reinach did; however, many of these were destroyed by his nephew, Joseph, on the morning of his uncle's death. He had been warned by Quesnay de Beaurepaire, the attorney general, that the Baron's arrest and trial could no longer be postponed and, not knowing that the Baron was already dead, sought to help him by destroying all of the damaging evidence he could find. Joseph's papers which, upon his death, were turned over to the Bibliothèque Nationale with the proviso that the first twenty-three bundles be not opened before January 1, 1951, and the twenty-fourth not before the year 2010, may some day expose Herz's motives, if there were any other than sheer greed.[42]

41 In Bruno Weil's recent (1934) account of the Panama scandal Herz is the devil of the piece, while Reinach is his not innocent, but pitiful, victim. There is even a slight tinge of sympathy in Drumont's account of their feud in *La Libre parole* of Nov. 21, 1892 (*De l'or, de la boue, du sang*, 67-70). Barrès' picture of Reinach in *Leurs figures* is hardly less black than that of Herz.

42 Bruno Weil, *op. cit.*, 482.

But if people were kept in the dark concerning his motives, the story of the extortion that he practiced upon the Baron became public property along with the many other sordid details of the Panama scandal. From 1880 to 1886 Herz had come to Reinach soliciting loans. Small at first, only 2,000 francs in 1880, the loans that the Baron granted him increased in size (that of 1885 was 200,000 francs) until their aggregate amounted to 500,000 francs in 1887. Meanwhile in 1885 Herz had secured the contract from the Panama Canal Company, with Reinach as its surety, and, having collected 600,000 francs in 1886, he had returned the contract to the Company. But he made no effort to pay Reinach what he owed him. In 1887 the latter secured judgment against him, the court ordering the sale of his furniture, etc. Herz now wrote a letter to Reinach warning him to be careful. It was so effective that Reinach not only took nothing from Herz for himself, but also paid most of what he owed the other creditors who had joined him in the legal action. But Herz was not satisfied. He now informed the Baron that he would ruin him unless he turned over to him the ten million francs due him from the Panama Canal Company; having done that, he would pay him what he owed him. These were the terms of the agreement of 1888 which Reinach was forced to make. But it was scarcely made before more threatening letters came. To avoid exposure, Reinach in July of this same year told Herz that his debts to himself and to his bank had been canceled. The total of gifts and canceled loans now amounted to about four million francs. Having done exceedingly well thus far, Herz demanded two millions more, saying he had classified the letters and would print them. The two millions were sent. In November, 1888, another million was sent. By July, 1889, the Baron had turned over to his extortioner 9,072,175 francs;[43] but the flow of menacing letters and telegrams continued. Reinach in an agony of fear and in the blind rage of despair hired an ex-policeman

43 *Ibid.*, 427. Alexandre Zévaès in *Le Scandale du Panama*, 196, says the total amount extorted was over eleven million francs.

to murder his tormentor, but the assassin and his employer failed in their dark design.

Herz continued to live, not only to prolong his victim's agony, but to intensify it by carrying out what he had repeatedly threatened to do. Although a Jew himself, he was not above using the anti-Semites to achieve the destruction of a fellow-Jew, while they, in turn, were not above accepting information from a Jew to attain their end: the ruination of the Jews as a class. Although Drumont had already in 1890 published a fairly lengthy history and criticism of the Panama Company,[44] his effort was in many respects similar to that of a blind man probing about with a stick, sometimes hitting the path and sometimes not. Soon after the founding of *La Libre parole* his articles began to reflect either an improvement in his powers of sight or good guidance, or both. Ferdinand de Lesseps, who in the former was the culprit, the "monstrous egoist" who should shed tears for the 800,000 poor wretches whom he had reduced to poverty,[45] was now replaced as arch-criminal by a subject more to his liking: Reinach, the Jew. Drumont's violence was extreme, though little more so than that with which *La Cocarde* took up the same campaign.

Reinach was really in hot water now. In order to turn the attack from himself and to frighten men in office from giving heed to the campaign against himself, he sent his friend, Andrieux, to make a deal with Drumont. The latter was to cease attacking him and in return would be given *bona fide* information concerning certain corrupt politicians. Drumont agreed, and for a time turned his guns upon the latter. *La Cocarde,* however, attacked with greater ferocity than before. The Baron, on the verge of a nervous breakdown from worry and inability to sleep, sought diversion on the Côte d'Azur; but distance only made his danger loom larger. Informed from private and public sources that the issue could no longer be delayed, the day of Delahaye's interpellation having been set, he hurried back to Paris, determined to make one last effort to

44 *La Dernière bataille,* 323-460. 45 *Ibid.,* 420.

stop the press campaign that had forced the reluctant ministers to agree to the interpellation. Herz and Constans, who now controlled *La Cocarde,* were behind it. He would therefore see them and attempt to persuade them to call their dogs off. He prevailed upon Rouvier, the minister of finance, and Clemenceau to accompany him. They visited the arch-enemy first, but they found him in no relenting mood. To Reinach's fervent plea he replied that he was ill and that he could not stop the campaign if he were well and really made the effort. Rouvier took leave of them as they now went to the home of Constans, the minister of the interior. Upon their arrival, Reinach, drained of physical strength as well as hope, fell upon a couch and asked Clemenceau to speak for him. Telling Constans that he must surely be aware of the rumor that he was the master of *La Cocarde* and was responsible for the campaign it was conducting against the Baron, Clemenceau asked him to desist.[46] Although Constans vehemently denied the charge, he did say in polite but clear French that there was no hope for the Baron. The latter arose with difficulty and, without saying a word, left with Clemenceau, whom he begged to stay with him; but Clemenceau insisted that he was expected at home. They separated. The Baron, crushed with despair, ordered his driver to take him home. Here he found Joseph with the warning from Beaurepaire that legal action would follow shortly. Joseph, who saw in this the ruination of his own career, reproached his uncle for the misdoings that had brought them to this plight. Other members of the family chimed in; so the Baron sought the more congenial company of two women whom he kept in an apartment nearby. He returned to his home at about two in the morning, went to his room, and the next morning was found dead. He had taken an overdose of the sleeping drug he had been using.[47]

46 If Constans's motive was, as George Adam avers (*The Tiger: Georges Clemenceau,* 100), to discredit his colleagues and seize the power for himself, he failed singularly.

47 Bruno Weil, *op. cit.,* 158.

What a striking confirmation all this was of what Drumont had been saying about the Jews! There was Herz's unscrupulous pursuit of an end determined upon, unhindered by conscience or sympathy; there was Reinach's widespread corruption of politicians and newspapers, now exposed in the Chamber by the incorruptible Delahaye, freshly armed with information given him by two emissaries of the Company to divert the popular anger from itself to the politicians; there was Reinach's almost excusable willingness to resort to murder; there was the supineness of the government in its unwillingness to prosecute a known criminal. The one illustrated the cold, steely nature of the Jew; the next, the methods he used in bending political power and influence to his will; the next, the lengths to which he permitted himself to go; and the last, the extent of his political power. It is small wonder, therefore, that Drumont gloated over the situation with an I-told-you-so,[48] or that his followers now looked upon him as a prophet and seer. Nor is it surprising, in view of the inflaming effect created by the relatively light punishment meted out to the guilty members of the Company and by the government's efforts to save a discredited parliamentary system by bringing charges against only ten of the 104 senators and deputies implicated and convicting only one of these because he foolishly admitted his guilt, that two years later an innocent Jewish captain was wrongfully convicted of selling military secrets to Italy and Germany, that he was sent to Devil's Island and kept there in close confinement for more than four years, and that, to use Clemenceau's terms,[49] "reparation" was not made for this "iniquity" until almost twelve years had elapsed after his conviction and France had been convulsed by a "civil war." This is not to say that there were not other factors, such as,

48 That was the tone of his article of Nov. 21, 1892, in *La Libre parole*, reprinted in *De l'or, de la boue, du sang*, 67-70.

49 His first volume of the reprinted articles on the Affair is entitled, *L'Iniquité*, 2nd edition (Paris, 1899); the second, *Vers la réparation*, 2nd edition (Paris, 1899).

for example, the partisan interests of the anti-parliamentarians and the monarchists, with their mixed attitude of unreasoning, yet highly utilitarian, reverence for the army; the interests of the Clericals; and the equally partisan interests of their opponents, with their preference for such ideal concepts as Justice, Truth, Liberty, and Law over reasons of state and authority. But the fact remains that the two camps into which the nation was divided were named after a Jew: there were Dreyfusards and there were anti-Dreyfusards.[50] Finally, it is no subject of wonderment that Barrès, who, after the failure of Boulangism in 1889, was conscious of the need of a nationalist doctrine and who, according to his own statement,[51] formulated such a doctrine in 1894, was profoundly influenced by the ideas, now apparently so thoroughly substantiated by recent events, of one whose slogan was " France for the French." [52]

50 Writing Sept. 1, 1898, Clemenceau with insulting logic called the latter. "Esterhazists," but the name was not popular (*Vers la réparation*, 117).

51 *Scènes et doctrines du nationalisme* (Paris, 1925), I, 14; *Le Voyage de Sparte* (Paris, 1906), 29; *Un homme libre* (Paris, 1912), 257.

52 During the Dreyfus affair, in some notes from a letter to Drumont, he said, " Il y a bien longtemps que nous nous connaissons. Vous vous rappelez que j'ai été un des premiers à vous saluer. Votre 'A bas les Juifs!' ne me choque pas. Nous allions le vendredi saint les tuer... Je vous aime surtout, parce que je suis né nationaliste" [*Mes cahiers* (Paris, 1929-31), II, 118].

CHAPTER IV

EMERGENCE OF THE NEW SYNTHETIC NATIONALISM OF MAURICE BARRES

IF Drumont's hostility towards the Revolution be excepted and allowance be made for certain other influences to be mentioned later, Barrèsian nationalism may be described as a union of (1) Boulangism (*revanche*, moral and material armaments, allies, Caesarism), (2) Drumontism (anti-Semitism, anti-Free Masonry, anti-Protestantism, anti-cosmopolitanism, though not anti-Clericalism), (3) Taineism (environmental determinism, regionalism), and (4) a lyrical exaltation resulting from the acceptance of a discipline.[1] Each of these elements involves both some theory and some practical policy. In the realm of policy the *revanche* of Boulangism has first place; it is not only the *raison d'être* of the other policies that are advocated, but also of the theories taken individually or together. In the realm of theory, on the other hand, it is Taineism that rules and controls all but the last of the four elements enumerated above—namely, the acceptance of a discipline. This quite illogically demands a volitional acceptance for which there is no place in the determinist theory of Taineism. But strict logic was a small sacrifice for one who was interested in a practical and " satisfying " doctrine; [2] and thus an emotional exaltation

1 Barrès, of course, rejected Taine's belief in an "independent reason existing in each of us," and reproached him for his lack of "piety towards France" (*Scènes et doctrines du nationalisme*, I, 17, 112); he also rejected Pascal's God, though Pascal was likewise one of his masters. It is not, therefore, the intention of the present writer to suggest that Barrès (and Maurras after him, in some instances) accepted all that these "isms" implied, or that there was in each instance a logically integrated doctrine or philosophy embracing all knowledge. They are solely meant to serve as convenient symbols or labels of the elements which Barrès assembled and synthesized into his doctrine of nationalism and, at the same time, to indicate their source.

2 "Le converti croit parce qu'il aime... Les assises d'une France fondée sur la logique ne me satisfont pas; je les veux sur la sensibilité" (*Mes cahiers*, II, 177).

is put above the " law " and, in a sense, made to dominate the other elements.[3]

The low state of France after 1870 "commanded my rôle," Barrès said in *Mes mémoires* shortly before his death.[4] He was but eight years old when the German troops overran his home town of Charmes in Lorraine and instituted an occupation of it that lasted over three years.[5] His father, a prosperous mechanical engineer, and his maternal grandfather, the mayor of the town, were among the hostages held by the Germans to prevent civilian firing upon their troop trains. German soldiers found lodging in his home, as in others, and one of them, taking a kindly interest in the boy, frequently escorted him to his school.[6] Since he was too young to understand the significance of events, his response to the tears of sorrow, anguish, and indignation of his elders was probably the more poignant. Writing of this period toward the close of his life, he said, " When we are all seated in church, each with his thoughts, what is our common thought? We do not want to be Germans. The principal religious thought at home, at Sion, everywhere, is patriotic." [7] This " religion " of not wanting to be German was no doubt more keenly felt in the part of Lorraine that had so narrowly escaped annexation than in other sections of France; people here were eyewitnesses of the large-scale emigration of Frenchmen from the annexed provinces; they did not want to give up their homes, their *terre et morts*, as Barrès

3 It seems to be a necessary element of nationalism. Waldemar Mitscherlich says, " So birgt die Idee des Nationalismus zwei wichtige Elemente in sich: erstens ein Verstandesmässiges: ein " Wissen " um die Zusammengehörigkeit, ein Erkennen der völkischen Lebensgemeinschaft, und zweitens ein gefühlsmässiges: ein Empfinden dieser völkischen Lebensgemeinschaft " [*Der Nationalismus Westeuropas* (Leipzig, 1920), 252].

4 *Mes cahiers*, I, 8.

5 Paul Lesourd, in *La Terre et les morts de Maurice Barrès* (Paris, c. 1925), gives an interesting historical sketch of the town and a description of it and the surrounding country.

6 Victor Giraud, *Les Maîtres de l'heure: Maurice Barrès* (Paris, 1918), 13.

7 *Mes cahiers*, I, 14-15.

later expressed it. It is not surprising, therefore, that when Barrès came to Paris, ambitious to become a man of letters, he was conscious of a certain superiority in the matter of *revanche*. In less than two years after his arrival he called upon the men of his generation to work and plan for it. Their elders have felt a "terrible anger," and they themselves feel that the honor of the country rests in the marching regiments; they are reminded of the "exiles" by the waving flags and military fanfares; their "fists clench"; they want to make themselves "provocative agents." Then he adds, "our special task, as young men, is to recover the seized land, to reconstitute the French ideal. . . . Our fathers failed one day; it is a task of honor that they have left us. They have pushed so far ahead of the *patrie* into the land of the spirit that we can, if necessary, devote several years to the one care of reconquering the exiles. It will require only a little blood and some grandeur of soul. . . ."[8]

This "one care," to which he devoted, not "several years," but the greater part of his life, determined his adherence to the League of Patriots and to the Boulangist movement. If additional urge was needed, it was furnished by his studies. Shortly after his arrival in Paris he had become enamored of the writings of Stendhal, for in them he discovered some of his own sentiments: the sentiment of honor; the taste for glory, boldness, and brilliant exploits; the cult of great men; the passion for voluptuous beauty.[9] Finding these sentiments so eloquently confirmed by this "French Nietzsche"[10] and,

8 *Les Taches d'encre*, Nov. 5, 1884, quoted by Victor Giraud, *op. cit.*, 33.

9 *Ibid.*, 39; Agathon (Henri Massis and Alfred de Tarde) *Les Jeunes gens d'aujourd'hui*, 12th edition (Paris, 1919), 55.

10 Agathon, *op. cit.*, 55: "Stendhal, ce Nietzsche de notre race..." Was he already under the influence of Nietzsche in 1882 and 1883? Probably not. He complained of the passion of some Frenchmen for him in 1892 (*La Figaro*, July 4), but in the space of a decade was frequently quoting him with approval in *Mes cahiers*, III (1902-1904) and in *Scènes et doctrines du nationalisme* (1902). *Cf.* Pierre Lasserre, *La Morale de Nietzsche* (Paris, 1902), App. I, "Nietzsche en France."

seeing them embodied in Boulangism to a considerable extent, he joined the General's movement with the greater enthusiasm. He "snorted with glee," as he said later, "at the violence of approval and disapproval"; he "tasted profoundly the pleasure of being in a mob"; he was "dazzled by the war" that so many expected and hoped would come. But because of a conflict of enthusiasms, he lacked the "sentiment that a spirit attached to a great truth ought to have"; he "had not untangled the symphony of life." [11]

He had learned that he ought to be enthusiastic, that he ought to be in a state of exaltation, which perhaps heightened his fervor for Boulangism at certain moments; but his great enthusiasm, the one he placed before the public gaze and analyzed with amazing frankness in his first trilogy of novels, was his own ego. "Ego worship" was the name he chose for the series. In the first (*Sous l'oeil des barbares*, published in 1888), Philippe, the hero, discovers his *moi* and the barbarians that surround it. Since they have an ideal opposed to his and want to change his *moi*,[12] they must be resisted to the utmost by building defences around the *moi* — high walls and ramparts.[13] Asked what evidence he has that he is a god, he refuses to answer lest he limit himself.[14] In the second story of the series (*Un homme libre*, published in 1889), Philippe submits to a regimen of self-glorification as a means of attaining happiness. Since enthusiasm makes for the greatest happiness, and, since analyzing this ecstasy intensifies the pleasure derived from it, he must needs analyze as much as possible in order to feel as much as possible.[15] The shades of Loyola and Pascal must have grimaced at this perversion of their rules of devotion! But Philippe's punishment is not long delayed; he who has considered himself a god discovers through his analysis

11 *Mes cahiers*, I, 39-40.

12 *Sous l'oeil des barbares* (Paris, 1910), 23.

13 *Ibid.*, 282.

14 *Ibid.*, 244.

15 *Un homme libre* (Paris, 1912), 11.

that his *moi,* taken alone, is quite sterile, and is, therefore, not a fit subject of exaltation. He goes to Lorraine, knocks on the stones in the churches where his fathers rest, and awakens the dead in his conscience. He feels their heart beat across the centuries.[16] He senses the Lorraine conscience which, though not asleep, "hesitates to affirm its personality";[17] it suffers from having accepted the barbarians.[18] He is now in a walled garden instead of on an ivory tower, as before, and can bring in those who have sentiments and interests analogous to his.[19] But the barbarians still assault the garden walls with their "vulgar influences."

In the last narrative of the series (*Le Jardin de Bérénice,* published in 1891), while still opposing his besiegers, he opens the strong gate and admits a beautiful young girl named Bérénice. He even, with the chivalry of a true lover, names the garden after her. As is to be expected of the friend of the egotist, she is no ordinary young lady; she "objectifies the sentimental part" of his *moi*;[20] she is the "popular soul, or the Unconscious";[21] she is to him what Beatrice is supposed by some to have been to Dante. After studying and analyzing her with the aid of Edouard von Hartmann,[22] Philippe concludes as follows in a letter to his friend, Simon: "In coming near these simple folk, I have seen how under each of my acts a subconscious activity collaborates with the conscious activity, and that it is the same as that which one sees in animals and plants; I have simply added to it reflection. . . . It seems to

16 *Ibid.,* 102.

17 *Ibid.,* 108.

18 *Ibid.,* 136.

19 *Ibid.,* 107.

20 *Sous l'oeil des barbares* (Introduction to the 1911 edition), 33.

21 *Ibid.,* 30.

22 *Ibid.,* 28; *cf.* Edouard von Hartmann, *Philosophie des Unbewussten,* 4th edition (Berlin, 1872), 55, 341, 610-613; also Ernst Robert Curtius, *Maurice Barrès und die geistigen Grundlagen des französischen Nationalismus* (Bonn, 1921), 17.

you that the power of reflection is a great thing! What a little thing, in truth, compared with the omniscience and omnipotence which the subconscious manifests in its slowness!" [23] Small wonder, therefore, that he names the garden after "her," since his reflective *moi* is but a "little thing," while "she" is "omniscient and omnipotent!" These coarse, simple, ignorant folk with whom, in real life, he came in contact as a successful Boulangist candidate in 1889, sponsoring a socialist program, these "sublime professors" have taught him that the "instincts are far superior to analysis"; [24] they have revealed to him the "sap of the world," the source of "creative energy." [25] Have the barbarians scaled the garden wall and brought in their "vulgar influences?" Not at all. These "professors," though "they have made him touch the foundations of humanity," [26] live in Nancy, the capital city of Lorraine; it is a Lorraine Bérénice, the Lorraine subconscious, the "Lorraine soul," that has been admitted. He now understands that he represents but a moment in the development of his race, only an instant of a long culture, only a gesture among thousands of a force that has preceded him and will survive him; [27] but he has a feeling of harmony and a sense of security that were lacking before.[28] He has found a worthier subject of exaltation.

Just as Barrès, the romancer, built high walls around his *moi* first, and then around his "garden" of Lorraine, Barrès the Boulangist deputy and journalist, was concerned over the pitiful state of the walls around the "garden" of France. In an article of 1892, entitled *La Querelle des nationalistes et des cosmopolites*,[29] he chides the French for their passion for Walt

23 *Le Jardin de Bérénice* (Paris, 1910), 197-198.

24 *Ibid.*, 198.

25 *Ibid.*, 202.

26 *Ibid.*, 202.

27 *Ibid.*, 201-202.

28 *Sous l'oeil des barbares*, 33.

29 *Le Figaro*, July 4, 1892.

Whitman, Tolstoy, and Nietzsche; they no longer attempt to understand as Taine did; they pretend to create works which are daughters of the literatures of the North and of the South rather than of the national tradition. "It is, in a word, to substitute the European soul for the French soul." And what is the European soul? Pouvillon, with "delightful irony," has called it the Belgian soul. The *nationalistes* contend that these popular foreign writers have been influenced by French writers. They hold that all the tenderness, passion, and sadness that any literature can present may be found in Racine. His friends, Moréas and Maurras, have founded the *Ecole romane* precisely to sustain this opinion. Since they would give the entire Bibliothèque Nationale for the masterpieces of Racine, they are a bit extreme; but he agrees with them to a certain extent.

This article is considered important in the history of French nationalism because it is said to represent the first instance of the definite use of the word *nationaliste* in its later sense,[30] as distinguished from the connotation it had had since the days of the Second Empire when it first came into general use.[31] Until Barrès, it had been used to refer to a person (or policy) that supported by word or deed the principle of nationalities. Such a person favored the principle of self-determination and its corollary, the equal rights of peoples;[32] he advocated freedom of intercourse between nations unhindered by the high walls of strong fortifications, heavy armaments, protective tariffs, and restrictions against the admission of foreign labor or foreign literature; he took a kindly altruistic interest in less fortunate nationalities; in short, he was a "liberal national-

30 Charles Maurras, in *Le Soleil*, Mar. 2, 1900, said, "C'est Maurice Barrès qui détourna *nationalisme* de son sens européen. Il le fit dans un article qui parut au *Figaro* d'alors sous ce titre 'La querelle des nationalistes et des cosmopolites' (D. P. & C., III, 169). *Cf.* Jean Herluison, "Maurice Barrès et le problème de l'ordre," *Revue critique des idées et des livres*, XII (1911), 264; Maurice Barrès, *Mes cahiers*, II, 118.

31 René Johannet, *Le Principe des nationalités* (Paris, 1923), 4.

32 Henri Hauser, *Le Principe des nationalités* (Paris, 1916), 24.

ist."[33] *Nationaliste*, and with it *nationalisme*, now experienced a peculiar metamorphosis so that in general parlance it came to mean the opposite to what it had formerly stood for.[34] And to Barrès is given the credit for having initiated the change.

Having appealed to the good sense of French littérateurs to cease their undignified mimicry of foreign authors and to take their inspiration from the French tradition, in 1893 he appealed to parliament and to the public for legislation to discourage the employment and presence of foreign workmen in France. The tariff law of the year preceding, with its high and numerous specific duties, its retention of high duties on agricultural products, its increase of duties on textiles, and its high minimum rates in general, was pleasingly protectionist.[35] But, as the strikes of French workmen at Liévin and Lens in August, 1892, showed, French laborers wanted protection as well as French farmers and industrialists. To one to whom walls were a specialty, this constituted a serious gap in the wall around France. Barrès therefore gave the measures that were introduced in the Chamber to deal with this problem his full support, both as deputy and as journalist. To arouse the public to the importance of the question, he published a series of articles under the title, *Le Nationalisme implique la protection des ouvriers français*,[36] which illustrates the new use to which the word *nationalisme* was being put. Statistics, he states, show that there are 1,300,000 foreigners in France, and that of these only 65,000 live on money brought in from abroad. They also show that the number is rapidly increasing. France should be hospitable? She is too much so; hence " the cosmopolitan charlatans like Cornelius Herz and Reinach who encumber Paris;

33 Carlton J. H. Hayes, *The Historical Evolution of Modern Nationalism* (New York, 1931), 159-160.

34 René Johannet, *op. cit.*, 5.

35 Percy Ashley, *Modern Tariff History* (New York, 1920), 332-333; Maurice Barrès, *Scènes et doctrines du nationalisme*, II, 191.

36 *Le Figaro*, May, June and July, 1893; republished in *Scènes et doctrines du nationalisme*, II, 186-207.

the twenty thousand foreigners condemned by our tribunals each year; the work of nocturnal Hospitality, which brings ten thousand foreigners to Paris, while many of our unfortunate compatriots remain on the streets for want of beds." [37] Hospitality should begin with the latter. French workmen have as much right to protection as French industrialists and agriculturalists. Moreover, they are at a disadvantage in competing with foreign laborers because the latter are generally excused from military service. "The idea of the *patrie* implies an inequality, but to the detriment of the foreigners and not, as to-day, to the detriment of the nationals." [38] Hence the desirability of taxing employers who use foreign labor, of imposing a military tax on foreign workmen, of expelling foreigners who have become public charges, of forbidding their employment in government enterprises or by privileged companies, and of not permitting the employment of French workmen abroad but bringing them back to France. Is it wrong? No, because "nationalism rules the universe." [39] But the proposed measures were not adopted. He persisted, however, in advocating them despite his defeat in the campaign for re-election several months later.[40]

Freed unwillingly of his parliamentary duties, he now had more time to devote to the problem of "untangling the symphony of life." In view of the nature of the solution which he found, it can be said that he had already made considerable progress in his first trilogy of novels. His discovery of the Lorraine dead and of the Lorraine conscience, or soul, in the *Un homme libre*, was an important stride in the direction his thought later took. The emphasis of instincts, of the subconscious, in *Le Jardin de Bérénice*, was another, for he discovered

37 *Ibid.*, II, 188.

38 *Ibid.*, II, 193.

39 *Ibid.*, II, 201.

40 Maurice Barrès, "Le Sentiment nationaliste," *La Cocarde*, Nov. 18, 1894; "Le Programme de Nancy" (1898), *Scènes et doctrines du nationalisme*, II, 160-163.

the source of the creative energy of the Lorrainers. His *moi* was at once inflated and deflated, and the process gave him a pleasant feeling of harmony and peace. He remained an individualist to the end; but his ego worship now ceased, as did also the dilettante's quest for pleasure as an end in itself. He left the guidance of Renan, the dilettante,[41] for that of Renan, the Breton,[42] and especially for that of Taine, the determinist.

41 Emile Faguet, *Politiques et moralistes du dix-neuvième siècle* (Paris, 1891), III, 360; Victor Giraud, *op. cit.*, 39: "Taine . . . et Renan . . . ont appris . . . à 'caresser sa petite pensée', à vouer à son moi un culte de latrie, à mépriser profondément les 'Barbares'"; Charles Maurras, "L'Influence de Taine," *Le Soleil*, August 21, 1897 (D. P. & C., V, 317): " . . . Je crois même qu'on l'appelle quelque part mademoiselle Renan."

42 Ernest Renan, *Essais de morale et de critique*, 4th edition (Paris, 1889), 382: "Nulle part la condition des morts n'a été meilleure que chez les peuples bretons; nulle part le tombeau ne recueille autant de souvenirs et de prières. C'est que la vie n'est pour ces peuples une aventure personnelle que chacun court pour son propre compte et à ses risques et perils: c'est un anneau dans une longue tradition, un don reçu et transmis, une dette payée et un devoir accompli." *Cf.* Maurice Barrès, *Huit jours chez M. Renan* (Paris, 1913), 60-61.

CHAPTER V

TAINE'S SPECIAL CONTRIBUTION TO BARRESIAN NATIONALISM

TAINE had invented his *race-milieu-moment* method of criticism to serve his philosophy which was based upon the principle of Locke and Condillac that man knows by means of his senses only.[1] Man can divide and add, analyze and generalize; but the result is an abstraction, not truth. Abstraction and metaphysics "suppose"; they do not "know."[2] All that men "know" of the world, therefore, reduces itself to a quantity of matter which is ruled by inflexible and unchanging laws. Everything is determined; the so-called accidents of existence are the result of exact and precise causes.[3] Man himself is no exception; he, too, is governed by these laws. If he has a design, he has probably been forced to make it. If he has a design, the world should also have one; but all one sees is that it acts solely from cause and effect. It is strictly determined; it has no liberty, no personality, no soul; it is unmoral. Man is an automaton whose actions are ruled (1) by the hereditary characteristics of his race; (2) by environment, which largely molds the race, especially, if it is still in its primitive stages when it comes under its influence;[4] and (3) by the epoch, or *Zeitgeist,* of the period in which he lives. He differs little from other animals; he is the "ferocious and lascivious gorilla" that his first ancestor must have been; his "mental organization," it is true, is more highly developed than that of animals or primitive men; but it is generally too weak to save him from

1 Emile Faguet, *op. cit.*, III, 244, 269; Kurt Macard, *Taines Milieutheorie in Zusammenhang mit ihren erkenntnistheoretischen Grundlagen* (Kiel, 1910), 42, 66; H. A. Taine, *History of English Literature*, translated by H. van Laun (Philadelphia, 1896), I, "Introduction."

2 Emile Faguet, *op. cit.*, III, 247.

3 *Ibid.*, III, 250.

4 Kurt Macard, *op. cit.*, 26, 29-30.

hallucinations and inventions of the imagination.[5] Only a few escape from this general mediocrity because of their more complex mental equipment, their more intensive mental activity. It is the superior person's *faculté maîtresse*, his *loi unique*, just as a special instinct is that of the animal or of an inferior person. But this "monomania of the spirit of man," as Faguet describes it,[6] is not an "accident"; it is the result of hereditary or racial characteristics and of the influence of the *Zeitgeist*.[7]

Such, briefly, were the general characteristics of Taine's philosophy and method. Neither was entirely new to his informed readers. He owed much to Montesquieu, Comte, and Herder.[8] Montesquieu had stressed the importance of studying racial and climatic influences as determinants of the "spirit" of the institutions and laws of particular nations; Comte had spent the greater part of his life combating the dominant metaphysical idealism of his time and attempting to substitute for it his Positivist determinism; he, too, had said that man was but another animal, a "prolongation of nature," and that he should be studied as such; finally, Herder had not only emphasized the importance of environment in explaining historical events, but had also, in a sense, anticipated Taine's method.[9] Nor was Taine uninfluenced by the intellectualism, the "abstraction," of his own *moment* or epoch; and, to the measure that he submitted to his influence, he was inconsistent with his premise that knowledge is gained only through the senses and that man as a consequence is a mere automaton.

5 Emile Faguet, *op. cit.*, III, 257-259.

6 *Ibid.*, III, 273.

7 Kurt Macard, *op. cit.*, 34.

8 A. Aulard, *Taine, historien de la Révolution française* (1908), 3-4.

9 *Ibid.*, 4: a quotation from Herder's *Werke*, III, 123: "Was ist das Hauptgesetz dasz wir bei allen grossen Erscheinungen der Geschichte bemerken? Mir dunkt dieses: Dasz allenthalben auf unserer Erde, was auf ihr werden kann, Teils nach Lage und Bedürfniss des Orts, Teils nach Umständen un Gelegenheiten der Zeit, Teils nach den angeborenen oder sich erzeugenden Character der Völker."

He was an ardent individualist and believed that the moral world had its inescapable laws as well as the physical world; he criticized the Jacobin program for attempting to impose the ethics of pre-Christian times upon a people each of whom had a conscience, a personality, and a concept of absolute justice as well as the tradition of individualism derived from the position of the feudal lords.[10] "M. Taine," said Barrès in criticizing his master, "as M. Renan, as all the masters who have preceded us, believed in an independent reason existing in each of us and permitting us to approach the truth." [11] Simultaneously, as a disciple of the other Taine, he opposed this article of faith with the arguments of the determinist school.

The war of 1870 and 1871 troubled Taine terribly. Rejected as a volunteer for military service because of physical infirmities, he determined "to acquit himself of that which he considered a duty towards this ailing France which he loved with a tender and silent passion, the duty of aiding its cure by making the general diagnosis which a philosopher-historian could present after a long study of its extensive constitution." [12] Hence the voluminous *Les Origines de la France contemporaine* to which he devoted the rest of his life, though it remained unfinished at his death.[13] The method by which he arrived at his "diagnosis" was his old one, that of a naturalist, of one who examines and tabulates the "metamorphosis of an insect." [14] He might well have named his studies *Le Milieu ancien, Le Milieu révolutionnaire*, and *Le Milieu moderne*.[15]

10 H. Taine, *La Révolution*, 23rd edition (Paris, 1901), I, 153-162.

11 Maurice Barrès, *Taine et Renan*, edited with comments by Victor Giraud (Paris, 1922), 101; *Mes cahiers*, I, 153-154; IV, 119-120.

12 André Chevrillon, in the "Avant-propos" of volume III of *Le Régime moderne* (Paris, 1901), xvi-xvii.

13 *Ibid.*, ii; he had planned to consider "L'Association" and "La Famille" in the last volume of *Le Régime moderne*.

14 H. Taine, *L'Ancien régime* (Paris, 1901), I, viii.

15 Taine planned to write a book that was to be called *Le Milieu moderne*. It was to present the general characteristics of the period into which European societies had just entered (André Chevrillon, *op. cit.*, x).

And though he had, in his own words, " no other purpose " than to " describe these three states with exactness," [16] his philosophy affected his diagnosis, as did his method.[17] His view of man had been a somber one; but his study of the revolutionary man, with his " crocodile worship," this worship of a god who naturally preferred " fat victims," but whose appetite was so voracious that he blindly devoured thin ones as well,[18] did not make man less abominable in his estimation. " Nothing is more dangerous," he said, " than a general idea in narrow and empty minds. . . ." [19] And what was this general idea? It was, in the words of Rousseau, " the complete alienation of each individual, with all his rights, from the community. . . ." [20] Since the minds of the revolutionists were " narrow and empty," they had no way of opposing the general idea.

Under the influence of the " classical " spirit,[21] they conceived of an abstract man and an abstract community which differed radically from their historical counterparts. They undertook to force the real man and the real community into their ideal molds. Now if science had been further developed, it would have taught them that there are certain general facts, certain traditions which have grown up from a long accumulation of experiences, that do not submit to reason. Indeed, they embody a reason of their own, a blind form of reason that mocks at their " reasoning reason." They are subject to

16 H. Taine, *L'Ancien régime*, I, viii.

17 A. Aulard was probably wrong to question his good faith, however (*op. cit.*, 327). Emile Faguet, while admitting that he had the secret purpose of again studying man (*op. cit.*, III, 279), insists that his *faculté maîtresse* was " probity " (*op. cit.*, III, 237).

18 *La Révolution*, I, i-iv.

19 *Ibid.*, I, 86.

20 *Ibid.*, I, 87, quotation from *Le Contrat social.*

21 *L'Ancien régime*, I, 288-318. He was probably wrong in using this term, for though Boileau had said, "Aimez donc la raison," he meant the imitation and observation of nature, not metaphysical reason. *Cf.* Emile Faguet, *op. cit.*, III, 285-292.

change and, if bad, should be modified; but, if one attempts to destroy or suppress them by the stroke of a pen, they have an inconvenient way of bobbing up again and of remaining, though weakened and half dead. One may take the bark off the "human tree," but the "tree" itself remains.[22] In short, traditions from their very nature have a certain imprescriptible right that cannot be ignored or suppressed. It was precisely this that the Revolutionists, seeking to mold life according to the vague chimeras that floated about in their empty minds, tried to do; and their effort did incalculable harm to France. They destroyed, or seriously weakened, the sources of energy of the community which lay in the social organization that had grown up in the course of centuries in response to necessity and convenience. In 1789 the nobles still had important privileges, though admittedly little power; the Church was still powerful and enjoyed important "liberties"; the provinces and communes were still "collective persons" in fact as well as in law;[23] the family was still important because of the traditional principle of hereditary selection and succession. Since these vital forces of the nation could not be suppressed completely, but remained to trouble the dream of their would-be destroyers, the result of the effort has been the subsequent unstable history of France, as well as a decline of its power under the continued and growing centralization and multiplication of the government's services. "If the law takes from the interested the direction of the ship, if it installs upon this vessel, which belongs to them, a permanent foreign crew, alone commanding and operating it, then the man of the boats, reduced to the humble position of the simply administered and of the passive tax-payer, no longer feels at home, but feels as though he were in the home of another; since the intruders have all the authority, let them take all the pains; the management is their business, not his; he looks on as a spectator, having neither the desire nor the idea of giving a hand; he folds his

22 *Ibid.*, I, 316.

23 *Le Régime moderne*, II, 222.

arms, remains idle, and becomes critical. . . . All these effects result in paralyzing the better half of the soul of the nation, much worse, in misleading the will and perverting the public spirit, in transforming the generous impulses into malevolent blows, in instituting, to stay, inertia, boredom, discontent, discord, weakness and sterility." [24] With authority concentrated, the administration centralized, ubiquitous regimentation, uniformity, and the like, the individual is left with no purpose to live except to be a prominent member of the "foreign crew"; but so many fail in this that they have a new reason for being dissatisfied.[25]

This diagnosis of France's "malady," coming, as it did, from one of the most authoritative writers in French letters, had no little influence. Admirers of de Bonald, Chateaubriand, de Tocqueville, Comte, Le Play, Proudhon, La Tour Du Pin, and others who had voiced opposition to the extreme centralization of the government of France, saw their ideas verified in varying degrees in this study, while the Felibrians found in it an eloquent justification of their efforts to revivify local sentiment. The schism of 1892 in the *Félibrige de Paris* over the question of decentralization,[26] the slight parliamentary concession of 1890 to the principle of communal and departmental autonomy,[27] and the campaign of 1892 and 1895 for a scheme to decentralize university instruction were, no doubt, in part, the result of Taine's influence.[28] But few were affected more profoundly than was Barrès, who was both an admirer and imitator of Chateaubriand and a Felibrian.[29] Boulangism had been only a "fever"; what was needed was a "national conscience." [30] Boulangism had followed an image of "the ideal

24 *Ibid.*, II, 206-207.
25 *Ibid.*, III, 224-225.

26 Charles Maurras, *L'Etang de Berre* (Paris, 1924), 119-134.

27 Charles Maurras, *L'Idée de la décentralisation* (Paris, 1898), 13-14.

28 *Ibid.*, 15.

29 Charles Maurras, *L'Etang de Berre*, 119. On the Felibrians, see below, p. 185 *et seq.*

30 Maurice Barrès, *L'Appel au soldat* (Paris, 1911), 283.

France"; what was needed was an idea of the "real France." Too many Frenchmen had only an "administrative patriotism"; what they needed was a "patriotism of the soil," of the hearth, of the commune, and of the province.[31] Once Frenchmen were conscious of these, the "real France," they would be better Frenchmen; they would love the soil of France and defend it zealously; they would love her customs and institutions, though varying in different sections of the country, and would protect them from contaminating foreign influences. Since decentralization would release the energies of the nation, Barrès joined the federalists in agitating for it.

This he did both as journalist and as novelist; and as the director of *La Cocarde*, of Boulangist and Panama fame, from September 5, 1894, to March 6, 1895, he was in a position to do this effectively. In the first issue of the new *Cocarde* he announced that it would be an organ of Republican opposition, stressing patriotism and social solidarity, and grouping around it socialists and intellectuals.[32] In the next number he declared "free and profound individualism" and "social solidarity" were its "double care" and the source of its ideal.[33] Finally, in taking leave of the paper, he summarized its program: "individualism and solidarity," between which there was no real opposition; "federation and contract"; "the maintenance of national unity by the cult of great men"; and "the party of to-morrow has a tradition—'48—'51—'52."[34] At first glance there seems to be little here to justify the statement of Maurras that "the editors of *La Cocarde* had the opportunity to apply and defend the methods and teachings of Taine," and that "in seeking the concrete form of their nationalism its editors felt themselves to be federalists . . . , provincialists,

31 Charles Maurras, *L'Idée de la décentralisation*, 16.

32 *La Cocarde*, Sept. 5, 1894.

33 Henri Clouard, "La 'Cocarde' de Barrès," *La Revue critique des idées et des livres* (Feb. 10, 1910), VIII, 210.

34 *La Cocarde*, Mar. 7, 1895.

and traditionalists. . . . "[35] But if it be considered that the individual and society sink their differences in the local governments, corporations, and associations that are made possible by the principles of federation and contract, it would seem that Barrès was seeking a theoretical justification and explanation of a means of tapping the "sources of energy" that Taine had valued so highly. His method, it is true, was less that of a naturalist than that of a manipulator of ideas. Just as Proudhon, using Hegel's dialectical method, had found a synthesis of authority and liberty in "federation and contract,"[36] so Barrès discovered in Proudhon's "federation and contract" not only a system that permitted change, but also a synthesis of collectivism and anarchism, of solidarity and individualism.[37] "Federation and contract! The geographical groups (regions, communes), the moral groups (aggregations, professional or of all orders), rise up only by themselves in the federation and regulate themselves within by contracts analogous to transactions and exchanges: that is what conciliates individualism and solidarity, that is what reunites while avoiding all idea of restraint."[38] It respects moral and physical differences; it permits the individual to set up tolerable relations with other individuals.[39]

But the decentralization that was to make this social individualism possible was to be introduced "under the protection of nationalism," which in turn was in need of decentralization.[40] A strong, authoritarian government, an elected dictator, would keep the federated regions and associations in their re-

35 Charles Maurras, *op. cit.*, 17.

36 P.-J. Proudhon, *Du principe fédératif* (Paris, 1868), Chs. VI, VII and VIII.

37 Maurice Barrès, "De Hegel aux cantines du Nord" (first published in *Le Journal* of Nov. 30 and Dec. 7 and 14, 1894, and republished in *Scènes et doctrines du nationalisme*, II, 243-254), *Scènes et doctrines du nationalisme*, II, 249.

38 *Ibid.*, II, 251-252.

39 *Ibid.*, II, 253.

40 Henri Clouard, *op. cit.*, VIII, 226.

spective places, while not robbing them of their vitality, as did the top-heavy administrative and parliamentary system. Contrary to the view of the orthodox economists and of the collectivist socialists, the idea of the *patrie* was "beautiful, good, legitimate" and, therefore, it should affect the social economy, politics, and public education alike.[41] Hence the plea for the exclusion of foreign workmen,[42] for the liberation of French workmen by means of decentralization,[43] for the abolition of parliamentary rule, for the cult of heroes, and the denunciation of the Opportunist-Radical coalition as a "syndicate of Panamists, of master black-mailers and of traitors."[44] Drumont, it was held, had rendered "a famous service in propagating, with tenacity, with an abundance of arguments, and with an incomparable emotion, this doctrine that we can understand each other only because foreigners have not minds made like ours."[45] But it must be accepted, recognized, and acted upon; and, if the campaign for decentralization, the effort "to create and fortify the energy by which man becomes conscious of his soil, of his race, of his traditions, and of his national group" should fail, "France would disappear, pilfered by the foreigners within (the Rouviers, the Reinachs, and other exploiters), or by foreigners from without."[46]

The owners of *La Cocarde* were, however, so displeased with the policy and conduct of its editors that they sought to interfere. This resulted in the resignation of Barrès and of most of the contributors he had attracted as the director of the paper. Next day the owners announced that they were abandoning

41 *Ibid.*, VIII, 227 (*La Cocarde*, Oct. 24, 1894).

42 Maurice Barrès, "Le Sentiment nationaliste," *La Cocarde*, Nov. 18, 1894; Henri Clouard, *op. cit.*, VIII, 227, 229.

43 Henri Clouard, *op. cit.*, VIII, 226.

44 Maurice Barrès, "Reflexions: le premier mot de l'année," *La Cocarde*, Jan. 1, 1895.

45 *La Cocarde*, Oct. 22, 1894, quoted by Henri Clouard, *op. cit.* (Feb. 25, 1910), VIII, 334.

46 *La Cocarde*, Dec. 19, 1894, quoted by Henri Clouard, *op. cit.* (Feb. 10, 1910), VIII, 229.

" vague political theories " and " noisy pronouncements " and that the journal would henceforth limit its purpose to giving a simple daily account of political events.[47] This brief Barrèsian experience of the paper was quite different from any it had had or any it was to have.[48]

Though he continued to contribute articles to the press, Barrès now turned to what was possibly his most important effort in his self-imposed task of stirring up national sentiment, the writing of his second trilogy of novels, *Le Roman de l'Energie Nationale*, which he had planned the year before.[49] Somewhat autobiographical and certainly didactical, this series of narratives gives the experience of six young Lorrainers in Paris in the decade following their arrival there in 1883. It is also something of a political chronicle, for the second and third parts give lengthy accounts of the Boulangist movement and of the Panama crisis respectively. It is, finally, a fairly complete statement of his doctrine of nationalism, containing in varying degrees the four elements (Boulangism, Drumontism, Taineism, and the lyrical exaltation) mentioned above.

47 *La Cocarde*, Mar. 8, 1895.

48 Henri Clouard, *op. cit.* (Feb. 10, 1910), VIII, 208.

49 Victor Giraud, *op. cit.*, 61.

CHAPTER VI

BARRES' ROMANCE OF NATIONAL ENERGY

ALTHOUGH Taineism in a sense dominates the whole of Barrès' *Le Roman de l'Energie Nationale*,[1] it is especially conspicuous in the first narrative, *Les Déracinés*, which may be characterized as an artistic version of Taine's determinist philosophy, of his criticism of centralization, and especially of the sixth and last book of *Le Régime moderne*, the topic of which is *L'Ecole*. Since the days of the First Empire the University has been a powerful instrument of the state, its task having been to uphold the established order.[2] Under the Third Republic it has made it its business to glorify the Revolution. In doing this it has slighted rhetoric for philosophy. Gambetta is its master of political philosophy, while Kant is its master of pure philosophy. Now Bouteiller (in real life Auguste Burdeau, Barrès' philosophy professor at Nancy, later minister and at least morally implicated in the Panama scandal), whose business it is to teach philosophy to the Lorraine boys whose experiences Barrès is about to relate, is a dutiful and inspired disciple of Kant and Gambetta. Instead of recognizing and utilizing the prejudices and natural tendencies of these Lorraine youths and thereby adding to the "spontaneity and to the variety of the national energy," he denies or ignores them and takes his students into the realm of the abstract where "one reality exists": the moral law.[3] To say that France was a "gloriously conquered" nation is no fit basis of a nationalism that requires "earthy foundations marked by genius."[4]

1 "Nous sommes," says Barrès, "des botanistes qui observons sept à huit plantes transplantées et leurs efforts pour reprendre racine . . ." [*Les Déracinés* (Paris, 1920), II, 174].

2 *Ibid.*, I, 12-13.

3 *Ibid.*, I, 21, 26.

4 *Ibid.*, I, 38.

Worse still, to " uproot these children, to detach them from the soil and from the social group, where everything binds them, in order to place them outside of their prejudices into abstract reason "[5] is to trouble them profoundly by the restraint it imposes upon their natural tendencies. His talk of humanity and of the duty of the individual to sacrifice himself for the community brings them to tears; his accent and his image dominate them; their desire to be as great as is their admired master is their only remaining social sentiment.[6]

Having been trained to frown upon their old prejudices, upon their own Lorraine, six of the seven turn their backs upon it and go to " happy Paris," each carrying in his soul " a dead young Lorrainer," for they are simply individuals now.[7] Recognizing no other responsibility than towards themselves, they wander about the Latin Quarter without a directing thread, " free as the beasts in the woods."[8] One of the more studious of the six, Roemerspacher, has written and published a none too friendly study of Taine and is visited by the latter.[9] Taine questions his failure to make allowance for ethics in his scientific studies and expresses surprise that his Kantian master has failed to give him a conception of duty. But the young man scoffs at the idea of duty and at the idea of recasting society according to the principles of pure reason.[10] Taine appears to be pleased and states that he has come to the

5 *Ibid.*, I, 21-22.

6 *Ibid.*, I, 40-41.

7 *Ibid.*, I, 138.

8 *Ibid.*, I, 139.

9 Pierre Chardon (D. P. & C., V, 320): " Charles Maurras publia dans *l'Observateur français* du 29 décembre 1890 l'article ci-dessous. A la suite de cette publication, le grand historien se rendit au journal, 10, rue du Bac, et y laissa sa carte en l'absence du jeune auteur. Charles Maurras se présenta donc rue Cassette afin de rendre cette visite, fut accueilli et, quelque temps plus tard, raconta l'entrevue dans une lettre à Barrès. Celui-ci utilisa ce texte dans les *Déracinés*, et mit l'aventure au compte d'un de ses personnages principaux: Roemerspacher."

10 *Les Déracinés*, I, 216-217.

conclusion that the " best school, the social laboratory, is the group, the free association ";[11] then, pointing to a tree, as they are strolling near Les Invalides, he says, " This tree is the expressive image of a glorious existence. It has not known immobility. . . . It has not been necessary that a master from without should intervene. . . . See what pure health it has! No predominance of its trunk, of its branches, of its leaves; it is a rustling federation. It is a law unto itself. . . . This powerful mass of verdure obeys a secret reason, the most sublime philosophy, the acceptance of the exigencies of life. Without denying itself, without abandoning itself, it has taken the best and most useful part of the provisions furnished it by reality. From the largest branches to the smallest radicles it has achieved the same movement throughout. . . . And now this tree, which each day confidently increases its store of energies, is going to disappear because it has reached its perfection."[12] Shortly after, while describing the interview to his friend Sturel, Roemerspacher remarks that Taine's sympathy for a beautiful tree, which he understands in all the stages of its growth, is an epitome of the best use that a man can make of his intelligence: " to order his mind, to conceive all the manifestations of organic and inorganic nature and our soul itself as parts of the universal soul which unites all, as individual parcels of the great bodies of the universe! Such is the sole task of those who wish to live nobly."[13] But Sturel sees in this a servile doctrine of renunciation, and accuses Taine of making his friend a pantheist, one who looks upon nature as a living unity, as having its own principle of action. The individual is not simply nothing and society all; nature is " an ensemble of independent energies " which by coöperating produce " the universal harmony."[14]

11 *Ibid.*, I, 221.

12 *Ibid.*, I, 222-224.

13 *Ibid.*, I, 230.

14 *Ibid.*, I, 233, 261-262.

In contrast to the plane tree that Taine has pointed out and described, France is a picture of dissociation. The bureaucratic administration destroys initiative; there is religious divison and strife; economic life is unorganized and is, therefore, a prey of international finance and subject to the inroads of foreign goods and workmen; there are all sorts of associations, but they are more interested in their own several tasks than in the common welfare of the French community. For this situation the bureaus are responsible. The bureau of teaching belittles the *petite patrie* and spurs men on to emulation without giving them a religion which might serve as a social bond, while the administration prepares men only for its own service; but many are refused and become antagonistic.[15] If a man were subject to a comparable dissociation, he would be "impaired, if not annulled, by it."[16] He would be decerebrated just as "France is decerebrated" by the existing anarchy.[17] Instead of working at cross purposes, Frenchmen ought to recognize that in principle personality is purely an accident, that "the veritable essence of the Frenchman is a common nature, a social and historical product, possessed as shares by each of us."[18] "The problem is simply one of entering into partnership with the national energy, of discerning its direction and accepting its various degrees of progression."[19]

Sturel, saddened by the assassination of his mistress, and worried over the imprisonment of two of his Lorraine colleagues for murder, joins the crowd that has lined the streets to witness the procession of officials and friends escorting Hugo's remains from l'Etoile to the Panthéon. "Hugo will rest henceforth upon the Ararat of national classicism. He will raise the refuge higher. He will be one of the elements of the sacred mountain that will give us safety, even when the lower

15 *Ibid.*, I, 266-269; *cf.* H. Taine, *Le Régime moderne*, III, 224-225.

16 *Ibid.*, I, 270.

17 *Ibid.*, I, 272.

18 *Ibid.*, I, 270.

19 *Ibid.*, I, 276.

parts of our territory and of our spirit will have been invaded by the Barbarians. Let us apply ourselves," continues Barrès, appealing directly to his readers, "to contemplate the *patrie* each day in the reserves of its powers and help to unfold them. Let us reflect that France owes all her grandeur to the men who are buried in her soil. Let us worship them and thereby augment ourselves." [20] Sturel, sensing the unity of feeling in the crowd, is reminded of Roemerspacher's statement, "I am a social man." [21]

But Sturel feels this more profoundly, when later, in the full tide of the Boulangist movement, he accepts the invitation of Saint-Phlin, the only one of the seven Lorraine youths who remained at home, to visit him, and is initiated into the cult of *la terre et les morts*. As Sturel represents in a general way the Boulangist Barrès, and Roemerspacher the Taineian Barrès, so Saint-Phlin stands for the sentimental and pseudo-scientific addition which Barrès made to the Taineian determinism: his Chateaubriandian love of the dead and of the graveyard atmosphere and the ideas obtained from Edouard von Hartmann and Jules Soury.[22] Hartmann, whose influence upon Barrès' *Le Jardin de Bérénice* has already been noted, had experimented with decerebrated frogs and chickens and had discovered that the spinal ganglia have a volition of their own independent of the brain; hence the importance of the subconscious.[23] But more important still, at least from the standpoint of Barrès' doctrine, was his statement that children inherit the ganglia and spinal formations of their parents.[24] Soury propounded

20 *Ibid.*, II, 236.

21 *Ibid.*, II, 237.

22 Barrès in *La Cocarde* of Jan. 20, 1895 expresses his debt and gratitude to these two men and refers to the latter as "un de nos maîtres les plus chers" (Henri Clouard, *op. cit.*, VIII, 211). *Cf. Mes cahiers*, I, *passim.* Camille Vettard in "Maurice Barrès et Jules Soury," *Mercure de France* (Mar. 15, 1924), CLXX, 680, holds Barrès was more indebted to Soury than to Burdeau, Taine or anyone else.

23 Edouard Hartmann, *Philosophie des Unbewussten*, 55.

24 *Ibid.*, 341, 610-613.

the same idea in his writings [25] and in his lectures at the Sorbonne, which Barrès audited as late as 1896,[26] although he was already acquainted with his ideas on the subject. It was probably after one of these lectures that Barrès wrote the following note: "That which is transmitted hereditarily is the structure of the nervous centers. Thrown into the same environment with the same equipment, we ought to react in the same manner. . . . The prejudices of the theologian, of the politician, of the moralist are reflexes. Not one of our journalists or orators thinks by himself. Perhaps a Goethe, a Voltaire? We are not masters of that which we think, feel, wish. We are only automatons. Only our machine is more complex. As long as we have our brain, we react in an appropriate manner." [27] And the value of this theory lay not only in the fact that it confirmed Taine's theory of determinism, but also in its sentimental possibilities. These were especially attractive to Barrès. Referring to Lorraine a few years later, he said, "At first I did not love her. She began to please me when I reflected that she had her dead." [28]

"Yes, François," says Saint-Phlin upon Sturel's arrival, "this soil has produced a family: all of my people have drawn from it by their roots; and my soul is made of the total of their souls, of the nature of the soil and of the circumstances of history. But I shall make you see a 'tree' of another amplitude! It is exactly for this reason that I have invited you, and you will be pleased." [29] They agree that children should be impregnated with the "knowledge of their dead and of their

25 Jules Soury, *Les Fonctions du cerveau* (Paris, 1891), 350-351. Later publications in which the same ideas are advanced are, *Lettre à Charles Maurras* (Paris, 1899), *passim*; (An article on the dead, dedicated to Renan), *La Gazette de France*, Nov. 2, 1900; *Campagne nationaliste*, 1899-1901 (Paris, 1902), 65, 125-139. *Cf.* Eugène Fournière, "Le Nationalisme: Lettre à M. Jules Soury," *La Revue socialiste* (July, 1902), XXXVI, 1.

26 Maurice Barrès, *Mes cahiers*, I, 73.

27 *Ibid.*, I, 154-155.

28 *Ibid.*, II, 237.

29 Maurice Barrès, *L'Appel au soldat*, 269.

soil" instead of being taught the "vague, floating, unreal humanities." [30] How well-ordered and forceful Frenchmen would be, once they accepted their "predestination!" [31] But would it not make for division? Sturel asks. He has already noticed a difference between the Parisian and Lorraine consciences.[32] To show that they may be combined into a national conscience, the host takes his guest to Metz to visit the graves of the French soldiers who died there. The lesson of the pious pilgrimage is that all Frenchmen should take cognizance of the fact that they have a responsibility towards these poor dead and towards the living in the lost provinces as well. They should also oppose the "incessant infiltration" of Germans into France because "they compromise our natural destinies." [33] And, since a "nation is a territory where men possess memories, customs, and an hereditary ideal in common," it is lost if it ceases to strive for this ideal; it will melt away in the fusion with the foreign people whom it accepts as the center of things, just as Lorraine once became French and Metz is now in danger of becoming German.[34] So instructed, Sturel returns to Paris more Boulangist than ever, for Boulanger has given the two Lorraines, the annexed and the French, more confidence in France and a greater desire to live.[35]

Five years later, in response to Sturel's request for money and for a plan of action, Saint-Phlin lauds the Lorraine discipline, the Lorraine "nurture." The normal school at Nancy should train the future teachers of their children in things Lorraine by promenades in the country, by visits to neighboring industrial establishments and places of historical importance, by showing what she owes and has contributed to French

30 *Ibid.*, 301.

31 *Ibid.*, 301.

32 *Ibid.*, 315.

33 *Ibid.*, 330.

34 *Ibid.*, 392.

35 *Ibid.*, 402.

culture.[36] They should be instructed in the qualities of the Lorraine race, in its local habits, in its entire heritage. They must love them as well as know them; they must love the soil and the dead.[37] Once they have this Lorraine discipline, "this Lorraine backbone," they will never be uprooted, though they leave their canton and plunge into the most "devouring environment"; they will remain the "continuity" of their fathers and will benefit from the "apprenticeship" they have made in their veins before being born.[38] Sturel, disgruntled over the failure of Boulangism, enraged over the Panama scandal, and displeased with the "general paralysis" created by the "decerebrated and dissociated" condition of France, concludes that the best thing he can do is to make himself more and more a Lorrainer. He will help his Lorraine traverse this period of weakness intact so that, "despite the maladies of the whole, this part will remain capable of producing Austrasian fruits."[39]

But he has not given up Boulangism; he has merely substituted "reality" for "generosity of soul";[40] he has joined to the Boulangist will to live, the will to strive for an ideal France, a positivist nationalism that should give Frenchmen "real" reasons for loving their country and new energy and power in striving for their ideal. Sturel, who, as has been noted, is Barrès' Boulangist counterpart in the series of narratives and is, in many respects, more nearly like the author than any of the other characters, distinguishes himself in *Les Déracinés* as a devotee of hero worship. Napoleon Bonaparte is his hero.[41]

36 Maurice Barrès, *Leurs figures* (Paris, 1911), 225.

37 *Ibid.*, 226.

38 *Ibid.*, 229.

39 *Ibid.*, 294.

40 Maurice Barrès, *L'Appel au soldat*, 283-284.

41 René Benjamin gives a delightful description of Barrès' work room in which a large portrait of Bonaparte, with "feverish eyes," stood facing the entrance. On the mantlepiece reclined a huge, bronze, Egyptian cat whose "satanic sneer" contradicted everything the portrait told Barrès ["Le Soliloque de Maurice Barrès," in his *Grandes figures: Barrès, Joffre* (Paris, 1931), 37-41].

When Roemerspacher tells him of his interview with Taine and takes him to the tree that the master has pointed out, he notices that it is standing directly opposite the Invalides. As they stand in the square contemplating the "two contradictory ethics" represented by the "little verdant bouquet" and the "glorious gilded cupola," glittering in the rays of the setting sun, Sturel's preference is easily the latter.[42] Soon after, he persuades his friends to accompany him on a pilgrimage to Napoleon's tomb, where he reverently relates the story of his life and suggests that they regard him as their "professor of energy."[43] Another energetic and masterful leader, such as Napoleon was, would give unity of purpose and a new energy to the present "decerebrated and dissociated" France. He later sees in Boulanger the hoped-for leader and joins his movement with enthusiasm. And now he discovers that Taine and Bonaparte are not so opposed to each other after all, for it is a trait of the French people to have a man who incarnates their sentiments.[44] Thiers, despite his thick spectacles, has been hailed the "Liberator of the Territory," and Gambetta has been proclaimed the "Rampart of the Republic"; "but a general is more expressive of power than an orator because he can lock up the babblers."[45] And how much more entrancing to a "warlike nation" is the young minister of war, riding his black charger, than the diminutive, bespectacled lawyer, Thiers! The former's vigorous words and deeds not only strengthen his own power, but call forth the energies of the French people.

The unity of sentiment that Boulanger represents is not only a question for Germany; it is also the "negation of parliamentarism." The German government and the parliamentary majority, therefore, coöperated in bringing about the fall of the Goblet ministry in order to strike down the popular min-

42 *Les Déracinés*, I, 229.

43 *Ibid.*, I, 248.

44 *L'Appel au soldat*, 53.

45 *Ibid.*, 53-54.

ister of war.[46] Parliamentarism is a mental poison comparable to "alcoholism, plumbism, syphilis," which by its "verbalism and vacuity . . . intoxicates all Frenchmen";[47] hence their blind unconcern over the distribution of places without regard to talent and the constant sacrifice of the public good to private interests; likewise their complete disregard of the future.[48] Boulanger's electoral victories in 1888 are defeats of the system,[49] just as are the Panama exposures of 1892. Sturel shows how, in the latter period, the deputies wait in the corridors of the Chamber for the arrival of the three-o'clock edition of *La Cocarde.* When it comes they devour it with great interest, just as in the morning they throw themselves upon *La Libre parole* and *L'Intransigeant* to see if they have been denounced. "Their faces," he continues, "which they wish to make serene, betray the beating of their hearts; the wrinkles of their foreheads, their idiocy, because they exhaust themselves figuring why the ministry should protect them."[50] But despite their obvious guilt, all but one of the *chéquards* are protected by the government, and most of them are also re-elected in September, 1893. It is exasperating. A friend of Sturel is so enraged at these people, "these *bourgeois*, these mollusks, these inert beings," who by their apathy prevent the realization of a great idea, that he is in the mood to begin throwing bombs.[51]

And what a service Drumont has performed for his country in exposing the sordid traffic of Reinach and Herz in men and

46 *Ibid.*, 58.

47 *Ibid.*, 104.

48 *Ibid.*, 109.

49 *Ibid.*, 118. How near the Panama scandal came to destroying parliamentarism in France is seen in Alexandre Zévaès' discussion of Numa Gilly's exposures in 1888. The deputies who came to Paris as poor as he and spent thousands per year he denounced as "Wilsons." But Raynal, Roche, and Baïhaut sued him and had him condemned in the name of outraged virtue, even though their souls were said to have been as black as hell [*Au temps du Boulangisme* (Paris, 1930), 118].

50 Maurice Barrès, *Leurs figures* (Paris, 1911), 25.

51 *Ibid.*, 180.

money! It is in *Leurs figures*, the third and last narrative of the trilogy, that Barrès depicts these men in the blackest colors. Because Reinach was the victim, he quite naturally attracts sympathy; but there is no compassion for him in Barrès' account. Reinach is the "poisoned rat" who, in his feverish desire to save himself, started the rumor that Delahaye could make a fortune if he would but listen to reason, and who spent his last evening galloping in the darkness as would a poisoned rat behind the wood pile.[52] But after all, theirs is a different race. Their *patrie* is not the French soil or the French dead; "it is the place where they find their greatest interests."[53] In pursuing these they remain the "continuity" of their dead.

But this psychological and environmental determinism of the dead and of the soil is not, it appears, a complete determinism or a constant one; for it may be ignored, forgotten, or even replaced by vague, floating abstractions. This is precisely what is wrong with Kant-ridden France. Frenchmen have chosen to follow the pillar of light in the sky as did the ancient Hebrews at one time; they strain their eyes and advance as fast as they can to keep it in view, forgetting that the real is under their feet and in the tombs of their ancestors. Now it is not enough that they be instructed in these realities; it is not enough that they be told that these realities constitute their determinism, their "predestination"; nor is an elegant Chateaubriandian reverence for and attachment to tombs, though it, too, is useful and necessary; what Frenchmen need is an emotional "acceptance" of these realities, an emotional "submission" to their determinism, comparable to Pascal's idea of a "true conversion."[54] They must prostrate themselves be-

52 *Ibid.*, 69.

53 *Scènes et doctrines du nationalisme*, I, 67.

54 *Leurs figures*, 222. Pascal: "La conversion véritable consiste à s'anéantir devant cet être universel . . ." In "Sur la conversion du pêcheur," the sinner finds rest only after prostrating himself before the throne of God; he meditates upon His kindness and upon the meanness of men who reject Him; he considers His grandeur and falls into an access of humiliation and adoration

fore their dead and their soil, and, in the spirit of a penitent, accept their designs. And what "a magnificent sweetness" will "appease" them! They will gladly accept all their "shackles," even death. " He who permits himself to penetrate these certitudes abandons the pretention of thinking better, of feeling better, of wishing better than his fathers and mothers; he says to himself: 'I am they themselves.' And what consequences he will take from this consciousness! . . . It is all an intoxication in which the individual destroys himself to rediscover himself in the family, in the race, in the nation." [55] Having had this experience, Frenchmen will consider themselves one; and, what is more important, they will *feel* themselves one; for " emotion is the great human quality " and nothing really great has been achieved without being accompanied by an extraordinary emotion.[56]

[Ernest Havet, *Pensées de Pascal* publiées dans leur texte authentique, 4th ed. (Paris, 1887), I, 194; II, 317-318].

55 *Scènes et doctrines du nationalisme,* I, 18-19.

56 *Leurs figures,* 268.

CHAPTER VII

THE ANTI-DREYFUSARD AGITATION

ALTHOUGH the three parts of *Le Roman de l'Energie Nationale* were not published until 1897, 1900, and 1902, the work was planned in 1894 and contained substantially the doctrines Barrès had assembled and advanced by that time.[1] The last two parts, *L'Appel au soldat* and *Leurs figures*, undoubtedly benefited from the " emotion " generated by the Dreyfus crisis, not only in Barrès, but in thousands of Frenchmen as well, with its street brawls, suicides, duels; heatedly partisan newspaper articles, bizarre cartoons, the conversion of former friendships into bitter hatred, and the division of Frenchmen in general into two hostile camps. Drumont thundered imprecations upon the Jews, Protestants, and Free Masons more loudly and vociferously than ever,[2] while Déroulède, who had resigned his seat in the Chamber in 1893 in disgust and had gone into retirement because Millevoye had, contrary to his promise, read out the parts of the bogus Norton letters which implicated the latter's friend, Rochefort, as well as Clemenceau, in the supposed treasonable relations with England, now returned to the political arena. The formula of this quixotic patriot, which Barrès described as "truly very powerful," was, " There is no probability that Dreyfus is innocent, but it is absolutely certain that France is innocent." [3]

If brevity, simplicity, and clarity enhance the power of a statement, this one had all these qualities. To the Boulangists (now simply plebiscitarians or nationalists, for the old name was no longer popular), to the anti-Semites, and to the royalists, there was no choice in the matter of taking sides. On the

1 To Doumic's charge that Barrès was busy rebuilding the altars he had torn down, the latter replied, " Ils peuvent témoigner que dans *la Cocarde* nous avons tracé avec une singulière vivacité, dont s'effrayaient peut-être tels amis d'aujourd'hui, *tout le programme du 'nationalisme'* que depuis longtemps nous appelions par son nom (*Scènes et doctrines du nationalisme*, I, 15).

2 He was elected to the Chamber of Deputies in 1898.

3 *Ibid.*, I, 32.

one hand was a Jewish captain, convicted of treason and supported by vague concepts of Truth and Justice; on the other was everything they loved and respected: the army, the honor of the *Patrie* and of the flag, the authority of the state. Even if Dreyfus had been condemned wrongfully, as few of the above would admit, what was a mere Jew's comfort compared with the French army, the "glorious repository" of the vital interests of France?[4] But neither side was prompted solely by altruistic considerations, whether patriotic or humanitarian. Many monarchists had "rallied" to the Republic after 1889, even before the appearance of Pope Leo XIII's encyclical of 1892. After the Socialists made considerable gains in the election of 1893, they were opposed by a coalition of the Center and the Right: of the Progressists, who now replaced the older Opportunists; the monarchists (royalists and Bonapartists); anti-Semites and Nationalists. The groups of the Right, therefore, had considerable political power.[5] Their control over the army, in which they were interested for partisan reasons as well as patriotic, was almost complete. Although they complained that a revision of the decree of the court-martial of 1894 would be a blow to the army and that it would weaken France's power of resistance to Germany's overweening military strength, they were also interested in the continuance and growth of their political power, which should ultimately bring either a plebiscitary republic or a monarchy. As for the anti-Semites, whether they were republican followers of Drumont or royalist followers of Jules Guérin, they hoped, as enemies of the Jews, the Free Masons and the Protestants, to restore the quondam power of the Clericals.[6]

The Dreyfusards or Revisionists (Radicals, Socialists and, after Colonel Henry's confession and suicide, the Center), with

4 See the Declaration that was subscribed to by the men in 1898 who later organized *La Ligue de la Patrie française* [Charles Maurras, *Au signe de Flore* (Paris, 1931), 96].

5 *Ibid.*, 58; Alexandre Zévaès, *L'Affaire Dreyfus* (Paris, 1930), 9.

6 Alexandre Zévaès, *op. cit.*, 9.

all their vaunted idealism, had their political interests and ambitions. The Socialists, despite their gains of 1893, were still effectively excluded from power. Moreover, they opposed the army as a mainstay of capitalism. Many of them, and some Radicals as well, such as Ranc, had felt its power during the Commune of 1871. They disliked compulsory military service and, in general, shared or sympathized with the views and sentiments so graphically expressed by Joséphin Péladan,[7] Abel Hermant,[8] and Lucien Descaves.[9] This is not to say that they

7 *Curieuse*, Vol. II of *La Décadence latine*, Paris, 1886. Péladan described in this novel the brothels of Paris, ascribing their existence to the three-year military service law. Men were not permitted to marry during the service period. If they were married before, the wife and children were reduced to wretchedness. To keep their children from starving, wives were frequently reduced to a life of shame (pp. 153-161). Reverting to his own experience in the army, he said, "Pourquoi n'avoir rien écrit jusqu'en 1880? Parce que, devant la caserne, cet enfer sans justice, j'aurais fui jusqu'en exil! Je revois ce jour odieux où on me fit dépouiller de tout vêtement: on viola d'un examen de maquignon la nudité de mon corps; on me toucha, on me toisa, comme on eut fait d'un cochon, moi tabernacle d'une âme immortelle, crée à l'image de Dieu, méditateur prématuré de l'*Apocalypse!* Heureusement, les yeux abîmés par l'étude, l'organisme débilité par l'excès cérébral, je n'avais plus assez de sang pour la boucherie; je n'avais plus assez de muscles pour les travaux forcés, et bête de rebut, dédaigné par l'abattoir et refusé par le bagne, on me déclara incapable de service actif. Douce France où la presque cécité est un bienfait du ciel! Douce France où l'éclopé seul échappe à l'abrutissement! Douce France où les mères, à leur prière du matin et du soir, implorent de la Vierge Marie une infirmité pour leur enfant! Douce France où je n'ai pu rester que comme animal de rancart! Douce France, cette plume brisée témoignera de ta douceur devant l'histoire" (p. 334).

8 *Le Cavalier Miserey* (Paris, 1887). Hermant's hero also was ordered to disrobe on entering the service. He was ashamed of his nudity and blushed as his examining physician chuckled to himself: "C'est mou... pas formé... C'est anémique... Avec ça, un gars à femmes... Encore une recrue pour la rue des Cordeliers" (41-42). He forms an attachment with the captain's mistress and is irregular in his duties as a consequence. He suffers imprisonment. He deserts with his mistress, both fleeing to Belgium. He returns and receives the horrible sabre-whipping. He steals to pay a new mistress for her favors. He is degraded and expelled from the army because the stolen watch has been found on his person. The narrative ends with Miserey on his knees, a despairing suppliant, with arms outstretched towards his regiment as it marches by in superb order.

9 *Sous-offs* (Paris, 1892). First published in 1889, this novel of Descaves

approved the wrong of 1870-1871, though they rejected the idea of *revanche*. "The beneficent growth of European democracy and of the proletariat" would, according to Jaurès, right the wrong of Alsace-Lorraine as well as those of Poland and Finland.[10] Truth and Justice were, apart from the Dreyfus affair, the weapons by which they hoped to introduce the socialist state, as they were in this instance the slogans of the Radicals, who hoped to recover the political power they had lost in the election of 1893. The alacrity with which they took sides in the Dreyfus affair in November, 1897, was no doubt due in part to the fact that the general elections were to take place in the following May. It is true, however, that Mathieu Dreyfus did not learn until November, 1897, what Picquart had discovered a year earlier, that the evidence pointed to the guilt of Esterhazy instead of his brother, Alfred.[11] Zola's famous "Letter to Félix Faure," which Clemenceau fittingly named, "I accuse!", was no doubt inspired by considerations of justice rather than by political motives; but its publication in *L'Aurore*, Clemenceau's paper, was not without political implications. The same may be said of the founding of the *Ligue pour la défense des droits de l'homme et du citoyen* on Febru-

purports to be a laboratory study of army life. Favières, a Parisian recruit, has his pockets emptied the first night he spends in camp. He finds he is an object of hatred to the provincial soldiers. Two Parisian recruits commit suicide within the first two weeks (p. 16). Once the Parisian receives officer's stripes, the provincials become more friendly. Much of the book is devoted to the relations of Favières and his friend, Tétrelle, with lewd women: first their assault upon two old women in a dark street of Dieppe; then their relations with a mother and her fourteen-year-old daughter; and finally their regular frequentation of a nearby brothel, where each has his favorite. This place is known as "44." "Et la vie militaire, enfermée entre le 44 et la caserne, trahit un nouvel aspect, en une vision nette et concise (that is, to Favières after a night spent there). Deux prostitutions se partagaient le soldat, regulièrement, sans relâche. La Maison se couchait quand s'éveillait le Quartier; l' alternance des services était combinée à souhait pour l'hygiène et la récréation du serviteur de l'irréfragable Patrie" (104).

10 Quoted by Charles Maurras in *Kiel et Tanger* (Paris, 1921), 280.

11 A. Charpentier, *Historique de l'affaire Dreyfus* (Paris, 1933), 117.

ary 20, 1898. Its progenitor, the *Société des droits de l'homme* of 1888-1889 had been organized to combat Boulangism and, as its inaugural proclamation stated, it was to last as long as the movement it was opposing constituted a danger. There was danger again; hence its revival. Its members feared the independence and arrogance of the higher army officials and their friendly relations with the parties of the Right. Many Radicals, as Free Masons, though not discarding the spirit of *revanche*, had no faith or hope of obtaining it by means of the army. They carried on a systematic fight against German militarism and what they considered to be German autocracy in the hope of establishing a world brotherhood which would center in Paris.[12] Opposing German militarism on national and international grounds, they opposed French militarism for partisan as well as humanitarian reasons.

While it is true that the elections of May 8 and 22, 1898, did not turn on the Dreyfus issue,[13] and that the lines between the Dreyfusards and their opponents were not clearly drawn until Waldeck-Rousseau formed his cabinet in June, 1899, with the support of the parties of the Left (Socialists included) and many moderate republicans, the political atmosphere was colored somewhat by it prior to the 1898 elections. The Nationalists and anti-Semites put candidates in the field against the moderate republicans, and some moderate Dreyfusards withdrew their support from the Méline ministry. The seven Catholic groups divided; but the strongest, which was dominated by the Fathers of the Assumption, attacked the Republic and asked its candidates to combat the Jews. The results of the elections, however, made no appreciable difference in the rela-

12 J. Kühn, *Der Nationalismus im Leben der dritten Republik* (Berlin, 1920), Ch. III, "Der Nationalismus in der französischen Freimauerei," by Hermann Gruber, pp. 127-158. He goes so far as to assert that Freemasonry "was in reality less peaceable than the sword-rattling, chauvinistic nationalism of other French circles" (157).

13 Charles Seignobos in E. Lavisse, *Histoire de France contemporaine* (Paris, 1921), VIII, 198.

tive positions of the parties; those on the Right were only slightly stronger than they had been.[14]

The excitement increased. Duels, trials, acrid articles and speeches, and ministerial crises added fuel to the fire in the "furnace." [15] Déroulède revived the League of Patriots, which had been dissolved in 1889, and led it in street brawls. In this work of driving the "foreigners of the interior" off the streets of Paris,[16] they were aided by the royalist and anti-Semite *camelots* of Jules Guérin, the *Jeunesse anti-sémite* of Dubuc, and the *Comités de la jeunesse royaliste* of André Buffet.[17] Colonel Henry's confession of forgery on August 30, 1898, his subsequent suicide in prison, and the flight of Esterhazy demoralized the forces of the Right. Brisson, the Prime Minister, now became a revisionist, as did many moderate republicans. Drumont even softened a bit,[18] though he insisted with Cavaignac and other anti-Dreyfusards that Henry's confession of having forged a letter in 1896 had no bearing on the trial of Dreyfus in 1894.

It was a young and, until then, a relatively obscure journalist, Charles Maurras, who gave the extreme "patriots" their cue. Convinced that Henry was the victim of an evil conspiracy or of cruel circumstances, he sought the permission of the editors of *La Libre parole* and of *Le Soleil* to describe him so in their columns, but was refused.[19] *La Gazette de France,* however, gave him permission to do so; and on September 6-7, 1898, it published his brief for Henry. Its title was, "The First Blood." Although he did not use the words, "patriotic

14 *Ibid.*, VIII, 199.

15 Maurice Pujo and Henri Vaugeois referred to the space between the Opera and Montmartre, "le quartier des journaux, qui était aussi, à cette époque, le quartier des manifestations," as the "fournaise" (Charles Maurras, *Au signe de Flore*, 88; Coudekerque-Lambrecht, *op. cit.*, 41).

16 Maurice Barrès, *Scènes et doctrines du nationalisme*, I, 106.

17 Alexandre Zévaès, *op. cit.*, 136.

18 Charles Maurras, *op. cit.*, 82.

19 *Ibid.*, 78.

forgery," ascribed to him by his opponents,[20] he implied as much; Henry had forged to prevent the revelation of a supposed letter of William II and had thus prevented war; he had forged to protect the army from the foreigners within as well as those outside the country.[21] He was not a criminal, but a hero, a martyr, every drop of whose "precious blood" reeked wherever "the French heart palpitates" and cried for expiation. Far from having been a disgrace to his country, he had honored it; and his remains and memory deserved to be so treated.[22] Although some anti-Dreyfusards were shocked by this bald approval of forgery, many, hoping to make the best of a bad situation, took up the young journalist's refrain. *La Libre parole* even collected a hundred thousand francs in the "martyr's" honor, which were used, not to erect a monument to commemorate his name and deed, but to defray the expense of legal proceedings against Joseph Reinach.

The anti-Dreyfusard forces were far from submission. When parliament reconvened on October 25, 1898, after the vacation, they defeated the Brisson government on the ground of its alleged campaign against the army. Dupuy, the next Prime Minister, was more tractable. When the Court of Appeal declared its readiness on October 29, only four days after they had caused the fall of the Brisson ministry, to consider a demand for the revision of the Dreyfus judgment, they were angry beyond words. They displayed their feelings in violent demonstrations until Félix Faure intervened and suggested that a measure be enacted providing that criminal cases be reviewed by all the chambers of the Court of Appeals and not simply by

20 *Ibid.*, 82; A. Charpentier, *op. cit.*, 182.

21 A. Charpentier, *op. cit.*, 182; Charles Maurras, *op. cit.*, 80.

22 It closed with these words: "Dans l'état de désordre où sont les partis nationaux, nous n'avons pu vous faire les grandes funérailles dues à votre martyre. Il fallait secouer sur nos boulevards la tunique sanglante, ainsi que les lames souillées, promener le cercueil, arborer le drap mortuaire en manière de drapeau noir. Ce sera notre honte, de ne l'avoir pas essayé. Mais le sentiment national, bien que dispersé et multiplié contre lui-même, encore incapable d'action, n'en est pas moins resuscité" (*ibid.*, 81).

the criminal chamber. This was finally done in the following February. Faure, true to the sentiments he harbored in 1882 when he helped found the League of Patriots, was their friend; but, unfortunately for their cause, the President died suddenly on February 16, 1899, in very embarrassing circumstances (embarrassing, at least, to Madame Steinheil and his friends, if not to him).[23] The election of Emile Loubet as his successor three days later was a signal victory of the Dreyfusards. The anger of the nationalist groups in Paris was so intense that they insulted the new President upon his return from Versailles and begged Déroulède to lead them to the Elysée. This the latter refused to do, saying there was a dead person there whose memory he respected; but he asked them to be on hand on the day of the funeral.[24]

In the three days that followed, Déroulède organized his *coup d'état* to the last detail. He sent out 4,000 cards to members of the League of Patriots, inviting them to be at the Place de la Nation at 3:00 February 23, 1899.[25] He tried to get the support of Guérin and Buffet, whose youthful followers would have furnished valuable aid. They, however, preferred to organize a *coup* of their own. Guérin was to recruit a mob that would march behind a general to the Elysée, while the Duke of Orleans was asked to come to the Franco-Belgian border to be ready for eventualities.[26] Déroulède had some difficulty finding " his man." As before, he sought him among the generals. All replied that they would willingly be seconds, but not the leader, until he came to Pellieux, a monarchist, who promised his aid despite his dislike of Déroulède's plan to have a constitutional convention elected.[27] He also consulted the politicians who could help and with their aid worked out

23 A. Charpentier, *op. cit.*, 199; Joseph Reinach, *Histoire de l'affaire Dreyfus* (Paris, 1904), IV, Ch. VII.

24 Jérôme and Jean Tharaud, *op. cit.*, 115.

25 A. Charpentier, *op. cit.*, 200.

26 *Ibid.*, 200.

27 Jérôme and Jean Tharaud, *op. cit.*, 116-117.

the personnel of the provisional government; but he gave them no information on how the *coup* was to be brought about.

Accompanied by Barrès and Barillier, at three on the afternoon of February 23, Déroulède left his hotel, entered a closed cab, and made several detours on the way to the rendezvous as a measure of precaution against the police. But unfortunately for Dèroulède and his cause, General Pellieux was "afraid at the last moment," as Boulanger had been a decade earlier.[28] According to the plan, he was to return from the burial of Félix Faure at the head of his troops, meet Déroulède and his Leaguers at the Place de la Nation, and lead them all to the Elysée. Instead, he returned to the Ecole militaire alone in a roundabout way. He had been so agitated during the funeral exercises and had seemed so ill that his superior officer, whose suspicions had been aroused by rumors, ordered General Roget to conduct the troops back to their barracks. It was he, therefore, whom Déroulède and Barrès, who was still with him, saw approaching at the head of the soldiers at the Place de la Nation. Déroulède decided on the spur of the moment to go on with his plan, hoping Pellieux was behind; but Roget refused to be intimidated or persuaded into adopting a treasonable course. Déroulède, however, persisted and was arrested, as was also Marcel Habert, another deputy. Although they were unanimously acquitted in the following May of the charge of having incited the soldiers to mutiny, the fiasco seriously injured the cause of the nationalist groups.[29]

It was the more exasperating to the latter because their hopes had been raised by the popularity of the newly organized *Ligue de la Patrie française*, which was gaining new members at the rate of a thousand a day [30] and ultimately had a hundred thou-

28 Joseph Reinach, *op. cit.*, IV, 592; Maurice Barrès, *Scènes et doctrines du nationalisme*, I, 249.

29 Charles Maurras, *Au signe de Flore*, 112: "Avec lui échoue le triple mouvement plébiscitaire, royaliste, antisémite qui n'a pas été combiné ou qui s'est désarticulé au dernier moment: cela fait sauter tout obstacle officiel à la révolution dreyfusienne."

30 Maurice Barrès, *Scènes et doctrines du nationalisme*, I, 73.

sand.[31] Among them were twenty-five members of the French Academy.[32] "The real inventor of the new League," however, was Charles Maurras.[33] Several weeks after Maurras' famous article on Henry appeared, one of his friends, Frédéric Amouretti, remarked that he knew a history professor, Gabriel Syveton, who had been impressed by the defense of Henry, and who shared the view that as many intellectuals as possible should be brought together in some sort of organization to oppose the Dreyfusards the more effectively.[34] Syveton visited them, bringing with him Louis Dausset, another professor. They discussed the availability of several other persons who might aid them. Maurras then asked, "Why not begin by informing Barrès?"[35] This was agreed upon. Maurras wrote to Barrès, saying he knew two professors who shared their preoccupations and suggested that he meet them.[36] The meeting took place in the offices of *Le Soleil,* where Maurras and Amouretti worked. The presentations were made. More names were considered, among them those of Henri Vaugeois and Maurice Pujo, who, with several others, had on the preceding April 8 (1898) founded the *Comité de l'Action française.* This was the first time Maurras had heard of the men who were later to become the founder and director, respectively, of the *Action française.* Upon the suggestion of Barrès that they be seen, the professors, though they had named them, advised against it. Dausset, however, lost little time in notifying Vaugeois that Maurras was busy collecting anti-Dreyfusard signatures. This was laudable, he added; but since he was a royalist and possibly a little unbalanced mentally, as his defense of Henry seemed to show, Vaugeois' efforts would be compro-

31 Coudekerque-Lambrecht, *Léon de Montesquiou: sa vie politique — L'Action française* (Paris, 1925), 29.

32 Maurice Barrès, *op. cit.*, I, 69.

33 Joseph Reinach, *op. cit.*, IV, 500.

34 Charles Maurras, *op. cit.*, 85.

35 *Ibid.*, 86.

36 *Ibid.*, 86; Maurice Barrès, *op. cit.*, I, 73.

mised if he coöperated with him.[37] So the two groups worked separately, connected only by Syveton and Dausset.

The declaration for which they secured signatures seemed peaceable enough. It lamented the deleterious effect of "the most baneful of agitations" upon the army and upon the vital interests of the French *patrie*. The signatories, therefore, agreed to work toward the maintenance of the traditions of the *patrie*, whilst conciliating them with the progress of ideas and manners; to unite and, without sectarianism, by word and example to strive to attain this end.[38] And to do this effectively, they wanted the support of the authority of as many distinguished intellectuals as possible. "The essential," said Barrès, "is that people shall no longer be able to say that intelligence *and the intellectuals* . . . are on one side only."[39] Intellectuals they actually secured in considerable number, as the names of the committee and of its officials indicate.[40] The honorary president was François Coppée and the president, Jules Lemaître, both of whom were Academicians. At the first meeting on January 19, 1899, Lemaître made a statement of clear, uncompromising hostility towards Dreyfusism, which was hailed by Barrès as a "magnificent discourse."[41] Déroulède was so favorably impressed by it that as president of the League of Patriots he took a thousand francs from the League's treasury and sent them to Lemaître, asking that they be used to give the speech the publicity it deserved.[42]

With its rapid increase of membership, the new League's prospects seemed bright. But its size hampered its effectiveness. Its membership was so heterogeneous that agreement on any particular doctrine was an impossibility;[43] it was, there-

37 Charles Maurras, *op. cit.*, 93.

38 *Ibid.*, 96.

39 Maurice Barrès, *op. cit.*, I, 69.

40 *Ibid.*, I, 76.

41 *Ibid.*, I, 72.

42 *Ibid.*, I, 77-78.

43 Brunetière, for example, was quoted by *Le Temps* as having said,

fore, forced to restrict its efforts to electoral activities, which were, in turn, displeasing to some. As a royalist later expressed it, " To wish to save a country by elections whilst maintaining universal suffrage, is to wish to put out a fire by blowing under it." [44] A fortnightly review was launched, but soon ceased to appear, apparently because of the absence of doctrinal agreement.[45]

Political events also weakened the new League's influence. Déroulède's pathetic failure in his attempted *coup d'état* of February 23, 1899, has been mentioned. On the following June third the Court of Appeals, despite the participation of all the chambers, which had aroused the hopes of the nationalist groups, unanimously voted the annulment of the judgment of December 22, 1894, against Dreyfus. The anti-Dreyfusards were furious. One of their number, Baron de Christiani, distinguished himself next day by vigorously applying his cane to the hat and head of President Loubet at Auteuil. While it, no doubt, gave pleasure to many of his friends, the Baron himself was arrested and was given a sentence of four years' imprisonment, during which time he might ponder over the wisdom or lack of wisdom of his act.[46] A week later the Dupuy ministry was defeated by a resolution, criticizing it for failing to protect the President of the Republic. The parliamentary crisis

" Nous repoussons avec énergie la doctrine antisémite et la doctrine nationaliste. Nous ne sommes pas la ' Ligue des patriotes '; nous formons une Ligue de patriotes. Ce qui n'empêche pas que les antisémites et les partisans de M. Déroulède seront reçus parmi nous." Barrès, who quoted this statement, added, " Je m'inscris contre la première phrase de cette citation " (*ibid.*, I, 71). " Il pouvait parler pour lui," said Maurras later, " mais que voulait dire son *nous?* M. Brunetière se croyait déjà maître en chef. En quatre mots, Barrès lui fit comprendre qu'il n'était pas chez lui. Il finit par donner sa démission, le 21 février suivant. Personne ne voulait de ce pédant de carnaval " (*op. cit.*, 103 and 118).

44 Coudekerque-Lambrecht, *op. cit.*, 29.

45 *Ibid.*, 29. Its appearance was frowned upon by other " patriotic journals " such as the *Echo de Paris*, the *Eclair*, and the *Libre parole. Cf.* Charles Maurras, *op. cit.*, 121.

46 A. Charpentier, *op. cit.*, 207.

that ensued was one of the most important of the many that have occurred in the history of the Third Republic, for Waldeck-Rousseau's success in forming a ministry of republican concentration, with the Socialists represented upon it by Millerand and the moderate republicans by General Galliffet, the scourge of the Communards in 1871, gave the Dreyfusards a decided political preponderance over their opponents. It also ushered in a period of political prosperity for the parties of the Left, particularly for the Radical Socialist Party. The violence with which the new ministry was received in the Chamber upon its first appearance there on June 26, 1899, by the parties of the Right emphasized the importance of the new Prime Minister's achievement. They might win more victories in street brawls and a partial victory in the verdict of a court-martial, but their opponents had made the decisive conquest in getting control of the government. Short of resorting to arms and real warfare, there seemed little left that they could do. Much against their will, Dreyfus was brought back to France and was retried by a second court-martial at Rennes in the following August and September. Rioting and street warfare were the order of the day in Paris in this period, while Rennes experienced all the excitement of a *cause célèbre* which reached its height when a fanatic attempted to murder Labori who, with Casimir-Périer, had been conducting the defence of Dreyfus before the court. This quite naturally angered the Dreyfusards as did also the verdict of the court, which again declared Dreyfus guilty, though "with extenuating circumstances." The sentence was reduced, therefore, to ten years' detention. When, however, a week later, the President granted the defendant the remission of the part of the ten years he had not already served and the legislature subsequently passed an act of amnesty for Zola, Picquart, and other Dreyfusard victims, the anti-Dreyfusards again had cause for wrath.

But their anger was now one of despair. Having freed Dreyfus from the fulfillment of the ten-year term, which his opponents considered a generous modification of his previous sentence, the Dreyfusards, with satanic irony, imposed the same term of banishment or imprisonment upon several of their leading opponents. On August 12, 1899, four days after the opening of the trial at Rennes, Déroulède and Buffet were arrested for plotting to overthrow the government. Guérin resisted arrest and was taken only after he had withstood a siege of the police for a month.[47] Tried by the Senate for treason, they were found guilty of the charge, and were condemned on January 3, 1900: Buffet and Déroulède to ten years' banishment and Guérin to ten years' imprisonment. And, as if this blow were not sufficient, Déroulède, in exile, made the demoralization of the parties of the Right the more complete by openly accusing the royalists of responsibility for the failure of his attempted *coup*. This Buffet denied with warmth, and a duel ensued between the fellow-exiles at Lausanne. The duel itself was harmless; but the affair seriously weakened Déroulède's hold upon his followers, many of whom now turned against him as a confirmed trouble-maker. To defend himself against his own friends, he converted the weekly organ of the League of Patriots, *Le Drapeau*, into a daily and placed it under the editorship of Barrès;[48] but it soon became an object of daily irritation to him. He was too far from Paris to direct it properly; the promised financial aid failed to materialize; and so he stopped its publication and washed his hands of all electoral cares. He was never again the popular leader he had been. The Chamber that was elected in 1902 was more hostile towards him than its predecessor had been, despite its tardy approval of the Senate's amnesty bill in October, 1905, by a vote of 541 to 3.[49] But this, as well as his triumphal return to Paris, when some 300,000 Parisians joined in welcoming him back, was more an act of defiance to Germany than an ex-

47 Sixty-seven persons were arrested in the month of August, but forty-five of them were freed after a brief investigation. The government's vigor in defending itself overawed the opposition.

48 Jérôme and Jean Tharaud, *op. cit.*, 145.

49 *Ibid.*, 162.

pression of love and admiration for Déroulède, for now that he was back friends and foes alike enclosed him in a halo of silence which he came to look upon as a new form of exile.[50] He was invited to make speeches at times and to participate in ceremonies, but more as a symbol than as a leader: a symbol of militarism and of *revanche*, which again was "Queen of France."

With their leaders gone or partially repudiated, with the moral disadvantage of having failed in the struggle for political power, and lacking the proper cohesion, the anti-Dreyfusards could do little more than protest against the reduction of the military budget and of the terms of service and against the anti-Clerical legislation that followed in the first years of the twentieth century. They disliked the reversal of the Rennes decision by the High Court on July 12, 1906, and the honors that were heaped upon Dreyfus and Picquart; but, again, they could do little more than voice their sentiments. Many, recognizing the futility of carrying on the struggle, became apathetic; others, prompted either by considerations of political expediency or by a change of heart, made peace with the new régime. Some, on the other hand, "kept up the good fight." Among these, the most consistent, vigorous, and daring were the men associated with the *Action française*, which was a development both of the *Comité de l'Action française* and of the *Ligue de la Patrie française*.

50 *Ibid.*, 165.

CHAPTER VIII

BEGINNINGS OF THE ACTION FRANCAISE

The *Comité* had been merged into the *Ligue* upon the founding of the latter; but, when the League drew up a program that was calculated to please everyone, " even the most blind," as Vaugeois expressed it,[1] in order to win an electoral majority, the Committee was revived in April, 1899.[2] "That is why," said Vaugeois, " letting the *Ligue de la Patrie française* attend to its electoral organization, I made up my mind to group together those of its adherents who were concerned above all with advancing the intellectual, moral and political reorganization of France in this *Action française*. . . ." [3] These he called together at frequent intervals to discuss a plan of action; or, as Maurras remarked, they met " in order to found something." [4] By June 20, 1899, they were ready to announce their decision. That evening Vaugeois, after reaffirming their "anti-Semitic, anti-Masonic, anti-Protestant, anti-parliamentary, and, finally, anti-democratic nationalism," presented to a considerable audience " the idea of a new French Republic, more or less modified in an oligarchic, aristocratic sense, where the power, having again become personal and responsible, would be exercised by the heirs of the revolutionary ' dynasties ': the Cavaignacs, the Carnots, the Cambons, etc. . . . France was to be governed, not by ' laws,' but by living heads, or even by one head, though it had to be cut off from time to time in the course of history. . . ." [5] As a true Boulangist and Drumontian nationalist he declared himself to be a " sincere re-

1 Henri Vaugeois, *La Fin de l'erreur française* (Paris, 1928), 292.

2 Charles Maurras, *Au signe de Flore*, 122.

3 Henri Vaugeois, *op. cit.*, 292.

4 Charles Maurras, *op. cit.*, 121.

5 Quoted by Maurras from a later account of it by Vaugeois (*ibid.*, 122-123).

publican," but a Frenchman first and foremost.[6] And, closing his address, he announced the formation of a stock company to publish the *Bulletin bi-mensuel de l'Action française*. This speech constituted the first number, which appeared on July 10. In the second Vaugeois declared, "The *Action française* will be 'nationalist.' It is destined, in the thought of its founders, to aid in the organization, already begun, of a new party. It is an organ of combat, because, above all at this time, the necessity obtrudes to combat, to conquer, to drive from our midst in a sufficiently brutal manner, so that he will harbor no desire to return, an enemy to whom the abominable carelessness of our representatives has ended in delivering us. . . ."[7] That it has remained nationalist and that its methods are often brutal, friends and foes alike agree—the former with pride and the latter with dismay or disdain.

Critical of the "practical" program of the *Patrie française,* the aim of the founders of the *Action française* was to formulate and popularize a doctrine that would continue independently of electoral success or failure. This they obtained, for the most part, from Barrès.[8] According to the latter, the Dreyfus affair was an "orgy of metaphysicians."[9] The True and the Good were not absolute, but merely relative concepts. "The assertion that a thing is good and true must always be clarified by a reply to this question: with reference to what is this thing good and true?"[10] In proposing a doctrine for the *Patrie fran-*

6 Coudekerque-Lambrecht, *op. cit.*, 30; Charles Maurras, *op. cit.*, 131.

7 Henri Vaugeois, "Réaction d'abord...," *L'Action française* (Aug. 1, 1899), I, 1.

8 Léon de Montesquiou, writing in 1914, said: "Qui alors nous a offert une doctrine pour soutenir de raison les sentiments que nous éprouvons devant le chambardement de la France, une doctrine à opposer à la métaphysique révolutionnaire dont les juifs et leurs alliés cherchaient à empoisonner les Français afin de les dominer plus facilement. Qui? Maurice Barrès. Maurras n'avait pas encore atteint le grand public..." (quoted by Coudekerque-Lambrecht, *op. cit.*, 38, from *L'Action française*, Mar. 9, 1914).

9 Maurice Barrès, *Scènes et doctrines du nationalisme*, I, 84.

10 *Ibid.*, I, 64.

çaise in March, 1899, Barrès therefore insisted that they repudiate "the philosophical systems and the parties they engender"; they should base their efforts upon reality and not upon caprice; they should "judge things as historians rather than as metaphysicians" and help to restore moral unity or a national conscience. Since nationalism consisted in "solving each question with reference to France," it was essential to have a common definition and idea of France.[11] Secondly, in order to secure the acceptance of this realistic view of the *Patrie*, he stressed the necessity of developing ways of feeling that were natural in the country. "At the root of everything, there is a state of sensibility," which he considered a necessary complement of reason; for, if the latter is alone used in the quest for truth, it always finds new reasons for putting things in question anew. Hence the value of a sentimental attachment to the soil as a sort of anti-intellectual discipline, as likewise of a similar attraction to the dead, of whom, in the last analysis, we are but a prolongation.[12] This view of the dead led logically to his third point: the restriction of the right of naturalization. Foreigners who came into France were after all the continuation of their fathers; and, despite the best efforts to live and think as Frenchmen, they were unable to do so because of the ineluctable law of psychological determinism. Frenchmen of too recent date had seriously troubled the national conscience in late years.[13] A sentimental attachment to the soil, on the other hand, led logically to a regionalist organization, his fourth point. The soil, too, spoke to them, as did the dead, and collaborated with the national conscience. It was by means of its "action" that the ancestors transmitted completely the accu-

11 *Ibid.*, I, 84-90. Barrès: "La vérité allemande et l'anglaise ne sont point la vérité française et peuvent nous empoisonner ... Il y a des vérités lorraines, des vérités provençales, des vérités bretonnes dont l'accord, ménagé par des siècles, constitue ce qui est bienfaisant, respectable, vrai en France et qu'un patriote doit defende" [Jean Dietz, *Maurice Barrès* (Paris, 1927), 136].

12 *Ibid.*, I, 90-94.

13 *Ibid.*, I, 94-96.

mulated heritage of their souls. The measures of the administrator and of the legislator were therefore to be inspired by this sentiment and by the principle that " the *Patrie* is stronger in the soul of a rooted citizen than in that of an uprooted." [14] Finally, in order that this national conscience have efficacy, he recommended that it be expressed in a visible authority.[15] But above all, they were to " clarify opinion on the great interests of the country." [16]

In a second discourse before the same group in the following December, Barrès discussed one of the " great interests " of France — the problem of Alsace-Lorraine. Although they were separated from France politically, they were still bound to her by moral ties. It was the duty of his auditors to work for their retention in the French consciousness; it was their duty to fortify France, and, having armed and organized her, they could be certain that, at the moment France deemed favorable and made a gesture of appeal, " an immense cry of love would rise up " from the other side of the frontier; and, finally, it was their duty to clarify the French conscience by basing it upon the soil and the dead. In this way they could " persevere usefully for the annexed." [17]

Such was Barrès' doctrine as he outlined it in 1899 in the hope that it would be accepted by the *Ligue de la Patrie française*. He, too, entertained doubts concerning the wisdom of restricting its program to electoral activities. Several months after resigning from its directing committee in October, 1901, he said, " I expected nothing from electoral action; I expected an intervention of another kind for which we were to prepare opinion." [18] In an article in *Le Journal* of October 30, 1899, he had painted a dark picture of the divided state of the national

14 *Ibid.*, I, 96-97.

15 *Ibid.*, I, 99.

16 *Ibid.*, I, 99.

17 *Ibid.*, II, 28-29.

18 *Ibid.*, I, 100.

conscience and had stressed the need of a doctrine, or a "national education." [19]

The members of the editorial committee of the *Action française* were profoundly impressed by this article—so much so, in fact, that they drew up a formal statement of such a doctrine as Barrès called for, a "charter" as Maurras characterized it,[20] and sent it to him. Barrès thus became a sort of "repository" of their *credo*.[21] He gratefully published it in *Le Journal* and thus gave it wider publicity than its publication in the *Action française* of November 15, 1899, alone would have given it. In introducing the four points of the statement, the authors referred to the desire Barrès had expressed in his recent article that the young patriots group themselves in a publication to help in the work of national education, and to his contention that there was no "possibility of restoring the commonweal without a doctrine." They continued in these words: "M. Maurice Barrès rightly adds that, for his part, he has striven to glorify and sustain 'that which the hereditary influences, the Soil and the Dead, create in us.' These strong words, which translate the program of the *Action française* too well to pass unnoticed," had given rise to the discussion that had ended in agreement on the four points that followed.[22]

The first point stressed the importance of society to the individual; for "every social peril involves serious perils for the individual." The second emphasized the importance of the nationality and of the nation as social units. International relations, whether of a political, moral, or scientific nature, depended upon the maintenance of nationalities. "If the nations were suppressed, the highest and most precious economic or spiritual communications of the universe would be equally compromised and menaced: we would have to fear a recoil of civi-

19 *Ibid.*, I, 101-102.

20 *Au signe de Flore*, 260.

21 *Ibid.*, 291.

22 Maurice Barrès, *Scènes et doctrines du nationalisme*, I, 104.

lization. Nationalism is, therefore, not only a fact of sentiment: it is a rational and mathematical obligation." The third point read as follows: "Among Frenchmen, citizens of a state obviously betrayed by the faction that governs it and menaced by formidable rivalries, all pending questions, all divisive problems ought to be coördinated and solved *with reference to the nation.* The natural groups of Frenchmen ought to gather around the common national element. Above their political, religious, and economic differences, they ought to rank themselves according to the greater or less intensity and depth of their French faith." [23] In the fourth and last point, it was declared that, "The duty of Frenchmen, conscious of these verities, is to-day to formulate them as publicly and as often as possible in order to retrieve their blind or negligent compatriots." [24]

Although this document already reflected the growing influence of Maurras' ideas,[25] insofar as they differed from those of Barrès, the manner in which it appeared and its general content were a tribute to the latter. Barrès valued the review's contributions to the cause of anti-Dreyfusism and especially its work among students in the Latin Quarter. He aided it in this work. He presided over the first meeting of the *Association nationaliste de la jeunesse* on the request of Camille Jarre, a member of the editorial committee of the *Action française,* in February, 1900, and supplemented Vaugeois' remarks, which constituted the discourse of the evening, with a brief but spirited address.[26] On the following July 11 the *Action française* sponsored the first dinner of the *Appel au soldat,* named

23 *Ibid.,* I, 104-105; Charles Maurras, *op. cit.,* 256-257.

24 Maurice Barrès, *op. cit.,* I, 105; Charles Maurras, *op. cit.,* 257.

25 Especially the emphasis on society in the first point, the "rational and mathematical obligation" of the second, and the solution of problems "with reference to the nation" of the third. Maurras perhaps claimed more originality for his "with reference to the nation" (*op. cit.,* 259-260) than was justified, since Barrès had used the expression: "with reference to France."

26 Maurice Barrès, *op. cit.,* I, 111-113.

in honor of Barrès' recent book. Since the author had refused to attend a great literary fête in his honor, a more serious evening was planned: a dinner to which only some thirty guests were invited. In his account of the events of the evening Maurras began with these interesting words: "The *Action française* believes in the virtue of iron. It does not cease to demonstrate the necessity of an energetic 'intervention' in contemporary France. But when the first organizer of the nationalist doctrines, in a veritable masterpiece, established this evident necessity, the *Action française* could not escape the desire of thanking him for it and thus declaring its own sentiments." [27] After the dinner and speeches by Vaugeois, Bourget, who presided, and Barrès, most of the guests registered for the periodical dinner of the *Appel au soldat* that was now planned. At their second dinner, February 7, 1901, Barrès defined the purpose of the study evenings of the *Appel au soldat* which were planned for every Tuesday of the ensuing year. They were to be a "laboratory of nationalist studies." They were to be thought of as a "constantly stretched spring." They would be not only an "explosion of sentiment," but also a "constant leaven in the country." [28] Their task was to study certain men who might be deemed the fathers of conscious nationalism. It was a "great security" to know that the movement was in harmony with the ideas of Auguste Comte. Maurras' campaign against romanticism, against what was little French and little durable in their literature, might serve as a "very vigorous point of support" to the special studies. "Nationalism, in effect, ought not to be simply a political expression; it is a discipline, a deliberative method of attaching ourselves to all that is really eternal and which ought to develop continuously in our country. Briefly, nationalism is a classicism; it is in every respect the French continuity." [29] Its advocates

27 *Ibid.*, I, 119; Coudekerque-Lambrecht, *op. cit.*, 51 (from the *Action française* of Aug. 1, 1900).

28 Maurice Barrès, *op. cit.*, I, 127.

29 *Ibid.*, I, 129.

should do for their generation what Victor Hugo had done for his. Under the Second Empire young men had been intoxicated by his writings. The powerful pages of *Les Misérables* had " incited a band of the Café Voltaire to take in hand the direction of the country." Some of his auditors, Barrès proceeded to point out, went back of Comte to de Bonald and de Maistre, neither of whom he himself knew. For his part, he would be happy to show them some day how the thoughts of Blaise Pascal confirmed the nationalist doctrine. He wished that every studious person could read Maurras' *Enquête sur la Monarchie.*[30] " I am not a monarchist," Barrès continued, " but I find that it is impossible to conceive a book of political literature wherein one finds more satisfaction for reasoning and high culture. That is what justifies your plan of instituting a political laboratory. However, I ask you to note well that we are assembled, not upon the idea of the monarchy, but upon the expression, the *Appel au soldat.* We find an ambiguity here that satisfies us. Our adversaries spit upon the army; on the contrary, we take a certain pleasure in saying to the soldier: 'Come, therefore, soldier, you, the material force, you, the sword of Brenn, be on our side.' We do not think that this country can be liberated by elections of the arrondissement." [31] If the soldier and circumstances failed to establish a harmonious France, they could at least have it within themselves. Some nationalists, he admitted in the anniversary address of the *Action française* on the following June 15, regretted the absence of complete agreement upon the past, present, and future; but, in any event, they were united in their " complete disgust " for the present and for the parliamentary régime.[32] Moreover, they were united when they turned to the past of France, the France eternal which had been creating them in the course of the centuries.[33]

30 *Ibid.*, I, 130. It had appeared in *La Gazette de France* from July 25 to September 27, 1900.

31 *Ibid.*, I, 130.

32 *Ibid.*, I, 131.

33 *Ibid.*, I, 132.

Such were the relations of Barrès with the *Action française* in its early days. He was their honored and respected master, and remained so in a less direct sense after November 1, 1901, when Vaugeois announced his own adherence, and therefore that of the review of which he was the director, to the royalist cause.[34] The movement then became and has remained the organ of the Maurrassian doctrine of "integral" nationalism which, however, owes much to Barrès. This is well illustrated by the article in which Maurras first used the expression, "integral nationalism," and explained it.[35] He credited Barrès with having given the word nationalism its new meaning in the French language. He had opposed the cosmopolitans in literature and had led the way from literary nationalism to political nationalism. "Nationalism," he continued, "reacts against the egoism of the Old Republican Party, just as it reacts against the indifference of that party to the great national interests. A nationalist, conscious of his rôle, admits as a ruling system that a good citizen subordinates his interests and his systems to the good of the *Patrie*. He knows that the *Patrie* is the basic condition of his well-being and of the well-being of his fellow-citizens. Every personal advantage which results in a loss for the *Patrie* appears to him a mistaken and false advantage. And every political problem that is not solved with reference to the general interests of the *Patrie* is to him a problem incompletely solved. The nationalist, therefore, prescribes to the diverse questions that are placed before him a common denominator which is no other than the interest of the nation.

34 Louis Dimier, speaking of the *Institut d'Action française*, founded in 1905 and of which he was the director, said, "Nous donnions des noms à nos chaires: à celle du nationalisme, le nom de Maurice Barrès; à celle des provinces, le nom de Louis XI . . ." (*Vingt ans d'Action française et autre souvenirs* (Paris, 1926), 94). Vaugeois' conversion came relatively late. "Telle était," said Coudekerque-Lambrecht, "à peu près, la composition de ces soirées (at the Café de Flore) 'où,' dit Maurice Pujo, 'sous les coups mortels de Charles Maurras, succomba tour à tour le républicanisme de chacun de nous, en cette année 1900 qui fut l'année de l'hégire pour *L'Action française*'" (*op. cit.*, 44).

35 "Le Nationalisme intégral," *Le Soleil*, Mar. 2, 1900.

As in the case of the Roman of whom Bossuet spoke, the love of the *Patrie* eclipsed everything in him." Maurras had seen near the eastern façade of the Parthenon the débris of the temple which the Romans had raised to the goddess of Rome. At first this had impressed him as a sort of profanation; but, after reflecting upon it, he had found in it a "sublime audacity." Then, adverting to the present, he remarked that the English had this "Roman virtue," and added: "French nationalism is tending to revive among us a similar religion of the goddess of France." This was scarcely possible, however, unless it approximated the sentiment of the French royalists; for the hereditary monarchy was the "only possible solution of the central power" in France. Without a king all that the nationalists wished to conserve would weaken and perish. The monarchy was at once the condition and the "normal and indispensable complement" of the reforms they desired.

But royalism was complete, or integral nationalism, not because the hereditary monarchy offered the sole means of realizing the reforms demanded by the nationalists, though that was important, but because it summed up the hopes and aspirations of the other nationalist groups. "Like the Catholic party, the royalists are Catholics (from reason, from sentiment, or from tradition) and they believe in the primacy of catholicism. Like the anti-Semitic party, they are anti-Semites. Like the party of M. Paul Déroulède, they desire a strong and responsible power. Like the moderates and the decentralizers, they wish autonomy of teaching, the liberties of the communes and of the provinces. But instead of wishing this through an accident of caprice or of passion, they wish it through logical necessity and as the simple consequence of the fact that they desire the return of the national monarchy. Royalism corresponds essentially to the diverse postulates of nationalism: it is itself *integral nationalism.*" Nationalism and royalism were, therefore, identical. It was the duty of the royalists to work for the success of nationalism and to support the defenders of the nation as they would if the enemy were at the frontier.

"In days of yore," he concluded, "to serve the king was to make oneself useful to the *Patrie;* to-day, inverting the expression, to make oneself useful to the *Patrie* is really to serve the cause of the king."

It should be noted in conclusion that Barrès likewise was a qualified friend of Catholicism;[36] that he, too, was an anti-Semite; that, as a follower and personal friend of Déroulède, he also wanted a strong political authority at the center of things; and that, finally, he was an ardent regionalist. He merely refused to accept the monarchy as a "logical necessity."[37] It would appear, therefore, that integral nationalism in its final form was Barrèsian nationalism with a king substituted for an elected dictator. According to Sir Leslie Stephen, John Morley once said, when comparing the views of Hobbes

36 Barrès, like Maurras, Anatole France, and others, rejected the Christian God. He was also apparently critical of Catholicism until the Dreyfusards used their political power to weaken it. At the height of the Dreyfus affair, in some reveries on the declaration of the *Patrie française*, he said tradition need not have a reactionary meaning. The government, he held, should be anti-clerical and militaristic (*Mes cahiers*, II, 91-92). He later championed the cause of the persecuted Clericals in the Chamber and in his writings. *Cf. La Grande pitié des églises de France* (Paris, 1914).

37 He held the monarchy was a German idea (*Mes cahiers*, II, 159). The "decisive union" of Lorraine to France came as the result of the material advantages obtained by the Lorraine peasants and bourgeoisie from the Revolution and from the "fraternity of combat and glory" in the republican and imperial wars (*Scènes et doctrines du nationalisme*, I, 88). In his letter to Maurras for the latter's *Enquête* he noted the absence of a popular French royal family such as the Germans and Russians had; also the lack of its concomitant, a popular and powerful aristocracy. He did not date the history of France from a century ago, but no more did he ignore the more recent periods [Charles Maurras, *Enquête sur la monarchie* (Paris, 1925), 135]. He questioned the patriotism of some royalists. He had heard Bourget say that they owed all to the Bourbons and nothing to France. "Je dirais volontiers: 'que devons-nous à la famille royale? Rien. Tout à la France, à sa culture" (*Mes cahiers*, II, 250-251). Discussing Maurras in *Le Gaulois* of July 9, 1905, he noted his influence upon men predisposed against the idea of hereditary power. He invited them to reflect upon a monarchy that would be neither clerical, nor aristocratic, but national. "Et les plus rudes lui disent: 'On n'a pas besoin de votre médecin. Mais qui sait? J'en prends tout le même l'adresse" (Jean Herluison, "Maurice Barrès et le problème de l'ordre," *Revue critique des idées et des livres* (Feb. 10, 1911), XII, 270).

and Rousseau, " Strike the crowned head from the monstrous figure which is the frontispiece of the Leviathan, and you will have a frontispiece that will do admirably well for the social contract." [38] While this statement is open to serious objections, one would do but little more violence to truth if he were to paraphrase it as follows: " Strike the crowned head from the frontispiece of Maurrassian nationalism, and you will have a frontispiece that will do admirably well for Barrèsian nationalism." [39]

Having reviewed the background of Maurrassian French nationalism, we shall deal with its elements in greater detail in the pages that follow. If the words " complete " and " integral " admitted of degrees of completeness and integralness, we might say by way of anticipation that Maurras' nationalism was more completely nationalistic in some respects than that of Barrès.[40]

38 *History of English Thought in the Eighteenth Century* (New York, 1876), II, 191.

39 Barrès, of course, wanted an authoritarian government; but it was to be plebiscitary. If the frontispiece of the *Leviathan* and that of the *Enquête sur la monarchie* be interpreted as the negation or complete annihilation of the individual, most objections disappear.

40 This is especially noteworthy in his unbending hostility towards romanticism and democracy which, in his opinion, were basic causes of French weakness.

CHAPTER IX

EARLY LIFE OF CHARLES MAURRAS AND HIS DEVELOPING EPICUREANISM AND AESTHETICISM

JUST as Barrès had some difficulty "untangling the symphony of life," so too Maurras was some time building a "system of ideas," a conception of life that satisfied him. Born in 1868 in the small fishing town of Martigues in Provence, about midway between Marseilles and the actual mouth of the Rhône, he was but two years old when the Germans invaded the departments to the distant north and was, therefore, less able to sense or understand the troubled feelings of his elders than was Barrès.[1] Indeed, as he averred later, his early years were "years of delight." [2] And outstanding among the pleasures of this period were the singing, dancing, and versification of his father, tax-collector for the Empire and later for the Republic, to whom, though he died in his son's sixth year, Maurras ascribed his "passion for little verses." [3] To him he was also beholden for his "taste for seeing, knowing, and, in general, that which relates to feeling," while he ascribed what "seriousness and determination" he had to his mother.[4]

His name, Charles Marie Photius Maurras, has given rise to speculations, both flattering and malicious, concerning his origins, which should be given some consideration in dealing

1 Sense them, however, he did, apparently. "Strasbourg et Metz tenaient à mes plus anciennes pensées. Né si loin du théâtre de la dernière guerre, je me rappelais qu'elle avait occupé tous les premiers fonds de ma petits enfance; bien avant le milieu de ma troisième année, j'avais vu mon père et ma mère, front contre front, et les yeux pleins de larmes, suivre, sur un grand atlas le cours irrésistible de l'invasion" (*Au signe de Flore*, 42-43).

2 *La Musique intérieure* (Paris, 1925), 1. (Hereafter, in citing the works of Maurras, we shall give the titles only, without his name.)

3 *Ibid.*, 4.

4 *Ibid.*, 4.

with a traditionalist and nationalist in whose philosophy "blood" and heredity play so important a rôle. The third name, Photius, an hereditary name in the family of his paternal grandmother, might conceivably suggest Greek ancestry;[5] but, in the light of our knowledge as to how the name was introduced into the family,[6] it seems purely fortuitous that one whose given name is Photius and who has spent much of his time and energy seeking to restore the ancient Greek idea of beauty should, therefore, be a descendant of the Phocians who established a settlement at Marseilles more than twenty-five hundred years before he appeared upon the scene.

This impression is heightened by the briefest consideration of his family name, usually a surer index of family origins. Maurras himself tells us that it means "great Moors or bad Moors, according to the augmentative or pejorative character of the 'as'," that a mountain near Gréoulx bears this name,

5 "The explanation is reasonable," says Maurras (*Au signe de Flore*, 2). André Maurel is more positive on this point. In his *Les Ecrivains de la guerre* (Paris, 1918), 97-98, he retells the old legend of the arrival of the Phocions in Provence. They found the Ligurian king at the point of giving his daughter away in marriage and were kindly invited to attend the banquet. After the repast the king gave his daughter, Gyptis, the goblet of pure water which, according to their custom, she was to offer to him whom she chose as husband. To everyone's surprise, she offered it, not to the man to whom she had been promised, but to a young stranger, Protis, the leader of the Phocions. Maurel then adds, "Je ne prétends point que M. Charles Maurras soit un descendant direct de Protis et de Gyptis, mais je suis sûr qu'il est issu d'un de ces Phocéens venus avec Protis aux bouches du Rhône."

6 *Ibid.*, 2-3. The father of his paternal grandmother wanted to have a son christened Phocion. The rector of Roquevaire, however, apparently not knowing of the Athenian orator and general of the fourth century B. C. and knowing only of the heretical and schismatic Phocion of the eleventh century A. D. who separated Byzantium from Rome, was both shocked and angered by the request. Not wanting a Phocion among his parishioners, he suggested Photius, an honored name in martyrology, as a better name for the boy. In the argument that ensued he is said to have told the father that his child would be "Photius, or nothing." The father, anxious that his son have a name, gave way; and so "Photius" began its uninterrupted career in the history of the family. Maurras was pleased to note that one of his saintly namesakes had lost his life defending the "plastic arts" against the Iconoclasts.

that it is a common family name in this vicinity and that his father never failed to make a " sort of pilgrimage " to it when he was conveniently near it. He has done the same, he adds.[7] How did " these Moors who called themselves Moors," these Maurrases, happen to be in Provence? Pursuing his version farther, we find that Martel's victory at Poitiers did not result in the immediate extinction of Islam in France; the war, as we know from historical records, continued in southern France, especially along the coast, for some centuries. In the course of this prolonged fighting the Moors of the Maurras were encircled by their enemies and isolated from their kinsmen and co-religionists. For many years they remained largely to themselves; " it was less difficult to baptize them than to make them come down from their rock for other purposes than for battle or booty." [8] Formerly " nomads " or pirates, they now became invincible mountaineers (*gavats*).

Lest, however, the pleasure of his enemies be too undefiled and the chagrin of his friends be too complete at seeing so stark an anti-Semite and so powerful a denouncer of the foreign residents in France (the *métèques*, concerning whom more will be said later) referring to these Moorish mountaineers as *mes gavats*, he hastens to relieve his friends and, in turn, to embarrass his enemies by saying that these mountaineers "could not have been Arabs." [9] They had been in Africa before the Semites came from Tyre and were " cousins " of the first natives of Provence. Hellenized and Latinized, as were the latter, they had later been oppressed by the Vandals and swept by Islam to the Provençal shores where in time they were transformed from tyrants into guests. Fortunately, as they left their mountain fastnesses to fight or plunder, " there were living and human preys!" In time they recognized their distant kinship with their victims and supposed enemies; amal-

7 Charles Maurras and Joanny Drevet, *Paysages et cités de Provence* (Grenoble, 1932, preface by Maurras), 6.

8 *Ibid.*, 7.

9 *Ibid.*, 6-7.

gamation followed, and they soon lost their identity in the "common crucible of Provence."[10]

While writing this version of the origin of his people, he must have been conscious of the fact that he was making the best of a patently bad situation; and, though it doubtless relieved his friends, it obviously failed to convince such critics as Urbain Gohier.[11] Certainly, there is truth in his statement that the blood of the Provençals was already "highly mixed" before that of the Moors was added and melted down with it in the "common crucible of Provence";[12] but it is far less certain that no Arabic or even Jewish blood figured in the fusion of the Moorish with the Iberian, Celtic, Greek, Roman, and German stocks.[13] Indeed, his emphasis on the "Latin gravity" of his father's countenance in the portraits he has of him appears to belie a certain uneasiness on this point.[14]

That, however, is a question which must, from its very nature, be left an open one. Bereft of his father, concerning whom his younger brother remembered only that he "sang and danced" for him, his appreciation of song and poetry grew apace with the advancing years. Servants, mother, aunts, and playmates facilitated this development until an incident occurred that inspired him with a mixed feeling of horror and disdain for song. A little girl, Tisthée, who was but a year or

10 *Ibid.*, 7. *Cf.* "A Martigues," in Léon Daudet and Charles Maurras, *Notre Provence* (Paris, 1933), 167.

11 His *Les Gens du roi: Sidi Maurras ben Ma'aras, ou le maure pion* (Paris, 1926) is the most virulent castigation of Maurras the writer has seen. In the following passage (p. 6) his scurrility reaches its height: "Le copronyme 'Maurras' dénonce des siècles de sales origines, où l'on voit s'accoupler les pirates maures, les écumeurs du littoral, les Juifs du Ghetto, les mokos, les ma'aras et les sidis du Vieux-Port, les nervi et les prostituées du quartier réservé de Marseille, les Zingaris et Gypsies qui viennent écroulles, leurs avaries aux Saintes-Maries-de-la-Mer. Dix générations de purulence et de crime, sans une goutte de sang français . . ."

12 *Op. cit.*, 7.

13 *Ibid.*, 15. Both the family of his father and that of his mother had "cousins of German descent."

14 *La Musique intérieure*, 5.

two older than Maurras, distributed among her playmates some lilacs and green branches which she had gotten at the church; then, after arranging the children in two rows, she asked them to sing "I am a Christian, it is my glory." While the other boys obligingly joined their voices with hers, Maurras alone remained silent. Tisthée, angered by his refusal to coöperate, expelled him from the group and prophesied that when they had grown up the others would know everything and he nothing. Troubled, he went to his mother with Tisthée's malediction and was overjoyed to learn that a child who was wise and worked hard could become as wise as the others without singing all their airs. He now made it a point to avoid song and strove not to permit himself to be affected by it. Knowing that the power of song often brought him to the verge of tears, he apparently became obsessed by the fear of permitting himself to become effeminate.[15]

But to "serious poetry," as if by way of compensation, he developed a greater attachment. His mother's recital of Racine's *Esther* was a memorable event in his life. It remained his favorite poem until he entered the Catholic College of Aix, whither the mother had moved in his eighth year to give her sons better educational advantages. Enraptured by a translation of the *Odyssey*, he now lost his sense of shame and his scruples about enjoying sensations engendered in him by music.[16]

This joy of savoring the delights of poetry was heightened by sharing it with a schoolmate, René de Saint-Pons, with whom he became more and more intimate. Together they devoured the poems of Musset (his "error of youth"), Lamartine, and Mistral. But "supreme beauty" tempted him "only to a certain point." "However," as he said later, "some propitious god guided me, as if by hand, step by step, towards the temple and altar where there were only good Muses."[17]

15 *Ibid.*, 13.
16 *Ibid.*, 23.
17 *Ibid.*, 30.

He saturated himself with Homer and with Virgil, but, "more than any other," with Lucretius, to whom he was introduced by Abbé Penon.[18] The Abbé's references to and interpretation of the *De Rerum Natura* "determined the predilection of my life for the sad arborial nook in the luminous field of the two antiquities." [19] Only here did he find the tragedy and the bitterness of human life recognized frankly; only here were these painful exigencies of life equalled by a tranquil power vigorous enough to deal with them; and here alone was there "clear understanding of our relations with destiny and with ourselves." [20] These tributes were written almost half a century after the event. He then remembered Lucretius as the perfect interpreter of his own "Christian pessimism." He was especially attracted by the "murmur of the man hostile to himself," and yet "consoled by the serene temples of knowledge." [21] "No ancient has ever been nearer to me," he adds. "With Pascal, with La Fontaine, whom Mgr. Penon also discovered to me, Lucretius has remained my companion at all hours. But I have deserted Pascal more than once; Lucretius, never. He contains all that is of service to me. Having him, ancient and modern poetry may repeat to me its *quid machiner inveniamque?*" [22]

18 *Ibid.*, 31: ". . . celui de mes maîtres auquel je dois le plus . . . " When the Abbé was consecrated Bishop in 1911, Maurras referred to him as the "first inspiration" of his "taste and desire for order" [*L'Etang de Berre* (Paris, 1924), 247]. *Cf. Quatre nuits de Provence* (Paris, 1931), 107.

19 *La Musique intérieure*, 31.

20 *Ibid.*, 31.

21 *Ibid.*, 32. How useful it was in an hour of real danger, when he, his brother and a friend were in danger of drowning on Aug. 3, 1885, is shown in his account of their experience in the "year of the cyclone" of Martigues, in *Quatre nuits de Provence*, 137-153.

22 *Ibid.*, 32. His reference to Horace as "superior to the sparkling and somber Lucretius" in the *Gazette de France* of Oct. 9, 1903, was probably a temporary lapse, rather than a desertion. In this same article he said, "Ame élevée, raison droite, coeur également incliné à la religion des ancêtres et à toutes façons de cueillir la fleur de la vie, Horace nous personnifie le véritable esprit d'Epicure, dans son honnêteté et sa grâce", [*Barbarie et poésie* (Paris, 1925), 291-292].

If we exclude the blow that was dealt his ambition to become a naval officer, when in his fourteenth year he was smitten with deafness, this discovery of Lucretius may well be regarded as the most important event of his life; for, in time, it gave him his canons of taste in art and poetry and those of order in sociology and politics, and became the lodestar of his nationalism.[23] "In time," we say, because the logical implications of Epicureanism with which he was eventually to build a philosophical system that embraced virtually the whole gamut of human knowledge came to him gradually. His tastes and enthusiasms were still undisciplined. While, on the one hand, he drew inspiration from Shakespeare, Dante, and Racine, he felt, on the other hand, a youthful enthusiasm for Baudelaire, Leconte de l'Isle, and others whom he was later to revile.[24] Similarly, his religious and social views were not immediately affected; for, in his twelfth or thirteenth year, he became a devotee of Lamennais' social gospel.[25] Enthralled by its phil-

23 In his "Reflexions préalables" of *Barbarie et poésie*, xi, he said, "Une polémique littéraire lucide conduisait à une polémique sociale et politique. Telle était la volonté des circonstances, on n'avait pas le choix. Déjà, de fort loin, il est vrai, les règles de la vie collective et les lois du gouvernement m'avaient beaucoup intéressé. Ces règles et ces lois ne sont pas sans rapport avec les principes qui président à l'art du poète quand il met en ordre son peuple d'idées et de mots, de couleurs et de sons; ainsi le veut l'unité de l'esprit humain. Cette analogie des deux plans m'a rendu des services continuels, et l'habitude d'évoquer toûr à tour leurs images complémentaires, m'aura aussi aidé à rendre moins indifférents à la chose publique les esprits passionnés pour l'ordre universel. Aujourd'hui tous les intérêts politiques et mentaux coïncident si parfaitement qu'il peut être bon de montrer ce qui était dit de leur convergence dans une série de travaux vieux de vingt et trente ans." But in his "L''Action Française' et la religion catholique" which constitutes the last section of his *La Démocratie religieuse* (Paris, 1921), 446, he had insisted (in 1913) that his political movement "n'a point l'objet immédiat de guérir des dissentiments qui portent sur l'être premier et dernier de toutes choses," that he had produced no "particular philosophical or religious teaching" (461), that "en esthétique, en politique, j'ai connu la joie de saisir dans leur haute évidence des idées-mères; en philosophie pure, non" (462). *Cf.* "*L'Action Française*" *et le Vatican* (Paris, 1927), 264.

24 *La Musique intérieure*, 32-37.

25 *Au signe de Flore*, 8.

osophy of liberty and its incitement to insurrection as the means of attaining it, he saw in the world only "oppressors and oppressed, exploited and exploiters," and was convinced that all the rich were necessarily bad and the poor "divinely good." His piety and love of what he vaguely conceived as divine justice made of him a "theocratic republican" who had no quarrel with the logical consequences of his position: community of goods, equality of parents and children, etc. This "madness," as he later designated it, accompanied by similar vagaries in romantic literature, "lasted some three or four years." [26]

But, according to his own account, he began to sense the "absurdity" of his position when observation and a naissant reason showed him that "the epoch of faith, the Middle Ages of Saint Louis, had not even conceived of the direct government of God or of the Pope." How incongruous it was, therefore, in his own day when faith in the "Master of things" had been narrowed down to the "conscience of a minority!" [27] However, no other régime seemed to be based upon justice, though he recognized the impossibility of attaining this ideal. He entered upon a period of indifference and skepticism which lasted from his sixteenth year to the approach of his twentieth. "I was tired," he informs the reader of his *Confession politique*, "of adhering to sentiment and caprice, and political quarrels appeared to me to be fantasies doomed to eternal contradictions. This skepticism was religious in source and, when I had lost faith, I persevered in a state of non-partisanship, or presently in that of a half-Buddhist contemplative." [28] He had, in fact, after having suffered the onset of deafness, referred to above, and accepted the kind offer of Abbé Penon to give him special lessons to enable him to complete his course of study

26 *Ibid.*, 9.

27 *Ibid.*, 9.

28 *Ibid.*, 9.

at Aix,[29] "hesitated at the crossroads," but he had been forced to conclude that "the most anciently built was the best." [30]

However, having made this choice, his skepticism was already considerably impaired; he was certainly no longer skeptical of the value of the way "most anciently built." He read the ancient masters with so much enthusiasm and showed such remarkable critical powers that Abbé Penon encouraged him to take up a literary career and persuaded Mme. Maurras to move to Paris with her sons so that Charles might ply his newly chosen trade in the best possible place.[31] This she did in 1885, in his seventeenth year. Unable, because of his defective hearing, to benefit from the lectures offered in the schools of the literary and cultural metropolis, he assumed himself the direction of his further education and plunged into an "almost complete philosophical absorption" from which he emerged some four or five years later.[32]

29 Coudekerque-Lambrecht, *op. cit.*, 45.

30 *La Musique intérieure*, 91.

31 Coudekerque-Lambrecht, *op. cit.*, 45.

32 *La Musique intérieure*, 37. According to a later account, this period began some six months before he arrived in Paris. Early in the summer of 1885 he accompanied other older students of the College of Aix on a three-day visit to the country house of the Jesuits at Saint-Joseph-du-Tholonet, not far from Aix. Here he experienced what may justly be described as the most important of his "four nights of Provence"; for here, and at this time, it came to him forcibly that Baudelaire's vaunting of the Law and the Rule profited only Sin and Transgression and that Lamennais' Faith was merely a stimulant to Anarchy. He was enchanted. "Qu'ai-je éprouvé alors? . . . Troublé? Enivré? Apaisé plutôt. Et même fortifié dans la possession vague et dans la maîtrise diffuse de biens spirituels qui me promettaient le salut." Poetry and reason combined to reveal to him the high maxims which have since saved him from the discomfort that pride, intrigue, hopes and the desire to dominate inevitably bring. "Cinq ans plus tard, le même réflexion fut poursuivie et complétée sur la terrasse du chateau de Pau: dès cette nuit de Tholonet, je nommai par leurs noms les bas lieux d'où m'avait chassé mon mouvement le plus naturel. Ce sont les lieux où l'on contracte, comme une maladie, l'habitude et le goût de se tenir pour mesure de soi et pour soleil du monde." He resolved definitely not to permit himself to be deluded by Love, Curiosity or Ambition. "Ne le reçois point sous le masque, ou religieux, ou philosophique, ou moral. Ne crains pas de leur arracher barbe et manteau. Si tu ne veux pas être trompé sur elles, mets-les toutes nues! Et sourtout

If Epicurus and his great apostle, Lucretius, could by some miraculous perversion of their doctrine have hovered over or followed their Provençal disciple during this period, they would, in all probability, have found little and decreasing cause for displeasure. Indeed, according to the Abbé Lugan, when, in 1892, or 1893, Maurras brought *La Bonne mort* to Brunetière in the hope of having it published in the *Revue des deux mondes*, he avowed to the famous critic that he had broken the last threads by which heredity and education had bound him to the infinite and had come to Paris "resolved to live his own ideas and to assure their triumph." [33] While he later frowned upon the experience of this period, of which he retained a lively recollection some thirty-five or forty years later, as a sort of aberration ascribable to youth's love of extremes, the fact that he noticed Aristotle's dictum on "contemplation considered as the height of happiness," tested it to the point of self-intoxication, and concluded that contemplation and happiness are identical, is suggestive of the Epicurean character of the ideas he had already "resolved to live." [34] This is borne out by his description of Charles Jundzill in his *Auguste Comte*, the autobiographical character of which seems clear, since Jundzill is described as representing "with much clarity the discomfort experienced by almost all spirits who, born in the Catholic tradition, have become strangers to the Catholic faith." [35] As a student in Paris, Jundzill was impressed with

prends bien garde de ne les croire qu'à demi quand elles te racontent qu'elles sont le Bonheur." (*Quatre nuits de Provence*, 110-129.)

33 A. Lugan, *Horizons d'âmes* (Paris, 1926), 73.

34 *La Musique intérieure*, 37-38. *Cf.* Diogène de Laërce, "Vie d'Epicure," in *Les Six Livres de Lucrèce de la nature des choses . . .*, translated by Michel de Marolles, abbé de Villeloin, 2nd edition (Paris, 1659), 374 and 377 (in the letters to Pythocles and Menoeceus), and Lucretius, *De rerum natura*, with translation by W. H. D. Rouse (New York, 1928), 172-173 (III, 28-30) and 442-443 (V, 1430-1435) for the Epicurean view of *vera voluptas* which comes from contemplation and is "divine" rather than "animal"; also George Depue Hadzits, *Lucretius and his Influence* (New York, 1935), Ch. VIII, especially pp. 153-159.

35 In *L'Avenir de l'intelligence* (Paris, 1927), 104; also in *Romantisme et révolution* (Paris, 1925), 95. *Cf.* A. Lugan, *op. cit.*, 75-76.

the foolishness of the interminable investigation that was going on; for what should have been only a means to an end had become an end in itself. He suffered because it offered him no principle by which he might order his private life; it gave him no basis of selection, no rule by which he might classify useful and true ideas. But his discomfort was already gone, for the most part, when he described it in a letter to Comte, of which Maurras pretends to give a *résumé*. Philosophy or science, or both, had undermined his faith in God and had forced upon him the conclusion that he was incapable of faith as the Catholics understood it. " It would be using," he continues, " truly inaccurate language to say that he lacked God. Not only was God absent from his spirit, but his spirit felt, if one may so express it, a rigorous need of *being without God:* no theological interpretation of the world and of man was endurable to him." [36]

But Jundzill and " his like," no longer admitting the existence of God, discovered a need almost as " rigorous " of " order in their thought, of order in their life, of order in the society " of which they were members [37]—an order based upon the realities of this world, not one based upon the vague unrealities of the supernatural and the infinite. It was doubtless Comte's effort to " naturalize " morality, to synthesize the natural and moral sciences without the benefit of gods invented by man after his own image or equally unreal metaphysical abstractions, that constituted his chief attraction to the young student whose breviary was *De rerum natura.*[38] However, Comte was to be more an ally than a master; for, as we shall see, certain fundamental parts of his *physique sociale* were either rejected outright or interpreted by Maurras to meet his particular needs.[39] Nevertheless, aided by Taine, Le Play, Jo-

36 *Ibid.*, 104. The italics are Maurras'. The fundamental Epicureanism of this " rigorous need of being without God " need scarcely be noted.

37 *Ibid.*, 104.

38 Emile Faguet, *op. cit.*, II, 363.

39 " Le Positivisme lui-même, abordé à la fin, n'a jamais pu me rallier à

seph de Maistre, de Bonald, Bossuet, Renan, and others, as well as by Comte and Lucretius, Maurras gradually erected these scaffoldings of his philosophical system: first, that man has a passion for changing raw nature, for transforming its rough products, as if he must needs humanize them before consuming them; second, that men do not start out equally endowed from the same point of departure at one and the same time, and that there are, therefore, personal differences and differences of means and fortunes; and third, that man's work does not end with himself, but that he "takes pleasure in building up and transmitting reserves of material savings, call them Capital, or spiritual reserves, call them Memory or Tradition, which preside over politics and over morals, over the sciences, over poetry and over the arts."[40]

"Tradition" with a capital "T" must not be interpreted as meaning just any or all of the spiritual reserve that man has built up and transmitted to later generations.[41] Some of it was, from its very nature, harmful or ugly and, therefore, not deserving of long life, while much, on the other hand, was not only beautiful and beneficent and, assuming that man is and will continue to be intelligent, enduring, but also more pleasurable to the "builder." Having culled out the latter from the whole reserve, he called it "Tradition."

Although he was vitally interested in the moral, social, and political elements of this spiritual reserve, and methodically selected what he deemed "the best," his prime concern was with its artistic and poetic ingredients, even in this period of "philosophical absorption" in first and last things which lasted

son dogme central: j'ai toujours contesté à Auguste Comte le passage nécessaire de l'esprit humain par la série des trois états de théologie, de métaphysique et de science" ("L' 'Action française' et la religion catholique," in *La Démocratie religieuse,* 462). "En effet à l'*Action française* les Comte, les Sainte-Beuve, les Taine sont adaptés et, pour ainsi dire, emmanchés au système d'une doctrine" (*ibid.,* 509).

40 *Au signe de Flore,* 10-11.

41 "Le nom de Tradition ne veut pas dire la transmission de n'importe quoi. C'est la transmission du beau et du vrai" (*Barbarie et poésie,* iii).

roughly from 1885 to 1890. Indeed, it proved to be his abiding primary interest, despite some later evidence to the contrary.[42] That it was fundamental, at least in the earlier period, may be inferred from his behavior; for his first important literary " action " was a vigorous espousal of the poetry of Jean Moréas, especially his *Pèlerin passionné*, and of the principles of the *Ecole romane* which Moréas founded in 1891 with Maurras and several others. In his *Jean Moréas* of the same year Maurras hailed the poet as a *Renaissant*,[43] who was " sensible of being perfectly happy," because he had " found the Sovereign Good." [44] This, apparently, was no less true of Maurras; for the verve with which he attacked the opponents (Decadents, Symbolists, Parnassians, and wilful critics) of this renewal of the "ancient Roman synthesis in which Gallic strength and the tradition of ' Rome the Great ' existed side by side," [45] came from conviction as well as from the heat of battle. Incidentally, it is noteworthy that this little brochure was dedicated to the author's "dear master," Anatole France, who had first acclaimed the poem in question.[46] This distinguished man of letters had taken kindly to Maurras a year or so earlier when the latter had ventured the opinion that France's recently published *Thaïs* embodied "an idea of different visions of living." [47] They became friends as master and disciple, a relationship that was valued the more highly by Maurras, not

42 *Le Chemin de Paradis*, xxxvii-xxxviii. In 1895, when this, his first book appeared, Edouard Herriot expressed the opinion that at the first alarm Maurras would take refuge in " some beautiful myth." Maurras, writing in 1920, says, " Grave erreur, en un sens : mon maître France l'avait vu, les lois de la beauté nous faisaient aussi penser aux lois de la vie, l'ordre de l'esthétique à celui de la politique." *Cf.* Abbé Cl. Mauriès, *Maurras et l'ordre chrètien* (Lyon, 1933?), 18-19.

43 " L'Avènement de Moréas," in *L'Allée des philosophes* (Paris, 1924), 234.

44 *Ibid.*, 228.

45 *Ibid.*, 256.

46 *Ibid.*, 224-225. His sympathetic support was also, no doubt, an important factor in convincing Maurras that he was on the right track.

47 *Anatole France: politique et poète* (Paris, 1924), 9-10.

merely because it was flattering to him, an obscure but ambitious young writer, but because he admired the "taste, charm, restraint, and forcefulness" of Anatole France's artistry and liked the "plastic tradition that animated" all his works.[48] And, though their disagreement over the issues raised by the Dreyfus affair ended their personal friendship, the disciple's gratitude towards his "first guide" continued undiminished.[49]

Maurras' conception of the "Sovereign Good" was "perfect happiness" engendered by "sacred beauty,"[50] or sometimes the latter alone. It was not enough, however, simply to contemplate or enjoy this divine Beauty, or to enhance the enjoyment by searching for and finding its laws and principles; there was a moral quality about it that demanded action and living.[51] Hence his rôle in the *Ecole romane* which, in a sense, was but the opening gun of a life-long campaign to rehabilitate and regenerate the morale of the French people. But, apart from his participation in 1892 with his friend, Frédéric Amouretti, in the effort to turn the *Félibrige de Paris* from its purely literary and cultural program to the practical one of political and administrative decentralization,[52] and his coöperation with

48 *Le Chemin de Paradis*, xviii.

49 In an interview with Robert Bourget-Pailleron in 1924, he said, "France a été mon premier guide, et je ne vous dirai jamais assez l'admiration pleine de gratitude que j'ai pour lui..." (*Anatole France: politique et poète*, 54). The following passage, also of 1924, and in the same brochure (p. 10), is suggestive of the extent of this admiration: "Plusieurs de ses poèmes sont des chefs-d'oeuvre qui mûrissent une fois pour toutes la gouttelette extrême du suprême suc de la vie et de l'âme..." One of his attractions was his opposition to Christianity. See page 23 for his high praise of France's *Leuconoé.*

50 "Pour soutenir ta voix qui dit la *beauté sainte*..." From the second stanza of Anatole France's *A Charles Maurras*, in *Le Chemin de Paradis*, v; also in *La Revue critique des idées et des livres* (Apr. 25, 1911), XIII, 130.

51 See *La Musique intérieure*, 37-46, for an interesting description of his early efforts to write poetry. The rhythm within not only continued alongside his abstract studies, but actually "nourished" them.

52 *L'Etang de Berre*, 119-134; *Au signe de Flore*, 34-37.

Barrès in *La Cocarde* in 1894 and 1895 in an effort directed toward the same end,[53] his "action" was largely the literary and intellectual campaign of a critic imbued with a passion for Beauty and a desire to cleanse French art and literature of what, to him, was its manifest ugliness and weakening effect. This was true until 1897, when he began to act upon the decision which had been forced upon him by observation and reflection during his visit to Athens in the preceding year.[54] This decision was that since the intelligence of France was weighed down by the "ignoble yoke" of rule by the masses, buttressed by their two "friends," the German and the Jew, and since the genius and taste of the Athenians no longer achieved anything, once their "best" had lost their independence, "it was necessary to shake off the yoke or accept its natural effects." Since the latter was out of the question, Maurras concluded that his battle line had been too short; "a lucid literary polemic led [therefore] to a social and political polemic." [55]

Although this decision necessitated the removal of batteries and men to new emplacements, the older sector was by no means evacuated nor wholly neglected in the years that followed. His energies were divided, it is true; but the ultimate end remained essentially the same.[56] Since the second polemic grew out of the first and was, in a sense but an extension of it, we shall now turn to the principles for which he fought in

53 In addition to contributing articles on decentralization, Maurras supplied the reader with information regarding new books and articles and occasionally he denounced the foreigners in France. *Cf. Au signe de Flore*, 37.

54 The first article found by the present writer in which Maurras openly espoused the monarchical form of government appeared in *La Gazette de France* on June 3, 1897, under the caption, "Défense éventuelle de M. Maurice Rouvier"; *Au signe de Flore*, 43.

55 *Barbarie et poésie*, xi.

56 "Aujourd'hui tous les intérêts politiques et mentaux coïncident si parfaitement qu'il peut être bon de montrer ce qui était dit de leur convergence dans une série de travaux vieux de vingt et trente ans" (*ibid.*, xi, written in 1925).

the first in the hope of being better able to understand those of the second.

Maurras' statement that his philosophical studies led him to no final conclusion, but merely to "some extremely subjective syntheses," and brought him only "some satisfactions of malicious criticism or of rather sterile clarity,"[57] seems so utterly out of place in his writings, so absolutely contrary to fact, that it must be regarded as an expression of temporary petulance or opportunism. It may most probably have been prompted by a desire to quiet the fears of his Catholic friends and allies, who were accused by hostile Catholic critics of consorting with a Pagan. Actually, the true Maurras, Maurras the aesthete and lover of order, who compared a thought to a physical molecule that embraced a "whole world of impressions, of sensations and of sentiments," had as complete a philosophy as its basic Epicurean (and Comtian) principles allowed.[58]

Having denied the existence of God, and still demanding order in his thinking, Maurras was constrained to reorganize his thought not only without God but also without any metaphysical equivalent, such as the Absolute, or the sovereignty of the individual Conscience. But since order implies selection and gradation, hierarchy and unity, a theology of a sort was inescapable, even though Maurras was determined to accept no solution of the problem which was not in accord with the "laws" or "order" of nature. Comte, who had faced the same problem, had discovered a satisfying solution in the Great Being, Humanity. Interpreting Humanity as the "human élite," those who have contributed to mankind's great work,[59]

57 "L' 'Action française' et la religion catholique," in *La Démocratie religieuse*, 462.

58 *Prologue d'un essai sur la critique* (Paris, 1932), 59, first published as "Essai sur la critique" in *Revue encyclopédique Larousse* (1896), 969-974.

59 "Cette nombreuse élite humaine n'est pas une image vaine. Elle forme ce qu'il y a de plus réel en nous. Nous la sentons dès que nous descendons au secret de notre nature" ("Auguste Comte," in *L'Avenir de l'intelligence*, 118-119). Comte also selected, but his principle was apparently love or the

and stressing the naturalness of the Positivist religion in the sense that man cannot possibly escape the rule of nature's laws, Maurras concluded that, so conceived, it was a "good" religion.[60] Greatest and best among the élite, those who constituted its core—the real élite—were, in his opinion, the ancient Greeks and their cultural heirs. This was true, not because they were Greeks and their heirs, but because of the high quality and perfection of their work:[61] in short, they were members of divine Humanity because of the exquisite beauty of their art. Having created and tasted such beauty, theirs must have been a calm and a peace—in short, a happiness—comparable to that of the gods of Epicurus and Lucretius.[62]

For beauty is the road to happiness. If one were inclined to cavil, one might with some justice, after noting how beauty is made the criterion of selection, conclude that here we have

"social instinct" ["Introduction" by Ch. Le Verrier, in Auguste Comte, *Cours de philosophie positive* (Paris, new edition, 1926), I, xli]. The following comment of Faguet would seem to apply to Maurras' concept of God almost as well as to Comte's: "Comme c'est lui qui fait son Dieu, et comme il le fait à son image, c'est l'humanité divinisée qu'il adore; c'est l'humanité épuré, subtilisée, purgée de tout ce qu'elle a de mauvais, centuplée en tout ce qu'elle a de bon; mais ce n'est pas autre chose que l'humanité. Seulement c'est l'humanité adorée indirectement; et voilà la supériorité de la religion théologique sur la religion humanitaire. C'est l'humanité adorée sans que l'on croie que ce soit elle qu'on adore. De tout ce qu'il a de bon dans l'humanité on a fait un être extérieur à elle, détaché d'elle, bien autrement imposant, bien autrement séduisant aussi, auquel on s'attache de coeur, d'âme, avec passion ..." (*op. cit.*, II, 366-367).

60 "Auguste Comte", *L'Avenir de l'intelligence*, 119.

61 *Anthinéa* (Paris, new edition, 1926), ix and 104.

62 "L'âme chagrine et mécontente qui fit de l'homme l'inventif et industrieux animal qui change la face du monde, cette âme de désir, cette âme de labeur ne sera jamais satisfaite par un nombre quelconque d'oeuvres ou de travaux, tout nombre pouvant être accru: c'est la qualité et la perfection de son oeuvre, qui lui donnera le repos, car toute perfection se limite aux points précis qui la définissent et s'évanouit au delà... Source d'exaltation et d'inhibition successive, elle trace aux endroits où l'homme aborde l'univers ces figures fermes et souples qui sont mères communes de la beauté et du bonheur" (*ibid.*, 104). *Cf. De rerum natura*, II, 646-651; and George D. Hadzits, *op. cit.*, 113.

to do with another metaphysical entity similar in many respects to an absolute. One would, of course, be told that beauty is expressed objectively in statuary, building, picture, poem, and song. But is not this the same sort of reply that the idealistic philosopher makes when such absolutes as Justice, Duty, Conscience, and the Individual are placed in doubt? Are they not reflected in and do they not dominate human behavior? The empirical aesthete counters that all the latter are vague imaginings that have no real existence other than subjective, whereas beauty is objective. Be that as it may. But what can one say for happiness, the *raison d'être* of beauty and the coping-stone of this hierarchy of thought? [63] Is not that a finality similar to those for which the metaphysicians are reproached? It is true that the question of first causes and that of personal immortality are excluded from this order of thought; it is, therefore, not strictly theological. But happiness, to be what it implies, must, it would seem, be subjective. Moreover, nature and natural laws, with which all must be in accord, are but "metaphysical entities" themselves; for the aesthete, finding raw nature crude, remakes and remodels it to bring it into accord with a "higher nature." [64]

63 *La Musique intérieure*, 96, 100; *Prologue d'un essai sur la critique*, 54.
64 Emile Faguet, *op. cit.*, II, 358-359.

CHAPTER X

THE "CLASSICAL," "PAGAN," AND "RATIONAL" AESTHETICS OF MAURRAS

OUR purpose here, however, is less to question than to seek to understand the aesthetic—and traditionalist—assumptions of Charles Maurras. To begin at the beginning, one may properly ask, "What is the nature of his 'happiness' and what are its philosophical implications?" Enough has been said to show that it is not sensuous or animal in character. The "sad joys of the flesh" are a delusion, as is also the hope of attaining happiness by making or securing the possession of more and bigger things.[1] Real happiness is possible, indeed, only to a relatively small number of "chosen persons." [2] Only to these is it given to know the calm repose or the sweet intoxication that is "wholly exempt from sadness" and disillusionment.[3] This exaltation, though it approach the point of intoxication, differs radically from the pleasures of the common herd in that it is rational throughout; the intellect never loses command. That Maurras has known such moments of extreme pleasure may well be imagined. When, as a youth, he stood before the ruins of the ancient theatre of Arles, he was so moved by their beauty that he made the pious vow that he would make an annual pilgrimage to this "sacred place." [4] But more compelling and, therefore, more conducive to happiness, was the greater beauty of the ruins of the Acropolis. Here he was so affected by the exquisite lines and splendor of the first column of the Propylaea that he embraced as much of it as his out-stretched arms could encompass, and, taking care that a nearby group of noisy Americans would think he

1 *La Musique intérieure*, 137; *Anthinéa*, 48, 104; *Principes* (Paris, 1931), 32.

2 *Anthinéa*, 48.

3 *Ibid.*, 41, 85, 104.

4 *Ibid.*, 40-41.

was measuring its circumference, he kissed it as a loving friend. This moment of "lyric folly" in which he "revelled with infinite pleasure" was one of the most memorable of his life. Since "it signified a pleasure wholly exempt from sadness, a free movement and a pure act," he was in the presence of something that "to the letter" fulfilled the requirements of a god. "A simple accident of life and nature, it summed up and explained both." Rare and unique, it was at the same time common and universal. It was the work of an industrious hand and of the unifying power of man's reason, "crowned by the tenderest of fortune's smiles." "Insolent happiness" had decreed that it be beautiful amidst the ugly. Into chaos it injected a rhythm, assured of its own law, and from infinite hostility it wrenched an "immortal accord." Hence the "ineffable sweetness" of this moment. His intelligence, far from frowning upon his delirious happiness, abetted it; for it told him he would never again have so justifiable a thrill.[5]

The contemplation and appreciation of beauty are means to happiness; but happier still is he who creates it; for he is, as it were, a "suspended spirit that travels ceaselessly between earth and heaven, carrying communications from one to the other."[6] His happiness is, indeed, a necessary condition for the creation of true beauty, just as the latter is, in turn, necessary for true happiness. He must not be in constant fear of sin or death, a basic condition of happiness; he must not be fearful of hurting others;[7] he must choose, for no one loves contrariety in his thinking;[8] he must have confidence in the choice made, and in his taste for having made it; in short, he must be without the least suspicion that he can be wrong.[9] Free from doubt and fear, his spirit moves with verve and

5 *Ibid.*, 40-42.

6 *La Musique intérieure*, 116.

7 *L'Anthropophage* (Paris, 1930), *passim*.

8 "Dans le choix réside l'essence, non seulement de tous les arts, mais de la vie elle-même" (*Prologue d'un essai sur la critique*, 41).

9 *Ibid.*, 45.

decision, which is evidence of his joy and happiness. But this freedom of action and expression is not just any urge that enters an undisciplined body or mind. He has a taste which almost instinctively, or "mechanically," makes him say or do the right thing at the proper time without the least vacillation or trouble of soul before each move.[10] This taste is a disciplined sensibility or, to use Maurras' expression, a "reflective sensibility." [11] It embraces his whole being. Being a man, he is a reasoning animal. In common with other animals, he has passions, sentiments, even morality. His reasoning powers alone distinguish him from the animals proper.[12] If his taste and style are to be good, his animal ardors must be strong; for they furnish at once the motive power, or movement, and the raw materials, "fine, rich, strong, and rapid impressions," with which he creates beauty.[13] This is done by reason which orders and polishes the materials thus supplied. It must not, however, be permitted to get out of hand lest it "wither the animal" and thus "exhaust its own sources." [14] It must, on the other hand, never lose control by letting the animal passions or sentiments usurp the directing rôle, while, on the other hand, it must guard itself from the vain pursuit of metaphysical "clouds." There must be, not an equilibrium or balance of these forces, for they are not equal, but an *order,*

10 "Bienheureux, dira la sensibilité clairvoyante, celui-là dont les oeuvres toujours répandues sur les choses ne sont rien qu'effets machinals, liaisons d'habitudes, inertes mouvements et totales occupations!" (*Le Chemin de Paradis,* lxxxii). *Cf. Anthinéa,* 67-68.

11 *Prologue d'un essai sur la critique,* 55. In a note of "L'Avènement de Moréas" he expresses his gratitude to Charles Morice for referring to Moréas' poems as "sentiments pensées" (*L'Allée des philosophes,* 252).

12 *Prologue d'un essai sur la critique,* 50-51; *Principes,* 40.

13 *Prologue d'un essai sur la critique,* 40; *Les Amants de Venise* (Paris, new edition, 1926), 287-289. "Le vrai poète est celui-là qui, goûtant, le plus énergiquement possible, le plus grand nombre d'impressions justes, les possède, les gouverne et les distribue. La nature infinie, si on la laisse règner en nous, devient un terrible maitresse d'énervement et d'imbécilité" (*Barbarie et poésie,* 224-225).

14 *Prologue d'un essai sur la critique,* 51.

which is simply the "conformity of a being with all the elements of his destiny." [15]

So reason which, as we have seen, was present even in his moment of supreme happiness, must be the artist's guide and counsellor in the creation of beauty as well as in its appreciation. It dictates or at least supervises the choice, in which "resides the essence, not only of all the arts, but of life itself." [16] That the fickle, restless, wretched Greeks should have given birth to Pallas and thereby "effected the ancient discovery of Reason," was natural, but none the less admirable. Because they experienced all life and all passion, the Athenians were constrained to seek a standard of behavior elsewhere than in life and passion. Sentiment disturbed their conduct; so they placed reason upon their altar. "The event is the greatest in the history of the world." [17] Pallas made men, while the latter made use of reason, which the Athenians possessed "to a degree of unique strength." [18] It enabled them to reconcile "measure and enthusiasm," "reason and power"; [19] it revealed to them the fact that art has its point of perfection just as nature has its point of maturity and bounty; and it directed them to this point of "maximum vigor and density which dominates and which incloses the rest." [20] It not only enabled them to create beautifully and perfectly, but made it possible for them to express their own thought perfectly: "a human thought superior to the variations of history and of nature." [21] "The influence of Athenian reason has created civilization and can doubtless recreate it." All the progress of our species consists only, therefore, in transmitting and developing the

15 *Ibid.*, 52.

16 *Ibid.*, 41.

17 *Anthinéa*, 102-103.

18 *Ibid.*, 72, 101.

19 *Ibid.*, 60, 74; "Invocation à Minerve," in *L'Avenir de l'intelligence*, 269.

20 *Anthinéa*, 54, 104.

21 *Ibid.*, 72. "La beauté parfaite est un . . . signe de vérité . . ." (*Barbarie et poésie*, 291).

priceless boon which the bounty of the Athenians has bequeathed us.[22]

They modestly prayed to Pallas and gave her, whom they had created, the praise for the perfection that reason made possible; but in so doing they were really invoking their best selves, while, at the same time, they were praying to something other than themselves.[23] And so must Maurras' prayer to the same goddess under her Roman name, his *Invocation à Minerve*, be interpreted.[24] Having praised her for her part in the work that lasts eternally and thanked her for the hours of forgetfulness of self that man, distracted by her, spends, he expresses gratitude for her " gift " to the Athenians. It has been variously labeled: " At one time it was called Wisdom; at another, Measure, or Perfection, or Beauty, and perhaps Taste. Others prefer Rhythm, Harmony. And others, Reason. Is it not also Modesty? Is it not the fire of eternal Composition? The precision of Number, clear and sweet Quality? It has been represented as a mysterious Band around a sheaf, as the Bit placed in the mouth of celestial horses, as the pure Line surrounding some noble effigy, as a living Order which fittingly distributes each portion." [25] These are but "melancholy images" and an " imperfect allusion " to the splendors of this gift and of Minerva herself. Vulgar men may think; but he who has found this boon " thinks well " and knows what it is to " be right, live suitably, die properly." Such was the nature of the gift which the Greeks or, more specifically, the Athenians gave to mankind.

Reason is not only the principal partner, with sensibility, in Beauty Incorporated, but it is also, in a sense, beauty itself. This close identity of reason and beauty even a cursory survey of the attributes of beauty will demonstrate. Chief among them

22 *Anthinéa*, 54, 104.

23 *Ibid.*, 102.

24 In *L'Avenir de l'intelligence*, 265-272, and *Romantisme et révolution*, 227-232. *Cf.* " L'Ame des oliviers," in *Anthinéa*, 233-238.

25 *L'Avenir de l'intelligence*, 269-270.

are purity, clarity, forcefulness, harmony, and durability, each of which is present proportionately as reason has been actively engaged in the creation of the work of art.

Purity, as an attribute of beauty, represents a choice, a filtering, a rejection of the dross, and a retention of only the Simon-pure: an eminently rational procedure.[26] The classical is, as a result of this process of elimination, " the purest of the exquisite and the beautiful," [27] and Anatole France's *Leuconoé* is " one of the warmest, purest, and most significant " songs of the French language.[28] Purity is, it is true, susceptible of degrees, until it reaches perfection itself. Some of the latter's poems " bring to perfection once and for all the last little drop of the supreme sugar of life and of the soul." [29] However, " there is but one place where perfection exists, there are not two ": it is the Acropolis of Athens. " What can we have to do with a Gothic ditty in the place of perfection?," Maurras asked by way of objecting to Renan's *Prière*, which he took along to the Acropolis to read and which the shades of the " little people of Greece " would not let him finish. " One does not repeat before a goddess, with four repetitions of '*you alone*' (alone young, alone pure, alone sacred, alone strong), in order to wish for her, in parting, a ' larger ' head with the means of embracing 'sundry types of beauty.' Either the words are simple puffs of wind, or they represent no sense, since one cannot write, 'When I saw the Acropolis, I had the revelation of the divine,' if one must conclude that the pieces of dried mortar of Byzantium, in their way, produce a 'divine effect.' " [30] Renan's trouble was impure thinking, and consequently an impure taste, in the presence of purity itself. He would even have had it impure!

26 Abbé Cl. Mauriès, *op. cit.*, 20.

27 *Barbarie et poésie*, 343. "A l'Acropole, il n'y a guère que des ouvrages archaïques ou semi-archaïques, et des chefs-d'oeuvre purs" (*Anthinéa*, 75).

28 *Anatole France: politique et poète*, 23.

29 *Ibid.*, 10.

30 *Anthinéa*, 46-47.

And why is the beauty of the Acropolis pure? It is pure because it is rational, because it embraces only what is in accord with nature, because it has substance, is solid, opaque, and palpable.[31] Its solid marble has no room within for the floating clouds of metaphysics; nor is there room for the vagaries of uncontrolled passion. Its parts are fixed: they are, and remain, where reason would have them, and the whole is but a figure of reason itself. Though common and universal, it is also pure and unique because it perfectly represents a thought that was pure. When impurities of thought were brought over from Alexandrian Asia in the form of Adonis- and Mithra-worship, the Greeks were barbarized and lost their former taste. Since their thought, and consequently their taste, was no longer pure, and since their artistic creations thereafter were only half Greek, they may be neglected as one disregards the copies of originals.[32] Although, in his study of the sculpture of this period, Maurras found some works that approached the sublime, the general impression with which he took leave of the athlete, straining his "pretentious muscularity," the adolescent boys with exaggerated arms, and the trembling and too flexible Aphrodites, was that the truth was represented too truthfully and the false too falsely. He sensed an air of dissolution mixed with some vestiges of restraint and saw "Epicurus and Zeno face to face and sometimes clashing in the same marble." An air of the unfinished over against an appearance of the too consciously finished marred these productions. The old certainty and its resultant freedom of movement had slipped away with the pure tradition.[33]

But to return to "the place of perfection," to the creations that Pericles ordered made. They are Greek and, because they are Greek, are unspoiled. Though their ruins may remind the visitor of a vast cemetery full of parched bones, or of a gigan-

31 Abbé Cl. Mauriès, *op. cit.*, 19-20.

32 *Anthinéa,* 59-60.

33 *Ibid.*, 76-77.

tic sculptor's rock-yard,[34] the white marble, whether fallen or broken or still standing, is solid and opaque. It reflects the bright light of the Mediterranean sun and the brilliance that was once Athens'. But the visitor is impressed by the forms and figures, which stand out in their high luminous setting, quite as much as by the purity of the materials or the purity of style, of which there is still ample evidence. There is no mixture of style here, no evidence of division of thought, no wavering, but a bold simplicity that goes directly to its end. Hence their clarity, another important attribute of beauty.

Clarity demands a clear and distinct outline: definite lines that set the work apart from its surroundings, whilst they make it as natural and as universal as nature itself. It is the lines that create form; and, in doing it, they limit and perfect. "All perfection limits itself at precise points which define it and vanishes beyond." [35] One of the disturbing qualities in the religions that came from Asia lay in the fact that they rebelled against lines. "'*In the beginning,*' . . . say the Jewish books"; the artist says, "at the end and only at the end of the work of art. . . ." [36] The artist loves finish and perfection, not chaos, which remains chaos in the absence of lines. Now, since art and the thought it expresses are inseparably one,[37] it is the peculiar virtue of the severe lines of the Attic style that they stress the necessity of limit and of death. Before Epicurus, whose "words of gold, ever most worthy of life eternal," proclaimed the nature of things and drove the terror of the Acheron from men's minds,[38] these lines, in their ineffable

34 *Ibid.*, 44.

35 *Ibid.*, 104.

36 In a letter from Maurras to Barrès of Dec., 1905 (Maurice Barrès, *Mes cahiers*, IV, 300).

37 "Une chose est certaine, la substance de la pensée et la manière de penser ne font qu'un... Une beauté formelle indépendente de l'esprit qu'elle rayonne et de l'intention qui l'anime, c'est une rêverie de professeur d'écriture" (*Anatole France: politique et poète*, 6-7). *Cf. Prologue d'un essai sur la critique*, 57-59.

38 *De rerum natura*, III, 13-17.

beauty, proclaimed the same message. "The peculiar quality of this wisdom is that it places man in accord with nature without drying up nature and without crushing man." [39] It tells us to accept our natural setting and its laws, one of which is death, interpreted not as the end of our transitory sojourn here and the beginning of a happier or sadder life in eternity, but as the final and complete end. This acceptance of "death immortal" and its resultant feeling of at-oneness with nature bring the sweet repose and peace which, as we have seen, is the hall mark of happiness. Since the end of beauty is happiness, both are served by the definite line and by definitive death. Reason, which must be empirical, is also served; for it may get out of hand and soar aloft into the great unknown of metaphysics. This death prevents by standing by as the ever-present sentinel whose duty it is to keep reason and beauty within the confines of nature. It is in this sense that the following passage in the "Préface" of *Le Chemin de Paradis* must, it seems, be interpreted: "I have dared to evoke in the presence of a thousand errors the finished types of Reason, of Beauty, and of death, triple and unique end of the world." [40]

Death, indeed, is not only necessary to beauty, reason, and happiness; it is itself beautiful. It must be admired as well as not feared. It is not the dead who departs; it is his friends, parents, wife, children, brothers, and sisters who leave him.[41] It is not the dead who moves; he is calm. It is the survivors who are moved to tears.[42] Death irritates and brings consternation because it destroys, because it does violence to form. This latter it really does not do, whatever happens to matter; for the laws of form are fixed and durable.[43] The human form is at its point of perfection at the point of transition from

39 *Anthinéa,* 104.

40 xc. *Cf.* J. Vialatoux, *La Doctrine catholique et l'école de Maurras* (Lyon, 1927), 18.

41 *Corps glorieux ou vertu de la perfection* (Paris, 1929), 13.

42 *Ibid.,* 14.

43 *Ibid.,* 18.

adolescence to manhood or womanhood. The dead at this point are most beautiful because the " realities are taken and retained . . . at their best point. . . . Who has not seen on a funeral bed the beautiful faces which death had been able to keep youthful at twenty years? It has brought them back to the peak of their perfection." [44] And how beautiful the " Lamented Young Man " is in the National Museum at Athens! " Ripe adolescent, grown, brought to the supreme moment of his virile springtime," he is in repose, though not standing or sitting. " The soul, as firm as the flesh, gives off emotion without receiving any in return. A faithful dog has lain down, whilst scenting some distant trace of the life that has evaporated. A prostrate little slave conceals his sorrow. And, especially, standing near him, more rigid than he, his old dejected father, with a hand on his beard, suppresses a sob. Is the hero aware of his three friends in tears? They shall not succeed in taking him from his new order. For, if they sigh that he is no more, do they not hear him reply, ' No. I am?' " [45]

Form and beauty, therefore, are exempt from "death immortal," from the "dead death," and may be expected to survive so long as there is art and so long as the world has a heart, or, having lost it, wills to recover it.[46] This art perceives, as does the true philosopher, that life and death are but parties to a cycle of realities that must be reconciled, not placed over against each other in positions of mutual hostility, as does the sophist.[47] The enlightened artist-philosopher knows that " the essential character of life . . . is to conspire to die." [48] And, having associated and compounded these apparent opposites " in the interest of a higher good," having come to admire death rather than to fear it, and no longer trembling before the imaginary threat of dire retribution in this life (no other

44 *Ibid.*, 23.

45 *Ibid.*, 20-21.

46 *Ibid.*, 45.

47 *Le Chemin de Paradis*, xli.

48 *Ibid.*, lxxviii.

is recognized) from an angry, jealous providence, equally imaginary, his thought and style — his life itself — assume a character of bold directness and simplicity, impossible under less favorable conditions.[49] His thoughts, in whatever type of art expressed, will be great and profound; for mediocre thoughts rarely have the courage to put themselves forward naked and alone.[50] On the other hand, though these great thoughts be simple, direct, and forceful, they will not be devoid of measure; they will not take wings into the unknowable, because, as we have seen, death is at hand to confine them to this world.

The power that is implicit in simplicity and, therefore, in clarity, though measured, may be, and in last analysis must be, brutal and violent.[51] It is not, it is true, simply a case of violence for violence's sake, but for a proper and necessary object.[52] It is said that the critic, who is no less an artist than the poet,[53] should always be courteous, or moderate, even frigid. "This is a way of obtaining sterility." Debonair critics, they describe the rude Demosthenes and the ardent Bossuet as having been "vehement," a virtue which these gentlemen would call violence if good French did not inspire them with fear. The violence of all of these great men remains patent. They were honest people who were incapable of insipidity, and they did not mince terms. They would have had a good laugh, and Racine with them, had one chirped to them that reason, meas-

49 "Quel profond moraliste l'a dit: vous serez jeunes tant que vous aimerez le risque de mort! Je n'ai pas vécu en momie. J'ai agi, travaillé, tenté de conseiller ou d'orienter. Peut être à tort. Et probablement à raison" ("Avant-propos," 1920, in *Le Chemin de Paradis*, xl).

50 *Prologue d'un essai sur la critique*, 72-73.

51 "Cette tradition classique qui est nôtre, passe toutes les autres. Elle montre, en effet, une force de la vie égale, en flamme, en coloris, *en brutalité ingénue* ou en fière délicatesse, à ce que put trouver le reste du monde, depuis les steppes de Russie jusqu'aux plages de la Guinée..." (*ibid.*, 83).

52 *Barbarie et poésie*, viii.

53 "Le poète faite si l'on veut l'abrégé de la substance de l'univers. Il traduit, il nous rend sensibles les beautés possibles ou réelles du monde. Mais le critique extrait l'essence de cette essence de beauté" (*Prologue d'un essai sur la critique*, 20).

ure, and humanity consisted in referring to everything with hints, as a confidante of Bérénice." [54] No, this circumspection, bordering upon fear, is not a moral virtue, or even intellectual refinement. The beautiful and the infinite are separate and distinct, and a morality based upon the latter warps and destroys the aesthetic sense. Christianity has doubtless created some new sentiments; "but it has not created a new sense any more than a new idea of the beautiful." An artist's moral excellence, or lack of it, is, therefore, of no concern to the critic.[55] And, since it is the purpose of art to save beauty, moral virtue must not be permitted to "supplant, exclude," or "disinherit" it.[56]

The Athenians were wiser than our modern moralists. They saw that, "if it is important that the soul be mistress of itself, it is necessary also that it seek to find its boon and, having attained it as the result of a happy effort, that it pluck it." Their maxim was: "Neither laxness nor harshness, no virtue without pleasure, and no pleasure without virtue . . ." [57] Understood "in its most penetrating sense," this means that violence is not harshness when it is necessary, that virtue and pleasure go hand in hand, and that it is virtuous, for example, to seize your booty. "Having seized our Quesnoy (true beauty), we die gay and content; if not, we hasten to take it: the necessary accomplished act is the only benefit that does not deceive." [58]

In a broader sense violence seems to be an indispensable concomitant of, and means to, art. As purity demands choice, so too does simplicity. There is no room here for misguided sympathy. The simple may, and should, give the impression of ease as well as of strength. This quality, however, is not

54 *Barbarie et poésie*, vii.

55 *Prologue d'un essai sur la critique*, 33-36.

56 *Corps glorieux ou la vertue de la perfection*, 45.

57 *Anthinéa*, 103.

58 *Barbarie et poésie*, ix.

easily attained.[59] It presupposes a patient analysis of the subject to be portrayed and a careful ordering of the materials to be used: the essential has been found, the unnecessary totally rejected, and the rest ranked according to the importance of each of its elements in terms of the essential. These lesser materials, or ideas, may have special claims upon the artist's sensibility, but they must be placed in inferior positions in order that the whole be orderly, logical, and simple.[60] Supposing they were individuals and were able to express their disappointment, their vigorous protests would seem justifiable.[61] But that is precisely the mistake that the romanticist makes, as is explained later. Furthermore, supposing that some concession is made to these less specific claims, the resultant work of art will be complex rather than simple, amusing rather than enchanting.[62] If, however, the artist's aim is to create as perfectly as possible in the hope of attaining and disseminating the highest form of happiness, he will avoid such concessions. He will arrange the materials in accordance with the mental image of order which his reason, or tradition, affords him as a channel for his sensibilities which, as we have seen, furnish the raw materials of his art. This law, or order, far from robbing him of his freedom of thought and action, as does the belief in the supernatural and in personal immortality, once he has made it his own, or has accepted what tradition has already given him, enhances his verve and gives him real liberty. Moreover, his faith and conviction in its rightness inspire him with a zeal for action.

59 *Anatole France: politique et poète*, 4-5.

60 "La tristesse dantesque est intérieure au poète: son ouvrage rayonne la paix et la joie. L'homme est triste en raison de toutes les limites opposées aux violences des sens et du coeur par son intelligence, à la fois serve et libre d'une volonté passionnée" [*Le Conseil de Dante* (Paris, 1920), 78].

61 This is admittedly fantastic when applied to sculpture, architecture, painting, poetry, and the like; but it becomes a dire reality when the aesthete applies his principles of beauty to the reorganization of society and the state.

62 *Prologue d'un essai sur la critique*, 75.

But what of the materials that are classified and ordered with so much decision and firmness? Is it not violence? No. It is, rather, a sort of charity. Not least among the virtues of Dante, the "Catholic Lucretius," is that he, no less than Goethe and Leonardo da Vinci, makes one feel "that the law takes precedence over things, that the being dissolves when it lacks its law and that the law is rigorous in proportion to the soul which it is called upon to govern. For the strong soul, a stronger law in order to accomplish the design."[63] True of the artist, it is no less true of the work of art and its elements. John Addington Symonds reflects but little understanding of Dante and of beauty when he objects to what he calls the absurdity of placing people in labeled, isolated cells for all eternity, since all that lives is mobile, pliable, and changing. It is Symonds who is absurd, not Dante. "This irrational changing would be tantamount to non-existence, and it is in order that they exist in all plenitude that a great poet lays down some definitions as certain as possible, *certi fines*, for each of the objects of his song."[64] In short, the elements die, or vanish into a vacuous non-existence, in the absence of the law which gives them being and an aesthetic immortality.

Moreover, when these elements are conscious and are endowed with the ability to think and feel, they are gratefully conscious of this truth. That, at least, was the feeling of Crito's slaves. How overjoyed they were upon rejoining him and resuming their services for him in the Elysian Fields, after years and centuries of vain efforts to find him![65] And how troubled they were when Mercury came and volunteered to take them all back to Athens, and Crito seemed to be at the point of accepting the offer when told that the city lay in ruins! While Crito was questioning Mercury, he recalled the words he had seen on the tables of Destiny as he was on his way to

63 *Le Conseil de Dante*, 44.

64 *Ibid.*, 45-46. "Ses têtes d'anges ont un corps. Elles ne flottent pas" (*ibid.*, 48-49).

65 "Les Serviteurs," in *Le Chemin de Paradis*, 208.

the Styx. There he had read, "*A Hebrew christ will come to the world, will ransom the slave, and, deposing the strong from the throne, he will place the first lower than the last in order that his glory be sung in life eternal.*" [66] To Crito's question if this had transpired, Mercury replied that it had. Crito sighed, although "he little understood how the absurd had thus triumphed." [67] Mercury added that since "the Hebrew had cried on the cross, 'It is finished,'" the slaves had been masters of their souls and had had no yoke other than living and dying. Assuming that they wished to return, Mercury busied himself with a few necessary preparations to lead them back. And, when the slaves tremblingly inquired where he was going to take them, he glibly replied, "To liberty, my friends." Whereupon Andocles, the dean and spokesman of the slaves, threw himself down before Crito and, embracing his master's knees, begged him not to renew their misfortunes. Describing conditions on earth, the "merciless tedium" in the absence of order, the indignities imposed upon the former masters and the pervading ugliness of the scene, all of which Mercury confirmed, the slave concluded, "I am not divining, Mercury, I am reasoning. But you, Crito, I beseech you. Say that we are not going back to the starving declassed. We are not going to drown in the throng. Here we shall cleave to you as the valleys to the mountains. The most humble of us is not unrelated to the brilliance of your golden hair and of your divine figure: he sustains one and plaits the other. *We are members of a beautiful body which you excel in directing, being its head and its thought*. It seems to us that at certain times a god exhales us from you." [68] All the slaves applauded, whilst Crito, still undecided, sighed again; then Mercury's three softly-spoken words, "Andocles is right," promptly settled the question.[69]

66 *Ibid.*, 202. (Maurras' italics.)

67 *Ibid.*, 221.

68 *Ibid.*, 226. (The present writer's italics.)

69 Compare with this his criticism of Tolstoy's *Master and Servant* in *Barbarie et poésie*, 120-122.

As the slaves of Crito were unhappy away from their master, and were in constant danger of being engulfed by the chaotic multitude, so too are the materials used by the artist, if severed from their law or order. Indeed, they are happiest when they fulfil the message which the artist "inscribes upon the shoulders of each in divine letters." [70] This is not, therefore, violence or tyranny on the part of the artist, or submission to an intolerable yoke on the part of the materials, but a liberation from the tedium of an erstwhile ugly, disordered existence and from the threat of complete extinction. Each is happy, therefore, in its proper place and, in consequence, vibrates with the "inner harmony" which pervades the whole and which a god seems to "exhale" upon it.

"Order is everything," [71] whatever the type of art, since it is the sign *par excellence* of the artist's submission to the law and of the mastery of reason over the senses. Without order, instead of having a "superior architecture," such as was Dante's, one has but a formless mass or a monstrous eccentricity. Without order the qualities of purity, clarity, simplicity, forcefulness, harmony, the sublime—all beauty and all art—are not only frustrated, but are made impossible, and one has but a murky, chaotic mist, or else sheer emptiness.[72] However, it is a "reasoned order," not an order for order's sake, that is so powerful an agent and so important a part of beauty. Just as death stands by to keep reason from flying away into the unknowable, so reason stands by to prevent order from drying up the sources of life. An unrestrained order, or law, might conceivably destroy itself. To prevent such an outcome, reason reconciles order and sensibility, and the result is a "living order," beauty and perfection.

70 *Le Chemin de Paradis*, 215.

71 *Barbarie et poésie*, 128.

72 There may be some "elements of beauty," but they will be disconnected. "Sans l'ordre qui donne figure, un livre, un poème, une strophe n'ont rien que des semences et des éléments de beauté" ("Le Romantisme féminin," in *L'Avenir de l'intelligence*, 199).

What is the basis of this authority which reason exercises over the imperious demands of order and the ineluctable claims of sentiment? Having found the beautiful and, consequently, the true, reason is upheld by a conviction that verges upon the mystical. Based upon a "realistic sentiment of things," this mysticism, which may be defined as the "quintessence of spiritualism,"[73] is serene: i.e., passionate, and yet calm, cold, and calculating, not perturbed or fanatical.[74] If the artist has arrived at his view of the beautiful by looking into his own soul, he may easily be moved to fanatical enthusiasm, or anger; but if his certainty has resulted from a careful study of nature and human experience, if it has come after a careful analysis of things without, rather than within, and he has found the true order with which his best self feels an instinctive kinship and to which he must adapt his life and thought,[75] he can be, and is, calm and serene, because he knows that the forces that are fighting for his order, this beauty and truth, are strong. They have known defeat, but never extinction; they have had their glorious epochs, and will have more.

For nature and tradition are the artist's allies. Not nature in the raw, nor all or just any tradition—for reason is selective, as are nature and tradition[76]—but nature "humanized" and tradition with a capital "T."[77] Both are, however, none the less real. In a sense they are one, for the Greeks first humanized nature and did it so perfectly that their work became and has remained *the* tradition since the days of Homer.[78] To the modernist, who is proud of our industrial and scientific

73 *Barbarie et poésie*, 134.

74 *Ibid.*, 136. "Fanatique et mystique ne sont point synonymes. Etre ému et mystique sont deux états distincts" (*ibid.*, 133).

75 *Principes* (Paris, 1931), 33.

76 "La vraie tradition est *critique*, et faute de ces distinctions, le passé ne sert plus de rien, ses réussites cessant d'être des exemples, ses revers d'être leçons" (*Action française*, June 3, 1909, in D. P. & C., V, 333).

77 *Prologue d'un essai sur la critique*, 79; *Barbarie et poésie*, iii.

78 "La patrie est une société naturelle, ou (*ce qui revient absolument au même*) historique" [*Les Lumières de la patrie* (Paris, 1931), 60].

achievements and looks upon them as both the evidence and the essence of progress and evolution, this is admittedly rank heresy. Believing that industry, the plastic arts, poetry, and eloquence advance simultaneously and equally along parallel lines, not unlike Prussian soldiers, the modernist is unable to understand how an age and a people, so backward in the industrial arts, could have wrought so perfectly in art. His trouble is vanity, for no one but a progressive or a fool could believe in the synchronous development of the arts.[79] Steam, electricity, and aviation are marvellous; but they have not changed human nature. People still rob, rape, and kill in automobiles, airplanes and tile bathrooms, fitted with the best of modern plumbing, just as they did elsewhere before these conveniences were invented. And the Romans who knew the *De rerum natura* by heart probably had the moral equivalents of tobacco and cocoa.[80] No, experience points to the "essential conformity of times." The materials and the relationships are the same. There are no new laws; they are all old, and those of human nature have not changed any more than those of nature itself.[81] History shows that a man is a "stable compound"; and "all art, thought, and civilization is based upon the belief that he and his surroundings are stable and essentially unchanging. Although chaos and confusion seem easiest and most likely to dominate, the 'miracle of order' has prevented this up to now," and has again and again proved the truth of the old axiom, *Eadem sint omnia semper!* "The human race depends upon this protection which enfolds its undertakings. Imperfect, alas! they are but the concurrence of an arrangement that is good, if not the good pure and simple."[82]

79 *Anthinéa*, 53-54. "C'est (i. e. progress) un dogme surnaturel, puisque les lois de la nature ne le contiennent pas" ("La Politique religieuse," in *La Démocratie religieuse*, 214).

80 *Le Chemin de Paradis*, l-li.

81 *Ibid.*, xlix-l; *Prologue d'un essai sur la critique*, 70-72.

82 *Le Chemin de Paradis*, liv-lv.

To the Greeks progress was advancement towards perfection, not the amassing of more and more things, the building of bigger and bigger material structures, or the invention of faster and faster means of communication. Wanting and aiming at perfection, they achieved a beauty that has never been equalled and which, because human nature is still fundamentally what it was in the days of Homer and Phidias, is still the most natural and human art that we have. So true is this that, if a man finds this beauty boresome, he will, if he is honest, examine himself and seek to correct his fault.[83]

83 *Anthinéa,* x. " Tout le progrès de notre espèce ne consisterait qu'à transmettre et à développer ce bien sans prix, une fois que les parties détruites en auraient été recouvrées. La mémorable impulsion donnée par Athènes ne s'est communiquée jusqu'à nous qu'assez faiblement. Elle s'est beaucoup altérée. Il ne nous reste pas grand'chose de la haute et délicate sagesse pratique qui maîtrisa et qui consola Ulysse à travers ses épreuves en l'empêchant de croire stupidement que les voluptés sont sans borne ou qu'on ne puisse composer avec les dieux. Le rhythme exquis d'un Phidias anime bien quelques poètes, mais ils sont clairsemés, dans l'histoire moderne ; et, encore que notre France, favorisée d'un Racine et d'un La Fontaine, en ait la meilleure part, les survivants sont peu en comparaison de ce qui a péri. Seul, à travers la méconnaissance et l'insulte, Aristote, ' L'Incomparable Aristote ', comme dit Comte, est continué dignement ; barbares de goût et de moeurs, nos modernes tiennent du moins à l'enchaînement du savoir, mais on s'occupe beaucoup plus d'en accroître la somme que de l'ordonner et de la distribuer à propos " (*Anthinéa,* 104-105).

CHAPTER XI

MAURRAS' INTERPRETATION OF THE LATIN HERITAGE

If a man is Latin in race or culture the task is easy, for it was Rome that gave the Greek tradition a new fatherland and spread it widely; although, unfortunately for Rome and later ages, it was already sullied by oriental impurities that brought about the downfall of Greece and later of Rome itself.[1] Had the Romans accepted the teachings of their great Lucretius, the outcome would probably have been a happier one. Though they failed to root out the oriental religions, indeed, later facilitated their expansion, though their idea of beauty was somewhat elephantine,[2] though they "had the impudence" to build a temple on the Acropolis and dedicate it to their own Goddess of Rome,[3] and though their adoration of this Goddess was "slightly brutal," as compared with the "masculine bashfulness and humility" which the Athenians evinced in the presence of Athena,[4] the Romans must nevertheless be credited with having served the Greek tradition powerfully. They sent their sons to Athens, where they imbibed in varying degrees the Greek taste for beauty while finishing their studies in philosophy and eloquence. Greek influence upon Roman life and thought was prodigious, even though it was more mixed than was necessary, or healthy. When the end came, one of the "Semitic leprosies" was powerful enough to exercise a weak preponderance.

1 "Hélas! tout compte fait, le monde romain s'acquitta mal auprès de la Grèce. A quoi pensaient-ils donc, ces administrateurs modèles, qui ne sauvaient pas leur éducatrice des pièges que lui ouvraient son intelligence et son ouverture d'esprit? Ce furent de mauvais tuteurs. Non seulement ils ne surent point la guérir des lèpres sémites, mais, tout le mal qu'Alexandrie n'avait pu faire au monde grec, Rome, on peut le dire, le fit. Il est vrai que Rome, à son tour, périt du même mal, en entraînant son lot d'hellénisme et d'humanité" (*ibid.*, 77-78).

2 *Ibid.*, 48.

3 *Ibid.*, 47.

4 *Ibid.*, 101-102.

Having grown up and spread in the Roman Empire, this "Semitic leprosy" was not, however, an unmixed curse; for, with some exceptions, it proved to be essentially what its name implied: Roman and universal. Its priests and monks, it is true, failed to distinguish the "pure Hellene from the contaminated Hellene" and welcomed and extended the contagion that had come from Asia. They unfortunately held Semiticism in high esteem, with its "convoy of buffoons, of prophets, of necromancers, of agitated and agitators without fatherland."[5] Nevertheless, wittingly or unwittingly, they were missionaries of Romanism and Hellenism, as is evident from the authoritarianism, the hierarchy, the canon law, the scholastic theology, the sacraments, the hagiology, and iconolatry of the Church. It was the mistress and the architect of the Latin culture of the Middle Ages and modern times, a splendid civilization that was well-nigh universal in the known world and which imposed a strong discipline upon the souls of men.[6] Its twofold maxim was "experience and tradition, order and progress."[7] Nothing was left to chance; everything was ruled and regulated: even visions and mystical ecstacy. There was, therefore, no lost motion, and every movement may be said to have been progress.[8] It was, indeed, more Roman than Christian, for the Christ of the Catholic tradition was and is, the "sovereign Jupiter who was crucified for us on earth."[9]

5 *Ibid.*, 225.

6 In the first edition of *Les Serviteurs* were these words, deleted from later editions: "Ici, le Psychagôgue manque de bonne foi et le dieu des voleurs se montre aussi le dieu des sophistes. Mercure aurait dû ajouter (car le bon Andoclès n'en pouvait rien prévoir) que la besogne des esclaves fut, durant plus de mille années, accomplie grâce à la servitude volontaire des ordres religieux aidés par la chevalerie, par des confréries d'ouvriers et d'artistes habilement organisées pour la prosperité de tous. L'harmonie de cet univers ne courut vraiment de danger que depuis deux ou trois cents ans" (*Le Chemin de Paradis*, 223, footnote). *Cf. ibid.*, lxxxviii.

7 "La Politique religieuse," in *La Démocratie religieuse*, 343.

8 "Le Dilemme de Marc Sangnier," *ibid.*, 41.

9 *Le Chemin de Paradis*, lxxxviii-lxxxix. (Quoted from Dante.)

By means of the spirit alone the Church secured a temporal dominion comparable and superior to the empires built by hand. That this was possible was due to the fact that the Church was free from all that was not pure thought, that it was the "incarnation and the terrestrial apotheosis of Thought."[10] In a sense the Church was not only more Roman than Christian, but, in so far as Christianity was irrational, "Biblical," and subjectively emotional, it was also definitely anti-Christian.[11] It was, in fact, civilization's chief protection against the "Jewish spirit," against "Biblism"; and, if France had given way to integral Gallicanism, it, too, would doubtless have fallen into the morass of Protestantism, this "worst enemy of the Species," just as did the other national churches. The slightest departure from Rome would have been a proportionate approach to Jerusalem.[12]

Until the Reformation came with its devastating effect upon poetry, the arts, manners, and civilization in general, Latin and Catholic culture—i.e., civilization—was secure. Then came another wave of the leprous plague, with the German, Luther, in the forefront now, instead of the Jew, Paul. The Church, after a period of indecision, definitely and heroically took its stand at the Council of Trent for order and the Graeco-Roman tradition. And France, after a longer period of internal dissension, chose to stand by the Church in defence of this same tradition—i.e., Latin civilization, which is the only one France

10 "La Politique religieuse," in *La Démocratie religieuse*, 219.

11 That, at least seems to be the only possible interpretation of the following and its context: "Clovis ne se fit pas simplement chrétien: il évita expressément l'arianisme des Burgondes et des Byzantins, il se fit catholique, catholique romain. Mais, quand elle coupa la tête au successeur et à l'héritier de Clovis, la Révolution n'était point anti-chrétienne; elle était protestante et anticatholique" ["Le Dilemme de Marc Sangnier," (*ibid.*, 42)]. This is confirmed by Vialatoux in the following: "C'est que, redisons-le, la pensée de Maurras n'est pas que l'Eglise doit devenir païenne; mais qu'elle l'est, et depuis longtemps, et que là précisément est son mérite. Ce n'est point une mission nouvelle qu'il lui assigne; c'est une mission traditionelle qu'il lui reconnaît" [*La Doctrine catholique et l'école de Maurras* (Lyon, 1927), 27].

12 *La Démocratie religieuse*, 41, 195, 341.

has.[13] Indeed, her men of letters, Ronsard, Racine, and La Fontaine, to name only the best, went beyond the Church to the source of this tradition, to Homer, as Sophocles had done many years before. And so brilliant was their work, so refined their humanism and classical spirit, that France became at once the home and the citadel of taste and polite manners, a distinction which she has not lost since, despite the destructiveness of the French Revolution and of romanticism, its literary, moral, and philosophical counterpart.[14] Both, daughters of the Reformation and, therefore, Asiatic and alien to the true tradition of France, they have " only interpreted " this tradition, not destroyed it. It is still alive, and with cultivation and care will again flourish.[15]

That it has not succumbed before the onslaughts of the religious reformers, the social and political revolutionists, and the romanticists, is due to the fact that this tradition is essentially natural to France. If French blood is not Latin, as some would have it, the others certainly cannot prove that it is German. As to the Celts, the most authentic forbears of the French, they are a mystery because so little is and can be known about them. With but a few relatively unimportant exceptions, the popular dialects of France are Gallo-Roman. If France to-day is one, it is because she was united by classical architects who gave her a literary language that is Graeco-Latin and a sense of order. These are the natural forces that hold France to the Graeco-Roman tradition.[16]

So powerful and so efficacious are these natural forces that it seems that all the French artist needs to do is to be well disposed towards them, and the result will be happy.[17] As he perceives the ease and naturalness with which beauty comes to

13 "... la France étant notre nom de nation, Rome est celui de notre civilisation" ("La Politique religieuse," *ibid.*, 195).

14 *Prologue d'un essai sur la critique*, 69-81; *Principes*, 33-34.

15 *Principes*, 34.

16 *Prologue d'un essai sur la critique*, 81-82.

17 *Ibid.*, 82.

crown his work, and knows why this is so, he may be pardoned, if in an access of filial piety, tinctured with no little pride, he intones the following laudation: [18]

I am Roman, because Rome as early as the Consul Marius and the divine Julius up to the dying Theodosius hewed out the first outline of my France. *I am Roman*, because Rome, the Rome of the priests and popes has given eternal solidity of sentiment, of customs, of language, of religion, to the political work of the generals, of the administrators and of the Roman judges. *I am Roman*, because, if my fathers had not been Roman, as I am, the first barbarian invasion between the fifth and tenth centuries would have made me to-day a sort of German or Norwegian. *I am Roman*, because, if it had not been for my tutelary Romanity, the second barbarian invasion which took place in the sixteenth century, the Protestant invasion, would have converted me into a sort of Swiss. *I am Roman*, since I am full to overflowing with my historical, intellectual, and moral being. *I am Roman*, because, if I were not, I would have almost nothing else French. And I never experience any difficulty feeling myself thus Roman; the interests of Roman Catholicism and those of France almost always blend and are in no particular contradictory. But other interests besides, more general, if not more pressing, constitute a law for me to feel myself Roman. *I am Roman* in so far as I feel myself a man: an animal that builds cities and states, not a rodent or gnawer of roots; a social animal, and not a lonely flesh-eater; excelling in capitalizing the acquisitions of the past and also in deducing therefrom a rational law, not an errant destroyer by hordes, nourished by the vestiges of the ruin he has wrought. *I am Roman* out of all the positive reality of my being, out of all that enjoys pleasure, work, thought, memory, and the poetry of men lived and assembled before me. Through this treasure, the lodgment of which she received from Athens and transferred to our Paris, Rome incontestably denotes civilization and humanity. *I am Roman, I am human*: two identical propositions.

18 "Le Dilemme de Marc Sangnier," in *La Démocratie religieuse*, 26. *Cf.* "Le Ciment romain," *La Gazette de France*, Mar. 9, 1899.

Having repeated these words, his emotional mood lingers. He muses further on the advantages of being French: "A new-born babe, according to Le Play, is a little barbarian. But when he is born in France this little barbarian is called upon to receive through education a delicate extract of all the works of the species. One can say that his natural initiation makes of him a man of quality in the strict sense of the word. Some of our neighbors and rivals doubt this. . . . The Germans are barbarians and they know it. I am not speaking of Muscovites and Tartars. The human race, it is our France, not only for us, but for the human race. That can be the measure of our obligations toward her." [19]

However, unfortunately for France and for the human race, since the Revolution or, if the Huguenots be considered, since the Reformation, there has been some division of opinion among Frenchmen regarding these views. France, it is true, thanks to the old tradition, was able to withstand the onslaughts of the sixteenth-century invasion of Hebrewism to which Germany and England, less well insulated by "Catholic humanism," weakly succumbed.[20] She not only suppressed religious dissent at home, but also, by taking advantage of the religious troubles of other nations, made herself the first power of Europe. Towards the close of the seventeenth century her king, his palace, her art, literature, and language were both admired and imitated throughout Europe. Then, some three decades later, Voltaire and Montesquieu made their regrettable visits to England. Each was more curious than cautious and inclined to place too much importance upon simple mediocrities which attracted them because they were new. The result was that they brought back to France the seeds of the fever and anarchy which the Jewish and German spirit had implanted in England. But, since both were men of taste and common sense, neither

19 *Principes*, 34-35; *cf.* "Le Romantisme féminin," in *L'Avenir de l'intelligence*, 208-209.

20 *Romantisme et révolution*, 4.

was seriously affected by this scourge.[21] The seeds, however, played havoc with Rousseau, and, through him, with France and Europe.

Taine, who complained of the difficulty of reading Comte, paid dearly for not having read him well. Otherwise he would never have made the mistake of arguing that the classical spirit was one of the major causes of the Revolution.[22] The classical spirit, far from having caused the Revolution, successfully repelled the Reformation and opposed the Revolution, which grew out of it. The affinity between these two lay in their common individualism. It was Rousseau, the Genevan, who really popularized Hebrewism in France and ushered in the period of romantic and revolutionary unrest. "Folly, savagery, crime,— these the adventurer, nourished on the Hebrew revolt, called virtue. This virtue of an ego of sordid quality was made the just judge of the human race. It proposed as model an uncultivated nature, vicious and mean. His worthless and plaintive sensibility, set up in the manner of law, was appealed to as the court of last resort against the universe. The lower his sincere abjection and natural villainy, the more he pretended

21 *Ibid.*, 5.

22 *Ibid.*, 2-4. The revolutionary bibliography included but few Greek works other than Plato's *Republic* and Plutarch's *Parallel Lives*, both of which were profoundly influenced by Semiticism, or other "Asiaticisms," and neither of which represented the wisdom of Athens and Rome. The tradition to which Phidias and Aristotle contributed so mightily, the classical tradition, had nothing to do with bringing the Revolution. " La Révolution est venue d'un toute autre côté: la Bible de la Réforme, les statuts de la République de Genève, les théologiens calvinistes, le vieux ferment individualiste de la Germanie auquel la Suisse trilingue servait déjà de truchement européen, enfin les élans personnels d'une sensibilité qui n'était retenue ni par des moeurs héréditaires, ni par une raison très saine, voilà les humbles causes des idées qui naquirent dans l'esprit de Rousseau. Par la magie de l'éloquence, elle entrèrent avec lui dans la vieille société française; loin d'y déterminer aucun état d'esprit classique, elles allèrent à détruire cet esprit de progrès et d'ordre. Qui niera que Rousseau n'ait ouvert l'ère romantique? " (" Note I," *ibid.*, 269-270). *Cf. Quand les Français ne s'aimaient pas*, 33; *Les Origines de la France contemporaine*, " L'Ancien régime," I, 288-318; II, 1-45; also Edme Champion, *J. J. Rousseau et la Révolution française* (Paris, 1909), *passim.*

that one ought to accept everything from him, and obey him and adore him." [23] And this "savage, this half-man," used the glory of France and the hegemony of Paris to spread his mad meanderings! Some hearts that were too tender and some spirits, too cultivated, were attracted by him; but it was the ignorant and lowly and the less advanced parts of the world that gave him an enthusiastic reception. Among the lower circles in France and more generally in Germany his preachings were particularly popular: for they elevated ignorance and weakness into virtues. So Germany and democracy now, with unspeakable insolence, proclaimed their right to empire. And France, tired of pleasures, tired of power, was seized by the strange desire to walk on all fours and eat hay, as Voltaire expressed it so well. She did just that, nothing less, whilst the old canons of taste, the old customs, and the great tradition were discarded or openly opposed where they were still treasured. The result was that her people found themselves in a wilderness of their own making, and their pillar of fire, not unlike that of the Jews of old, was Rousseau's hateful trinity of Protestantism, romanticism, and republicanism. More Protestant than were the Protestants themselves, he taught them the religion of the "inner God," without cult, priest, or doctrine. By his silly affectation of "nature," he sapped the defences of classical culture and opened the way to romantic sensibility within and to the invading hordes of barbarians without. Finally, his ridiculous ebullitions in political theory — the social compact, the general will, and the like — incited them to substitute an anarchic republicanism for the old traditional order. Nothing is clearer than the direct interconnection of the hateful trinity.[24]

This triple interrelationship was maintained by Rousseau's followers and disciples. At first blush this would not seem to be true of Chateaubriand, one of his most distinguished disciples,[25] who passed as an ardent Catholic and monarchical

23 *Romantisme et révolution*, 6. 24 *Ibid.*, 7-8.

25 "Chateaubriand fut des premiers après Jean-Jacques qui firent admettre et aimer un personnage isolé et comme perclus dans l'orgueil et l'ennui de sa liberté" ("Trois idées politiques," *ibid.*, 245). *Cf. ibid.*, 271-272.

opponent of the Revolution. He is said to have provoked a Catholic renaissance. But this he could not have done for the simple reason that he did not know what Catholicism was. He failed to realize that the Catholic tradition—the Christian sentiment regulated by the Graeco-Roman discipline — was the natural order of humanity. Far from having been a Catholic Epicurean, as he has been named, he was a " shameful Protestant clothed in the purple of Rome." [26] He passed as an adversary of the Revolution. He was, in fact, greatly beholden to it. Having taken leave of the savages in America and returned to France, he was profoundly moved by the ruins he saw. But he did not weep: he wrote. His pages were, however, so grandly and so pathetically tearful that their sound moved him to tears.[27] His selection of things to weep over is revealing. Things that were not completely or hopelessly destroyed, where there was still something that could be done to save them, he passed by. The more complete and irreparable the tragedy, the more certain it would be of calling forth the tears of his readers, and the greater the justification of his own, which he found so enjoyable. A republican he was not in the exact sense of the word, but his emotional instability made him an unruly and bad subject even after the Restoration. When the Legitimists were forced out in 1830, and when it appeared that the Duke of Bordeaux might die, he considered it safe to be devoted to their cause. The new régime inspired him with horror. " But he loved horror." [28] " He died in the delights of despair," amidst the political and social troubles of 1848. " . . . Rapacious and solitary bird, lover of charnel-houses, Chateaubriand never sought in the dead and in the past the transmissible, the fertile, the traditional, the eternal: but the past as past and the dead as dead were his unique pleasures." [29] Far from conserving, he needed widespread and com-

26 *Ibid.*, 246.

27 *Ibid.*, 246-247.

28 *Ibid.*, 248.

29 *Ibid.*, 248.

plete destruction to give him surer reasons for regrets. His sole concern in all things was their power to move—especially himself. His aim was to make the universe bow to him. Although he was and is the idol of many conservatives, he was really the incarnation of the genius of the Revolution.[30]

And the great Victor Hugo? He was worse, if possible, than his distinguished forerunners. Coming at a time when the masses were learning to read, he, of all the writers of his time, "corresponded best with the rusticity of the new readers."[31] Before his time common sense in French literature was not "vulgar sense"; now it became so. Even Chateaubriand was shocked by the chaos that Hugo introduced.[32] When anthropologists tell us that the auditory centers and the regions corresponding to verbal memory of his brain were highly developed, while the centers where thought and the association of ideas arise were less developed than among many intellectuals, they are merely confirming what is evident from the most cursory analysis of his works.[33] "The delicate and the sublime of the intellectual life escaped him. His was a great verbalistic imagination."[34] He freed the phrase and, especially, the word. He insisted that caprice was far more important than the genius of the language or the order of style; he substituted the idea of character for that of beauty and the idea of originality for that of perfection.[35] His "unknown deformities" were newer and more original, and consequently less traditional. His aim appeared to be to spoil both the French language and the French taste. "He dissolved its armature to bend it to his caprices. He fettered it with a prodigious multitude of useless expressions."[36] Although he thought he was

30 *Ibid.*, 248.

31 "Le Centenaire de Victor Hugo," in *Pages littéraires choisies* (Paris, sixth edition, 1922), 55.

32 *Barbarie et poésie*, 317-318.

33 *Pages littéraires choisies*, 58-60.

34 *Ibid.*, 59.

35 "Lorsque Hugo eut les cent ans," D. P. & C., II, 254-255.

36 *Barbarie et poésie*, 317.

making great discoveries and was opening up new vistas and new horizons, he " simply led his admirers back to the sensation of chaos, the troubled state of the pure savage or of the child." [37]

After the " battle of Hernani " of 1830 Hugo's influence mounted and spread rapidly, despite a stubborn rear-guard action of the diminishing classicists and of the more respectable romanticists, such as Chateaubriand and Lamartine, from the vantage point of the Academy. By 1841 he had " crashed " this citadel, and his type of romanticism was thus given formal recognition. Its power soon verged upon the despotic; for, with the exception of Sainte-Beuve, Merimée, Balzac, and later Taine and Renan, none of whom was entirely immune from the " microbe of romanticism and revolution," [38] Hugolian romanticism was the source and inspiration of French art in the nineteenth century. Although exemplified in varying degree, this was true of the naturalists, and also of the impressionists, the symbolists, and the Parnassians. It was not until toward the close of the century that the old tradition again raised its head, in the poetry and art of Anatole France [93] and Jean Moréas,[40] and partially in the aggressive, purposive, though essentially personal and therefore romantic art of Barrès.[41]

37 *Pages littéraires choisies*, 64.

38 *Barbarie et poésie*, 318-320; *cf. Le Chemin de Paradis*, xix.

39 *Ibid.*, xviii-xix; *Anatole France: politique et poète*, 52-53.

40 " L'Avènement de Moréas," in *L'Allée des philosophes*, 224-257.

41 " Grand écrivain d'humeur, artiste d'amour et de haine, ce profond moraliste français ne disait rien de l'âme qu'il n'eût reconnu par l'épreuve directement. *En lui et en lui seul, il aura procédé à la découverte du monde, de la nature humaine, des lois impersonnelles qui mènent ceci et cela.* Rien donc n'est plus précieux que la haute matière dont ses livres sont faits " (*Le Chemin de Paradis*, xvii; present writer's italics). " Le Bouteiller de Maurice Barrès ne fût peut-être point né sans Victor Hugo: est-il bien national, est-il conforme à notre passion pour la renaissance française, aux espoirs que nous avons mis dans le vingtième siècle, de répéter avec Bouteiller qu'Hugo est un dieu? Une fête était admissible, non pas ce culte de latrie " (*Pages littéraires choisies*, 69-70).

Protestantism, Kantianism, romanticism, democracy and "Hugocracy" — all barbarities — were interdependent; and, allied with one another, they dominated thought and art in the nineteenth century, and continued to do so despite the salutary reaction just noted.[42] What was a young man, who was convinced that the Greeks had invented beauty, a beauty that until relatively recently had brilliantly stood the test of time, who knew that the tradition of this beauty had been taken over by the Romans and by them had been implanted in France, that there was but one "France eternal," but one strictly French culture, and who knew in his heart from repeated confirmation in the realm of fact that there was a "hierarchy of pleasures, a nobility, and a plebianism of sentiments" [43]—what was such a person to do but look upon the dominant barbarities of his day with a mixed feeling of anger and contempt? Given an acute analytical mind, a strong will, and a flair for dialectics and polemics, his was not simply to choose the best and saturate his soul with it, as an Epicurus would probably have done; his was to fight for the "transmission of the beautiful and the true," [44] as did Lucretius.[45] What does the physician do with a patient who has been poisoned? He fights the "subtile little morbid atom," that is multiplying so rapidly, with strong medicine or with surgery. And so Maurras felt called upon to fight "the microbe of romanticism and revolution" in order to save the beautiful and the true. That the "microbes of the gangrene" should yell and protest, like so many devils, against the blows thus administered, was to be expected. "But Tradition, taking the point of view of the entire man and of the interest of his life, laughs at them." [46]

42 *Ibid.*, 69.

43 *Ibid.*, 70.

44 *Barbarie et poésie*, iii.

45 George Depue Hadzsits, *op. cit.*, 150-153; *De rerum natura, passim.*

46 *Barbarie et poésie*, v.

CHAPTER XII

MAURRAS' OFFENSIVE AGAINST ROMANTICISM

THE war against "alien barbarous romanticism," and in behalf of the inherently French traditions of classical aesthetics and civilization, was to be fought vigorously, even violently, but not blindly. "Even in art," Barrès had said, "there is no profit in being an imbecile."[1] True in art, it was equally true in a campaign in the interest of art. Reason and intelligence, so necessary in the appreciation and creation of beauty, were equally useful even in the heat of battle—particularly so. In a task so prodigious as the reorientation of a great nation's art and thought, reason suggested the wisdom of having allies. Nature and the Graeco-Roman-French tradition, which, as Maurras firmly believed, are really identical, were at hand, ready to help; but, long neglected, and in some respects not dissimilar to the ruins of the Acropolis, it was precisely to restore them to their just heritage that was the task in hand. The old tradition needed the red blood of living Frenchmen, while the latter were in need of its order and beauty. The Catholic Church, which had contributed so largely to its development, was also at hand. It was, moreover, still active and powerful, though relatively not so much so as it once was. It would make a valuable ally despite its Christian connections.[2] Admirers and disciples of Comte, Taine, and Renan,

1 "Taches d'encre," quoted by Maurras in *Anatole France: politique et poète*, 53.

2 "L'alliance des catholiques me semble désirable pour tout homme de bonne foi, et surtout s'il est né Français ou si une raison quelconque l'intéresse au maintien de l'héritage latin ou helléno-latin: sans l'alliance catholique, c'est un trésor dont l'humanité peut faire son deuil" ("Avant-propos," written in 1920, of the *Chemin de Paradis*, xxxvi). *Cf.* "Préface," written in 1894, *ibid.*, lxxxvii-lxxxviii. The following remark of Vialatoux would, therefore, seem to be true: "Redisons-le, si étonnant que cela paraisse, Maurras aime et chante l'église catholique parce qu'il croit voir en elle la seule ouvrière

though they were not "complete" classicists,[3] would be likely friends and allies. Anatole France was a Parnassian, but he was the first to restore Racine to a high place.[4] He was also a fearless opponent of Christianity, and his style was undeniably clear and beautiful: therefore, classical. Barrès was more romantic than Anatole France; but, though his heart dictated his art, his heart was essentially right, for he saw the need of a renaissance of French pride.[5] His end was right, but his

heureuse de la déchristianisation du monde, l'authentique forme païenne de notre ère" (*op. cit.*, 25). These words were written by a Catholic opponent of Maurras. Barrès, a friend, and likewise an "infidel," said, "On peut trouver notre attitude vis-à-vis de la monarchie peu logique, mais c'est une attitude analogue que me semble avoir Maurras au face du catholicisme" (*Mes cahiers*, III, 8).

3 He criticized Lemaître's campaign against Ibsenism as "incomplete" (*Pages littéraires choisies*, 160).

4 *Anatoles France: politique et poète*, 52.

5 *Le Chemin de Paradis*, xvii. In a letter to Barrès in December, 1905, apropos the latter's *Au service de l'Allemagne*, Maurras said he was not hostile toward his doubts and perplexities. "Tous les détours, tous les méandres, tous les va-et-vient d'une pensée et d'une sensibilité trop émues pour se fixer et se formuler, mais trop amies de leur unité supérieure et profonde pour ne pas la rechercher désespérément est encore un aspect du miracle grec, croyez-le" (Maurice Barrès, *op. cit.*, "Appendices VII," IV, 299-300) ! It would be interesting to know how Barrès reacted to the words, "Greek miracle," obviously meant as a compliment, since he had said, "L'art grec était religieux. Je ne sais pas cette religion, et je ne la sense pas. Alors quoi! dans la mesure où je suis compétent, professionnel, j'admire. Mais cela me parle moins que l'art chrétien, que la petite église (tout auprès avec les tombes féodales) qui me permet de relier mes idées. Maurras, lui, a un peu cette religion. Que sentirait-il en Lorraine" (*ibid.*, II, 207) ? His voyage to Greece, contrary to that of Maurras, was disappointing because it gave him an idea of perfection it was necessary to set aside, life not being long enough to entertain it. Moreover, it would demand his denial of Hugo and Lorraine. It was even destructive. "Mais a-t-on compris l'action destructive d'Athènes sur un homme que cette ville invite à se renier? L'invitation au suicide. Elle me supprime à mes propres yeux ma raison d'être, selon moi, de former des êtres selon ma discipline et que juge ma discipline misérable auprès de celle d'Athènes. Mais Maurras s'est mis à l'école d'Athènes et veut s'en faire de par le monde le missionarie. Moi, j'aime mieux oublier cette leçon. Mot de César: le premier dans une bourgade des Gaules, plutôt que le second dans Rome. Seulement, j'ai vu Rome qui me travaille, me sape, me taraude ..." (*ibid.*, II, 267-268).

method was faulty; coöperation with him, therefore, demanded a considerable sacrifice of principle. A purer classicist was Moréas, after his conversion to the Racinian tradition in his *Pèlerin passionné* in 1890. His was not only a "conscious reaction" against the current romanticism with which he himself had been thoroughly saturated,[6] but it was also a sort of atavism, for he was born in Athens and his ancestry was Greek, not French.[7] This doubtless made his poem the more attractive to Maurras, who in a jubilant and somewhat arrogant mood joined his "friend" and "master" in the literary scuffle that followed. And, looking upon Moréas as the "living sign of the national poetry," he gladly joined him and several others in founding the *Ecole romane* and enthusiastically coöperating with them in their avowed aim of restoring the classical tradition.[8] Still other allies were his friends of the Felibrian movement, of which more will be said presently. Although some of its leaders were not free from the "romantic microbe,"[9] Roumanille and Mistral particularly represented the Graeco-Roman tradition and their work fits into the more general reaction against "German and Hebrew cosmopolitanism."[10] Such were the allies to whom Maurras could turn in this great task. His coöperation with them represented a compromise in almost every instance, whether in art or in thought; but, having made these concessions and loving beauty,

6 "Si vous aviez lu les *Cantilènes* (1886) et les *Syrtes* (1882), vous connaîtriez que la divinité de M. Moréas est de date récente. M. Jean Moréas fut autrefois un homme. Il connut le Mal, eut des heures de tristesse chrétienne et de réflexion ennuyée" ("L'Avènement de Moréas," in *L'Allée des philosophes*, 250).

7 His real name was Papadiamantopoulos.

8 "Qui sera prince des poètes?," *Barbarie et poésie*, 169; "L'Avènement de Moréas," *L'Allée des philosophes*, 224-257; *La Musique intérieure*, 42-46; "La Mort de Jean Moréas," *L'Etang de Berre*, 343-352. For the "Declaration" of the *Ecole Romane*, written by Moréas and La Tailhède in 1891, consult Charles Maurras and Raymond de la Tailhède, *Un débat sur le romantisme* (Paris, 1928), 126.

9 *Cf. Théodore Aubanel* (Avignon, 1927, written in 1888), *passim.*

10 *Ibid.*, 4; *L'Etang de Berre*, 155, 195.

he jealously guarded against further concessions and at times cautioned his allies when they too flagrantly yielded to the enemy.[11]

Having friends and allies not only made the movement with which he was identified appear more imposing, it also prevented his being alone, one of the chief characteristics of the romanticist and of Rousseau's "noble savage." Civilized man was a "social animal," not a "lonely flesh-eater." And, as reason dictated more or less rigorously, though not without compromises, his selection of allies, so too it governed his choice of enemies. Although reason indicated clearly that romanticism, Protestantism, and revolution were closely bound together, a natural dislike of politics and a feeling that the "democratic distemper" was "definitive and insurmountable," or a feeling that, since this was so, it would be wise to accept it as such, made him willing to compromise for a time in regard to the political implications of the "unholy trinity." He looked upon Leo XIII's order to French Catholics to accept the republican form of government as a shrewd political stroke and doubtless found in it a justification of his own policy of ignoring this contradiction in his own thought and action.[12] His campaign was, therefore, until 1896 or 1897 almost wholly moral and literary, or simply intellectual. As late as 1895, drawing upon Barrès' new application and interpretation of the word "nationalism," he labeled it "intellectual nationalism"[13] and, at the same time, described its aim and strategy as follows: "Intellectual nationalism can only formulate itself clearly in the French language if it has first perceived how cosmopolitan romanticism was among us and how ugly it was."[14] Its task was first to understand how loathsome and alien this romanticism really was and then to expose the wide-

11 See page 150, note (4), above; Charles Maurras and Raymond de la Tailhède, *op. cit., passim.*

12 *Au signe de Flore*, 16-17.

13 See pages 60-62 above.

14 *Pages littéraires choisies*, 160.

spread inroads it had made in the nation. In exposing the ugliness of romanticism, Maurras' method was not simply to denounce; he appealed to the reader's intellect and sensibility by showing why the classical is beautiful and wherein the romanticist violates the precepts of beauty and why, therefore, the result is and must be far from sublime.

As we have seen, thought and style are inseparable. This is as true of the hideous as of the beautiful. Having a false philosophy, the romanticist cannot possibly have a beautiful style. And the word that sums up this erroneous philosophy, the word that embraces the underlying thought of romanticism and its religious and political counterparts is individualism. It is the root of their common ugliness. According to the romanticist, the individual must extract from his inner being his own law. He is and must be a law unto himself. He must accept no other law, lest he lose his dignity as a human being. To accept any other would be to accept "pure restraint" which, in turn, is "pure immorality." One may submit to an outer law, but one should *accept* no other than his own; for it alone deserves to be called moral law. The self, or *moi*, is thus an exalted "inner god" in the face of whom laws, manners, customs, and institutions have little authority or value. The social heritage is essentially bad, and its transmission baneful. The just, the noble, the brilliant, and the proper thing is to re-create the world each morning according to the individual's caprice of the moment, or simply to begin this task each morning by questioning, discussing, and verifying everything. The more completely everything old has been rejected or destroyed the better will be the result. Destruction, complete destruction, is, therefore, the individualist's first duty. Such is the effrontery of this "hateful self" in the presence of the "products elaborated and filtered in the course of generations" by the great critic, time![15] Nothing is sacred to it other than itself and such principles as freedom of conscience, freedom of in-

15 "La Politique religieuse," *La Démocratie religieuse*, 238-239; *Barbarie et poésie*, 21.

quiry and liberty in general: principles which facilitate the general destruction and serve the divine ego. And this is as the "inner god" says it "ought to be," which is another potent "cause of impiety towards that which is."[16]

In religion this doctrine assumes the form of Protestant Biblism; in politics, revolution and democracy; and in art it has given rise to the "aesthetics of character." Christians and romanticists make much of virtue, of disinterestedness, of devotion, sacrifice, and abnegation. This is all beautiful, but it is "more insufficient still than it is beautiful." So long as it is simply a question of fighting, they have what is required. The crusaders showed that. However, it is not simply a question of fighting. "It is necessary to conquer. It is necessary to profit from the victory." This the crusaders failed to appreciate. They lacked the virtue of order, of organizing the results of their victory. An excess of heroism is as harmful as too little; it has its time and place as has everything else. Instead of straining one's whole being to be constantly sublime and heroic, in petty affairs as well as in important ones, instead of trying to be supernatural at all times and in all places, which we know is beyond the powers of the best, one would do well to recognize that human powers have their limits and reserve one's enthusiasm and abnegation for great moments.[17] This wise rule is, however, ignored. Although experience and an intelligent view of life show clearly that good sentiments alone are not sufficient for the attainment of a happy, well-ordered life, that egoism and self-interest are the driving forces of human behavior, Protestants and romanticists stubbornly, even hypocritically, persist in their belief. This is well illustrated by the famous George Sand—Alfred Musset—Pierre Pagello affair. Caught between her system of ideas, based upon a virtuous benevolence, and the actions to which the fire in her blood drove her, George Sand was again and again placed

16 *Le Chemin de Paradis,* lv.

17 "Le Dilemme de Marc Sangnier," *La Démocratie religieuse,* 51-58.

in the position of having either to disavow herself for the love of these ideas, or to sacrifice the latter for the love of self. Although she never denied herself, she lied often and shamelessly in order to appear to be what she really was not.[18] Her experience, which was anything but a happy one, should, therefore, have taught her that kindly sentiments cannot "suffice to put order and happiness in the life of a woman";[19] but she clung desperately to her ideas despite the constant hiatus between them and her actual behavior.

This refusal to recognize human limitations may lead to the worst sort of hypocrisy, or to an equally loathsome desire to confess, even to the point of the indiscreet. In the one instance, the theory is that one must be good and, if the desires of the flesh overcome a frail will, one must still appear to be good; in the other, being good or bad is not as important as being frank and sincere. This latter was Rousseau's view, who at the head of his *Confessions* said, "I have told the good, the bad, with the same frankness." In short, the idea is that whether one is good or bad, the important thing is that one should be one's self frankly, openly, and sincerely.[20] Somehow the mere confession of the bad will make it good; or, if it will not convert it into the good, if accompanied by regret and repentance, it will at least bring satisfaction, pardon, or oblivion. "But religious faith alone gives virtue to these beautiful and noble fictions of the moral order. Nature does not forget: she cannot arrange that that which was has not been and, involved with the present, that it will not affect and determine the course of the future."[21] Nature goes its way despite our emotional desire for pardon, or our feeling that we have received it. "There, in the depth of everyone's being, the police of nature, which exerts itself through disgrace, through failure, through

18 *Les Amants de Venise* (Paris, new edition, 1926), 280; *cf.* "D'Emma Bovary au grand tout," *Barbarie et poésie*, 354-355.

19 *Les Amants de Venise*, 281.

20 "Le Romantisme féminin," *L'Avenir de l'intelligence*, 216.

21 *Les Amants de Venise*, 277-278.

sickness, through death, develops the simple consequences of our delinquencies. The succession of misfortunes, sprung from a first fault, accompanies us to the tomb." [22] But often enough the sordid confession wends its way without the slightest trace of expiation or repentance, not that it would make it any better. Despair there is, however, and it is very real. The soul is perplexed and sad because of the inconsistencies denied or admitted. This sadness may be tasted to the full and enjoyed, or the *moi*, having suffered and tasted everything, may desire to die and end it all.[23]

Since the essence of goodness and of kindly sentiments is to love, that is one of the most fertile sources of disillusionment and melancholy. And since, human nature's limitations being ignored, this love must be carried to the point of paroxysm, the disenchantment is the more poignant. This frenzied excitation is not passion proper, nor is it exaltation; it is simply emotional caprice that has escaped its master.[24] Yet love is supposed to be the great moral and social cement and the sovereign remedy for pain. But who has not seen or experienced the pain of love itself? [25] Who has not also observed that once the Protestant's or the romanticist's soul is freed from the thought of God, which "serves as surety, reënforcement, and multiplier of all the fantasies, passions, and reveries of the individual, the power of which, the value of which, are thus increased and exalted to the infinite," this soul becomes more sociable, more moral, and more open to loving his neighbor? This loving of one's neighbor is not the sum total of morality, it is true. It has never prevented a person's injuring himself by drunkenness or by other means; and it has never been shown that this love can effect or determine the behavior of men. Moreover, one of its effects may easily be the grossest

22 *Ibid.*, 278.

23 "Le Romantisme féminin," *op. cit.*, 217.

24 *Ibid.*, 216.

25 "Le Baptême de Jésus: un nouvel évangéliste," *Revue bleue* (Aug. 6, 1892), L, 186.

immorality or the purest baseness.[26] Love has been described as the "genius of the species" which possesses men and promises them happiness beyond anything they have imagined. It is also said that he who is the prey of amorous passion, though he appears to be pursuing a purely personal end, is really fulfilling the wishes of the species.[27] But "is there in the economy of this world a Genius of the Species?" It may well be doubted, for it is certain that the existence of such a mythical being will never be proved; "but there is in us, there is in every being down to the smallest atom an extraordinary tendency to depart from itself. Call it the Genius of eternal emigration, if you must have genii as in the Arabic tales: but is not this precisely Love itself?" [28]

This "Genius of eternal emigration" has its place in life: it enflames and renews, as knowledge and thought lull to sleep and pacify. Both effects are excellent. The fault of the romanticists is that they admit only one, and that not in its natural form. "That a love pretends to free itself from the order of nature and from the conventions of the world, that it boasts of astonishing the vulgar by surpassing and thus offending and disconcerting it: that indicates simply that it has neglected a certain kind of considerations, but it has not abolished the reality which they represent; more than any other love, this one will be thwarted unexpectedly by sentiments and interests unworthy of it, or by cares almost indelicate. In neglecting the grounds upon which all love moves, in treating it as a pure and mystical union of intelligences, without bearing upon material expedients and human media, the romanticists have gravely deceived themselves on the conditions of love." [29] They have even failed to understand its true nature despite their apparent interest in gazing upon it. "Natural love seeks happiness. It is, therefore, restlessness, impatience,

26 "Utilité de définir" (1895), *Barbarie et poésie*, 300-301.

27 This was the view of Jules de Gaultier in his *Le Bovarisme*.

28 "D'Emma Bovary au grand tout," *Barbarie et poésie*, 363-364.

29 *Les Amants de Venise*, 286-287.

desire. It is a pursuit of anything other than itself and, first of all, rushes from out itself. Whatever its passions or its energies, it is to their appropriate end, it is to a happy calm, to an agreement of peace and internal accord, that all these inner wars aspire. They will be less ardent without the will to escape and to be done with them. The amorous man furbishes the dressing of his sore only in attempting to extract from it a point that tears it open. In order to love well, it is not necessary to love love. It is not necessary to seek it; it is even important to feel some hatred for it. If it would retain all the sweetness of its charm and the force of its virtues, love ought to obtrude as an enemy whom one fears, not as a flatterer whom one beckons." [30] This is the wisdom of the ancients, who looked upon love as a demon, not a god.[31] The more powerful its hold, therefore, upon a person, the greater the need that it be bridled by reason. The romanticists, by giving way to it, have peopled Olympus with dissolute gods; by giving it aid and comfort and cultivating sadness and despair, they have veiled not enflamed this ancient demon, debased and not sublimated it. It may well be doubted whether they love at all despite their overmuch talk about it; for love is so constituted that it flees those who seek each other, and overwhelms and crowns those who have forgotten themselves.[32] Whether it be a love of love, as was that which exhausted poor Musset, or a "bizarre love of self," such as agitated George Sand, it is not really love. To love love is after all to love one's self,[33] and to do this consciously is not so much loving as thinking of one's self.[34]

The romanticist, cursed by his sacred ego, is thus denied the pleasure of love as well as the peace that comes to a life

30 *Ibid.*, 287-288.

31 *Ibid.*, 285.

32 *Ibid.*, 318.

33 "Le Romantisme féminin," *op. cit.*, 206.

34 *Ibid.*, 234.

lived in accordance with a humanly attainable standard of conduct. Moreover, this thought of self is but an unrelated segment of thought, not one that fits into a logical system. It is morose brooding that has as its subject the sad, unstable, and capricious "inner god," and it must, from its very nature, remain a segment of thought. It is impressionistic, as is all thought of the romanticist, if indeed it may be dignified by labeling it thought. Take the case of Michelet. If his spirit had been pure and free, it would have decided matters in accordance with definite reasons. But enslaved and impure, it "ordinarily ceded to a heap of impressions and conceits which are produced under the influence of the nerves, of the blood, of the liver, and of the other glands. These natural humors dominated him like alcohol. . . . More destitute among general ideas than was Robinson among the beasts and plants of his island, Michelet found himself in the same necessity of making tools without a tool, a method without a method, an art of thinking without a brain. Dying of a desire to reason, he took the shortest way. He turned his great heart to account. As he would have tilled the soil with the point of a knife, or cut out wooden shoes with a spade, if the whim of shoe-making or farming had come to him, Michelet created thought with his heart."[35] Of every particle of a general idea that came within reach this impressionistic heart made a god. It was not a finished god comparable to those of the polytheist, "balanced by a vast concert of other divine forces"; it was "a true God in the Christian sense, a God of the monotheist, clothed for several moments in all the perfections catalogued by the theologians."[36] Responding to his restless nature and to the needs of the moment, these temporary deities passed by successively as Life, Man, Love, Right, Justice, People, Revolution. And quite often these abstractions melted into a formless mass which was set over against a hostile mass, also formless, which,

35 "Trois idées politiques," *Romantisme et révolution*, 250-251.

36 *Ibid.*, 252.

as the situation demanded or the heart decreed, was labeled Death, Beast, Hate, or Authority. His Manichaeanism was uncertain because he was remarkably inept in the art of distinguishing, dependent as he was upon his senses only.[37]

In his impressionistic god-making, Michelet was not unlike Victor Hugo, who with his "infinite impressionability" elevated the word into a divinity and lived to help and see his underlings construct a theology of the "word-God." Loving, honoring, and worshiping the word as a "living being," they emancipated it from all bonds of reason and significance, whilst they elaborated a "theory of the word-color, of the word-perfume, of the word-thing." [38]

Both victim and slave of this "verbal sensuality," [39] the romanticist places a high premium upon the picturesque, the new, the foreign, the excessive, and the disordered.[40] Anarchy and chaos, the pre-social, the monstrous, and the unnatural are the preferred elements of his restless, dissatisfied heart; and the result is necessarily ugly in terms of all civilized criteria of beauty. The *moi,* moreover, for and by which these beneficent standards are neglected and degraded is not less ugly, for its chosen surroundings are but a reflection of the disorder within. Not only is it ugly; it is likewise cowardly, since it is too weak-willed, too soft and languorous to accept nature's challenge to reduce things and ideas, and our lives, to an order not in violent disagreement with it. Instead, it flees this responsibility which nature and tradition place upon us, though not without a persistent inner warfare and consequent sadness.

This "cowardly and ugly *moi*" is,[41] as a matter of fact, essentially feminine, for weakness and superstition are natural to women.[42] They also find it difficult to be impersonal, since

37 *Ibid.*, 252.

38 "Le Romantisme féminin," *op. cit.*, 212 (Note 1), 218.

39 *Ibid.*, 213.

40 *Ibid.*, 210-211; *Barbarie et poésie*, 34.

41 "Le Dilemme de Marc Sangnier," *La Démocratie religieuse*, 132.

42 "Le Romantisme féminin," *L'Avenir de l'intelligence*, 166; *Le Chemin de Paradis*, lxxix.

nature actually wants them to be intoxicated with themselves.[43] Inasmuch as their art is to begin love by creating an obsession, they both revel in their sentimentality and use it.[44] But their joys are not unmixed with sorrow. Perverting Descarte's famous phrase, woman says, "I suffer, therefore I am." [45] And, following the lead of the romantic doctors, she delights in confessing her sorrows and inner conflicts, which she has not only because nature has made her what she is, but also because she too subscribes to the "aesthetics of character." [46] However, in exposing these inner struggles, she betrays womanhood the world over; for the "unknown woman" is more beautiful than the indiscreet, unabashed woman who spends her time destroying the long-recognized virtues of woman: resignation, sweetness, and patience.[47] Over against these she invokes the "Right to love, the Right of him who is loved, or the Right of him who loves," and constitutes herself a court of love which is both party and judge in the case. This exaltation of sentiment for the psychological curiosities and aesthetic novelties that may be produced has exhausted the souls of women and has driven them to copy and play the man. A brilliant form of feminism it may be; but it is a menace to the whole human race, for, instead of loving as nature intended she should, she thinks of love, and, especially, of herself.[48] She who does this is doomed to "rapid destruction" for violating an elemental but nevertheless fundamental law of nature. Having escaped the order prescribed for her, she disappears; and the same fate will be in store for the human race, if women, generally, the world over, take up this unholy doctrine of "Rights," or simply think of love or self, instead of loving.

43 "Le Romantisme féminin," *op. cit.*, 220, 222-223.

44 *Ibid.*, 222.

45 *Ibid.*, 220.

46 *Ibid.*, 221.

47 *Ibid.*, 232.

48 *Ibid.*, 234.

Not only is this romantic feminism destructive of womanhood, and not only does it carry the poisonous bacillus that may eventually destroy the human race, it is also, here and now, destructive of manhood. Just as romanticism has inspired women with the desire to become men, so, too, it has moved men to copy and imitate women. "The women, so broken and humiliated by our manners, have avenged themselves by imparting to us their nature. Everything, from spirit to love, has become effeminate. Everything has softened. Incapable of disposing and of advancing ideas in harmonious series, one no longer thinks of anything but to submit." [49] Soft, decadent, and apathetic, prevented by his individualism from valuing the national institutions, customs, and traditions, and precluded from all positive action by his conscience, his persistent inner conflict, the effeminate romanticist turns to the chaotic, the barbarous, and the foreign to titillate his tired and exhausted soul. Exhilarated, he submits to them with abandon. He is thus doubly immune to the patriot's appeal to defend the cumulative capital of the nation: he sees nothing worth defending and, if he did, lacks the spirit and the will to do so. Moreover, what little spirit he has left he has freely and traitorously placed in the service of the national enemy. He boasts of his cosmopolitanism, which is to say that he boasts of his Germanism, of his vassalage to Germany.[50]

The loss of Alsace-Lorraine was but a "sensible image" of this vassalage and loss of spirit.[51] "The French of 1871, amidst a thousand errors, committed that of not defining themselves or circumscribing themselves." [52] They lacked a national theory, and the result was that they were penetrated from all sides. A theory they had, but it was cosmopolitan. It held that the French were a people without a definite character; they had all the tastes and, at the same time, none; they constituted

49 *Le Chemin de Paradis,* lxix.

50 *Quand les Français ne s'aimaient pas,* 1, 33.

51 "L'Annexion intellectuelle en 1895," *ibid.,* 31.

52 *Ibid.,* 33.

no distinct nationality, having no common racial origin, no physical unity; there was only a unity of desire, a unity of love. Their only claim to distinction was that they gave form to the ideas of Europe, that they were the announcers, ushers, and interpreters of the English savants and German philosophers. Giving passage to the rays from the South and to the blasts from the North, they regarded themselves as the "clarions of European thought." [53] And, though they suffered the disastrous defeat of 1871 for their troubles, they continued to treasure this rôle despite a short-lived thirst for revenge.[54]

What did the Germans do when they were similarly situated? They became enthusiastic converts to Fichte's doctrine. The *Ligue des Patriotes* would do well to have several million copies of his *Reden an die deutsche Nation* printed and to encourage their fellow-countrymen to read them.[55] If they found its language too abstract, the *Ligue* might set up special chairs where its lessons would be explained. It is, in fact, a mediocre book, and revolting to a man of taste, with its many spurious and declamatory statements. Unlike Leibnitz, Goethe, Heine, Schopenhauer, and Nietzsche, who knew how to guide and develop their thoughts, Fichte was a pure-blooded barbarian. The conception and the expression of his *Reden* were equally bad. He was a sort of misguided lyric in ontology. It has rightly been said that his philosophy was born of his character; for he not only admitted it, but proudly boasted of it. " His reflection was but the continual discharge of his humor." [56] That his soul was generous and inflated with beautiful desires, is true; but his abstract divagations were comparable to an " orgy of metaphysical words " devoid of any relation with strict logic. Since he had made romanticism and barbarism his servants, this was to be expected. If he had

53 *Ibid.*, 32.

54 " La belle idée de la Revanche a rendu d'immenses services; mais, mal administrée, son déclin fut rapide " (*ibid.*, xiii).

55 *Ibid.*, 23.

56 *Ibid.*, 25.

adhered strictly to his theory of the deified *Moi*, he would have been far above the relatively lowly exigencies of national life: he would have persevered in the cosmopolitanism which served as his point of departure. But he was guided by his emotions, not by a calculating intellect. He obeyed circumstances upon which he appeared to impose a system and, in so doing, was a good German. If he led his disciples into the coarse kingdom of irrationality, he discovered to them and, at the same time, to the whole nation a sentiment and an idea which, aided by other forces, brought the ignominious retreat and abdication of the proud and cruel conqueror.[57]

Frenchmen may well pass over the system of moral and metaphysical ideas by which Fichte promised to bring a renewal of humanity. Let them, however, note carefully that he followed the instinct of a conquered and injured people; let them take soundings of the violence with which he denounced the conqueror, of his contempt for the "Latin" languages and of his horror of the "Latin" spirit; let them take notice of his hate-inspired characterization of themselves as "German bastards" whose ancestors, instead of returning to the Rhine with their booty, remained among the "Gentiles" and, forgetting their own language, have learned to speak the language of serfs and of a conquered people and are, therefore, no longer masters of their own speech.[58] He congratulated the Germans upon their ignorance of the "bad things" of the Graeco-Latin culture, upon the purity of their language and upon its "immediate clarity"; for its words were formed directly from the concrete without recourse to foreign roots. The Franco-Latin language admittedly enjoyed an era of perfection in the seventeenth century; but, the German imperfection was preferable, for it was a sign of life. The Franco-Latin no longer created anything because the imprint of death lay upon its brow. The Germans would some day make largesse

57 *Ibid.*, 25-26.

58 *Ibid.*, 26.

of their vitality to their neighbors, even to the French, to whom a German renaissance was as necessary as to the whole world. Their name itself, *Allemands* (*All-Man*), clearly indicated that God had chosen them to represent the human race.[59]

One need not smile at these ideas. " If they do not count in themselves, they embrace and express a sentiment, fecund and bold. Bold, since it was born at the very time that Germany appeared to be in the throes of death under the heel of Napoleon. Fecund . . . , we ought to know well enough why." [60] Not all German hearts had stopped beating. The patriots became aroused and grouped themselves around the Queen of Prussia, Stein, Blücher, and Humboldt; they founded units of the *Tugendbund* in many places. Fichte, who inspired the *Risorgimento,* poor preacher that he was, would probably have organized the victory defectively; but he died in time, in the early days of 1814, before the victory was won. Some of his worst romantic, libertarian, and humanitarian logomachies survived him, but failed to spoil his work. The scholastico-social convulsions of Germany in the middle of the century dated from him. But " this vague political individualism " of Rousseau, which he renewed, was dammed up by the Prussian monarchy and was stopped in its course by Bismarck in a period of some thirty years.[61] Germany was fortunate in having statesmen who were capable of reducing and organizing the too divergent elements in her national expansion.

They were aided by the bad fortune or folly of France. Fichte's anarchism infected all of Europe, and France in particular. Within two years after he had delivered his famous *Reden* in Berlin, Mme. de Staël had accepted the sense of these declamations and had paraphrased them in a "pernicious work" which the Imperial police rightly described as " little French." " With the treatise, *De l'Allemagne,* the hesitating forms, unfinished conceptions, and confused reveries, scarcely having made

59 *Ibid.,* 28.

60 *Ibid.,* 28.

61 *Ibid.,* 30.

their obscure way from that which one ironically denominated German thought, began to come to us. It is since this date that disorder, impropriety, and the inconsequential have wholly taken possession of French thought, the sense of which they have deformed. In philosophy, in politics, in literature, the picture of the *indefinite*, of the *amorphous*, took shape, if one may so express one's self. Fichte capitalized himself. A stamp of clear words was placed upon the most confused theories. From 1825 to 1840 an alloy of Hegel was introduced. . . . It arose from the impoverishment of the spirits and it succeeded in augmenting the poverty. Thereafter, only German thoughts and sentiments were doted upon; some heads very well made, those of Renan and Taine, submitted to this shameful taste for the preposterous." [62] Such submission to the alien and barbarous was France's folly.

Barbarous though this perpetual logical frenzy was, it was at least embellished with a robust and naïve grace. The French, on the other hand, have acquired neither this grace nor this strength, whilst they have lost many of their best qualities. A quarter of a century has passed since they suffered a national defeat and humiliation of the first magnitude; nevertheless, the youth of France have in this period been brought up at the feet of Germany, their conqueror. They have been taught to admire, not her energetic nationalism which rallies the Germans to their tradition and gives them an absolute confidence in the special aptitudes of their race, but all the rest: the thought, language, and poetry of the Germans, even their socialism. The youth of France have been kept in ignorance concerning "the real cause of German superiority." [63] Hence the need of enlightening them on this point, of distributing Fichte's *Reden* in France and interpreting it in this sense; hence, likewise, the urgency, unless France wishes to die as an effeminate romanticist or a meek Christian, of showing them,

62 *Ibid.*, 30-31.
63 *Ibid.*, 31.

trained cosmopolitans as they are, that all ideas have their fatherland;[64] and, finally, the necessity that Frenchmen learn to "define" and to "circumscribe" themselves—in short, their need of a conscious sentiment, an integrated theory of French nationalism.

This need Maurras sought to fill, and it is to his theory of integral French nationalism that we now turn.

64 "La Jeunesse lettrée en 1895," *ibid.*, 12.

PART II

THE INTEGRAL NATIONALISM OF MAURRAS AND THE ACTION FRANCAISE

" Un nationaliste conscient de son rôle admet pour règle de méthode qu'un bon citoyen subordonne ses sentiments, ses intérêts, et ses systèmes au bien de la Patrie. Il sait que la Patrie est la dernière condition du bien-être de ses concitoyens. Tout avantage qui se solde par une perte pour la Patrie lui paraît un avantage trompeur et faux. Et tout problème politique qui n'est point résolu par rapport aux intérêts généraux de la Patrie lui semble incomplètement résolu. Le nationalisme impose donc aux questions diverses qui sont agitées devant lui un commun dénominateur, qui n'est autre que l'intérêt de la nation. Comme pour ce Romain dont parlait Bossuet, l'amour de la Patrie passe en lui toute chose . . . Le nationalisme français tend à susciter parmi nous une . . . religion de la déesse France . . . Comme le parti catholique, les royalistes sont catholiques (de raison, de sentiment, ou de tradition) et ils tiennent à la primauté du catholicisme. Comme le parti antisémitique, ils sont antisémites. Comme le parti de M. Paul Déroulède, ils souhaitent un pouvoir responsable et fort. Comme les modérés et les décentralisateurs, ils veulent l'autonomie de l'enseignement, les franchises des communes et des provinces. Mais au lieu de vouloir cela par un accident du caprice ou de la passion, ils le veulent par une nécessité logique et par la simple conséquence de ce fait qu'ils veulent le retour de la monarchie nationale. Essentiellement, le royalisme correspond aux divers postulats du nationalisme : il est lui-même le NATIONALISME INTEGRAL."

CHARLES MAURRAS, " Le Nationalisme intégral,"
Le Soleil, Mar. 2, 1900.

" En 1905, nul mouvement d'opinion n'a suivi le coup de Tanger : c'est qu'en 1905, *l'Action française* n'avait pas encore sa librairie, son Institut, son journal, ni sa forte prise sur la jeunesse et sur l'élite intelligente du pays. En 1911, au contraire, l'esprit public a réagit devant le coup d'Agadir : c'est que, en 1911, nous étions là, avec toutes nos forces, hommes et idées. Guillaume II n'était plus seul à stimuler la République ; une autre action que celle de la Wilhelmstrasse s'exerçait sur le monde républicain : par l'effort d'un jeune journal parisien, par son contrôle impitoyable, le monde républicain le plus avancé dut se mettre à penser et à parler à la française, dont il avait perdu l'habitude et le goût.

Sous la simple menace de l'empereur allemand, on n'avait guère fait que des réponses démocratiques et républicaines, c'est-à-dire discontinues et brèves, comme il convient aux êtres qui sentent à peine, enchaînent peu, ne pensent rien : notre oeuvre aura été d'éclaircir la vue du péril, et de la débrouiller, et de la rendre intelligible : d'en faire chaque jour un rappel très concret. Assurément, l'Allemagne de 1911 aura, plus qu'en 1905, pressé le bouton, mais nous l'avons bien remplacée dans l'intervalle des sonneries. Et c'est alors que le pays a répondu par des efforts de réflexion personnelle qui ont réorganisé toute sa pensée. De là est sorti ce qu'un publiciste a pu appeler une "*renaissance de l'orgueil français*" et qu'il faudrait appeler plutôt un retour de l'intelligence politique française."

CHARLES MAURRAS, *Kiel et Tanger* (Paris, 1921), 223.

CHAPTER XIII

THE PROVENCAL REVIVAL

Before he entered actively upon his campaign to extirpate from France the "microbe of romanticism," Maurras had identified himself with the Felibrian movement, to which he was doubtless first attracted by aesthetic considerations and through which he was first inspired to agitate for definite political ends. Although he had read the works of Frédéric Mistral before he went to Paris in December, 1885,[1] he had failed, while he resided in his ancestral home and province, to appreciate the significance of Mistral's work and of the movement of which this "rustic Homer," as Lamartine characterized him,[2] was the leader. At Paris, however, as the young Maurras and his still younger brother enthusiastically took up the study of the Provençal language and lovingly repeated the verses of its masters day and night, their mother twitted them for having had to come to Paris to learn Provençal.[3] Whether it was distance that made Provence dearer to Maurras, or new influences, such as the ideas of Comte, Taine, Renan, or of Amouretti, his friend, or whether it was both,[4] he developed a great love for the language of his native people, for their legends and proverbs which now impressed him as wise and poetic, and for their peculiar manners and customs. Other than reviews of books for periodicals, this love may be said to have inspired his first literary effort, his critical study of Théodore Aubanel, who died in 1886.[5] Written in 1888, it was crowned by the *Société des Félibres de Paris* in the same year, a year that was also noteworthy as that in which Maurras first

1 *La Musique intérieure*, 28-30.

2 Frédéric Mistral, *Mirèio*, pouèmo provençau avec la traduction en regard, preface by Lamartine (Paris, 1921), xvi; *cf.* the first stanza of the first song.

3 *Au signe de Flore*, 32.

4 *Ibid.*, 10, 32; *L'Etang de Berre*, 189.

5 Théodore Aubanel (Avignon, 1927).

met Mistral and Barrès.[6] On July 11 of this same year he was formally admitted into the Society of the Felibrians of Paris, although he was only twenty years old.[7]

This organization had been founded in 1879, three years after the formation of the *Cigaliers de Paris*, another society of southerners. Both groups made much of Mistral, when, in 1889, he came to Paris to see the centennial exposition of the Revolution. Two years later members of both societies made their first descent upon the South to dedicate statues and busts erected in honor of local heroes. At Martigues a bust of the medieval Templar, Gérard Tenque, was dedicated and a ceremony was performed by Charles Maurras in honor of Sainte-Estelle, patroness of the Felibrians.[8] The government of the Third Republic paid the travel costs; the busts and statues that were dedicated were furnished by the *Collège des Beaux-Arts;* the Felibrians and the Cigalians supplied only the speeches and the enthusiasm. Paris seemed to be assuming the leadership of this, a manifestly local movement, as of everything else.

But the pioneers, the heroes, and the real leaders of the movement were not Parisians, either from choice, from residence, or from birth. The Albigensian crusade in the middle ages and the subsequent policies of the Church and of the French kings had been destructive of much that had been distinctively " southern " in France, of much that had made the people of the *Midi* an incipient nationality. Not only was Catharism suppressed, and not only was the virtual political independence of earlier days largely lost, but the heavy penalty that the nobles of the South were forced to pay for having opposed the northern invaders was also destructive of the poetry of the *langue d'oc* and almost of the language itself; for, the poets, or *trouvères*, were no longer patronized by powerful and

6 *Sous l'étoile du mage* (Paris, 1931), 11; *L'Etang de Berre*, 189.

7 The speech which he delivered on this occasion appropriately dealt with "*Les Trente beautés de Martigues.*" The Provençal and French versions of this address are in *L'Etang de Berre*, 6-19.

8 Albert Thibaudet, *Mistral, ou la république du soleil* (Paris, 1930), 197.

wealthy lords, as had been the case before. Provençal poetry, it is true, was not completely wiped out; it was still written for and by interested members of the lower classes. But, written for a more subservient class of patrons, it lost its former verve, its former freedom; it savored of the pedantic and its lack of imagination gave it the air of routine workshop production. Not all the poets of the South were, however, long-faced and despairing. In 1323 *La Joyeuse compagnie* was founded at Toulouse. In the following year it was converted into the famous Academy of Toulouse which for almost two hundred years gave aid, comfort, and encouragement to poets of the Southland. In 1513, however, it began giving prizes for French works and did so increasingly until by 1694 it may be said to have become a French institution.[9] French replaced the *langue d'oc* as the respected literary language and local poets now versified in a crude *patois* instead of in the finer old Limousin. This was true, for the most part, until Jacques Boé, better known as Jasmin, wrote his poems in the first half of the nineteenth century. So popular was his four-volume collection of poems, published between 1843 and 1845, that the French Academy awarded him its grand prize in 1852.[10]

By this time the poets of Provence had become active also, as the publication of *Li Prouvençalo* and the Congress of Arles, both of 1852, indicate. Too far removed from Toulouse to benefit from its Academy during the period when it had been disposed to encourage poetic efforts in the *langue d'oc*, Provençal poets had been isolated from other southern poets and, lacking a common organization, had remained isolated from each other. Little good poetry was written, therefore, and the Provençal language gradually came to be looked upon with contempt and shame as the dialect of the socially inferior.[11]

9 Mauritz Boheman, *Précis de l'histoire de la littérature des félibres*, translated from the Swedish by Christian Lange (Avignon, 1906), 3-10.

10 *Ibid.*, 15.

11 Frédéric Mistral, *Mes origines: mémoires et récits*, translated from the Provençal (Paris, 1906), 222-223.

Early in the nineteenth century, however, the old latent energies were revived, partially in response to romanticism and revolution, and partially in reaction against the levelling centralization which the Jacobins and Napoleon had intensified.[12] Unsolicited and without leadership or organization, poets raised their heads in various parts of Provence to sing of the beauty of the local landscape and of the local customs. So considerable was this movement by 1823 that Claude Achard heralded it with the publication of *Lou Bouquet*, a collection of the best poems of the period and a work which marked the first effort to give the language a rational basis and a fixed orthography at a time when neither existed.[13] The *Prouvençalo*, similar in character and edited by Joseph Roumanille, registered the growth of the movement in the next twenty-nine years (thirty-one poets collaborated in it) and revealed the appearance of three remarkable Provençal poets: Roumanille himself, Théodore Aubanel, and Frédéric Mistral. It likewise gave further impetus to the movement.

Roumanille was the oldest of the three and was at this time the best known. His earliest efforts in poetry had been in French, much to the disappointment of his mother who had forgotten the French she had learned in school. She soon, however, experienced the greatest joy when he began to versify in the dialect she had taught him. His first collection of Provençal poems, *Li Margarideto* (1847), justified the change; for its success was immediate and impressive, especially among a generation of enthusiastic youth. Indeed, his ability to inspire others to take up the work of breathing new life into the old language was as remarkable as was the beauty of his verses. As professor and printer in Avignon, he attracted the interest and admiration of many young men of talent and awakened in them "a love of the beautiful, the true, and the good, of

12 Pierre Lasserre, *Frédéric Mistral: poète, moraliste, citoyen* (Paris, 1918), Chs. III and IV.

13 Mauritz Boheman, *op. cit.*, 18.

God, work, and virtue."[14] Of these young men, the most brilliant were Aubanel and Mistral.

Aubanel, the second member of the "generative trinity" of Felibrianism, was eleven years younger than Roumanille and one year older than Mistral. He was born in a family of Avignon that had reason to recall with pleasure the timely death of Robespierre, which alone had saved the life of his grandfather. It was but natural, therefore, that he shared Roumanille's antipathy toward the Revolution of 1848 and that he was a pious Catholic. Naturally inclined to sadness, he escaped despair and discouragement by "objectifying his affections," by saturating his spirit with the old Provençal language and folk-lore, and by forgetting himself in the apostleship of a common idea.[15]

But greatest, though the youngest of the three, was Frédéric Mistral, whose rural home was near Maillane, a village some twelve miles distant from Avignon. Here he was born in 1830 to his father's second wife, daughter of the mayor of Maillane. From her and from the laborers on his father's farm he learned to sing the old Provençal songs and was making verses of his own before he was sent to Avignon for more advanced instruction than could be obtained at home or in the nearby village.[16] Indeed, it was his practise of versifying in the local dialect that attracted the attention of Roumanille, one of his professors. One evening, as the latter accompanied the students to the vesper service, he discovered that Mistral, instead of listening attentively, was writing. Seizing the boy's paper, what was his surprise to find that he had been translating the Penitential Psalms into Provençal! Laudable though the exercise was in his estimation, he felt the time was ill-chosen and that his superior, M. Dupuy, should know about it. He accordingly

14 *Ibid.*, 23.

15 *Théodore Aubanel*, 51.

16 Before he went to Avignon he had rediscovered in Homer and Virgil the ideas and customs of his country and had secretly begun the translation of Virgil's poems into Provençal.

took the incriminating slip of paper to the senior professor and asked what sort of punishment should be meted out to the young offender. That M. Dupuy advised that there be no punishment, not even a scolding, may be ascribed in part to his informant. After the service Mistral, who was expecting the worst, was invited by Roumanille to accompany him on a walk around the walls of the city. As they walked side by side the young student was soon put at his ease, for nothing was said of his recent infraction of an important rule. Instead, Roumanille congratulated him upon his interest in Provençal, admonished him to pursue it farther and strike out upon a path of his own, instead of simply translating, and told him of the Provençal revival which was taking place, climaxing the evening and entrancing the youth with a recital of some of his own poems. " That was the dawn that my soul awaited to awaken to the light," declared the grateful Mistral many years later.[17] At seventeen he took leave of the school in Avignon and spent the next two years at home. His father then sent him to Aix to study law. Having completed the prescribed course in 1851, he returned home. Prepared and authorized to practise law, he disliked the prospect of a lawyer's life, though he wished to please his father. What was his pleasure, therefore, when his father now informed him that he felt he had done his duty by him in giving him an education such as he himself had never had and that he was giving him a free hand to choose the profession he desired to follow! "And there even," according to his own account, " —at this time I was twenty-one—with my feet on the threshold of the paternal country home, eyes toward the Alps, in and of myself I resolved: first, to restore, to revive, the sentiment of race which I saw annihilated by the false, anti-natural education of all the schools; second, to expedite this resurrection by the restoration of the natural and historical language of the country, against which the schools were fighting unto death; third, to

17 Frédéric Mistral, *op. cit.*, 115-116.

restore the vogue of Provençal by the influx and the flame of divine poesy."[18]

No grass was permitted to grow under his feet before he set out upon this threefold project. He contributed ten poems to the *Prouvençalo* mentioned above. At the same time his "love child," *Mireille*, upon which he was to spend seven years, began to take shape. He likewise coöperated with Roumanille in the Congresses of 1852 and 1853. To that of Arles, which Roumanille summoned, Jasmin refused to come, presumably from jealousy.[19] A schism followed. The Congress of Aix of 1853 was more general in its representation: northerners attended it, as well as southerners. Here an ugly rift appeared among the latter on the question of orthography. A second schism arose. Congresses seemed to be conducive to division among the southerners rather than unity. There were now two schools: that of Avignon and that of Marseilles. The former, led by Roumanille, desired a rationalized spelling of words, based upon their etymology; they were, therefore, known as the "Etymologists." The latter, who called themselves the "Naturalists," wanted words to have their old orthography, that with which they had been endowed by the *trouvères*, though it had in many instances long since passed into desuetude. Indicative of the spirit and vigor with which this word-war was fought was the ostentatious refusal of the Etymologists to label themselves *trouvères* any longer in the face of the taunt of their opponents that they were not good traditionalists.[20]

From the heat that was generated by this quarrel was born the *Félibrige*.[21] In the following spring seven poets, among whom were the three leaders we have mentioned, met at intervals in the chateau of Font-Ségugne, owned by Paul Giéra, their friend and something of a poet also. On May 21, 1854,

18 *Ibid.*, 194.

19 Mauritz Boheman, *op. cit.*, 38.

20 *Ibid.*, 38-43.

21 *Ibid.*, 44.

one of the seven poets was missing, thus leaving a total of seven, including Giéra, the host. After a hearty repast they agreed to form a union to give the Provençal language definite form and rules.[22] They accordingly set up an organization, the name of which they agreed should be vague and mysterious. Mistral then gave the gist of a story, the *Ouresoun de Saint Anseume*, which he had obtained from an elderly woman of Maillane. Saint Anselm, according to the narrative, found the Blessed Virgin upon his arrival in heaven telling her Son that she had suffered seven sorrows on his account. The fourth of these was when she had lost Him and had sought Him three days and nights unavailingly until she looked in the Temple, where He was disputing with the scribes of the law, "with the seven *félibres* of the Law." His colleagues promptly saw the point in the story and proclaimed themselves "the seven Felibrians of the Law." Each thereupon presented the form he would give to the name of their union, when Mistral interposed with the following statement: "I shall close with this national word: *félibrige, félibrige!* which will designate the work and the association."[23] It then occurred to one of the seven to utter what was doubtless uppermost in the minds of all. He said, ". . . We are the Felibrians of the Law. . . . But, the Law, who will make it?" "I," replied Mistral, ". . .

22 *Ibid.*, 46-47.

23 Frédéric Mistral, *op. cit.*, 223-226. But what does the word itself mean? asks Boheman. "Ni la vieille femme [who had told the story to Mistral], ni Mistral lui-même, ni personne autre ne le savait, et en dépit de toutes les tentatives d'interpretation, on n'a pas encore réussi à résoudre le problème d'une façon satisfaisante. On la fait dériver du grec 'philabros,' ami du beau, de 'philebraios,' ami de l'hebreu (ce dernier mot a chez les juifs la même signification que 'maîtres de la loi'); d'autres le font venir de 'felibris' ou 'fellebris' (de 'fellere,' protégé des Muses); d'autres encore de font venir de 'la fé libera,' la croyance libre, ou de 'fé-libre,' faiseur de livres; enfin, d'autres ont essayé de le faire dériver de l'espagnol 'féligrès': *filii ecclesiae*, paroissiens. Si l'on n'a pas encore réussi à découvrir la véritable étymologie félibréene et le sens exact de ce mot remarquable, il ressort pourtant de l'ensemble des explications qui précèdent, que 'félibre' doit avoir la même signification que 'maître,' c'est-à-dire 'versé dans l'Ecriture Sainte'" (*op. cit.*, 48-49).

and I swear to you that, if I must give the task twenty years of my life, it is my purpose, in order to show that our language is a language, to write out the articles of the law which governs it." [24] The outcome of this vow, so solemnly made and faithfully observed, was the *Trésor du Félibrige*, a Provençal dictionary which consumed much of his time and energy in the next twenty years. Before disbanding on that memorable day, already dear to them as that of Sainte Estelle, they agreed to make her their patroness.[25]

Their first coöperative enterprise was *L'Almanach Provençal pour le Bel An de Dieu 1855*, the first number of a projected annual publication which Mistral described as follows: "All the tradition, all the banter, all the spirit of our race found itself condensed in it; and, if the Provençal people should some day disappear, its manner of being and thinking would be found again just as it was in the Almanac of the Felibrians." [26] Knowing that they would have to win over the common people, if their movement was to be a success, they made an effort to give expression to the sentiments and feelings so dear to them. Jasmin, they readily admitted, was a great local poet and the leader of a formidable school of writers, " but he had not founded a literature " because the popular need had not been recognized.[27] The *Almanach* was designed, therefore, to attract the common run of people and to serve as an organ in which the principles of the new philology might be developed. The number of copies grew year by year from the original five hundred until it reached fifteen thousand, while the *Almanach* itself became increasingly a chronicle of the *Félibrige* and a

24 Frédéric Mistral, *op. cit.*, 225.

25 "... Et comme 'estello' en provençal signifie 'étoile' nous prîmes comme emblème l'étoile symbolique avec les sept rayons, dans l'espoir que, sous son éclat, les destinées du félibrige seraient vouées au succès " (Mistral, quoted by Boheman, *op. cit.*, 49-50).

26 Frédéric Mistral, *op. cit.*, 232.

27 Jasmin's school, *Lis troubaire*, did publish a little review, *Boui-Abaisso*, from 1841 to 1846, but its clientel was more or less select (Pierre Lasserre, *op. cit.*, 73).

bibliography of the productions of its members.[28] Its subscription list was enlarged and the general popularity of the movement was enhanced by the formation of kindred Felibrian societies in many other cities of the South. Aside from its glorification of local scenes, aside from its numerous banquets amidst the oratory, the pomp, and circumstance of dedications, and the "wines of honor," all so dear to the southerners, one of the greatest attractions of the movement was the glamorous halo in which it was wreathed by its poets, particularly Mistral. In 1859 his *Mirèio* (*Mireille* in French) was published in Avignon. It enjoyed an immediate and extraordinary success. What was the pride and pleasure of his fellow-Felibrians and of his fellow-southerners in general to see it hailed as a "masterpiece" and its author acclaimed by the great Lamartine as a "Greek poet," a "rustic Homer!"[29] And, upon reading this epic narration of the love of Mireille and Vincent, frustrated by the pride of her father and the harshness of nature, a pathetic story simply told, but with power and grandeur, many doubtless shared Lamartine's experience who, upon finishing it, was surprised to discover a smile on his lips and a tear on his hand.[30] At the fête of Nimes, in 1859, the enthusiasm for it and its author was unbounded. The *Félibrige*, having given to Provence and the South the nucleus of a restored literature, now passed from its formative period into one of more rapid progress.[31]

The acclaim with which *Mireille* was received made it clear that the cult of Beauty had returned to Provence. But, though some of Mistral's later productions were technically superior in respect to versification and purity of language, they never attained the popularity of his first great epic, his "love

28 Mauritz Boheman, *op. cit.*, 52.

29 Paul Brousse, *Frédéric Mistral: ses oeuvres, le Félibrige* (Perigueux, 1903), 10.

30 *Ibid.*, 20.

31 Mauritz Boheman, *op. cit.*, 58-59.

child." [32] *Nerte*, because its appeal was likewise general, though not as enthralling as was the pathetic *Mireille*, was more popular than were *Calendal* and *Le Poème du Rhône*, both of which were steeped in Provençal lore, oratorical, didactic, and encyclopaedic.[33] These qualities frequently tired the general reader, but they appealed strongly to the Felibrians proper.[34] How enchanting the lines of the "Invocation to the Soul of Provence" in the first song of *Calendal!* [35] How entrancing the paean of the Prince of Orange in the second song of the *Poème du Rhône* to the "Empire of the Sun!" [36] And how sweet the nostalgia for the energy and poetic skill of the knights and troubadours of old Provence in these and other poems! With one heart they had died for liberty, whilst their base descendants now cowered at the feet of foreign gendarmes. But from the Alps to the Pyrenees courageous poets were busy reviving the old Roman accent, the "family mark," "the sacrament that binds sons to their ancestors" and man to his soil, knowing that if a people, enslaved though it be, clings to its language, "it holds the key that will deliver it from its chains." [37]

32 Paul Brousse, *op. cit.*, 23; Pierre Lasserre, *op. cit.*, 123 and 167.

33 Paul Brousse, *op. cit.*, 34.

34 *Ibid.*, 24. *Cf.* Albert Thibaudet, *op. cit.*, 18; Charles Maurras, "Le Paysage maître de l'âme," *Revue encyclopédique* (1895), 199.

35 This great soul had withstood the northern knights; it had inspired the troubadours. And continuing, "Car les houles des siècles,—et leurs tempêtes et leurs horreurs,—en vain mêlent les peoples, effacent les frontières: —la terre maternelle, la nature,—nourrit toujours ses fils—du même lait; sa dure mamelle—toujours à l'olivier donnera l'huile fine; Ame éternellement renaissante,—âme joyeuse et fière et vive,—qui hennis dans le bruit du Rhône et de son vent!—âme des bois pleins d'harmonie—et des calanques pleines de soleil, — de la patrie pieuse, — je t'appelle! incarne-toi dans mes vers provençaux!" [*Calendal, Oeuvres* de Frédéric Mistral (Paris, 1886-1890), II, 5].

36 "Son portulan à la main—qu'il [the Prince of Orange, son of the King of Holland] feuillette, le prince transporté lors s'écria:—'Salut, empire du soleil, que borde comme un ourlet d'argent le Rhône éblouissant! empire de plaisance et d'allégresse, empire fantastique de Provence qui avec ton nom seul charmes le monde.'" Continuing, the Prince laments his not having been born in the days of chivalry and poetry (*ibid.*, IV, 47).

37 *Au poètes catalans, ibid.*, III (*Les Iles d'or*), 164-175.

It was to preserve this means of deliverance and therewith to exalt the past greatness and splendor of Provence and of the *Midi* that these poets were so active with word, pen, and pencil.[38]

The " Empire of the Sun " and the " Roman accent " implied more than simply a literary revival of the old Provençal and Limousin languages: a Latin federation was intended.[39] In 1867 the Catalans presented a cup to the Felibrians as a token of admiration and appreciation. Mistral in August of the same year indited a poem, *La Coupo*, to signal the event. From this " sacred cup," this " felibrian grail," [40] the Provençals would quaff the hopes and dreams of youth, the memory of the past and faith in the year that was to come; from it they would drink knowledge of the True and of the Beautiful, of the high pleasures that make sport of the tomb; from it they would imbibe poesy, the divine ambrosia, by which man is transformed into God. But the Provençals would not drink alone: the Catalans, their " accomplices " and " brothers," would join them in this holy sacrament.[41] In fact, all Latin peoples would partake of this cup, for they were all members of the great Latin family. It was, therefore, eminently proper that when, in 1874, the Provençal Felibrians celebrated the five hundredth anniversary of the death of Petrarch, Catalan, Italian, and Rumanian deputations participated in the festivities. In the following year a public-spirited Catalan instituted a prize for the best Latin poem of the year. That of 1878 was won by a distinguished Rumanian poet. In the same year Mistral suggested to a group of artists and Felibrians at Marseilles that " perhaps the *Félibrige* bore in itself the future of the Latin race." [42] But it was Baron de Tourtoulon of Montpellier and Berluc-Pérussis of Aix who led in this Latin orientation

38 Jean Charles-Brun, *L'Evolution félibréenne* (Lyon, 1896), 16.

39 *Ibid.*, 16-17.

40 Albert Thibaudet, *op. cit.*, 145.

41 Frédéric Mistral, *op. cit.*, III, 39-43.

42 Jean Charles-Brun, *op. cit.*, 17.

of the *Félibrige*. The former established the *Revue du monde latin* to promote the cause of Latin coöperation. Frédéric Donnadien of Béziers, inspired by Mistral's Marseilles address, wrote a brochure in which he listed and stressed the advantages of uniting peoples of the same race and expatiated upon the necessity of considering the *Félibrige* a "social force."[43] Though Avignon was the "cradle" of the *Félibrige* proper, it was Montpellier that became the center of its Latin proclivities. Its festivities were attended by distinguished Catalan and Rumanian poets to affirm the idea and sentiment of Latin kinship; A. Roque-Ferrier's *L'Idée latine et les fêtes de Montpellier* at once recognized its leadership in this phase of the Felibrian action and advanced the cause of Latin federation; here, also, in 1890 was founded the *Société du Félibrige latin* in the interest of Pan-Latinism.[44]

The *Félibrige* was thus becoming a "social force." But, if the principle of federation was useful as a means of binding together peoples of the same race or cultural background, regardless of national frontiers,[45] it was even more useful, so many thought, as a principle of organization within the French nation. Mistral, contrary to Roumanille and Aubanel, was enthusiastic over the events of 1848; he looked upon the Republic as the "breeding-cell" of future federations. But the *coup d'état* of 1851 completed the disillusionment he experienced on this score, which his contact with republican fanaticism, intolerance, and gross materialism had begun.[46] Embittered by the course of events and by his study of the history of Provence, he referred to the crusaders of 1209 as "traitors" in a strophe of the first edition of *Mireille* which he thought it wise to omit from later editions. In a note which he appended to the first song of *Calendal* he was less caustic,

43 *Ibid.*, 18.

44 *Ibid.*, 18.

45 That this Pan-Latin agitation was not without imperialistic implications seems clear. *Cf.* Albert Thibaudet, *op. cit.*, 175.

46 Frédéric Mistral, *Mes origines: mémoires et récits*, 156 and 201.

but none the less critical. He admitted that it was apparently necessary that ancient Gaul should have become modern France; but he added that it was not achieved in a manner desired by the southerners, who had never contemplated any fusion other than that of a federated state. "It is always a great misfortune," he continued, "when civilization must by surprise give precedence to barbarity, and the triumph of the *Franchimands* retarded the march of progress by two centuries. Because that which was subdued, mark it well, was less the South, materially speaking, than the spirit of the South." [47] The Provençals of old sensed an antagonism of race in Simon de Montfort's campaign. Religion, he thought, was merely a pretext; for the religious situation in the South did not justify the intervention of the crusaders. Moreover, the centralizing activities of Louis XI, Richelieu, and Colbert were regrettable in that they constituted a systematic war on all the traditional social forces, upon the natural peculiarities of different localities, and upon the former spirit of self-reliance and independence of the people of the South.[48] Strong as were his feelings on this subject and forceful as was his expression of them, he inaugurated no formal political campaign against the levelling centralization which he considered so harmful to the True, the Good, and the Beautiful — to civilization itself, as he understood it. He placed his faith in the revival of the old language, believing it to be the key to the door that barred deliverance. When, however, a campaign was launched to convert the Society of the Felibrians of Paris from a strictly cultural and literary force into a "social force," one that would openly espouse the cause of administrative decentralization, he gave it his whole-hearted support.[49]

47 Quoted by Pierre Lasserre, *op. cit.*, 139.

48 *Ibid.*, 138-153.

49 Albert Thibaudet, *op. cit.*, 213-214.

CHAPTER XIV

THE FEDERALIST CAMPAIGN AND MAURRAS' PART IN IT

SUCH a campaign, such an effort to persuade the Parisian Felibrians to pursue a course of political action, was begun by two of the Society's younger members: Frédéric Amouretti and Charles Maurras.[1] Maurras expressed the greatest respect and admiration for Mistral and his work: "In saving a language the poet has also saved a race. It is almost commonplace to repeat it, Mistral was first of all the doctor of our traditions. We have been unable to drink from his cup without having our thought captivated by the memory of the dead and by the lesson of the old men, by 'the hope and dream of youth. . . .' He has made us unite 'the memory of the past and the faith in the year that will come. . . .' As he thought for a whole people, he taught us to think historically."[2] Mistral, in turn, valued the work and friendship of his young compatriot, as his autographed portrait in Maurras' home at Martigues shows; for on it the poet inscribed, "To Charles Maurras who more than all has best understood my work."[3] But, according to Maurras' dictum, loving or hating too much compels one to desert sentiment for action.[4] In this instance literary action, such as that of the *Ecole romane*, appeared to be insufficient—a view that was shared by his friend Amouretti. The latter, who was five years Maurras' senior, was born at Toulon; but, having spent his years of childhood and early manhood at Cannes, he both felt and considered himself a

1 Berluc-Pérussis had, it is true, anticipated their demand for political action, but the program he contemplated was more social than political, envisaging the widespread establishment of Provençal stores, cafés, etc. (*ibid.*, 207-212).

2 *La Sagesse de Mistral* (Paris, 1926), 9-10; *Sous l'étoile du mage* (Paris, 1931), 18.

3 René Benjamin, *Charles Maurras, ce fils de la mer* (Paris, 1932), 236.

4 *Promenade italienne* (Paris, 1929), 168.

Provençal.[5] Prizing highly the cultural amenities of old Provence, he was convinced, and so persuaded Maurras, that their revival and maintenance was possible only by adding political action to the literary movement already begun.

Hence the " Declaration of the Federalist Felibrians " of 1892, prepared and signed by the two friends,[6] and read by Amouretti at a meeting of the Society of the Felibrians of Paris.[7] The older members were informed that the younger ones had long been developing ideas which the older had sown. They were now impatient to realize these ideas and were determined to announce them before political assemblies as well as to literary groups. Inasmuch as the rights and duties of the Felibrian writers and of their language proceeded from their autonomy, rather than creating or extending it, local autonomy was their first objective. Hence their demand for free communes, for the local control of their officials and of their essential functions. Instead of being merely " administrative circumscriptions," these communes were to have an intense life of their own and were to be mothers that inspired their sons with the virtues and " the ardent passions of the race and of the blood." Likewise, the " souls " of the provinces were to be freed from their departmental prisons. This demand was not inspired by " archeological regrets "; nor was it prompted by a desire simply to restore or copy the institutions of other days. Their purpose was " to complete and to perfect them." They, therefore, seconded the demand of the Bretons for a sovereign assembly and suggested others for Bordeaux, Toulouse, Montpelier, and Marseilles or Aix. These assemblies would be given power over the provincial administration, the courts, the schools and universities, and public works, such as the building of much-needed roads and canals. Provincialism alone could bring the great works desired for a hundred years

5 J. Berenger, *Charles Maurras et Frédéric Amouretti* (Cannes, 1913), 15-16; *L'Etang de Berre*, 294.

6 *L'Etang de Berre*, 120, 123.

7 *Ibid.*, 124-134.

but never achieved. Moreover, it might lead to the solution of the economic and social problems that were troubling France. They and their young friends expected much from the intellectual and moral renaissance of the South, but they desired something more: "the highest possible productivity of the marvelous riches of our soil." They were not two youths intoxicated with words and fine phrases. It was a "profound sense of the national interests" that inspired them to demand political action.

Such, briefly, was the tenor of the declaration. To some it appeared too ambitious, even dangerous. Among these was the prefect of the Seine who made representations to the president of the Society and thereby gave rise to a long and acrid dispute which two years later resulted in the expulsion of Maurras from the Society. By way of protest, some twelve "young Felibrians" resigned from the older organization and founded with him, under the presidency of Amouretti, the Parisian School of the Félibrige, which lasted until the Dreyfus affair divided and dispersed its membership.[8] This was not, however, before it had inspired the formation of the French Regionalist Federation and had aroused among the young Felibrians of Paris and in the South an enthusiasm that was heightened by the generous support given them by the great Mistral himself.

Their plan of action was to win such an overwhelming popular approval of their political principle that it would be forced upon the government.[9] While Amouretti was already a monarchist and believed in the efficacy of rule from above rather than from below, Maurras still subscribed to the democratic doctrine despite its inconsistency with his aesthetic and philosophical principles. The apathy and indifference with which their campaign for decentralization was received by the cities and towns and the open or concealed hostility of many poli-

8 *Au signe de Flore*, 35; *L'Etang de Berre*, 120-121.

9 *Au signe de Flore*, 38-39.

ticians doubtless helped to discredit the democratic idea in Maurras' thinking. Meanwhile in the articles which he contributed to Barrès' *La Cocarde*, many of which bore upon this campaign, he reproached the later Bourbons as well as the Jacobins and Napoleon for having introduced the administrative and political unity and uniformity from which France was suffering and by which it was being weakened.[10] But, having denounced those who had robbed the communes and the provinces of their former "liberties," and having shown the necessity of recreating them, he admitted the need of a strong central authority to curb any possible centrifugal tendencies of the newly freed communes and provinces. He even sensed a desire on the part of the French people to repose this authority or executive power in the hands of "someone."[11] In thus tentatively accepting Barrès' Caesarism, he seemed to question the ability of the masses to cope wisely with the problems pertaining to the nation as a whole, while, at the same time, he was convinced that the central government could not lay its heavy hand upon the local governments without destroying the vital sources of civic life.

These articles reveal two factors that attracted him to the movement in which he was engaged: one was aesthetic and in accord with the general philosophy he had come to accept; the other, allied with it, reflected the influence of Taine and Barrès.[12] In a review of a book by Rochegude, he excused himself

10 "Les Trois mensonges" (Du 'Pensiero'), *La Cocarde*, Jan. 2, 1895.

11 *La Cocarde*, Jan. 20, 1895.

12 "Il [Barrès] insista pour substituer au patriotisme administratif un patriotisme terrien et remplacer l'image de 'la France idéale', chère à quelques rhéteurs, par l'idée d'une France réelle, c'est-à-dire composée, comme dans la réalité, de familles, de communes et de provinces: tous éléments non point contrariés ou divisés entre eux, mais variés, sympathiques et convergents... *La Cocarde*, formée des éléments les plus divers, fut, malgré tout fédéraliste et nationaliste. On y poursuivit les Français de trop fraîche date, ces 'Métèques', qui font la loi chez nous. On appuya, bien que la feuille ne passât guère les fortifications, toutes les justes causes provinciales . . . La rédaction de *La Cocarde* eut l'occasion d'appliquer et de défendre les méthodes et les enseignements de Taine. En cherchant la forme concrète de

for repeating the names of so many aristocrats in a brief article by saying that they were the "substance of the national religion," that they signified "a reflection that was wise, prompt, full of audacity and harmony." Then followed a brief invocation to the "dear national Minerva, the little Roman Minerva," the source of all wisdom, grace, and thought. The goddess resided in every province, every city; and, one and indivisible, was everywhere, presiding over the whole body of the nation as well as over each hearth in it. "It is of such sentiments that the nationalism of many Frenchmen is constituted. And from thence," he added, "comes also our federalism." [13] Provençalism, in particular, was essentially Roman and, therefore, desirable; and, since federalism promised it freer scope and a chance to revive and develop, it was to him the first and immediate objective.

The second factor, though likewise not devoid of sentiment, was one of policy, of defense against the encroachments of Germanism and cosmopolitanism. Georges Thiébaud had noted how the English spirit, the German, and the Protestant had invaded France and had suggested that they be replaced by the "spirit of France." But which France? Maurras was prompted to ask. Answering his own query, he insisted there was only one France, a natural France, not an artificial one which was less a geographical or an historical entity than an "administrative label." This conception of France resembled the liquid which certain merchants of Bercy denominated wine, but the formula of which varied with the maker and which contained everything but the sugar of the vine. In this "artificial France" everything was included except the "thought, the memory, the vague dream of these thirty thousand communes and of their territory, of the varied rivers, of the shores of the ocean

leur nationalisme, ses rédacteurs s'étaient senti fédéralistes; ils se sentirent provincialistes et traditionnistes quand l'on essaya de donner de leur fédéralisme une interprétation en désaccord avec cette réalité concrète dont il resultait" [*L'Idée de la décentralisation* (Paris, 1898), 16-17].

13 "Fédéral-National," *La Cocarde*, Dec. 21, 1894.

and of the sea, of the valleys, the forests, the plains, and of the hills of which our France is in reality composed." [14] Many have accepted this concept of France, with its "fantastic uniformity" and "unreasonable monotony"; and, pursuing "phantoms," have become cosmopolitans, people without a country or fatherland. "The fatherland is a place in the world where one has ancestors of bone and flesh, fathers who have lived and who are dead. Civicism implies a city environed by a distinctive landscape and surrounded by familiar walls. It may doubtless extend and generalize itself in various ways: still one must needs exercise caution not to let the real groundwork, the natural point of departure of sentiments, disappear, if one would save them from dissolution." Abstractions die from barrenness when separated from the living concrete world. ". . . The Anglo-German element which M. Thiébaud wishes to eliminate will withdraw only with the return to life of those profound masses of the Province which Barrès declared . . . were still confined to the 'great empire of silence.'" M. Thiébaud, he thought, would do well to join them in the task of awakening these silent masses.[15]

M. Léopold Lacour had said that the provinces, the "natural circumscriptions," were dead. This would be a great misfortune, were it true. Mistral had shown, however, that, even though the melting-pot of time, with its tempests and storms, mixed peoples and effaced frontiers, old mother earth (or nature) still nourished its brood with the same milk. Nature had not changed its processes; it still conserved "this invariable (or varying only with infinite slowness) foundation which alone explains, bears up or sustains the infinite transformations of its appearance." The railway, the telegraph, and telephone had not overthrown the fundamental law of things, for their first effect was to "make the consciousness of our diverse fatherlands more sensible to the heart and more profound,"

14 "Quelle France," *La Cocarde*, Jan. 3, 1895.

15 *Ibid.*

as Bourget had justly shown.[16] No, the "natural circumscriptions" were not dead, even though the old frontiers of the provinces had changed. The Provençal dialect, for example, was still very much alive, Lacour notwithstanding. But how many "natural circumscriptions" were there? Lacour had suggested eight or ten; Le Play, thirteen; Comte, seventeen. Amouretti, who had studied the question exhaustively, had arrived at Comte's figure which, incidentally, coincided with the zones of influence of the press. But it was less important to determine upon a number than to respect the wishes and desires of nature, modified by the tendencies and habits graven upon it by history.[17] Was this simply intellectual federalism and Felibrianism, devoid of all sentiment? as Lacour had stated. Far from it. ". . . The slightest odor of the thyme of our hills, having mingled with the words of my declaration, will suffice to make such language look suspicious." [18]

It was with arguments such as these that Maurras contributed to the campaign of *La Cocarde* for federalism. Shortly after Barrès and his friends abandoned the journal, the *Ligue républicaine de décentralisation* was founded. To it Maurras seems to have adhered, though not Barrès, who disliked its moderate and rightist tone and complexion.[19] While Maurras found its program in general a "little vague," he liked its clear and forceful demand for the decentralization of the public services in accordance with the principles of regionalism.[20] He also welcomed the opportunity of closer contact with Paul Bourget, author of the famous *D'Outre-mer* which had appeared in the columns of *Le Figaro* about the time when Barrès and his friends had taken over the direction of *La Cocarde.* It had been a powerful ally in spreading the gospel of decen-

16 "Les Circonscriptions naturelles," *La Cocarde,* Jan. 11, 1895.

17 "Les Circonscriptions naturelles," *La Cocarde,* Jan. 13, 1895.

18 "Encore les circonscriptions naturelles," *La Cocarde,* Feb. 1, 1895.

19 *L'Idée de la décentralisation,* 21. Upon the suggestion of Bourget its name was changed to *La Ligue nationale.*

20 *Ibid.,* 21.

tralization,[21] and its author was now a prominent leader of the *Ligue*. Still another attraction that this moderate group had for Maurras was doubtless the work and influence of Madame Adam. Her *La Nouvelle revue*, in which Mistral's *Poème du Rhône* first appeared in 1896, worked powerfully in the interest of the movement, and, in fact, became a sort of provincial "headquarters." [22]

21 Paul Bourget, *Outre-mer* (*Notes sur l'Amérique*), (Paris, 1895), 2 vols., especially chapter XII, "Le Retour." After noting that democracy in France had meant the destruction or suppression of the individual by an oppressive majority, while democracy in the United States permitted and encouraged the completest development of the individual by restricting the meddling of the state, he declared that the Americans were but faithful to their origins. Founded by outlaws, rebels, and adventurers, the United States did not achieve democracy by reasoning; she merely confirmed it. He found a vast "patriotic cordiality," even in the South, and ascribed it to this loyalty to their origins. "C'est," he continues, "un leçon que nous pouvons recevoir de la démocratie Américaine; mais pour la pratiquer, il nous faudrait travailler dans un sens opposé à celui où marche depuis cent ans chez nous le parti démocratique. Nous devrions chercher ce qui reste de la vieille France et nous y rattacher par toutes nos fibres, retrouver la province d'unité naturelle et héréditaire sous le départment artificiel et morcelé, l'autonomie municipale sous la centralisation administrative, les universités locales et fécondes sous notre université officielle et morte, reconstituer la famille terrienne par la liberté de tester, protéger le travail par le rétablissement des corporations, rendre à la vie religieuse sa vigeur et sa dignité par la suppression du budget des cultes et par le droit de posséder librement, assuré aux associations religieuses, en un mot, sur ce point comme sur l'autre, défaire systematiquement l'oeuvre meurtrière de la Révolution Française. C'est le conseil qui, pour l'observateur impartial, se dégage de toutes les remarques faites sur les Etats-Unis. Si leur démocratie est si vivante et si forte, c'est parce que l'individu y est libre et puissant en face d'un Etat réduit à son minimum d'action. Si elle réunit toutes les volontés en un immense harmonie, c'est qu'elle est vraiment nationale. C'est pour avoir établi un régime où l'Etat centralise en lui toutes les forces du pays et pour avoir violement coupé toute attache historique entre notre passé et notre présent, que notre Révolution a si profondément tari les sources de la vitalité Française" (*op. cit.*, II, 320-321). Bourget's book was unquestionably influential, but Maurras may have exaggerated when, in 1897, he said that Bourget had done much the same service for the decentralizers that de Tocqueville had done earlier in the century. It is interesting to note that Bourget objected to democracy because it crushed the individual, while Maurras came to oppose it because it freed him.

22 *Sous l'étoile du mage* (Paris, 1931), 22; *l'Idée de la décentralisation*, 21.

Just as the end of the Barrèsian experience of *La Cocarde* had no disastrous effect upon the federalist movement in general, so, too, may it be said that it marked no interruption in Maurras' personal efforts to realize the coveted goal. His contributions to the *Revue Encyclopédique Larousse,* to *La Gazette de France,* to *Le Soleil,* and to other reviews and journals reflect his zeal to destroy romanticism and the centralized administration, both of which, he was convinced, were but different expressions of substantially the same thing, as they were both destructive of a strong and virile France. The essential unity of the causes he was advocating is perhaps exemplified best by an article of 1895.[23] In a sanguine and optimistic mood, he hailed the rise and spread of the love of the *terra patriae* as "just, reasonable, ancient, and natural." People again were becoming pagans, he exulted. Mother Earth was being worshiped anew as she had been at the beginning of the world. Only now she was more beautiful than she was in primitive times, having battened upon the ashes of their forbears, their arts, their industry, and their wisdom. "Works of art and civic virtues all proceed from the earth as they all return to it. We are disposed to consider its landscapes, its pure lines, its soft colors the true doctors of our soul." This paganism, this adoration of Mother Earth, was not pantheism, was not the worship of just any earth; it was Provençal earth, Angevin earth, etc. that were revered. Rather than pantheism, it was a "true polytheism." This religion rightfully stressed the importance of tradition which some objected to because the life and thought of the dead prevented the quick from thinking and truly living. They looked upon tradition as a great manacle or prison. Their mistake was failing to reflect that the most distant horizon limits our vision, that an innocent little flower or the soil of the earth itself may baffle us in the pursuit of our desires. This soil, though at times stubborn and recalcitrant, sustains us and gives our feet solid support. Moreover, the

23 "Le Paysage maître de l'âme," *Revue encyclopédique Larousse* (1895), 199-203; also in *Barbarie et Poésie,* 111-123.

horizon defines our world and gives it form. Half of our goods are formed and established by the limitations of circumjacent space. Almost all of the remaining half are derived from the experience of time. "Of the forces that bind us, those that do not proceed from the countryside come from the men who have preceded us here, or rather, those that do not flow from the natal soil today have issued from it in earlier days; and the tradition which has made us its repository is, therefore, a blessed thing, wheat from the divine earth." [24]

These natural and traditional forces were of priceless value to the nation as well as to the commune or province. Hence the need of all Frenchmen concerning themselves with the question, not whether foreign literatures had turned that of France from its traditional path, important as it was, but of distinguishing the good from the bad in the various ethnic influences that had come into France from the outside. "It is not a question," he said, "of pell-mell certifying to the classical influence which the seventeenth century wrought and to that of the Anglo-Germanic which the nineteenth century brought, but, rather, of determining if this Anglo-Germanic influence has not sterilized many noble spirits whereas the classical influence would have made them fruitful. In a word, the question is one of knowing if there is not a 'happy' way of national 'limitation.'" [25] Some Frenchmen, especially the youth of the land, already understood this. Tired of the subjective and anarchistic revery that had been brought in from abroad, they were now attempting to escape from themselves and were disposed to turn to a restored naturalism which was positive, scientific, and politic all in one. In accord with what was sound in Taine's *race-milieu-moment theory*,[26] and venerating the celestial and

24 "Le Paysage maître de l'âme," *Revue encyclopédique Larousse* (1895), 201.

25 *Ibid.*, 202.

26 "Je serais étonné que l'on me soupconnât d'illusions sur le sort des thèses de Taine relatives au milieu, à la race, au moment. Elles ont fléchi en partie, et je le sais. Néanmoins, il est une part de leur philosophie naturelle qui revient à la vie" (*ibid.*, 203). While rejecting Taine's system as too

terrestial forces beatified by August Comte,[27] this naturalism named them gods and would choose for itself " its true name, paganism." [28] Essentially pagan, as was also, as we have seen,[29] Maurras' Epicurean aestheticism, it harmonized with the latter beautifully.

In the spring of 1896, the next year, Maurras went to Athens, leaving France as a republican and returning as a royalist.[30] This change not only brought his political thought into fundamental agreement with his aesthetic philosophy; but it also gave him an air of greater certainty and conviction in advocating federalism as the means of insuring the free growth and permanence of the " pagan naturalism " he had discovered in the youth of France. No longer subject to the political tutelage of Barrès, whose individualism in art, philosophy, and politics was only too clear, he was now free to strike boldly at the thing which vitiated French politics as well as French art.

narrow, slow, and potentially arbitrary, Maurras accepted his fundamental thesis of natural and historical determinism. Critical of Taine's harsh treatment of the classical spirit, of his failure to grasp the secret of La Fontaine's aestheticism, of his advocacy of ideas not always established in conformity with his self-imposed method, and of his obsolete style, he, nevertheless, accepted him as one of his masters. " Malgré tout, M. Taine demeure notre maître; il conserve beaucoup de droits à l'attention et au respect " (" Influence de Taine," *Soleil*, Aug. 21, 1897, in D. P. & C., V, 317-318). Here, again, as in the case of Comte and others, he accepted much, but rejected what was contrary to the canons of his Epicurean preconceptions.

27 *Cours de philosophie positive* (4th edition, edited by E. Littré, Paris, 1877), V, 18; VI, 711-716. Comte here stressed the determining rôle of climatic and racial forces and advocated the union of biology and sociology because he was convinced of the need of studying man as an animal.

28 " Le Paysage maître de l'âme," *Revue encyclopédique Larousse* (1895), 203.

29 Chapter X, above.

30 " Je le (royaliste) suis devenu: beaucoup de mes amis ont jugé que ce fût par le péril soudain où la République impuissante jeta la nation en cédant tout aux Juifs dans l'affaire Dreyfus. J'ai dû le dire et le penser: rien n'est plus exact, sans l'être absolument. La conversion de mon esprit est antérieure d'un an à l'Affaire, elle date des premières semaines que j'ai vécues hors de France, mon voyage de Grèce du printemps de 1896 " (*Au signe de Flore*, 43).

He had hoped to force federalism upon a reluctant parliament by a "free reaction of the public." Many of his friends were still deluded by this "chimera." He was now convinced that it could be achieved only by an "energetic and wise Power" — in short, by a king — from above by means of a "skillful mixture of diplomacy and authority."[31] Moreover, some of his friends (Barrès *et al.*) had found support for their federalism in that of Proudhon.[32] While, as he readily admitted, the term federalism was more definite and precise than decentralization, it implied a certain adherence to the political theory of the *Contrat*, to the moral metaphysics of the anarchists that was most distasteful. Those who subscribed to the "divine right of the individual" were confusing ontological dreams and political realities. His idea of federalism called for a local autonomy based upon natural necessities, historical or economic, not one based upon a contract.[33] Instead of reasoning from the general to the particular, instead of beginning with a general idea of France and deducing therefrom the idea of its elements, he used the more realistic inductive method of arriving at the idea of France by way of the idea of its elements. "The Provençal thinks first of all of his Provençal France, the Angevin of his Angevin France. In fact, it seems natural to set out from the place where each citizen of the country finds himself in order to join them at the point where their thought meets; this process gives to patriotism concrete form and real substance."[34]

The old process, though useful as a means of confirming the unity of the nation, had now lost its *raison d'être,* since, for four centuries Frenchmen had lived together in this indestructible union. With one state, a language without a peer, a litera-

31 "La cause du fédéralisme étant juste et sainte, il fallait entreprendre de la servir par un autre biais" (*ibid.*, 39).

32 See p. 64, above; also "Le Système fédératif," *La Quinzaine* (Sept. 1, and Oct. 1, 1896), XII, 51-73; 296-317.

33 *Ibid.*, XII, 59-60.

34 *Ibid.*, XII, 66.

ture, an art and a poetry stamped by the tradition of Greece and Rome, a common way of feeling, and a "common sense" so general and so human that it was unique, France no longer needed a metaphysical corroboration of its unity. Jacobins and Caesareans, such as Déroulède, objected to the love of the federalists for their particular *patrie* as deleterious to the national sentiment; many anarchists, on the other hand, even went so far as to deny the roots of this attachment. As a matter of fact, experience had shown that there was practically no longer a single France once the diverse Frances had been suppressed. Who would go to war and have his head broken for a mere "word in the air?" If, on the other hand, you were to give a man a town, a steeple, a bit of sky, even a confused idea of all towns, of all steeples, and of all the neighboring skies, he would have something to live and to die for. Proudhon, who stressed personal affinities based upon professional and economic interests, pretended to free man by fictitiously removing him from his soil, his family and his race. He doubtless liberated his metaphysical person or *moi;* but that which really determined him was pitilessly damaged and diminished. "You strike the living man when you happen to touch his local institutions. It is our air that we defend when we defend our *patries*." [35]

This natural federalism had the advantage, first, of being practical; it despised the "quarrels of political ontology." Second, it was not opposed to patriotism, whereas Proudhon, with his bad point of approach, could deny the fatherland if he desired. This the "pagan" federalist could not do, for it would be as easy for a man not to be a vertebrate or a horse not a quadruped as for a Provençal not to be a Frenchman. "I have informed the patriots that federalism was the best boulevard of nationalism; but, in another sense, our Proudhonians are becoming more and more aware that federalism is the vanguard of the forces working for nationalism. The true name of the new party would be Federal-National if it

35 *Ibid.*, XII, 71.

did not rhyme unpleasantly with the name of one of the parties of the German Empire." [36] A third advantage was that it removed an "almost comical equivocation" — internationalism. Cosmopolitan internationalism which exalted the idea of humanity at the expense of the memory, the customs, laws, and traditions of the fatherland was really what Proudhon wanted. Internationalism properly understood called for the exchange of goods between nations and desired the abolition of hostilities between peoples; but these objectives postulated the maintenance of peoples and the conservation of nations. Europe at some future date might have to federate to hold its own against American commercial competition or to repel invading hordes from Asia. Of this there was but little likelihood, however. More to be desired was an Hellenic-Latin union which, while not destroying the traditions of the member-nations, would, nevertheless, permit a greater intellectual and cultural unity.[37] Fourth, and last, this type of federalism sought the establishment of autonomous territorial groups; it had no part in the "flagrant contradiction" of some federalists who, deluded by the principles of the liberty of association and the freedom of the individual, wished to establish the liberty of the commune only to impose upon this sovereign commune a régime of unrestrained individualism.[38] This federalism was not brought down from the top of Mount Sinai, nor was it invented to satisfy any universal postulates. It was advanced as the best means of meeting the needs of the fatherland.

Barrès was, however, essentially safe, as his recent publication of *Les Déracinés* indicated.[39] He, whose "anarchism," whose *Culte du moi*, was once disquieting, was now saying, "In principle, personality ought to be considered a pure acci-

36 *Ibid.*, XII, 298.

37 *Ibid.*, XII, 300-301.

38 *Ibid.*, XII, 302.

39 Reviewed by Maurras in "La Décentralisation," *Revue encyclopédique Larousse* (1897), 1076-1081; expanded and republished as *L'Idée de la décentralisation* (Paris, 1898).

dent." There were, in other words, but few persons; only seldom did a human being become the receptacle of the human soul. Whether this was good or bad was not the question. If true, it would not "be bad for the common herd to adopt a common law, an order superior to the individual passions." [40] When Barrès had two of his characters agree that a third had suffered from and had been "degraded by the individualistic and liberal *milieu* into which he had been thrown," he was giving things their true name and was a true disciple of Taine. He was not so good a pupil, however, in the case of Sturel's worship of Napoleon. For one thing, his method was bad. Certainly, hero worship was commendable; and there was no denying the need of "professors of energy." But they did not create energy; they simply called it forth from its latent state in their admirers and followers. Energy, itself, was the work of nature. And he who led a "vegetative life," close to his soil and to his natural medium, found his personal resources limitless, for what he used up he could replace from the inexhaustible supply of nature. Napoleon, himself, was doubtless such a man. He must have had strong roots to have been able to uproot the French, a point Barrès had apparently overlooked in reading Taine, for the latter had well shown that Napoleon had cut the French off from their traditions.[41]

France was indeed uprooted, disorganized, and unhappy, as Barrès had shown. Both the élite and the masses were dissatisfied. And the almost uniform hostility of the Jews, of the university professors, and of those, who, having discovered their souls, were assiduously cultivating them without profit to themselves or to society, towards *Les Déracinés* was particularly noteworthy. Emile Faguet, for example, while not unalterably opposed to administrative decentralization — he admitted that many things done in Paris might be done better in the canton, the arrondissement, and the department, but not

40 "La Décentralisation," *Revue encyclopédique Larousse* (1897), 1077; *L'Idée de la décentralisation*, 30.

41 "La Décentralisation," *Revue encyclopédique Larousse* (1897), 1078.

in or by the commune—was fearful of its possible effect upon the army and finance, functions which the federalists themselves considered national in scope and, therefore, beyond the pale of decentralization. His objections to federalism were similar to those Thiers had once advanced; in fact, he had repeated some of his arguments. They made one doubt the reality of the war of 1870 and of the German victory; for, if they were right, if the union of the civil and military orders was as close and rigorous as they insisted, France certainly must have been the conqueror. The truth of the matter was, however, that France's "centralized empire was defeated by a mere confederation of sovereign states for which customs and military bonds alone made for unity." [42] No, if Faguet was so inspired with patriotic solicitude, he would do well to observe how necessary the local spirit which he disdained was to the prosperity of the nation. Lacking this spirit, the nation itself was languishing. Barrès had given sufficient proof of this in his description of the progress of Germanization in the eastern provinces of France.

Critical and fearful of a thoroughgoing administrative decentralization, Faguet unreservedly conceded the necessity of restoring the provincial intellectual life by all possible means. But how could this be done? There was only one way: "to oblige all of the citizens to concern themselves with the local finances and . . . politics, to cease unloading them on an officeholder." [43] From these humble tasks they would pass, if capable or, if they liked, to intellectual cares. This last came at the end of the process of decentralization, not at the beginning; it was "a flower, not a root." Any other procedure would simply result in the creation of branch-establishments of Paris in the provinces, in setting up mirrors instead of lighting the home-fires. Fearful of local territorial associations, Faguet favored moral and professional associations as decentralizing agencies. The latter, unrestrained by the former, were already

42 *L'Idée de la décentralisation*, 35.

43 *Ibid.*, 36.

dismantling the frontiers of the country; they were, in fact, cosmopolitan. This was true of Catholicism, "so often accused of ruining patriotism," of Protestantism, of banking, of science, of the professions proper, and of labor. It was precisely at this point that the federalism of La Tour du Pin and Barrès was so ingenious, for it united "the two kinds of groupings, the territorial and the moral, in a strong and complex communal, provincial, and national organization." [44]

44 *Ibid.*, 37. That the reference to the Marquis La Tour du Pin La Charce was not a gratuitous one is indicated by a study of his principal work, *Vers un ordre social chrétien: jalons de route, 1882-1907* (Paris, 1909?). His plan of social reform as presented here was not one of Christian Socialism, for the two words taken together made no sense. His ideal was a "Social Christianity," or simply "Christianity," as deduced from the doctrines of the Catholic Church (38-39). No matter what a man's social position, a social order, if just, would insure him a home, the means of rearing his family, and the possibility of saving enough for old age. These the entrepreneur was not supplying the worker. What was needed was a corporate régime based upon old and tried principles which gave the members of the association, the association itself, and the state certain definite rights, duties, and functions, specified and protected by the law. In medieval times the worker, whether an apprentice, a journeyman, or a master, had his appropriate rights which the statutes of his association guaranteed and the magistracy protected. There was an "equal respect of diverse rights" which must be the basis of a social order worthy of the name. These rights were combined, not as a weapon of some against others, but as a protection of the interests of all. The corporation was not a private society; it had a definite place in the organization of the commune and, less directly, in that of the state itself. "The corporation, like the commune, is a state within the state; that is, it is bound to it by a moral contract which permits reciprocal powers and obligations. The public power does not dictate to it its rules, but it confirms them in order to keep them in a sphere of proper utility not detrimental to the public utility, while at the same time it protects it in their application against material difficulties or from oppression from without" (24). There was a vast difference between administering and governing. A country should never be administered. The administration of industry was the prerogative of the association. Its income would be derived from the "regulated contributions" of its members and from its investments in the industry, and its governing body would be made up of representatives from every interested element. Along with its other duties it would pass upon the professional ability of the entrepreneur as well as upon that of the worker. This corporative system would put an end to France's economic decline, for it would substitute for profit and quantity production the economic well-being of all. It would check the evident moral

France, to be again healthy and strong, needed to get away from the underlying principle of the institutions of the year VIII. Burdened by thousands of petty distractions, the central government was unable to perform its rightful functions properly. Moreover, this perpetual interference in the personal life of the citizens was arousing a feeling of disgust and hostility most destructive to patriotism. If patriotism was to be saved, the state would have to be conceived as no less "one," but united according to principles more in conformity with nature. "To the communes the affairs rightly communal, the provincial to the provinces; and let the superior organs of the nation, freed from all superfluous functions, preside with more of a spirit of continuity and vigor over the national destiny."[45] This would give the central government more stability and independence. As the guardian of the nation's unity, as the repository of its political traditions, and as the faithful trustee of the fortunes of the country, it would be able to conceive and undertake the long and vast designs "by which a people

decline of the country by conserving the home and restoring family life. Political decline would also cease because everyone would have a stake in the government (32-33). These corporations, although the workers might place their savings in them and thus become co-owners of the instruments of production, would be essentially associations of persons, not of capital. There would be a host of little autonomous states within the state, bound together by coördinating organisms, each exploiting its branch of industry in its local workshop under the protection of the state and in conditions guaranteeing the common good. In such a régime the usury and slavery of capitalism and socialism, respectively, would be obviated (93-100). The failure of several years of effort to organize the workers and employers on the basis of virtue or charity pointed to the necessity instituting the system by a law of the state (41). Such, briefly, was the plan of the Marquis to which Maurras frequently referred with favor in general terms, but which he never described in detail. Its essential agreement with his aesthetic view of order, with his emphasis of tradition, and with his federalist doctrine is, however, quite apparent. And now that Maurras was a monarchist their political views were similar. For the Marquis' anti-democratic views, consult his *La Représentation professionnelle* (Paris, 1905), *passim.*

45 *L'Idée de la décentralisation*, 44.

preserves and renews itself, remains free, and becomes powerful." [46]

It was somewhat in this manner that Maurras participated in the campaign for federalism and local autonomy prior to the outbreak of the Dreyfus dispute. We end our survey of his advocacy of federalism here, not because he ceased to support it, for he continued to plead for it at intervals both by presenting arguments for it and portraying the unique beauty of his own Provence and Martigues.[47] Among its aims, as we have seen, was the desire to tie his countrymen again to their roots, to give them something real to love, to stand and fight for as Frenchmen, and to prevent their being stifled and overcome by cosmopolitanism which, to him, was the negation of patriotism. Since the Dreyfus affair brought the issue of cosmopolitanism versus nationalism so sharply to the fore, it is now necessary to turn to the Drumontism in Maurras' nationalism.

46 *Ibid.*, 44.

47 Among the handy booklets in which these appear, are: J. Paul-Boncour and Charles Maurras, *La République et la décentralisation: un débat de 1903* (Paris, 1923), chapter II, "Que la république ne peut pas décentraliser"; Léon Daudet and Charles Maurras, *Notre Provence* (Paris, 1933), part II, "A Martigues"; *Quatre nuits de Provence* (Paris, 1930); *Corse et Provence* (Paris, 1930); *Les Secrets du soleil* (Paris, 1929).

CHAPTER XV

THE DRUMONTISM IN MAURRAS' NATIONALISM

ALTHOUGH Maurras had begun his attack upon the cosmopolitanism of French writers and artists early—it was, as we have seen, one of his objections to romanticism, as it was, likewise, one of his reasons for advocating federalism as a means of combating it—it was not until he joined Barrès at *La Cocarde* in 1894 that he showed unmistakable signs of Drumontism in a racial, economic, and political sense. In fact, he cast his first vote for the Jew, Naquet, even though, as he later insisted, he was already an anti-Semite at heart.[1] In November, 1894, Barrès warned his readers against the presence of 1,300,000 foreigners in the industries and professions of France. In an article which appeared in *La Cocarde* a month or so later Maurras gave these foreigners a name, *métèques* (metics), which he borrowed from the ancient Athenians and which has since come into more or less general use in France.[2]

What was a certificate of naturalization? he asked. Drumont had defined it as "a legal fiction which enables one to participate in the advantages of a nation, but which cannot in so doing give one its spirit." This, Maurras thought, was only too true. "Nature has intentions that assert themselves in the secret recesses of souls and bodies. . . . Such a naturalized person may be an excellent Frenchman from desire, from reflection, from consent, as the casuists say; but everything does not terminate with him; hence the importance of being on one's guard against his sons and grandsons. There is a physical life in them that may work against us." That this was not an idle ghost story was indicated by the behavior of these sons. Frightened or vexed by the blood tax, they chose the original nationality of their fathers, but remained in France to profit

1 *Au signe de Flore*, 17.

2 "Les Métèques," *La Cocarde*, Dec. 28, 1894.

from the common welfare which they refused to help defend. They likewise refused to serve their fatherland. One would think they would be ashamed of themselves, but there was an arrogance about them that was equaled only by the resignation with which they were being tolerated. In the evening they came as humble suppliants and the next morning the hospitable French awakened to find themselves their subjects and captives. But fortunately France was tired. They had abused her long enough. With nationalism and federalism making headway, thirty million Frenchmen were sighing for the departure or expulsion of thousands of these dangerous metics.

Athens had had her metics too. She tolerated them, even protected them by special laws. But she also imposed a special tax upon them so that they might not elevate themselves too high above the citizens proper. A special magistrate kept an eye on their conduct; they were asked to choose a patron and a surety from among the Athenians; they were not allowed to own Athenian soil; they were often forced to row the Athenian ships and to perform other laborious and humiliating tasks; their wives and daughters held parasols over the heads of Athenian women at the Panathenaic festivals. This was justice itself. Those who objected were, of course, free to leave. If the metics of France were forced to submit to a similar régime, they would doubtless be less insolent and less "daring in treason." Even the Dreyfuses would have a respect born of fear which a Jewish prophet once said was the principle of wisdom.[3]

3 "J'ai tenté," he said about a month later, "de montrer la gravité de ce mouvement. Et j'espère bien l'avoir fait sans passion personnelle. Le nom dont j'ai voulu désigner ces étrangers qui s'incorporent si difficilement à nos races était d'origine athénienne. Il n'enfermait point de mépris. Hospitalier, gracieux, cordial, même carressant, ce nom de Métèques veut dire: 'ceux qui habitent avec nous', 'ceux qui sont de notre maison (sans être tout à fait des nôtres)', 'ceux que nous souffrons volontiers sous notre toit'." France had no objection to their presence so long as they observed certain rules of modesty and decency. But the French were not protected as the Athenians had once been. Hence the following: "Il faut ou renoncer à sa sécurité et à la vie tranquille sur la terre des ses ancêtres au se résoudre à

"Nature has intentions that assert themselves in the secret recesses of souls and bodies. . . ." This suggests a racial determinism that makes the amalgamation of different peoples an impossibility. Nevertheless, we find Maurras saying not more than three months later that the Celts and the Romans had coalesced, that they had resisted the Normans as they had opposed the Goths and the Franks, and that they had imposed their language, their arts, letters, and political institutions upon their conquerors.[4] Their unity or uniformity of custom, spirit, language, and possibly blood had created *one* France. He ad-

faire sa police soi-même" ("Les Murailles d'Antibes," *La Cocarde*, Jan. 25, 1895).

It is only fair to say that while Michel Clerc substantiated most of the above in his *Les Métèques athéniens* (Paris, 1893), adding even the prohibition of the right of intermarriage between metics and Athenians (79), the duty of the male metics to carry vessels filled with honey and cakes for the Athenians at the Panathenaic festivals (154), and that their sons were not admitted to the gymnastic and military schools of the ephebus until the second century B. C. (38-39), he stressed the point that, except for the restrictions noted, they enjoyed the protection of the civil law of the Athenians, that the murder of a metic carried the penalty of exile rather than death (there was little to choose between them, he thought), that in commercial affairs there was no differentiation of rights (114), while in the matter of religion they were allowed by special permit to establish their own cults and to erect their own appropriate temples (120-121). "Sur ce point (religion) donc, comme en ce qui concerne la justice, Athènes s'est montrée fort libérale, par tempérament assurément, mais aussi et surtout par intérêt: rien ne pouvait plus contribuer à attirer et retenir les métèques que cette assurance qu'ils trouveraient à Athènes, entourés de compatriotes, leurs sanctuaires, leurs dieux et leurs rites nationaux" (123). Some were ambassadors; more were tax farmers and contractors for public works (ch. VIII). He did say that the people (*demos*) treated them as equals and that they demanded that the aristocratic citizens do likewise. Their presence, he added, weakened prejudices and pride and made for democracy as well as for economic development (448).

If these results followed from the presence of the metics in Athens despite the restrictions we have noted, it is not to be wondered that Maurras was gravely concerned over their greater numbers and greater freedom in France. For however Athens may have benefited from their presence, the weakening of her pride, the decline of her traditions, and the rise of democracy were too high a price in any event.

4 "Société d'ethnographie nationale," *La Gazette de France*, Mar. 26, 1895.

mitted that race in a physical sense had doubtless been exaggerated; but he declared that he, too, was a "racialist" along with Gaston Méry and others. He believed, as did they, that there was a "French race." [5] It, too, was born much as was France. "It is from the Gallo-Roman type, combined in the course of five centuries and augmented by barbarous elements earnestly assimilated, that it is necessary to proceed in order to conceive and define the French type." [6] Rome's work of assimilation and organization was later continued by the Church and the Capetian monarchs. It was from them that the French "race" derived its ability to organize and direct, its "masculine" traits; its "feminine" qualities came from Celtic and German sources. Gaul may have been a woman, but not France; for France, the "most beautiful force of modern times," resulted from the union of the "Gallic tumult" and the "Roman order." [7] If France was feminine, the Celtic soul was nothing less than anarchic. And, in view of the French Revolution and the destructive work of romanticism, it appeared that this original Celtic genius was reappearing everywhere and, with it, the spectre of civil war. France was in a dissociated and chaotic condition because this Celtic genius, having broken its former happy union with the Roman, had gotten out of hand. As for the metics and the alien ideas [8] with which France was encumbered, they were simply making the confusion the more confounded.

5 *Idem, ibid.*

6 "La Guerre des Gaules" (Nov. 3, 1901), *Gaulois, Germains, Latins* (*Extraits*), in *Les Cahiers d'Occident* (Paris, 1926), I, 1, p. 17.

7 *Ibid.*, 18-19.

8 Ideas, along with customs and institutions, were particularly vital "racial" factors. "Si l'on accorde aux moeurs d'une nation la moindre importance, il faut tenir compte des idées, qui en font, pour une part considérable, les ingrédients et les composants. Quelle part? J'avancerai que les idées sont peut-être le plus subtil, le plus délicat et le plus profond de la vie morale; elles sont à sa fleur en même temps qu'à sa racine. Et que le sort de ces idées esthétiques et directrices ait parfois dépendu de l'issue d'un combat [that between individualism and order in the religious wars of the sixteenth century], l'histoire entière me dispensera de vous le démontrer" ("La Guerre religieuse," *La Gazette de France*, Mar. 23, 1898).

Of the permanent chasm that persisted between the French "race" and some of the metics of France Maurras found a convincing demonstration in the history of the family of Gabriel Monod in which he became interested early in the summer of 1897.[9] Gabriel Monod, the author of *Allemands et Français* (1871) and latterly of *Portraits et souvenirs*, a leading opponent of Fustel de Coulanges in the latter's late years, currently director of the *Revue historique*, an influential figure among French historians, and something of an exponent of German historiography,[10] he had already attracted Maurras' attention, when, by chance, a book, *La Famille Monod, portraits et souvenirs*, written by Gustave Monod, the historian's uncle, fell into his hands.[11] Maurras' discovery of the foreign origin of this powerful and influential family left him dumbfounded. Here was an example, as if made to order, of the point he had made on the rôle of the metics in France in his article in *La Cocarde*.

He promptly began to denounce the family in strong terms in the columns of *La Gazette de France;* but, when the professor became a prominent Dreyfusard, Maurras saw greater possibilities in the materials he had at hand. He conceived a book of which the title would be *Les Monod peints par eux-mêmes* and had considerable amusement working on it in his spare time during the next few years.[12]

With an epigraph from Edouard Drumont at its beginning,[13] he dwells upon the dignities and honors of the historian,

9 *Au signe de Flore*, 150, 156; *cf.* "La Politique des Monod," *La Gazette de France*, June 27, 1897; "Autour de l'affaire Dreyfus," *La Gazette de France*, Jan. 9, 1898.

10 "Sentinelle allemande dans l'université," *Quand les Français ne s'aimaient pas* (Paris, 1926), 62-92.

11 *Au signe de Flore*, 150, 167.

12 First published at intervals in the *Action française* from Oct. 1, 1899 to Aug., 1902. The "essential" was published in *Au signe de Flore* (Paris, 1931), 155-240. *Cf. La Gazette de France* of Jan. 31, Feb. 1, and Apr. 26, 1899, in which the Monods are delightfully described as "a tribe of savages."

13 "Quand le jour du châtiment sera arrivé... ou la minorité qui se

upon his high praise of German music, science, and philosophy, and upon the reasons why, though a friend of the enemy, he was able to hold these important positions. This last is largely due to the fact that the French families have been reduced to father, mother, and child, with each more or less a free agent, while the Monod family is a " splendid, spontaneous federation, formed, it is true, of adversaries of the tradition of France, but solid and strong, it to-day numbers more than two hundred flourishing units." [14] Loyally grouped around their natural chiefs, impervious to the influence of French customs, they constitute a " tribe " of two hundred and fifty which is pitted against each single Frenchman.[15] This explains why three of the forty males of the family have chairs in the academies: one in the Institute, and two in the Academy of Medicine. Others stand high in French Protestantism, in business—even in the feminist movement. All Frenchmen are destined to succumb, therefore, to the blows of this tribe unless the Monod State within the French State is destroyed, and unless the French families are reconstituted. This last can be done most expeditiously by abolishing the law of equal succession. If it is asking too much to demand the restoration of the right of the oldest, a convenient minimum would be to accept the principle of the free testation of property. This would be a good beginning, but there must also be a revolt against Monodism, the civil, economic, and political predominance of a few foreign families among Frenchmen. " We are already the subjects of our metics. Are we to be serfs? Are we going to submit to another barbarian invasion?" This will transpire unless a methodical and energetic revolt overturns the Monod State.[16]

permet de tels actes, vous entendrez ces hommes, si grossiers dans le succès, si plats quand la chance a tourné, recommencer à bêler leurs discours sur la tolérance... (1886), *Au signe de Flore*, 155.

14 *Ibid.*, 161-162.

15 *Ibid.*, 163.

16 *Ibid.*, 166-167.

The constitution of this state is characteristically its family-tree. Jacques Monod, when Henry IV annexed Gex to France at the close of the sixteenth century, left his native country and moved to the canton of Vaud. His male successors in the seventeenth and eighteenth centuries moved their habitats in each generation. In 1765 Jean Monod was born. He emigrated to Copenhagen, where he married Louise-Philippine de Coninck who bore him one child in Switzerland, six in Denmark, and five in Paris, where they settled in 1808. Having no home or homeland, they flitted back and forth across the map of Europe. Now the French, who are no longer vagabonds, have a decent attachment for their paternal homes; not so the Monods who, like the Jews, are deprived of this sentiment.[17] The Jews, it is true, do have a mystical fatherland, their restored Jerusalem. The Monods, on the other hand, have neither fatherland, habitat, nor sepulchre. Nothing binds them to the soil. If they have roots, they are frail and short. Their bonds are personal bonds: caprice, desires, interests. Fundamental to them is the tribal tie of the Monod State. Modern France has pleased them; but it may cease to do so, for Gabriel is reported to have said in 1875 that, if the reactionaries won over the Republicans in their dispute over the constitution, he would prefer to leave France. More recently, when Dreyfusism seemed to be at the point of defeat, he again expressed a desire for a change of air. "Capricious, but exacting residents of the countries that have received them, they are not French. One need not complain about it. But one need not ignore it." [18]

"All immigration is not mischievous." A hundred Italian laborers settled at Istres in the middle of the nineteenth century. They have added to the beauty, health, and strength of the Provençals of the district. Their children are truly French. Not so the Monods. Upon their own admission, they are not handsome or beautiful. According to Adèle, one of the twelve children of Jean, her brother Valdemar was "ugly," resem-

17 *Ibid.*, 173.

18 *Ibid.*, 175-176.

bling a "monkey." [19] Their health has been no better than their appearance. Edouard, father of the historian Gabriel, died mentally deranged, having suffered several cerebral congestions. But it is Guillaume, known as Billy to his friends, who illustrates this weakness of the family best. He suffered from a disease which alienists labeled "religious monomania." He insisted that he heard a voice that revealed to him that he was the Christ returned to earth to save men and that he must act in that capacity. Upon one occasion he escaped from his caretakers and went to the Tuileries to protest the action of the Consistory in removing him from his pastorate and placing him under observation. He was held and later returned to his father's home with the request that he be placed in an institution for nervous diseases. He was placed in the care of an English physician near Bristol, was released upon a formal retraction of his claims, retracted his retraction, and, "to spare the king of the French another colloquy," he was persuaded to go to Switzerland, where he won a few disciples. Returning to Paris later, he had about forty converts at the time of his death. While Edouard's softening of the brain gives us an exact picture of the average mentality of the family, "this Guillaume was, by way of retaliation, a fool of some distinction." [20]

The French need not be alarmed over the purity of their race, with such "monkeys" and fools in their midst. The Monods guard their own racial integrity. They have no ambition to change the blood of their fellow citizens. Their hope is, in time, to replace the population of France. "M. Gabriel Monod, in a letter dated June 27, 1897, exposed this part of the program of his family: 'The other Frenchmen no longer having children, one can mathematically calculate the moment when we shall be the *only ones* in France . . . .' [21] The last of

19 *Ibid.*, 179.

20 *Ibid.*, 182.

21 "Le mot souligné enveloppe une délicate plaisanterie de professeur. *Monos* en grec veut dire seul, M. Gabriel Monod estime que ses congénères

the French, condemned to the fate of the Aztecs, will salute at death the face of a rejuvenated Gaul, renewed by a tribe of forty million gorillas, eighty per cent of whom will be subject to paroxisms of religious monomania or liable to the softening of the brain."[22] No one will object to this last figure when it is considered that two out of the twelve had mental diseases and that the ratio can be expected to increase in later generations. Proof of this is seen in the fact that of the two hundred and fifty living Monods only three have been able to refuse to place their names on the Dreyfus or Picquart lists.

How this Monod State introduced itself into the French State is well illustrated by a letter which Jean, father of the twelve, wrote to a Parisian bookseller in October, 1793. In it he ordered a list of books which he hoped to secure at a reduction in price. Judging from the list, his library shelves must have been empty. But the Revolution and especially the year 1793, when everything was sold for a bite of bread, created an enviable situation for those in a position to demand the libraries, furniture, and the like of the aristocrats at a reduction. Many Europeans were prevented from taking advantage of this situation by the war. But our Genevan pastor, citizen of a neighboring neutral state, was able to do so and was, therefore, among the "first foreigners who participated in the liquidation of France."[23] The revolutionists stole and plundered the national goods and sold them to the first comers. Old France was bartered away for money. Meanwhile the bourgeoisie became princes. Their good fortune, as well as that of the peasants and soldiers, blinded them to the slow and crafty conquest that menaced them. The old orders would have prevented this conquest, but they were destroyed; and the Rights of Man delivered both person and property to these insidious immigrant-conquerors.

justifieront l'étymologie. Les Uniques, les Seuls-de-leur espèce seront aussi les Seuls-en-France" (*ibid.*, 183).

22 *Ibid.*, 183-184.

23 *Ibid.*, 188.

Jean Monod's first contact with France was a profitable one. In 1794 he was recalled to Denmark to the home of his wife. He went, but with him went also the desire to take further advantage of France's weakness. In 1798 he made his first visit to Paris. Here, in addition to preaching to fellow Calvinists, he observed the affects of the laws of 1790 which emancipated the Jews and recalled the exiled Huguenot families. He likewise noticed the curious fact that the metics, because their coming represented an act of will, were ranked above native-born Frenchmen in the moral hierarchy. When, therefore, he received a call from Paris to serve there as a pastor, he was glad to change his habitat. Although he was paid by the state, its autocratic nature inspired him with a certain fear. He, therefore, daily prayed God to save the little Monod State against this monster that could so easily devour it. He should either destroy it outright or so weaken it that it would no longer be an object of fear. Whether or not God heard and executed the request, the desired development transpired. Liberal opinion saw to that, especially after 1830.

It is this weakness of the French State that has given the Monod State its power. Its enormous administrative machine, having usurped so many civic rights, has long ceased to function in the national interest. Uncontrolled by the Chambers, it has pursued its own interests or those of the metics who control it. University professors such as Anatole France's Lucien Bergeret are absolutely at the mercy of the Monod State despite their greater wisdom and erudition. They must conciliate the Monod State, as Bergeret was forced to do, if they wish to advance. This being the situation in education, how long will it be before the entire administrative system will have fallen into a state of slavery to a " foreign horde?"

In order to remain united, which is a necessary condition of the maintenance of their State and of its dominance, the Monods have carefully nurtured and protected the foreign in their character. That the Monod type is alien, non-French (whether it be Danish, Swiss, or Dutch is immaterial), is unquestionable. Their interest and their most deep-rooted sentiment has been to hold on to the other Monods. Together they can shut themselves up in their citadel until adverse winds have blown over. And what method has the Monod State used to insure the permanence of the alien character of its citizens? Its answer is, "By blood"[24]—that is, by marital alliances with foreigners or by inter-tribal marriages. It is true that Edouard, the fifth of the twelve, married into an Alsatian French family. Their children, because they were half French, were closely watched and carefully trained in the Monod tradition. The oldest, Fanny, married an English merchant of Russian origins.[25] Gabriel, her brother and our historian, who prates so much about his French mother in order to convince others of his patriotism, nevertheless married Olga Herzen, a Russian. Two of their children have given full satisfaction to the genius of their race. One, Edouard, has distinguished himself by his extreme hatred of the army, while the other, a daughter, is rumored to have named her dog after General de Boisdeffre.[26]

This implacable hatred of the Monod State for that of France began when, years ago, France committed a wrong against it that has not yet been expiated. Jacques Monod, who was a better nationalist than patriot, was driven from Gex when that district was annexed by Henry IV by his desire to remain a Swiss. The revocation of the Edict of Nantes by Louis XIV had no direct effect upon the Monod State because there were

24 *Ibid.*, 209.

25 "Est-ce bien russe qu'il faut dire? Il s'appelait Alexandre von Glehn. Il devait être au moin de quelque province baltique..." (*ibid.*, 215).

26 Gabriel Monod, in a letter, dated Feb. 3, 1900, objected to the charges made against his children, saying that they had had only one dog, named Flick, which died in 1898. His son, he asserted, was quite justified in his indignation in view of the admissions made by the officer with whom the trouble arose. Of the 103 marriages of the Monod family after 1793 only 22 were with foreigners, he said. Five days later, in another letter, he emphasized the fact that 81 of the 103 marriages were with French men or women. These letters only served to bring sharper shafts from Maurras' armory which, in turn, finally led to a duel (*ibid.*, 226-227).

no Monods in France at the time. When the Revolution added Geneva to the territory of France Jean Monod was in Denmark. But this annexation, nevertheless, legally converted him into a French citizen. As we have seen, he later came to Paris to take advantage of his new nationality. But he succeeded in having this quality limited to himself, even though his oldest son was born in Geneva. The latter was thus able, though nineteen years of age, to "dodge" Napoleon's draft law of 1813 which was applicable to boys of fifteen. The Monods, though they were prospering, refused to pay the blood tax. When, in 1814, the campaign was wholly defensive, Frédêric was twenty; but he found pleasure in repeating to himself that he was not French. Once peace was made, he suddenly became possessed by the desire to become French, for he had to be a citizen to become an employee of the State in the capacity of a Protestant minister. Meanwhile, the other sons and daughters considered themselves fellow citizens of their Danish mother until Benjamin Constant, also a Swiss citizen, announced in the "matchless" Chamber that, according to the law of 1790, all Frenchmen who were exiled in the time of Louis XIV on ground of religion were declared natural Frenchmen. They now busied themselves to discover a kinship with such an exile, or exiles, in the hope of obtaining the status of French citizenship. This they found, as if made to order, in an ancestress of their mother, a certain Rachel d'Amberbos. There was some difficulty in proving this to the authorities, for there was a delay of five years in granting their petition. The grant came only after the July Revolution. If their story is to be accepted, as it apparently was by the authorities, it is but a small and pale drop of French blood that flows in their veins. It is, as it were, an exile; but it has given the others a patent of fellow citizenship.

One would think that the Monods would be thankful for this exchange, since it has brought them so much. Instead, Dr. Gustave refers to his mother's departure from her paternal home in Denmark as a "painful sacrifice." God blessed the sacrifice, it is true, and, when he reflected upon the good fortune of the Twelve, his heart overflowed with gratitude toward his "parents and toward God." There is, however, not a suspicion of gratitude for the bounty of the soil or for the kindness of the nation that received and endowed them. On the contrary, in this book which was avowedly written "for the instruction and edification of the future generations of the Monods" he says, after referring to the fact that the oldest sons were considered Danes in 1813 and 1814, "The advantage was precious for my older brothers: it was in the last years of the first Empire, the time when Napoleon was draining France of all its young men to make of them cannon meat."[27] Then, after being told how they finally secured their coveted French citizenship, the reader is confronted with the following edifying passage: "It follows from these facts that, since 1830, we have enjoyed the rights of Frenchmen, even though we have not submitted to all the burdens. Our ancestors suffered enough from the crime committed by Louis XIV for this tardy and feeble reparation to have been due their descendants."[28] This is the official Monod tradition. France once wronged them; she must, therefore, make reparations and continue to do so to future Monod generations. Combining complaints and menaces, they demand the right to despoil France, meanwhile promising a pardon which they have no intention of giving. Such is the law of the Monodian conqueror.[29]

27 Quoted by Maurras, *ibid.*, 237.

28 Quoted by Maurras (*ibid.*, 238-239).

29 In 1912 the "ex-dictator" of French history teaching died, saddened by and despairing of the nationalism of the youth of France. There was therefore, no appeasement in his life time. It came later as the achievement of France herself. "De l'air français aux eaux, aux vins, aux fruits, aux arts et aux lettres de la patrie, du pur froment de France à la 'rose de France', une action convergente, extrêmement profonde et non moins étendue, s'exerçait sur les coeurs, les esprits, les corps des Monod" (*ibid.*, 242). Early in the conquest of Morocco one of the Monods was killed in battle. Other Monods fought heroically in the World War. Maurras was mollified. Writing in 1931, he noted that two Monods were members of the *Ligue*

As we have seen, the Dreyfus affair and, particularly, Gabriel Monod's rôle in it so stirred Maurras' wrath that he made much more use of the materials he had at hand concerning the Monod family than he had originally intended. This same affair and the spirit of combat that it aroused provoked anti-Semitic articles and statements from Maurras which Drumont must have prized highly. Bitterly partisan they were, though less hostile to the race, as such, than Drumont's writings. It was the political and economic power that the Jews wielded in France and the philosophy and its corresponding political system that enabled them to lord it over the French proper that aroused both his ire and fear. That Dreyfus was guilty went without saying. And when the press reported that the "traitor's" two brothers, Mathieu and Paul, had been called before the bar and had been formally accused, he hailed the news as "delightful music."[30] Commenting upon the observations of the Marquis de La Tour du Pin on the Jews, he welcomed them as verifying the statements of Drumont. The Jews were truly succeeding in their self-imposed task of decomposing the French nation and were dreaming of raising the walls of Solomon. Religion, family, and property were the foundations of their City which was less a place or habitat than a concept or "social *milieu*." Jehovah had promised them the empire of the world; and, given their essential unity despite their dissemination throughout the world and with their exceeding cleverness in finance, they were already well on the way to achieving it.[31] In fact their rise to world dominance had been relatively easy once they had destroyed the religious unity of the world by the Reformation and the political unity of the world by the Revolution. That France was conquered

d'Action française and that the Monods were no longer Simian in appearance, many even being beautiful. For these changes Maurras gave thanks "to the spirit and to the body of the common mother, notre France, maîtresse aux divines métamorphoses."

30 "Autour de l'affaire Dreyfus," *La Gazette de France*, Jan. 9, 1898.

31 "Intermède philosophique: la Cité juive," *La Gazette de France*, Jan. 4, 1899.

was only too clear. Their power in the French educational system, in politics, and finance was unquestioned. Moreover, their numbers were growing while those of the French were not. The Marquis rightly favored treating them as aliens, forcing them to abjure their errors, and excluding them from the economic and political life of France. "Certainly, a bloody repression is inevitable," Maurras concluded; "although certain inexpiable crimes entail the penalty of penalties, it must be as short and as moderate as possible." [32]

The Jews were presumably not all bad.[33] Some, certainly, were worse than others. Joseph Reinach, for example, was "the most authentic game for the guillotine" one could find on earth. "The daily outrage of this German Jew against the soul of the fatherland designates him for capital punishment. Let the penalty be inflicted as soon as possible. I desire and demand it . . . ," Maurras exclaimed.[34] He added, however, that, since he had no desire to suffer with him, he wanted it done with justice and reason. He, therefore, counseled wisdom, though violent measures would be necessary before long. They should husband their strength, for revolutions were troublesome and tended to get out of hand. Once the State were "methodically reconstituted," it would strike those who deserved it. In such a régime the mere mention of their crimes would entail death. Joseph Reinach, this "professor of impudence," [35] this "unparalleled model of hypocrisy and fraud" would be dealt with as his uncle should have been handled [36]—

32 "Intermède philosophique : les solutions de la question juive," *La Gazette de France*, Jan. 7, 1899.

33 The following, however, reflects his view. more faithfully : "Ces ennemis du genre humain n'y sont pas à leur place. L'idée de nation les insulte. Ils ne connaissent pour un peuple que le leur : de cent peuples fondus, dénationalisés, leur rêve d'avenir est de fonder une gentilité unique d'où ils puissent tirer l'esclave universel" (*Quand les Français ne s'aimaient pas*, 13).

34 "Sagesse ! Sagesse !," *La Gazette de France*, Feb. 9, 1899.

35 "M. Joseph Reinach," *La Gazette de France*, Apr. 30, 1899.

36 Henri Dutrait-Crozon, *Joseph Reinach historien: revision de l'histoire de l'affaire Dreyfus*, preface by Maurras (Paris, 1905, two volumes in one), I, ix-x.

that is, with quick, certain, and condign punishment. One who daily insulted the French army and, at the same time, claimed to be a better patriot than those who defended it deserved summary treatment. With an unbelievable effrontery, he argued that his patriotism and that of his Dreyfusard friends was purer and finer than that of the Nationalists, because, instead of rising from the soil, it came, as did Justice, from the purest recesses of the skies. The Jews, he claimed, were twice French, whereas the Nationalists were only once, for the French Jews were not only born French, they were also French from choice. Their one desire was to show their gratitude to the people who had freed them. The Nationalists would give up their lives for the fatherland; but the Jews loved it so much that they were prepared to sacrifice its " mortal image " and its territorial possessions. Moreover, they were better patriots in that they had a higher destiny for France. She was to be forever the " Christ of the nations," the sacrificial lamb on the altar of Justice. But this " simpleton " of a Reinach should have known that the progress of justice depended upon the maintenance of society, that, without it, there was no hope of justice, and that the " first justice is to respect it "—i.e., society. No one should be allowed, therefore, to claim the right to overthrow everything because of a supposed judicial error that has not been proved.[37] As for Reinach's history of the Affair, it was "one of the worst works in the world." That of Dutrait-Crozon, on the other hand, should either not exist at all or be one of the best in the French language. "It is," he concluded, " an anti-Jewish treatise. It is, therefore, in a word, a manual of patriotism. I do not know that, since the books of Drumont and of Barrès, anyone has written anything better for France." [38]

The foregoing clearly establishes, it would seem, the Drumontism of Maurras. Drumont, the Jew-baiter, was, it is true, an individualist; and his style, though strong at times in mat-

37 *Ibid.*, xix-xx.

38 *Ibid.*, xliv.

ters of detail, was weak in organization and consistency. But his glory was elsewhere: it lay in his having opened a passage into which high-spirited men of action could hurl themselves.[39] Writing in 1917, at the time of Drumont's death, Maurras, after repeating Léon Daudet's tribute to him, added, "Yes, the generation that was eighteen years old in the year of *La France juive* is wholly the debtor of Edouard Drumont. This great Frenchman oriented it toward the political truth. Completing and perfecting Taine, his just and profound criticism from the outset made the most important realities of the life of a people, the soil and the blood, felt. Completing and perfecting Déroulède, Drumont's work also showed what had to be done within the country in order to recover Metz and Strasbourg. The nationalist formula was thus born almost entirely from him; and Daudet, Barrès, all of us began our work in his light. We thanked him for it every day during his life. This admiration and this gratitude should have cheered him on his deathbed."[40] Maurras' foes, however great their hatred of him may be, cannot truthfully impugn his loyalty to his masters and to his principles.

39 *L'Observateur français,* Mar. 21, 1890, in D. P. & C., I, 394.

40 *Action française,* Feb. 6, 1917, in D. P. & C., I, 395.

CHAPTER XVI

MAURRAS' CONVERSION TO ROYALISM

EXCEPT for his Epicurean aestheticism which was the basis or pattern of his philosophical system, it may be said that Maurras was in substantial agreement with Barrès in respect to two of the basic elements of their common nationalism: Taineism and Drumontism. We may now ask if the same was true of Barrès' Boulangism.

When, in 1889, Maurras cast his first vote, it was, as we have seen, for the Jew, Naquet, one of Boulanger's ablest political lieutenants. That Maurras was on this occasion a better Boulangist than anti-Semite is evident. Although he described this period of his life as one of "almost complete philosophical absorption",[1] when his reaction to active politics was one of revulsion, he was not so completely engrossed in his intellectual pleasures or so disinterested in politics that he took no interest, for example, in the Wilson scandal of 1887. At this time he joined thousands of other Parisians, many of whom were Boulangists, in crying "Down with the thieves!"[2] However, as the party strife became more heated and the movement brought a national awakening, especially when it began to attract the conservative elements of the country, Maurras gradually lost his "horror" of politics and finally cast his lot with the movement. It was, indeed, his love for the General that determined his vote of 1889.[3]

The conservatives needed disciplining and here was the disciplinarian who could do it. Moreover, Germany needed to be reduced to her proper place in European affairs and here was the man around whom a united France could achieve the desired end. Maurras, it is true, had been younger than Barrès

1 Pages 113-114, above.

2 Nevertheless, his first reaction to the General's movement was one of dislike because of its "demagogic aspect."

3 "Confession politique," *Au signe de Flore*, 16-17.

in 1870 and had been far removed from the actual theatre of warfare; but, amidst the Boulangist agitation, he now recalled how, as a child not three years old, he had seen his father and mother, with tears in their eyes, bend over a great atlas as they tried to trace the course of the invasion. He recalled the refugees from Metz and other sections of the conquered provinces whom he later met in Aix and remembered how one family on certain days took from a lock-box small pieces of black bread, the bread of the siege, wrapped in scraps of silk, and piously passed them around from hand to hand as though they were relics. Several of his professors, moreover, were Lorraine refugees; and, though they were serious at times, it was their gaiety that astonished the youthful Maurras. In Paris, he sought out Barrès, René Marc Ferry, General Mercier, and other " men of the East." Wishing as a Felibrian to restore the liberties of his Provence as a means of bringing about the " reconstruction of the French energies," he quite naturally shared their desire to recover the lost provinces.[4]

In general, however, his distaste of politics was such that he gave it little time or thought. His activities as a member of the Ecole romane, of the Félibrige of Paris (even after 1892, when he and Amouretti sought to give its program a political orientation), and as a co-laborer with Barrès in erecting the " first bastions of the intellectual nationalism " [5] were predicated upon the principle of persuasion rather than that of force.[6]

4 *Ibid.*, 42-43.

5 " La Jeunesse lettrée en 1895," *Quand les français ne s'aimaient pas*, 14.

6 In this regard he may be said to have followed the strategy of another one of his masters, Le Play, who described the methods of his social groups as follows: " . . . Nous demandons uniquement à la persuasion la réforme qui, au milieu des grands événements de l'histoire, fut trop souvent imposée par la force " [Frédéric Le Play, " La Méthode d'observation," *Les Ouvriers européens*, 2nd edition (Paris, 1879), I, 290]. " . . . Nous avons fondé l'école de la paix sociale pour *enseigner* ' la constitution essentielle des sociétés ' " (*ibid.*, I, 595). "Les membres des Unions trouvent, dans leur Bibliothèque, un moyen utile de provoquer cette réforme; mais leur vrai moyen d'action est dans les exemples et dans les leçons qu'ils donnent à ceux qui les entourent " (" Les Ouvriers de l'Occident," *ibid.*, VI, 560).

By 1890 Boulangism was patently a failure. When, therefore, Leo XIII announced that the Catholics of France would do well to accept the Republic, Maurras considered it a wise move, for it severed the Church from the " corpse " of the old parties on the Right.[7] He was so impressed with the Pope's astuteness that he contributed a number of articles, chiefly on literary subjects, to the *Observateur français,* the chief organ of the *ralliement.* However, the Right Republican parties soon impressed him as being not much more alive than their neighbors to the right. He was, in fact, confused and frankly admitted to Barrès upon one occasion, that he did not know where he was going.[8] His own doctrine, to be sure, made reproaches; but, although he admitted that democracy was bad, he thought " it was definitive and insurmountable." [9] The idea implied by *Les Serviteurs,* written in 1891, was truth itself; but it was perhaps too idealistic. The monarchy was dead, he felt. The Count of Paris was known to favor parliamentary government and a parliamentary monarchy disagreed with the " essential postulates " of his studies quite as much as did the parliamentary Republic. Moreover, he had no faith in the possibility of an Orleanist restoration. A fifth dynasty there might be, but not that.[10]

That he was an ardent nationalist, that he wanted France to be great and strong, that he felt that she could be made so by reviving the classical tradition in art and literature, by decentralizing the government and keeping a heavy hand on the metics, that these were certainties to him is unquestionable. It was the form of the central government that France should have that gave him trouble. That, and the doctrine of Déroulède and his followers. They were zealous nationalists; they preferred an authoritarian or dictatorial government to parliamentary rule; they advocated a strong army and powerful allies

7 " Confession politique," *Au signe de Flore,* 17.

8 *Ibid.,* 18.

9 *Ibid.,* 16.

10 *Ibid.,* 17.

against the day when France should choose to strike for revenge—all of which was good from Maurras' standpoint. In this period of uncertainty and turmoil in his political thinking, therefore, the Boulangist plebiscite-dictatorship appeared to him to be the likeliest means of attaining the desired moral and material rehabilitation of France. As late as Jan. 20, 1895, in an article [11] in *La Cocarde,* he asked, if the federal system they were advocating were introduced, what form the central government should assume. His answer was that the people were clearly demanding "Someone." Hearing this cry repeated, almost as a chant, by the "heart of France," he reflected that, since history has always seen the apparently contradictory principles of "authority and liberty," "local autonomy and the strengthening of the executive power" grow and diminish in concert, they must "attract, require, and mutually postulate each other." Later, soon after Barrès and his friends had broken with the owner of *La Cocarde,* Maurras visited his friends, Amouretti and Joseph Bérenger, at Cannes. They discussed the possibility of reviving at Paris the *Réveil de la Provence* which his two friends had published locally in 1888 and 1889. It was to do much the same thing *La Cocarde* had done under Barrès except that the ideas of the nineteenth century masters of conservative reform, which the Rightists had permitted to disappear into semi-obscurity, were to be stressed again. They agreed that decentralization could be achieved only through the central government. Then, again, arose the question, "But what government?" Amouretti and Bérenger, both militant royalists, replied without hesitation that a monarchical (Orleanist) government was necessary. Maurras, however, asked "if their dynastic flag would not hinder precisely the impulsion of the movement desired," [12] in view of the fact that the royalists were weakened and discredited by the failure of the Boulangist movement and the action of Pope Leo XIII.

11 "Une France fédérative."

12 *Au signe de Flore,* 40.

Political strategy, therefore, attracted him to the solution advocated by Dérouléde and Barrés. This, however, demanded an elected dictator and was, therefore, predicated upon an essentially democratic principle. Feeling that democracy had come to stay, being too powerfully intrenched to be dislodged, Maurras was not prepared to flout it openly, even though it was the political and social counter-part of all that he considered bad in art and philosophy. He even gave it some lip-service. But, as he became increasingly convinced that the objectives he and his friends considered so necessary to the rehabilitation of France depended upon a political solution, he gradually overcame his earlier dislike of politics and became proportionately interested in political theory. He began, with the aid of Le Play, de Bonald, Joseph de Maîstre, and others, to apply his Epicurean-Comtian preconceptions to the field of politics. This was an interesting and fascinating game, though considerations of strategy delayed his acting upon the conclusions to which his studies led. That some of these were quite definite is indicated by his *Méditation*,[13] written in 1901. Since he has, however, described the first part of it as conforming to his sentiments as an isolated spectator" in the years from 1892 to 1895,[14] we may well give it some consideration.

This brief monologue was suggested by a statement of Hecateus of Miletus which he had found in a book of Henri Ouvré. According to the latter, the ancient logographer began one of his works with these words: "I, Hecateus the Milesian, I say these things and I write as they appear to me, because, in my opinion, the vain discourses of the Athenians are numerous and ridiculous." Ruminating upon the fearlessness of this ancient chronicler and upon the gratitude which hundreds of men in the ages since have had reason to feel for him, Maurras felt constrained to add the following words of praise to the many that had gone before with what may be regarded a touch of self-praise—certainly self-justification: "By his desire to

13 Republished with comments in *Au signe de Flore* (Paris, 1931), 19-30.

14 *Ibid.*, 27.

possess the truth, to extricate it from the 'it-is-said' and to isolate it from the contradictions of man, this clumsy critic, this humble and awkward collector of facts shares in the majesty of human knowledge. He gave it his contribution. . . . To be right is still one of the ways in which man perpetuates himself; to be right and to change the "numerous and ridiculous" discourses of one's fellow citizens, Hellene or French, in a small number of coherent and reasonable propositions, is, if one has achieved it only at one point, the master-stroke of energy." [15]

After noting the changes that analysis and knowledge have wrought in geography and history, fields in which Hecateus pioneered, Maurras admits that it was to politics, rather than to these, that his statement attracted his attention. For it is in politics that there is such a "frightful chaos of absurdities" that the ancient geographer, who lived in a time when political wisdom was almost as necessary as accurate commercial information is now, could have had no conception of it. In his day the homes were the foundation-stones of the cities, while in this it is difficult to persuade a small group of reasonable people to accept these two self-evident and interdependent propositions: (1) "The individual is not a social unit; (2) the first social unit is the family." [16] It is only by dint of endless discussion that one wins their acceptance of these truths. To say that minds are weak and brains soft, and that other interests occupy the wise, is to make excuses that have some value; but they are not sufficient. Some minds are good. Some strong spirits have even given this subject some thought and have "thought the truth." "We have," he informs Hecateus, "a mathematical philosopher, born in the South, who by the mathematical route has found and proven that, in reality, the individual is not a social unit and that the first social unit is the family. We have also had the same proposition discovered and demonstrated by a natural philosopher, born in the North, and

15 *Ibid.*, 20-21.

16 *Ibid.*, 23.

who has used in his discovery and proofs of this only the method of the experimental sciences. The first of these philosophers believed neither in God nor the devil. The other, dear Milesian, was a pious Christian. If the proofs of one or the other, if the proofs of the two together were not considered sufficiently strong, it seems to me that their juncture and their accord would present a phenomenon sufficiently remarkable to impress the public, or, at least, for want of the public, the leaders and the wisest." [17]

As to the public, being more numerous than in the time of his imaginary interlocutor, its vain discourses are also more numerous and more ridiculous. The Greeks in his day had chiefs and sages. There is nothing of the sort in France. "As it suffices to pass several examinations or to modulate a few confused cries under the pretext of speaking in order to be called a sage, the profession of chief, of magistrate, and of prince belong to the first comer at whom it pleases the multitude to look. You have no idea of that." [18] Having such a haphazard system of selection, it is not so surprising, perhaps, that the worthy representatives of this vain multitude recently voted almost unanimously to stamp on the public money a collection of "subterfuges and absurdities, composed a little more than a hundred years ago by the assembly of the poorest heads that our France has ever produced."

"The first article of this more than indigent statement declares that men are born free. Alas! Old Hecateus, before our leaders and among the best of these leaders, among those who sit at the right and who have merited the fine title of Cornichons you would be obliged to speak a long time before making them understand that, of all creatures, man is perhaps least free at

17 In 1931 Maurras injected at this point the following note: "Il n'a pas échappé à nos lecteurs que j'essaye ici d'attirer l'attention d'Hécatée, philosophe ionien, mort il y a vingt-cinq siècles, sur le théorème fondamental de la Poltitique, tel que l'ont formulé de nos jours Le Play, chrétien, normand, praticien de l'induction, et Comte, positiviste, languedocien, praticien de la déduction" (*ibid.*, 24).

18 *Ibid.*, 25.

his birth, being unable to walk as does the newborn chick, to discern or to take his nourishment round about him, or even to assimilate the least element from the outside. When, the cord having been severed, he has ceased to depend upon his mother, he comes to depend upon his nurse, then upon his teacher, then upon his father and upon his chief, all for his greatest advantage: he grows only on this condition. If the man of whom we speak is not a savage, if he comes from an opulent civilization, in proportion as this civilization is more advanced this man will be the more dependent, for he will be bound by a greater number of ties. Liberty is not at the beginning, but at the end. It is not in the root, but in the flowers and in the fruits of human nature, or, better expressed, of human virtue. One is freer in proportion as one is better. This it is necessary to become. Old Hecateus, how you will laugh! Our men thought they could arrogate to themselves the prize of effort by advertising everywhere, in their town-halls and their schools, in their universities and their churches that this prize is to be had without effort. But would it be worth even the shadow of a million to proclaim that everyone is born a millionaire?

"The same statement, Hecateus, also pretends that the end of all political association is the preservation of the natural and imprescriptible rights of man. We know that the end of every city is life, not only human life, but animal life, the individual life of everyone, none of us being likely to live without 'the political association!' The proclamation, approved by four hundred and six votes against eight, adds that, in principle, all sovereignty resides essentially in the nation: your time had not forgotten to note that all powers come from the gods, rulers of the world, in other words, from the profound natural laws which man has not made and to which man must conform, if he does not wish to perish! The proclamation said: law is the expression of the general will. You perceived that it is the expression of the necessities and of the exigencies of the safety or of the prosperity of the public: would you, otherwise, have maintained any priests at public expense or given heed to the sages who were your legislators?" [19]

Feeling that he has given the Milesian an idea of the nonsense that was acclaimed and extolled throughout France and of the folly of nobles and of beggars alike, Maurras again praises him for his enthusiasm for the truth and for his great services to later generations, exclaiming as he takes leave of him, "If we could but imitate you, and speak as well on the things that we know!"

"Know," he apparently did, but considerations, already mentioned, prevented his doing in politics what Hecateus had done in geography and history—what, in fact, he himself had already been doing as a critic. It was his voyage to Athens in the spring of 1896, so important to him in his quest for beauty, that brought decision, although a bold, forthright action based upon it came only several years later. That is why many of his friends, he wrote some thirty-five years later, were under the misapprehension that it came during the Dreyfus affair. True in a sense, it was not absolutely so; for, he added, "The conversion of my spirit came a year before the Affair, it dates from the first weeks that I lived outside of France, my voyage to Greece in the springtime of 1896." [20]

Since Maurras later, because of his acrid partisanship and zeal for the restoration of the monarchy, at times gives the impression, even to impartial readers, that his royalism was dearer to him than his nationalism, that the welfare of France was less important to him than the desired monarchical government, it is well that we consider the reasons for this "conversion" of one who held that reason should never abdicate to sentiment. As the steamer left Marseilles and he saw the shores of France recede in the distance, how small his country seemed, isolated and floating in a vast world as it was! He was frightened. Until now he had been proud of the statesmanship that had achieved the Franco-Russian alliance. He had not been in

19 *Ibid.*, 25-26.

20 *Au signe de Flore*, 43.

the East long before he discovered what France was having to pay in ill-will in this section for the Russian " protectorate " he had prized so highly. Moreover, he was struck by the unmistakable evidence he found here of Germany's prodigious scientific, economic, financial, political, and military development.[21] More imposing still, and fear-inspiring, was the preponderance of the Anglo-Saxons. Its growth was doubtless less spectaular than that of the Prussians, but it was none the less real. The English and the Americans had, in fact, " divided the universe in a great silence." Though they were masters everywhere, no one could measure their real power. Although his first reaction to the revival of the Olympic games as an International of sports had been one of opposition and fear, lest it profane a beautiful name and result, not in an intelligent and reasonable federation of modern peoples, but in the vague disorders of cosmopolitanism, he was now reassured, for he was convinced that when several distinct " races " meet and are constrained to associate with each other, they are mutually repelled and withdraw at the very moment they think themselves joined. One benefit, therefore, that should result from these games was that they would reveal to the Latin nations, so long blind to the silent growth of Anglo-Saxon predominance, " the number, the power, the influence, the growing ambitions, and, further, the weak or vulnerable point of these audacious pretendants to tyranny." The French might well give this subject a quarter of an hour of anxiety, for a people that is afraid of being afraid is pretty low.[22]

And what rabid nationalism these people evinced! Spiro Louys, the Greek winner of the Marathon, showed his joy too freely and thereby revealed his lack of taste and measure. But he was a model of restraint compared with his barbarous colleagues. " The silly people !," Maurras was moved to exclaim. " English, Germans, especially the Yankees, have no idea of

21 *Ibid.*, 44.

22 *Le Voyage d'Athènes* (Paris, 1929), 56-63; *Anthinéa* (Paris, 1926), 247-249.

the wild prattling that their hoarse or piercing voices make, with their *hurrahs* and their *hochs*. They are doubtless tolerated, even watched with a semblance of pleasure, because courtesy demands it. But all disinterested spectators have troubled hearts. These barbarous tongues are ill-suited to a place so compliant and so sweet. In ancient Athens the Scythians were used only as policemen. Several Americans have behaved like over-grown children. Their flag alone is seen. Their accent alone heard. Nationalism is a lovely passion. Nevertheless, one must mix it with civility when one leaves home! The Athenians have the good grace to notice nothing."[23] While Frenchmen would do well not to imitate the boisterousness of these barbarians, and though some friends had said many fine things about France, he was convinced that her "future and her grandeur" had been neglected.[24]

One friend, with whom he had discussed art and literature on a walk, when asked abruptly by Maurras concerning French influence in the Levant, promptly replied with the words which had long since been used in referring to Athens, *Graecia capta ferum victorem. . . .* Maurras, now thoroughly aroused, asked with warmth what Athens was worth after she had lost her liberty. Had, he now began to wonder, the Treaty of Frankfort and the loss of the provinces really reduced France to so low a state? That had occurred a quarter of a century ago. Why was it not partially repaired? Why partially forgotten? Moreover, before 1870, there had been 1815 and Waterloo; also 1805 and Trafalgar. Why was England mistress of the Mediterranean, France's sea? What was England doing at Malta in France's place? And when was Gibraltar last attacked by a French army? Returning to Athens, where he examined a reference book, he discovered that in the period from 1792 to 1815—twenty-three years of almost unbroken warfare—France had neither touched nor attempted to touch this stronghold, historically the vanguard of Britain's rule in the Mediterranean. The last time it

23 *Le Voyage d'Athènes*, 92-93; *Anthinéa*, 262.

24 *Au signe de Flore*, 44.

was besieged by the French was during the American war under the "tyrant," Louis XVI. However, other wars, in which thousands of Frenchmen had met violent deaths, had been fought since. But to what avail? France's democratic wars had been of no use. Under the "tyrants," upon the admission of the Committee of Public Safety itself in its report of Oct. 14, 1794, every war had brought a new province. At that time the Family Compact had given France a relatively strong position at Naples and Madrid. The acquisition of Corsica had served as a fitting prelude to the seizure of Algiers and the conquest of Algeria by other French kings. These reflections, pointing out, as they did, when France began her descent downward, upset his whole view of French history as well as his conception of the map of the world. The First Republic and the First Empire had lost the seas; the Second Empire and the Third Republic, the Continent. And the cause of this mischief was one and the same throughout.

This he announced in his "Fifth Letter" from Athens to *La Gazette de France*.[25] The Greeks were having trouble, too, he found. The country was the prey of parties. The number of the bourgeoisie seemed to be greater than the country could well sustain. It was feared that they would become charges of the state which was already burdened with too many civil servants, all of whom were active politically. Reduced to purveyor and foster-father, the state would disappear in civil ruin. "Such," aphorized the young reporter, "is the destiny of the countries where the mob has too much influence." These opposing parties made pacts to the detriment of the public credit. New quarrels would result and inevitably bring the foreigner upon the scene. Having no national dynasty, the Greeks had chosen a king from a foreign family. Pleasant, tactful, and discreet, he was rendering a useful service, comparable, in many ways, to that once contributed by the podestas in the Italian republics as neutrals in the factional quarrels of the cities. He was blamed by some for the too moderate use he made of his

25 Apr. 20, 1896.

constitutional powers; others opposed even that. Several did Maurras the honor of asking him his advice. This he refused to give for the following reason: " A secret shame held me back. Remaining silent in regard to it, I reproached myself for this silence. It was doubtless criminal, inasmuch as I felt intensely how the democratic, republican, and liberal error of all of these Greek patriots forebode more disappointments for them than the Tsar and the Sultan: but, in order to point out the mistake of the Hellenes, I would have had to expose the blunder of the French in the last hundred years of their history. I did not have the heart to humiliate my own people in this manner and it is in my innermost secret being that, with a penetrating bitterness, I have computed the unbelievable responsibilities assumed by the French Revolution in the deviation of the political spirit among the people it has instructed." [26] This statement may be deemed to represent a faltering effort on Maurras' part to imitate the great Hecateus.

Returning to France on a Marseilles steamer, he had an amusing experience that gave point to his earlier reflections. The captain and the crew were Provençals, while the passengers were mainly foreign, with a few scattered Frenchmen among them. The cook had written out the menu in an Anglo-French that was peculiar to himself. The result was that " rump steak " appeared as " roustec." Maurras' enjoyment of this " free and beautiful " translation was suddenly interrupted when, on the other side of the table, a woman, her cheeks painted and her teeth strong, seized a gold pencil from her bodice and, with the " fierce expression of a Great Britain truly queen of the seas," struck out the offensive Provençalism and wrote above it the " insular " form of the word. Maurras, unwilling to fight the proud woman, assumed the expression of a ruined man, of one, for example, who had been expelled from his home. Whether she saw and understood, he was unable to determine. At any rate, she refrained from laughing at his impotent rage. " A people threatened with eviction has only one right: to think

26 *Le Voyage d'Athènes*, 82-87; *Anthinéa*, 258-260.

with courage and to decide with resolution." France at this moment seemed to him an "orphan."[27]

What, then, did these proud Englishmen have that the French lacked? "Fidelity to their order and to the course of their safety." He had never denied this fidelity; he had never seen it. It had been lost for him by others before him. His national spirit had slipped to an inferior plane. That this was true was not his fault, nor was the blame to be placed upon contemporary Frenchmen. When one judges the good and the bad, or the progress and the retrogression of an individual, one must consider the average life-span of the people in general. So, too, in judging the state, one must take into account the life-span, not of men, but of nations. To have held the Frenchmen of 1896 responsible for the fact that they were not as active and as powerful as the English would therefore have been unjust, for one suffered and the other benefitted from an "accumulation of anterior circumstances."

What had united France's neighbors and rivals, friends and enemies through the successive generations? What, at the same time, had unbound, separated, and divided the French? In general, the successive acts of a people reflect in large measure the succession of the powers that have governed it. At London and at Berlin, in the period in which both flourished, the government was dynastic. The same was true of Paris when it prospered. It is dynastic succession that gives coherence to the powers of an empire. "Etymology," he reflected, "would decree, if history did not, not only because the dynasty averts the worn out system of electoral and parliamentary rivalries, but also because it is good and beautiful, that the authority of the sovereign chief be not a power forged by the hand of man, that it come to us from the most remote ages and that the centuries form, bring, and name it for us, impose upon us *ready-made,* as haloed by its right, this *right* of the chiefs upon which is based the major rôle which they played in the building of the country."[28]

27 *Au signe de Flore,* 46-47.

28 *Ibid.,* 48.

And who was the legitimate chief of France? For some four years it had been Philippe VIII: "ancient and ever new symbol of the constant renewals of an identical power by an identical blood, the living picture of the symmetry and parallelism of the destiny of born chiefs and of their nation, the same hazard of birth creating the nationals in the country, the kings in the dynasty. . . . Hazard, seconded by education, had not done so poorly!"[29] What, he found himself asking, would France's lot have been at this time had she remained faithful to her kings? In any event, he decided France must have a king, if he and his French contemporaries did not wish to be the last Frenchmen. If France was to live, she had to have a king.

While Maurras, in his *Confession politique,* from which we have drawn so heavily for the reasons that figured in his "conversion," says only that his own doctrine reproached him for his passive acceptance of political democracy,[30] his Epicurean-Comtian philosophy was doubtless an important factor also—perhaps fundamental. Having found his doctrine brilliantly confirmed in the art of ancient Athens, having as a consequence found beauty and happiness in contemplating its ruins, he was confident that, since they conduced perfection in art and in the artist, they would do the same for society. "The truth shall make you free," now almost trite from its frequent use and abuse as the burden of many a dreary homily, was again proved by his experience to be no mere idle promise. Just as, according to Maurras' doctrine, a sure taste disciplined by reason, controlled, in turn, by death, nature, or truth itself, gave the artist simplicity and directness of style—in short, freedom and power—so, too, did the certainty and self-confidence, inspired by his lyrical experience on the Acropolis contribute to Maurras' freedom—it gave him added freedom in art and a new freedom, a "conversion," in politics.[31] Some five years later he remarked

29 *Ibid.*, 49.

30 *Ibid.*, 16.

31 In regard to truth, Barrès was a pragmatist. He stated, for example, that there was a French "truth," a German "truth," an English "truth,"

that Barrés had publicly expressed astonishment that he had brought back from Athens so live a hatred of democracy. " If modern France," Maurras avowed, " had not persuaded me to this sentiment, I would have received it from ancient Athens. The brief destiny ot that which was called democracy in antiquity [32] made me feel that the peculiar quality of this régime is

etc. (footnote 11, p. 104, above). Not so Maurras, despite his Comtian hostility toward absolutes. To him truth had a mystical power and attraction not unlike that of beauty. Barrès objected to the impractical nature of the royalist campaign in his letter to Maurras in the *Enquête sur la Monarchie.* To this Maurras replied, " Mais on me permettra d'insister sur ce mot *pratique.* En trente ans de pratique pure, et de tâtonnements en tâtonnements, le système républicain a mené le pays à sa perte. Dès lors, il faut bien établir, par une vue d'ensemble et par des recherches directes, les causes des malheurs publics en même temps que les conditions du salut public. S'il n'y a point d'erreur dans notre vue de ces causes, dans notre mesure de ces conditions (et Maurice Barrès ne m'en signale aucune), une théorie ainsi faite deviendra la règle nécessaire de la pratique. Les praticiens auront sans doute le pouvoir de s'en écarter; mais chacun de leurs écarts sera payé par quelque nouveau revers. C'est une vérité abstraite et théorique que deux fois deux font quatre et deux fois quatre huit: je ne crois pas que nos financiers les plus pontifs la puissent négliger sans s'exposer à des dommages. Dans l'intérêt de la pratique, ne négligeons pas le cabinet du théoricien" [*Enquête sur la monarchie* (1925), 134-137].

This mistake Barrès was making, as Déroulède had already done: " Déroulède eut l'éclair d'audace qui avait fait défaut à son chef. *Mais il lui manqua une idée raisonnable.* Son idée plébiscitaire signifiait des éventualités si parfaitement anarchiques que les chefs de l'armée devaient reculer devant elle. Comme l'a fort bien dit Buffet, on ne sort pas du gâchis pour entrer dans le chaos" (*ibid.*, 419-420). (Present writer's italics.)

In insisting upon truth in politics, that is, that political ideas be in accord with human nature, Maurras was simply adapting one of his aesthetic principles to the realm of politics. " Ce que le philosophe peut exiger de la poésie, c'est seulement de ne pas contredire ce que la science révèle de certain sur la nature humaine. Sous cette condition, que la poésie ait champ libre! Elle ne pourra qu'ajouter pas ses ornements à la magnificence de la religion. Veut-elle attribuer aux corps des qualités imaginaires? Il suffit qu'elles ne soient point en opposition avec les qualités constatées..." ["Auguste Comte," *L'Avenir de l'intelligence* (Paris, 1927), 121].

32 Quoting several passages from the *Études d'histoire ethnique* of Paul de Leusse, he observed by way of conclusion, " La vive imagination du comte de Leusse nous réalise en numérations excellentes cette pensée, presque trop clair, que le régime antique fut l'aristocratie. Bien plus, dans tous les temps et toutes les villes où se montra une civilisation héllenique brillante, ce fut une

only to consume what the aristocratic periods have produced. Production, action required a powerful order. Consumption is less exacting: neither tumult nor routine hinder it much." Since all democracies make a "bonfire" of the accumulated products of the nation's past, he was unable to see how a person could be a nationalist and a democrat at one and the same time, for he could not wish to destroy and to conserve France's strength simultaneously.[33]

But to favor democracy and romanticism at one and the same time was consistency itself, for both were basically individualistic and, therefore, destructive of the best in tradition. That Maurras considered the principles of art applicable to society is clear. When, many years later, some of his friends complained that, having no sooner conquered important positions in his literary campaign, he had abandoned them for a political struggle, he replied that he had not deserted any positions, but had merely divided his effort. This, he added, was forced upon him by the circumstance that the barbarians, "Demos, flanked by his two friends, the German and the Jew," had placed a heavy yoke upon the intelligence of France. Two alternatives presented themselves: either this yoke must be shaken off, or its natural affects accepted. Since, for him, there was no choice in the matter, political action was necessary. "A lucid literary polemic led to a social and political polemic. . . . Already, from afar, to be sure, the rules of collective life and the laws of government had interested me very much. These rules and these laws are not without relation to the principles that preside over the art of the poet when he reduces to order his people of ideas and words, of colors and of sounds: so the unity of the human spirit demands. This analogy of the two planes has given me no end

aristocratie de l'aristocratie, une fleur de la fleur qui l'avait préparée et determinée. Aux moments dits démocratiques, c'est-à-dire quand le plus grand nombre des *citoyens*, quand la partie inférieure de l'élite prit le dessus, cette demi-démocratie fut une consomption rapide. Ainsi périt l'Athènes d'Alcibiade et de Périclès" ("Note II," *Anthinéa*, 281).

33 *Ibid.*, xii; *Le Voyage d'Athènes*, 11-12.

of service, and the habit of conjuring up successively their complementary images has also helped me to render the spirits impassioned for the universal order less indifferent to public affairs." [34]

34 "Reflexions préalables sur la critique et sur l'action," *Barbarie et poésie* (Paris, 1925), xi. Continuing, he said, "Aujourd'hui tous les intérêts politiques et mentaux coïncident si parfaitement qu'il peut être bon de montrer ce qui était dit de leur convergence dans uns série de travaux vieux de vingt et trente ans." In 1901 he wrote, "J'ai bataillé dix ans pour les traditions du goût français; mais je n'ai conçu l'esperance de les voir relevées que du jour où j'ai conçu le possibilité de rétablir l'ensemble de nos traditions nationales" ("La Politique et l'art nouveau," *La Gazette de France*, Dec. 12, 1901).

CHAPTER XVII

THE CONVERSION OF THE ACTION FRANCAISE TO ROYALISM

Maurras came away from Greece hating democracy, having already, with some hesitation, attacked it from his new spiritual and philosophical vantage point. But he did little about it for some months. Busy with his literary tasks, he became a political Hecateus only a year after his return. In the *Gazette de France* of June 3, 1897, he openly attacked the Republic for not punishing the Panama *chéquards,* and, answering his own question as to what would have happened to Rouvier under the monarchy, he blandly declared that he would have been hanged. Montesquieu had said the principle of republican government was virtue. Virtue in a hypocritical form, perhaps; but true virtue was impossible to republican statesmen, since republican government was necessarily based upon corrupt party rule. To say that the ministers and parliament were responsible to the majority of the electorate, which was itself not unlike running sand and could therefore not accuse anyone, was the rankest sort of cynicism. The system not only reeked with venality, but positively encouraged it. Three days later, in the same journal, he twitted Clausade, the sculptor, for portraying the heroes of the Revolution as giants in order to please the " little people " of his day, his patrons. To call them giants was, however, more complimentary to the old régime than to his Lilliputian friends, for it was the " old France, monarchical and traditional " that had produced them.

Although these articles were but harbingers of the campaign that was to follow, they do show that his earliest efforts to propagate his " positivist " royalism antedated the outbreak of the Dreyfus affair by several months. More incisive, more provocative, and more in the nature of a manifesto was an article which he wrote soon after the guilt or innocence of Captain Alfred Dreyfus became a public question. In the face of the excitement this question aroused and the apparent inability of the Republic to defend the nation's army, Maurras felt it was treason not to give expression to the ideas in which he was convinced national safety lay. How would a monarch have met this issue? he asked himself. What would a monarch do to prevent the recurrence of other such crises? Approaching his colleagues on the staff of *Le Soleil* with these questions, and, receiving encouragement from them, he wrote an article for the journal in which he attempted to answer the question, "How would a monarch help?" He showed that in decisive moments nothing was so important as to have the highest functions of the state (the army and navy, diplomacy and justice) concentrated in the hands of one living person who was above parliamentary deliberations and judicial formalities. A monarch could solve this crisis; for, contrary to the Republic which deliberately weakened the army because it was distrusted as a hotbed of royalism or Boulangism, he would defend it as his predecessors had done. Moreover, the monarch would never have permitted this question to have reached the stage of a crisis. First of all, the Jewish financiers and the Huguenot industrialists would never have been permitted to organize their system of extortion as was done by the democratic and parliamentary Republic. The very existence of this system clearly revealed the fact that authority had crumbled and that responsibility had disappeared. Party and group interests were considered more vital than the interests of the nation. Public opinion, controlled by Jewish bankers and Genevan mummers, was in command. This would not have been the case had there been a monarch. Frenchmen were really not so much concerned about justice as they were about public safety. This latter, however, required a first magistrate who would be a "living law, an intelligent authority" to all.[1]

Although its publication (it had not been carefully read by the editor) brought upon Maurras' head the displeasure of the management, royalist journal though it was, it likewise brought

1 *Au signe de Flore*, 64-67.

to its author many congratulatory letters. And, when several days later, Philip VIII issued a proclamation to the country in the rôle marked out for him in the article as defender of the army, Maurras' pleasure was truly great. Amouretti, he now felt, had been right all along in insisting upon the good qualities of the Prince. He was unquestionably the " public safety incarnate." Regarding him in this light, the young critic and journalist was proud to declare himself his faithful follower. He had " found his port," when he was to make excursions in the interest of king and country in the years that followed.[2]

Even now, however, his literary pursuits remained his primary interest, until, in September, 1898, upon his return from London, whither he had gone to study the treasures of Greek art in the Museum, he took up the defence of the suicide, Colonel Henry, as a martyr to the best interests of the country. Coming, as it did, at a moment when the anti-Dreyfusards were pretty well demoralized, it gave the less disaffected a rallying point. This and the unmeasured abuse that was heaped upon Maurras by the Dreyfusards made him something of a national figure. " At this point of my life," he later admitted, " when the end of a purely literary career coincided with the maturity of my thirty years and this action, the best and, in any case, the most useful of all those over which I have had reason to rejoice, I am bound to recognize that I was recompensed with an almost abusive hatred." [3] Not the sort to cringe under the attacks of men whom he despised and hated as enemies of the fatherland, he struck back by tranquilly continuing his defence of Colonel Henry. But, once in the thick of this battle of words, more and more of his time and energy was required by the political campaign upon which he was now definitely launched.

He now contributed regularly to the anti-Dreyfusard literature; he played so important a rôle in the formation of the *Ligue de la Patrie Française* that his arch-enemy, Joseph Reinach, flatteringly referred to him as one of its chief found-

2 *Ibid.*, 67-71.

3 *Ibid.*, 82-83.

ers; and, disappointed with the limited objectives and general obtuseness of this body,[4] he joined Vaugeois in reviving and reorganizing the *Comité de l'Action Française.*[5] Organized for study,[6] the membership of this smaller group had more points upon which there was general agreement. All were anti-Semites; all opposed Free-Masonry, Protestantism, parliamentarism, and democracy; and all but one (Vaugeois said "all") were in agreement regarding the proposed form the government should take: that is, an oligarchical or aristocratic republic with a powerful and responsible head chosen from one of the revolutionary "dynasties"—a Carnot, a Cavaignac, a Cambon, etc.[7]

This one, it scarcely need be said here, was Maurras. And perhaps his most significant and characteristic achievement in this period was the slow leavening influence of his ideas and personality upon certain select members of the group first, and eventually upon all. Nationalists of the Déroulèdian or Barrèsian stamp, and for the most part individualists in their thinking, their "conversions" were more far-reaching than that of their political and philosophical mentor had been. Vaugeois, for

4 To Vaugeois's complaints Maurras replied, "Ce sont des républicains. Leur coeur est bien français, mais le bon sens leur dit deux choses: tantôt qu'ils usurpent les fonctions de l'Etat quand ils se mêlent d'assurer l'ordre, eux qui ne sont rien dans l'Etat, et tantôt qu'à travailler trop exclusivement pour l'ordre, le drapeau, l'armée, la patrie, ils travaillent implicitement contre le régime. De là leur peu d'allant. De là, ces tiraillement et ce trouble. Je vous assure qu'ils auraient dû commencer par tomber d'accord d'un certain nombre de petites choses afin de pouvoir agir efficacement. Tel quels, ils ne peuvent pousser jusqu'au terme ni leur idée de la France, ni leur idée de l'Etat, ni leur juste critique des Droits de l'Homme et du Citoyen" (*ibid.*, 111-112).

5 Maurras would have preferred to name it the *Intérêt Commun,* Louis Dimier informs us in his *Vingt ans d'Action française* (Paris, 1926), 15.

6 Coudekerque-Lambrecht, *Léon de Montesquiou: sa vie politique, l'Action française* (Paris, 1925), 30.

7 *Au signe de Flore,* 123-125. Louis Dimier: "Républicains étaient pareillement tous ceux qui se joignirent à lui dans ces commencements, à l'exception de Maurras, royaliste déja, en qui se réalisait le type de blanc du midi, sauf la foi religieuse qu'il avait renoncée, quoique gardant à l'Eglise catholique son attachement et son respect. Seul de son parti politique, il ne devait pas moins y attirer tous les autres" (*op. cit.*, 11).

example, their leader, the founder and director of their review, the *Action Française,* had, before the Dreyfus affair, oscillated between German Marxism and the ideas of the French Revolution. As a student and professor of philosophy he had placed much faith in a possible moral regeneration of society. His outspoken anti-Clericalism and his Spinozism completed his outlook. Maurras was astonished that an anti-Semite could declare himself a follower of Spinoza. Vaugeois, in turn, expressed surprise that an unbeliever could be so well disposed toward Roman Catholicism.[8] The two were, in fact, poles apart in their thinking. Nevertheless, they were attracted to each other: Maurras by Vaugeois' fundamental honesty and zeal for the truth, the latter by the former's ideas.[9] They argued much—on one occasion through an entire night.[10] Maurras gave him a copy of his *Chemin de Paradis* and the next evening Vaugeois returned, giving to Maurras a history of his home town written by his great uncle. But when Maurras accepted this with a "You see, we *can* agree," his friend exclaimed, "*We* agree? With you! Never!"[11] When, on one occasion, Vaugeois told Maurras he was the only royalist in France, the latter replied, "Join me, we will be two."[12] The stronger will, aided by convictions based upon a doctrine that seemed to have been cut to measure for the times, gradually won out. Already in the second number of the *Action Française* Vaugeois' article, *Réaction d'abord,* reflected the doctrine of his friend. In a little more than two years he declared his own adherence and that of his periodical to the royalist cause.[13]

8 *Au signe de Flore,* 134.

9 In the midst of one of their many arguments Vaugeois exclaimed, "Vos idées, tant que vous voudrez?... Mais (le doigt tendu, l'oeil en flamme) vos passions, non, jamais!" (*ibid.*, 109).

10 *Ibid.*, 105-109.

11 *Ibid.*, 110.

12 Louis Dimier, *op. cit.*, 11.

13 For this last, Maurras apparently thought the time inopportune or opposed it as bad strategy. Louis Dimier: "Maurras était d'avis d'en ajourner l'aveu. Il y voyait l'inconvénient de nous couper des nationalistes. Je crois

Meanwhile, by means of discussions which he held with the members of the group and others attracted by them at the Flore café, Maurras gradually made converts of many others. Louis Dimier, who was one of these, has given us a description of him at this time.[14] According to this one-time friend and colleague, Maurras' mind was his chief attraction. Thin of body, with a sallow complexion under a thin black beard, he generally wore an expression of sadness mixed with distrust, possibly because of his inability to hear well. As a rule he was polite to a fault, but on occasion, when his nerves took charge and he lost his temper, he was not above throwing dishes at the waiter. But his keenly intelligent mind also had its turn. This, coupled with an extraordinary passion to convince others, which sharpened his dialectical skill, enabled him to overcome the objections advanced by his interlocutors or to use them to confirm his point. His sense of the practical, of what was possible, impressed his friends as equally remarkable. Moreover, there was a quality in his powers of speech that inspired confidence in his listeners that the desired end could and would be realized soon.[15]

qu'il avait surtout celui de nous ranger dans un parti. Jusque-là, nous n'avions paru céder qu'aux exigences des idées pures; ceux que nous combattions, même, en étaient frappés: cela nous donnait beaucoup de credit, cela ouvrait à notre campagne du côté des gauches, d'où presque tous les membres de l'Action Française étaient issus, un champ infini. Une profession publique de royalisme traversait ces facilités, comme associant à notre action les intérêts dont le prince était le centre, et le préjugé de ses adhérents. Mais comment l'éviter? Vaugeois n'était pas l'homme de ces sortes de précautions; puis, l'inconvénient tenait aux choses, le silence n'y eût point aidé" (*op. cit.*, 17). It won for them many old royalist supporters, he added.

14 Since this was written after his rupture with Maurras, after having worked with him more than twenty years, it may be assumed that it is less favorable than it would have been had it been written twenty years earlier. Aside from a rather severe treatment of his subject's character, he seems, however, to be remarkably impartial.

15 "La passion de convaincre, la plus forte chez lui et qui dominait sur toutes les autres, s'y exerçait au moyen d'une dialectique puissante, où l'esprit se donnait tout entier, s'offrant à la contradiction avec une bonne foi absolue, triomphant de l'objection au moyen d'arguments qui, faisant la lumière à mesure qu'ils avançaient, emportaient comme une palme la conclusion. Les vues d'exécution n'étaient pas moins frappantes. Il y avait chez cet homme

These gifts, coupled with the fact that he had a definite plan based upon what appeared to be a complete and logical philosophical system, in a time when other nationalists were confused in their thinking, making concessions here and there to the dominant liberal philosophy, though rejecting its conclusions, gave him a distinct advantage. Moreover, Déroulède's fiasco of February 23, 1899, and his subsequent mistakes as an exile doubtless strengthened Maurras' arguments powerfully. Regular visitors at the Flore café were Vaugeois, Pujo, Moreau, Bainville, Montesquiou, Mazet, Tauxier, and Robert Launay. Less regular, but interested observers, were Paul Souday, Paul Bourget, Maurice Barrès, and others.[16] Bourget is said to have christened Maurras " the healer of France." [17] Of those who attended these meetings regularly, Montesquiou's experience was doubtless typical. A national republican of the Barrèsian stamp,[18] the course of events and the influence of these conferences gradually converted him first into an " uneasy republican " and finally into a monarchist. Reminiscing in the *Action Française* on the eve of the World War (June 15, 1914), he said he was attracted to this group by its declared desire to " study." " I had earlier frequented the nationalist circles, I had seen several of the leaders near at hand. I had found myself bewildered, not to say, dismayed. The leaders did not know where to lead their troops. They inspired these forces with enthusiasm by shouting to them: ' Forward! ' but they did not

un sens de manoeuvre aussi délicat que ses principes étaient fermes et étendus : en sorte que, aux lumières de l'esprit, ses propos ajoutaient la confiance d'en voir réaliser l'objet. De là lui venaient un double empire, et une force d'ascendant à laquelle nous cédions tous " (Louis Dimier, *op. cit.*, 14; *cf.* Coudekerque-Lambrecht, *op. cit.*, 45-46).

16 Louis Dimier, *op. cit.*, 15; *Au signe de Flore*, 142-143.

17 Coudekerque-Lambrecht, *op. cit.*, 46.

18 In his reply to Maurras' *Enquête sur la monarchie* (246-247) of 1900, he favored a Caesarean republic as more likely to furnish the immediate action which the political situation demanded. It would take too long to revive the old faith in the monarchy, he thought. (This reply may also be found in Coudekerque-Lambrecht, *op. cit.*, 32-34).

know what road to have them take. So I hastened to those who openly declared that they did not know,—but added that they were going to look around. This investigation was led, it is true, by one who knew: Charles Maurras." [19] And, "knowing," he directed the study with the following result, so well expressed by Maurice Pujo: "Under the mortal blows of Charles Maurras, the republicanism of each of us succumbed one by one in this year, 1900, which was the year of the *hegira* for the *Action Française*." [20]

Since at the outset they were in general agreement in their attitude toward the Jews, the Masons, the Protestants, parliamentary government, and what might be termed democratic liberalism, much of their arguing and discussing turned upon the question of Caesarism versus royalism. In reply to the criticisms advanced by his friends [21] and with the approval and encouragement of Amouretti, Maurras, shortly after the wholesale arrests of August 13, 1899, wrote a declaration of royalist faith which dealt specifically with this point, as its caption, *Dictateur et Roi,* suggests. Rejected by his friend, Gustave Janicot, director of *La Gazette de France,* as too radical,[22] it

19 Coudekerque-Lambrecht, *op. cit.*, 30-31.

20 *Ibid.*, 44, quoted from the *Action Française* of May 24, 1910.

21 "Les adhésions nous viennent de tous les groupes de l'opinion et de tous les points du Pays. Elles arriveraient plus nombreuses encore sans un malheureux préjugé: quantité d'antidreyfusiens et d'anti-sémites, patriotes aussi énergiques que passionnés, se réprésentent la Restauration monarchique comme un régime trop effacé, trop tempéré, *trop parlementaire* pour mettre fin aux entreprises des factieux. Par la déclaration que voici, nous nous proposons notamment de détruire ce préjugé et de définir ce que nous entendons et avons toujours entendu par la Royauté" ("Dictateur et roi," *Enquête sur la monarchie*, 447).

22 Louis Dimier: "Le prince dont on demandait le retour fut représenté comme *dictateur et roi.* Sous un titre où ces mots se trouvaient associés, Maurras tint prêt, pour la *Gazette de France*, un article où se trouvait expliqué l'assemblage, et que Janicot ne voulut jamais laisser paraître. 'Qu'est-ce, disait avec horreur ce royaliste de 1850, qu'un dictateur? Un nomme qui vous prend tout.' Et, de ses deux bras allongés, il faisait le geste de tout saisir autour de lui" (*op. cit.*, 19).

was not published until four years later.[23] It was none the less useful, however. Clear and closely reasoned, he loaned it to his friends to satisfy their curiosity or to clarify moot points that arose in his many conferences. Its reading hastened or completed many a " royalist conversion." [24]

His friends wanted a dictator. Maurras would give them a dictator-king whose first duty would be to punish the state criminals whom the Republic permitted to go unpunished, even honored, and whose second would be to reconstruct and rule the state according to a principle of order natural to the French nation and in agreement with the dictates of universal reason. Instead of denying citizens the right to manage their private and local affairs and asking them to declare their views upon distant and complex national problems, this natural and rational order would restore the lower liberties and the higher authority. Unhampered by the task of selling non-inflammable matches or of distributing an " insane education," not weakened by a horde of " electoral courtiers," corrupt and corrupting, not enslaved by the Chambers, political parties, or by unforeseen events, the state would be free and strong in matters of national concern. The king, responsible to the individual interests of his family and of his people, would reign and govern with the aid of technical experts and local councils. This would insure unity, constancy, and permanence of policy and design. True, as compared with the unstable parliamentary republican régime, it would be true likewise in comparison with a plebiscitary or Caesarean republic, for the latter would also be dependent upon

23 *Action française*, Aug. 1, 1903.

24 " Mais plus d'une conversion royaliste fut hatée et mûrie par cette lecture. Le jour où l'on renonça sérieusement à la publication immédiate, une voix dit :—C'est dommage, c'était très clair ! . . . Jamais une oraison funèbre ne me fit autant de plaisir " (*Enquête sur la monarchie*, 447). " Les formules de *Dictateur et Roi* leur paraissaient donc établir une politique sensée. Maurice Pujo m'a avoué un jour que sa première tentation secrète de ralliement à la monarchie date de la soirée lointaine où je lui demandai avis et conseil sur les termes de ce factum. Et pourquoi ?—*C'est*, dit-il, *que j'y ai trouvé, exactement dosés, la logique et l'esprit critique naturels aux Français* " (*Au signe de Flore*, 274).

elections. If the elected dictator were chosen for a term of years, troubled periods of electoral agitation would follow. If chosen for life, assassination and revolution would follow, as was the case in Poland, since governmental competition would be extended to the entire country. Moreover, there would be nothing to prevent an elected dictator from compromising or sacrificing the future in order to appear successful in his lifetime—a danger for the country inherent in the system. Hence the wisdom of placing the sovereign power in the hands of a family, representative of the entire people, past, present, and future, and itself represented by a man, the king. Maurras had heard much nonsense about the hazards of birth. As though elections were free from hazards! The heir to the throne was at least trained for his job, which certainly was not true of the presidents of the Third Republic. The hereditary monarchy, furthermore, presupposed a "natural sentiment of domestic foresight" which would not readily gamble away the future of the dynasty. This prudence, so characteristic of fathers and heads of families, once distinguished the Capetian house and would do so again. They did not wager all on a single campaign as did the two Napoleons, each of whom left France smaller than he had found it.

Therefore, if France was to have peace at home and was again to be strong abroad, if the useless and dangerous electoral rivalries and periodic agitations were to be avoided, the sovereign power had to be placed in a family. And it was to the most worthy, the oldest and most illustrious family that this honor was due. No other family, however glorious its history, offered guarantees comparable to those of the Capetians. Theirs was the oldest dynasty in Europe and, more important still, it belonged to France. They made France. Without them there would have been no France at all. "Nature was satisfied to make this unity possible, not necessary, nor inevitable: these princes formed and fashioned it as an artist gives a personal touch to some chosen matter." And they did it by pursuing during a thousand years a continuous policy at home and abroad in a firm and an authoritarian manner. The Hohenzollern policy, so fatal to France, was but a good copy or a reasoned plagiarism of the old Capetian policy.

This ordered France, so natural to the French people and so in accord with the postulates of universal reason, was not an ideal France, comparable to that of the English, German, and Helvetic inspired rhetoricians who presided over the " republican Church." This France was a " reality, dearer and more beautiful than all." It was not a " murky idea." This reality and this beauty resided in its soil, its blood, its traditions, its interests, and sentiments. This being true, it required a monarchy led and dominated by the " House of France." This alone met the requirements of necessity. Many thoughtful Frenchmen had come to this conclusion and were now saying, " What our ancestors did from custom and sentiment we shall continue with scientific assurance and certainty from reason and from desire." [25]

Such, briefly, was the nature of this royalist-nationalist declaration to which he asked his friends to subscribe. That it and his conferences were having effect is seen in the first formal statement of principles that the editorial committee of the *Action Française* drew up and published in the issue of November 15, 1899. While it is true that this was done in response to Barrès' appeal in *Le Journal* of October 30, preceding, for a doctrine by which alone the " restoration of the common weal " would be possible and that it reflected his doctrine in part and was sent to him as if for safe-keeping or as a mark of respect, it also reflected Maurras' doctrine. This is seen in the emphasis of society over against the individual in the first of the four articles and in the statement in the second to the effect that nationalism was not only a " fact of sentiment," but also a " rational and mathematical obligation." [26] In the wording of the third article, over which there was some dispute, his influence is no less evident. Instead of indicting a formal definition

25 " Dictateur et roi," *Enquête sur la monarchie*, Appendix III, 446-463.

26 *Au signe de Flore*, 256; see pp. 98-99, above.

of nationalism, Vaugeois had simply written that Frenchmen should be classified according to the " intensity and depth of their French faith." To this Maurras objected, seeing in it a mark of fidelity to the " sentimental individualism of the university philosophy, illustrated rather than contradicted by the superior egotism of Barrès." [27] Too attentive to the image of the fatherland in their hearts, it neglected the fatherland itself, the object called France. It was an obligation of politics to make it endure with the aid of, or in spite of Frenchmen. Just as fish were protected from fishermen, so France itself was under the necessity of being protected from Frenchmen. He, therefore, insisted that they write that pending political questions be approached and settled " with reference to the national interest." In this he was humored, except that it read, " with reference to the nation," a wording Maurras disliked, but was persuaded to accept by his friends, Moreau and Amouretti.[28] Vaugeois' point on classifying Frenchmen according to the intensity and depth of their French faith was likewise retained. The fourth and last article simply stressed the duty of Frenchmen, conscious of these " verities," to " formulate them as publicly and as often as possible " in order to bring their blind or negligent compatriots back into line. Since the latter were the Dreyfusards, it was a counsel of anti-Dreyfus action to which Barrèsian and Maurrasian nationalists could well agree, one that can not well be ascribed to either leader.[29]

27 *Ibid.*, 259.

28 *Ibid.*, 259.

29 Meditating upon this period later and, especially, upon Barrès' relation to their group, he remarked that Barrès had postulated the need of a doctrine. But what doctrine? Maurras asked. That of Barrès was " clear and precise." With its powerful appeal to sentiment, it was indeed " profoundly moving." Going beyond the spirit and hearts of many, it penetrated the flesh, blood and bones of several generations. His customary exhortation to glorify the " soil and the dead " was full of magic and charm. But granting and accepting these, there still remained the question of the political direction they should be given. How use these sentiments when even the best among the dead were divided? How reconcile them? The soil itself bore the marks of their strife, while the moral and regional traditions were as divided as were the political. There were,

More impressive to those who remained obdurate in their individualism than the conferences at the Flore café or the convincing argument of the *Dictateur et Roi,* even though, as we have seen, there was a readiness on their part to accept some of the implications of his doctrine, was doubtless Maurras' *Enquête sur la Monarchie* of the summer and autumn of 1900 in the columns of *La Gazette de France.*[30] After the defection

therefore, only two alternatives: either to accept the "definitely superior benefit" and sustain it, or to resign one's self to the same eternal debates and conflicts between the individualists and those who stressed the value of social sanctions—i. e., to further quarreling between the nationalists and the cosmopolitans. It was to this crossroads of policy that all resolved itself in the last analysis. Barrès refused to see the necessity of a choice which Maurras considered imperative. It was, indeed, not necessary, with the country pitted against an external foe, as all who witnessed the influence of Barrèsianism during the World War know. "But face to face with the enemy within, nothing is possible if one does not know who is wrong, who is right," Maurras insisted. Moreover, Barrès thought highly of Déroulède. How could he subscribe to the idea of the plebiscite after the double failure of 1889 and 1899? And why did not a spirit as sharp as his conceive a distrust of the elective principle? "If the City is called a thing sacred, if the Fathers, the Soil, if the Race of the fatherland are confided to us as legacies not to dissipate or not to permit to be dissipated, would it be wise or would it not, rather, be foolish to intrust such treasures to the silly hazard of the ballots?" The first adherents of the *Action Française* were far from thinking in this manner. It is true, they gave Déroulèdism little consideration. They followed Barrès whose gifts were individual and personal. These they accepted, but, as was true in his own case, they were much less concerned about the rights of the individual than in his duties, limits, and in the conditions that in the last analysis permitted the individual to exist. As for himself, Maurras said he had made some distance in this sense and, preceding his new comrades, he was forced to stop to discuss the better. The result was the preparation and publication of the four articles noted. (*Au signe de Flore,* 254-255).

30 It appeared here several times a week from July 25 to Nov. 15, 1900. Another episode of some importance to the royalist orientation of the *Action Française* was the address which Lucien Moreau delivered to a group of young men at the café Procope on Mar. 29, 1900. (Published in the *Action Française,* May 1 and 15, 1900; the essential may be found in the "Préface de 1909," *Enquête sur la monarchie,* 9-20; *cf. Au signe de Flore,* 279-282). It was made at the request of Camille Jarre, a plebiscitarian nationalist, who asked that Maurras' "realistic politics" be explained to the group. This was the first time that Maurras' "organizing empiricism" and the doctrine that evolved from it, his "integral nationalism," was explained to a youthful

of *Le Soleil* to the Dreyfusard cause, *La Gazette de France* was practically the only important organ that the royalists had left. Although Janicot had rejected his *Dictateur et Roi,* he was interested in the group that Maurras was turning to the royalist cause. A personal friend of André Buffet and Count Eugène de Lur Saluces, both of whom were exiled by the Dreyfusard government for their partisan activities, and, knowing Maurras' flair for travel and inquiry—he had judged his voyage to Athens a success—he suggested in May, 1900, that Maurras spend a week or two at Brussels. Here he would speak to the two exiles with an open heart and report of their conversation what he thought would best help the cause. To get their views was almost the same as securing those of the Prince himself, for Buffet was the head of his political bureau, while Lur-Saluces was his delegate or proxy in the southwest. The exiles approved the plan and the voyage was undertaken. So, a second time within a five-year period the director of *La Gazette de France* was instrumental in giving direction to Maurras' life and activity. The voyage to Athens had brought him to the seat of beauty and had convinced him of the need of bringing his political views into conformity with it; the second, the visit to Brussels and the *Enquête* that grew out of it, bound Maurras, his doctrine, and his colleagues to the royalist party and, in turn, added to his prestige in the eyes of many of his nationalist friends who were more easily persuaded by the concrete evidence of outward success than by a clear and logical system of thought.[31]

audience. Maurras modestly stayed away, but it was agreed that his friends would meet him at the café de Flore at midnight. The evening, he was glad to learn, had been a success, for there was as much formal assent to his views as open opposition.

31 "Cette manifestation décisive fit franchir une grande étape. Mon effort royaliste au sein de *l'Action Française* cessa d'apparaître comme un simple caprice de jeune écrivain isolé. Mes amis commencèrent à le concevoir comme leur bien commun, qui était reçu avec honneur et bonté dans la pensée du Prétendant" (*Au signe de Flore*, 289).

This visit, in fact, consummated an alliance between Maurras' small, but militant group of royalist-nationalists and the old royalist party. The distinguished royalist exiles helped him prepare a useful and an interesting questionnaire and, by means of the series of interviews which they granted him, showed him and, in turn, enabled him to show his readers that the doctrine of the older royalists was for practical purposes essentially the same as that of Maurras and his group.[32] This rather lengthy presentation of the views of the official leaders of the party was followed by the publication, with comments of his own, of letters from Paul Bourget, Barrès, and a considerable number of others—several from members of the staff of the *Action Française*. Well conducted and shrewdly presented, the *Enquête* attracted widespread attention in the provinces as well as in Paris. Buffet, who had reliable sources of information, was so elated over its reception in royalist and non-royalist circles, so happy over the fact that the monarchy had become a favorite topic of general discussion, that he blithely informed Maurras that he was weighing his mail of a morning before opening it, it was so heavy.[33] He and the Prince now saw that their old strategy of spreading the idea of the king from the inclosure of a party to a group of hereditary friends could only result in the continued waning of their movement. Henceforth they could hope to secure recruits of exceptional militancy in the most unexpected quarters.

Although his nationalist friends for the most part agreed with him in theory, their replies revealed continued doubt as to the possibility of restoring the monarchy and questioned the practicability of seeking to do so in the face of the given state of public opinion in France. True of the replies of Barrès, Le Goffic, and Lionel de Rieux, it was likewise the position that was taken by most of his colleagues at the *Action Française*, of

32 "Chez nos exilés," Book I of the *Enquête sur la monarchie*, 31-101; *cf.* Commandant Dublaix, *Le duc d'Orléans: sa doctrine, son programme* (Paris, 1925), *passim*, or especially 46-61.

33 *Au signe de Flore*, 288-289.

Vaugeois, Moreau, Dimier, Montesquiou, etc. Bainville, who had already become a monarchist without benefit of Maurras' tutelage, expressed approval of the ideas ascribed to the two prominent royalist exiles. Soon, however, an ironical situation arose. Maurras, who had worked so hard to convince them of the truth and wisdom of his doctrine, and having finally done so, now begged them to delay the formal announcement of the *Action Française's* adherence to the cause of royalism, or "integral nationalism," as he had come to name it, lest they antagonize their nationalist friends by thus classifying themselves as members of a party.[34] This, he feared, would restrict their field of appeal. For some time this anomalous situation obtained, although Vaugeois' statements from March, 1901, onwards left little doubt as to what the trend of the political orientation of the *Action Française* was and what its outcome would be. In the issue of August 1, 1901, when electoral placards were being posted everywhere, he said the *Action Française* was not interested in them, that it was "devoted to integral nationalism." The number of November 1, 1901, reported Vaugeois' visit to the Prince at Carlsruhe and his formal adherence as well as that of the Action Française to the royalist cause.[35]

That this was a notable victory for Maurras and for his system of ideas, for "integral nationalism," need scarcely be stated.[36] As had been noted above,[37] in an article, entitled, "Le

34 See note 1, p. 250, above.

35 *Enquête sur la monarchie*, 172.

36 In an article in *La Gazette de France* of Feb. 23, 1902, entitled, "Encore la démocratie," he replied to those who reproached him and his followers for merely making language instead of pursuing a realistic politics, as they had promised, by saying that it was for the lack of a comprehensible language that royalism had been ignored by many cultivated and patriotic Frenchmen. He and his followers were trying, therefore, to translate the language of 1825 into that of contemporary France. In this work they had no scruples concerning the origin of the word or expression which they used. Who, for example, had appropriated more Jacobin or radical expressions for a royalist propaganda? "Nous avons pris *salut public* à la convention et *bien public* à M. Thiers, *nationalisme* à M. Maurice Barrès, *intégral* à

Nationalisme intégral," in *Le Soleil* of March 2, 1900, in which he first used this expression, Maurras interpreted the word " integral " in the sense of royalism completing and summing up nationalism as a " logical necessity." Nationalism, in other words, was not complete, was not nationalism in its entirety, without royalism, " since the monarchical institutions alone satisfied all the national aspirations, all the national ends, as the integral reproduced the sum of all the values of an algebraic function." [38] This adjective and name, aside from distinguishing its devotees from the republican nationalists of the Déroulèdian or Barrèsian persuasion, had two advantages: it retained for the new royalism its nationalist origins and early associations; the implied incompleteness of the older republican nationalism could be relied upon to bring more republican converts into the royalist camp.

Benoît Malon, et comme les mots sont les signes des choses que nous n'avons boudé aux mots."

37 Pp. 110-112.

38 *Au signe de Flore*, 281. Bernard de Vesins, President of the *Ligue d'Action Française*, said at the League's thirteenth congress, in 1926 " Pour se distinguer des patriotes qui, restant républicains, avaient pris le nom de nationalistes, l'Action française, dont le nationalisme ne pouvait pas se cantonner sur le terrain constitutionnel, résolue à réaliser les solutions de son nationalisme dans la constitution politique de l'Etat français, se dit nationaliste intégral parce que la solution monarchique satisfait à tous les besoins du pays, comme une intégrale en mathématiques représente la somme de toutes les valeurs d'une fonction algébrique " [*L' "Action Française" et le Vatican*, preface by Charles Maurras and Léon Daudet (Paris, 1927), 75-76].

CHAPTER XVIII

"INTEGRAL NATIONALISM" AS THE RESULT OF MAURRAS' "ORGANIZING EMPIRICISM"

HAVING described the elements of Maurras' nationalism as near as possible in the order in which he turned his attention to them—his campaign for decentralization (Taineism), that against the Jews and Protestants (Drumontism), that against parliamentary instability and weakness (Boulangism), and, back of all of these, his campaign in the interest of a " French renaissance " to restore the morale of the French by giving them a sane and realistic philosophy as a substitute for their effeminate romanticism and idealism, we must now attempt to show how, in his opinion, royalism or integral nationalism summed up as a " logical necessity " the elements noted.

In an article entitled, *Les Nouveaux organizateurs,*[1] written in 1899, he demonstrated his point in a characteristically mathematical way. There were, he said, several groups that were opposed to certain aspects of the doctrine of the French Revolution. Each had built up and was spreading abroad its respective critique. There was the criticism of the revolutionary succession law by those who wanted testamentary freedom and the reconstruction of the family; the criticism of the centralized rule of the municipalities by those who desired the reconstruction of the commune; the criticism of the departments by the same men who wanted, with the reconstructed communes, the restoration of local liberties—i. e., the reëstablishment of the provinces; the criticism of economic liberalism by those wishing the freedom of trade unions and the formation of professional groups or corporations; finally, there was the criticism of political liberalism by the plebiscitarians, the authoritarians,

1 First published in *La Gazette de France*, May 6, 1899; and republished later in *Petit manuel de l'enquête sur la monarchie* (Versailles, 1928), 201-203; also in *De démos à César* (Paris, 1930), I, 47-60.

and the anti-parliamentarians—men who wanted the " reconstruction of governmental liberty " and a strong national power. Add up these five criticisms, he suggested, and you will have a criticism of the whole liberal, parliamentary, and republican system. Add up the five " liberties," and you will have the five natural powers which were the basis of the constitution of ancient France. " Finally," he continued, " add to the hereditary institution of the *family* the permanent statute of the *commune* and of the *province,* the *professional* institution, and the stable principle of political authority: you will have the formula of the monarchy." [2]

Similarly, in the following year, in his comments upon Vaugeois' reply to his questionnaire on the monarchy, he gave in a brief and concise statement both a synthesis of the elements of his doctrine and an outline of his later work. All the elements were there, he held. All that was needed was a little synthesizing. The monarchy was traditional, hereditary, antiparliamentary, and decentralizing. By being all of these at once, it met the requirements of those who valued the national tradition and were, as Barrès expressed it, amenable to the suggestions of their soil and their dead; of those who wished to restore the family, the basis of which was the principle of her-

2 *De démos à César,* I, 57-59. It was doubtless such words as the following that Dimier had in mind when he referred to Maurras' power to make others believe in the practicability of his program: " Et toutes ces thèses sont professées, soutenues, appuyées par des fractions considérables de l'élite française, souvent même par des organisations puissantes.

Il reste à les unir, à les grouper, à les ordonner.

Et ce n'est pas fait!

Et les royalistes ne songent pas encore à le faire!

Si les royalistes voulaient!

Si les royalistes savaient!

En quelques mois, ils deviendaient les directeurs incontestées de la conscience française et la Monarchie serait faite, tout au moins devant l'opinion. In ne resterait plus qu'à la réaliser, comme le postulat de l'esprit public tout entier " (*De démos à César,* I, 59-60). The royalists " wished " and " knew," as their part in the *Enquête* in the year following showed; but France has clung to the Republic, accepting, in the meantime, much of his nationalist philosophy and spirit.

edity; of the nationalists who, almost to a man, desired to substitute a nominative, personal, and responsible government for the parliamentary system France had; of the flourishing decentralizing movement of the country. All might find a home under the monarchist roof. "To make it understood," he concluded, "that the Monarchy is all that and that it alone can achieve it all at the same time, that is the outline of our task. It seems very simple to me. A small group will suffice. If it is active, intelligent, and resolute, it can cause and secure at least the consent of the French army where the monarchist elements abound. . . ."[3]

Nationalism, therefore, if it was not to be a half-hearted nationalism, clearly demanded the monarchy, for it alone could achieve the objectives of the nationalist groups. Royalism was not only integral and complete nationalism, but its immediate objective, the monarchy, was likewise a "logical necessity," since it alone, and no other agency, could achieve the desired nationalist ends. Experience and reason clearly proved this.

It was this appeal to history and reason, this use of the inductive and deductive methods of reasoning that he denominated "organizing empiricism" in 1898[4]—two years after he had made use of the procedure in his reflections on the history of France while he was in Greece. It will be recalled that the history of France assumed a new aspect and meaning for him at this time. Little or nothing had been done after the Revolution to wrest Gibraltar and the supremacy in the Mediterranean from Britain's firm grasp; France had invariably bene-

3 *Enquête sur la monarchie*, 169.

4 "Trois idées politiques," *Romantisme et révolution* (Paris, 1925), 261-262. Had he been naming this method of reasoning in 1902, he would perhaps have christened it "ordering empiricism." Pour ma part, j'ai souvent critiqué les excès de l'organicisme et stipulé que le mot d'organisation doit être toujours pris comme une métaphore. Quand les Français seront devenus dignes de comprendre la portée et la profondeur du langage qu'ils ont hérité de leurs pères, ils retourneront au mot propre. Ils ne diront plus *organisation*, ils diront *ordre*. Au lieu *d'organiser, mettre en ordre* prévaudra" ("Science et prejugé," *Gazette de France*, Feb. 10, 1902; *De démos à César*, I, 118-119).

fited from the wars of the ancient régime by the acquisition of a province or two, but not so thereafter—her emperors in each instance left her smaller than they had found her; Berlin and London were flourishing under their monarchs, while Paris, without hers, was languishing. The lessons of history were as plain as a pikestaff. If France was again to be strong and great, her king had to be restored to power first. It was this sort of purposeful analysis that Maurras' " organizing empiricism " both constituted and demanded. It was an analysis toward a definite end, an end, though referred to in various ways, which was always essentially the same. It was the greatness, the power, the well-being, and the prosperity of France, attained and made secure by " public order " or " public safety." [5]

5 It was in Sainte-Beuve that he discovered a master of this method. In Maurras' comments upon him we find the following definition of it: " Cet Empirisme enseigne et professe en effet que l'ordre des sociétés, de quelque façon qu'on l'obtienne, importe plus que la liberté des personnes, puisque cela est la fondement de ceci; au lieu de célébrer l'égalité, même devant la loi, son attention se porte, instinctivement mais aussi méthodiquement, sur le compte des différences naturelles qui ne peuvent manquer de frapper un oeil d' analyste; enfin, quand tant d'instituteurs publics fatiguent les oreilles de cette vieille France avec l'éloge de la plus molle sensiblerie dans les lois et les moeurs, l'Empirisme loue, au contraire, comme normale, une saine mesure d'insensibilité morale et physique.

Qu'est-ce que tout cela au regard de la vieille France, si ce n'est une réaction contre les idées de Jean Jacques? Elle y reconnaît les principes de morale classique et de politique païenne qu'avait gardés si précieusement le catholicisme; et peut-être nos contemporains sont-ils mieux éclairés sur cet ordre d'idées que ne le furent les jésuites de 1857, lorsqu'un ami d'Auguste Comte vint leur offrir l'alliance positiviste. De ce qui est traditionnel ou 'vieille France', l'Empirisme organisateur n'exclut à peu près rien, sinon peut-être les abus du sentiment chrétien. Mais ces grands abus, l'on peut dire que l'Eglise elle-même les neutralise ou les combat, puisqu'elle n'a jamais cessé de renier les sectes ignorantines ou iconoclastes qui sont nées de la lecture des livres juifs. Enfin, cet Empirisme n'offre rien de sectaire. Il ne force personne. A peu près comme à l'Hygiène, il lui suffit que dépérissent tous ceux qui le négligent, personnes ou sociétés " (" Trois idées politiques," *Romantisme et révolution*, 262). Other " noble intellects " of Sainte-Beuve's family were Taine, Renan, Fustel de Coulanges, Auguste Comte, Le Play, Joseph de Maistre, de Bonald, Balzac, etc. Some years later, when replying to the charge of Paganism, he described his method in the following manner: "... La méthode réaliste, appliqué par nous à l'analyse de l'histoire,

Everything, in the last analysis, depended upon "public safety," for, without it, where would beauty, happiness, national power, national traditions, all the desirable things in life, even science be? Yet, paradoxical as it may seem, and though the preservation of science depends upon public safety, there were those who, in the name of science, would ruin the state simply to expose to the gaze of the public an "interesting" document.[6] Theirs was an individualism gone stark mad. But those who pretended to build up a science of politics upon the doctrine of individualism were but little less mad, inasmuch as their initial doctrine was the negation of society itself. No, a true science of politics postulated several fundamental principles. Among these were to be found the idea that law, understood in the sense of the totality of the institutions of a given society, arises from natural causes and situations—i. e., from considerations of expediency and necessity; that it is by organization that societies grow and become conscious of themselves; that this organization necessarily implies a social and political inequality which democracy, itself a "desert of sand," endeavors to suppress; that the *"individual is not a social unit,"* since society begins with the family; that societies are not made to last only through the brief span of one man's life, but to endure much longer; and, finally, that societies are good or bad in direct proportion to their prosperity or lack of it. A prosperous life is the criterion by which societies should be judged. And a political science worth its salt would define the conditions of the prosperity of communities. It would reject automatically all principles known to be destructive of the life and prosperity of communities. Not satisfied to show that inequalities exist and are, in fact, necessary in the nature of things, it would place

est la même que des croyants comme Le Play et Vogelsang ont appliquée à leur études sociales. Notre critérium historique est le leur: la prospérité. Nous jugeons d'une institution d'après ses fruits, ce qui n'a rien de bien contraire à l'Evangile" ("Le Droit et le fait," *Action Française*, Nov. 27, 1909; *De démos à César*, II, 92-93).

6 "Trois idées politiques," *Romantisme et révolution*, 261.

before the people two definite alternatives between which a choice was inexorable: " political inequality or the death of the country." [7]

Such a science of politics, recognizing the imperiousness of nature in the enforcement of its laws, would be critical in its analysis and severe in its judgments, but not more so than nature with which it would conform. It would seek to persuade men to give heed to nature's inexorable laws and try to spare them from the penalties nature imposes for infractions of her laws.

Reason and experience show that the progress of the sciences has brought war instead of peace. This should not be shunted aside as an unpalatable truth. It must be taken into account and proper provision made for it. The material wealth of nations is growing by leaps and bounds and it is reasonable to expect that the goods of the world will be disputed more fiercely in the future than ever. In view of the prodigious common interests that each fatherland represents and the rivalry that exists between these fatherlands for the control or possession of more of the goods of the world, it is clear that the people of France will either be happy together or suffer in common. " This is the positive foundation of modern patriotism." [8] Rome at one time united all the fatherlands in one empire and imposed upon them the *pax romana* which Roman Christianity continued to impose at least in theory later. Feudal and royal lords often fought, it is true, but all the while they recognized the greater organization of which they were a part. Then came the Reformation, and Christianity as the world order ceased to be. " Where is mankind, for every man? In his fatherland. It is not beyond it. The fatherland is the last solid political circle which, surrounding the others (family, commune, province), is not surrounded by any." [9] To be sure, the socialists sing about

7 " Science et préjugé," *Gazette de France*, Feb. 10, 1902; *De démos à César*, I, 118-124.

8 " Une campagne royaliste au 'Figaro,' " *Enquête sur la monarchie*, 472.

9 *Ibid.*, 473.

the International being the mankind of to-morrow, but it is really the work of the nations.[10] It has no existence of its own, no independence, no sovereignty, as was true of Rome and the Church. Even the scientific, literary, and mercantile relations, the treaties of arbitration and the postal conventions have no value apart from that of each race that sustains them. A nation that languishes may expect to see its international commodities decline likewise. "If it continues to weaken, it will disappear." The lower the degree of its political existence, the less secure will be life and property. Armenia and the Transvaal show how easily modern man, without a strong fatherland, may again relapse into a state of barbarism. It is not to be wondered at, therefore, that patriotic necessity becomes important to those who understand these things, that it has even given rise to a sort of religion.[11] " . . . This idea is the greatest power of the modern world," though it is relatively weaker in France than elsewhere.[12]

Given this rivalry between the nations, it behooves those who love France to give serious thought to considerations of national interests and of public safety. Her government itself must be regarded as simply a means to this end.[13] Is the government of the Third Republic a good or bad means? is the question. Both observation and analysis indicate that there is but one answer: it is irrevocably bad.

It is bad because it is based upon the revolutionary doctrine of individualism, upon a metaphysical abstraction that has no counterpart in nature or in the political world proper. It makes the individual man the one respectable object on earth and tolerates society as a "chain" which has as its sole *raison d'être* the progress and the perfection of the individual. No

10 One of the first principles of the *Action Française*, advanced as early as Nov., 1899, was, "Necessité moderne des nations pour l'Humanité" ("La Politique religieuse," *La Démocratie religieuse*, 244).

11 "Une campagne royaliste au 'Figaro,'" *Enquête sur la monarchie*, 473.

12 *Ibid.*, 472.

13 "On mettait le salut public au-dessus de tout" (*ibid.*, 476).

society is legitimate unless it has resulted from a contract or pact freely entered into by free, conscious, and rational persons. In doing this, they do not alienate their liberty, but they place it side by side with that of others " as small, similar cubes, equal in height, in dimension, and in weight." This liberty, the conscience, and the reason of the individual constitute the " prize, the honor, the boon of life." This being so, it is guaranteed by the state. That is its function.[14] But the state should be first and foremost a means to public safety rather than the guarantor of the so-called " natural rights " of the individual. It is because it has been prostituted to this end that the social ties of Frenchmen have been loosened or dissolved since the Revolution. Consequently, the French people are in a state of atomic division in which every individual lives isolated from other competing individuals.[15] All natural bonds save the nation, all secondary societies have been affected by this system and doctrine.

Nevertheless this idea is represented as justice, as the very essence of morality. Close analysis and a little perspicacity reveal that societies are formed to meet natural ends or needs. There is no question of justice in the inability of a son to choose his father, or in the fact that a citizen is thrown into a body politic without his conscience having been consulted. Similarly, if an idea, however well-intentioned, endangers the safety of a state, it is less important to decide whether or not it is just than to know how to avoid it. The most certain and reliable method of stirring up confusion and agitation in politics is to inject into it the concept of pure morality. That is why the revolutionary spirit has never failed to do precisely that.[16]

14 " La Politique religieuse," *La Démocratie religieuse*, 311.

15 *Ibid.*, 248.

16 The Dreyfus affair was a case in point. If nothing is more sacred than the living body of an individual, no matter who, a condemnation must *ipso facto* be suspect. Society, rather than the condemned, becomes the true culprit. Sympathy for the condemned is the romanticist's true rôle. The gallows and the jail are unjust. Hence the demand for revision; and, to obtain it, excesses are legitimate, for, in this case, violence and passion are proper. If

" . . . It has always lived on this mixture and on this confusion to the detriment of true morality as well as to that of true politics. Morality (i. e., the true) places itself above the wills: now, society arises not from a contract of wills, but from a fact of nature."[17]

Individualism is, therefore, not only a false doctrine, but it is conducive to the rise of disorder and chaos. It is its foster-child, democracy, which is the "anarchic element of the Republic."[18] It has made every Frenchman a king, charged with the duty, which he is unable to carry out, of providing for the public safety and looking after the most general conditions of the national development. "This task is absurd. . . ."[19] "Politics is too intricate and too complex, it has at stake interests too important, too distant, and too general to be abandoned to the caprice of everyone. Everyone is doubtless interested: but, because we are interested in wearing hats and shoes and carrying umbrellas, we do not feel obligated to make our hats, shoes, and umbrellas ourselves."[20] Just as specialized workers make these, so should specialized workers be allowed some discretion in politics. This is not done, however, and the result is confusion and irresponsibility.

This irresponsibility results from the fact that popular sovereignty is really a fiction.[21] It is used as a blind by those who rule. Elections, parliament, political parties, and the adminis-

individualism were true, which it is not, it might be just to disorganize the army, public opinion, and the laws of the state, to upset everything for one person. Being palpably false, it is not only unjust, but also contrary to the demands of public safety to do so (*ibid.*, 242).

17 "C'est ainsi," he continues, "que Vaugeois se trouve amené à s'écrier un jour, '*Nous ne sommes pas des gens moraux.*' Et, à le bien voir, il est impossible de rien faire de plus moral que cette honnête distinction entre deux ordres que l'on confond malhonnêtement" (*ibid.*, 246).

18 "Encore l'organisation de la démocratie," *Gazette de France,* May 4, 1899; *De démos à César,* I, 36.

19 *Enquête sur la monarchie,* 344-345; 454.

20 *Ibid.,* 345.

21 *Ibid.,* 521.

trative system, all the paraphernalia and trappings of this so-called democracy, are but the instruments by which this irresponsible group of conquering thieves first seized control of the government and now perpetuates that control. To ask the source of the false doctrine of individualism, is to ask who constitutes this group. An orientalism which the early Jewish Christians adopted as their own, it is a Jewish-Protestant doctrine [22] which has been prostituted by the Jews, the Protestants, the metics, and the Free Masons—the " four confederated states " to their several advantage. They are the true " kings of the Republic." [23]

How does this alien, cosmopolitan *bloc* rule? Its guiding principle is to divide and rule. Itself united in the interests of its petty, selfish ends against the interests of the nation, it uses the doctrine of equality, the elections, parties, and the like to keep the French divided and in a state of slavery.[24] The doctrine of equality keeps the conquered French from seeing clearly. It places " beneficent and maleficent, anarchic and organic, national and cosmopolitan doctrines on the same footing." In the family, " equality causes the forceful division, the liquidation of the properties, the instability of the homes." [25] Since

22 " Politique et biologie: l'égalité," *Gazette de France*, Jan. 28, 1904; *De démos à César*, I, 142. " Il ne viendrait pas à l'idée d'un bon catholique Français de tirer de saint Luc un encouragement au pillage et à l'insurrection. Et cependant, saint Luc se réjouit parce que ' le Seigneur déposa les puissants du trône ', parce qu'il ' exalta les plus humbles ', parce qu'il ' combla de bien les affamés ', et qu'il ' renvoya les riches les mains vides '.

De même saint Matthieu, dans le sermon sur la Montagne, donne ces paroles du Christ: ' N'appelez personne votre maître, car vous n'avez qu'un maître et il habite dans les cieux '; ' n'appelez personne votre père; car vous n'avez qu'un père, et il habite dans les cieux.' Heureusement, l'Eglise, l'antique Eglise catholique et apostolique de Rome, avertit son fidèle qu'il n'a rien à tirer de textes semblables contre l'autorité des pères de famille, ni contre les maîtres de la cité humaine " (" Une campagne royaliste au ' Figaro,' " *Enquête sur la monarchie*, 507).

23 " La Théorie des quatre états confédérés, maîtres de France," *De démos à César*, II, 33.

24 " Comment faire la monarchie," *Enquête sur la monarchie*, 418.

25 " Politique et biologie: l'égalité," *De démos à César*, I, 143.

equality makes for division and undermines the discipline of the army—weakens France itself—it has the blessings of this *bloc* of robber-states.

Elections serve the same end. The elective system reduces the government to a state of dependence upon the press, opinion, money, and the administrative system, all of which they control and dominate.[26] It creates a perpetual agitation and trouble;[27] so that the Republic may well be "denominated a system of chronic revolution and of constitutional anarchy."[28] Creating division as it does, this constant turmoil is a valuable means to power and to its retention.[29] Reserving the best and most important offices for themselves, they let the French fight for the crumbs that fall from their table. And those who win in this "scramble for employment,"[30] those who are elected to the minor offices or are appointed to the numerous administrative posts, must do as they are instructed to do, the doctrines of personal liberty and equality notwithstanding. These "electoral parasites,"[31] either to give the appearance that the cards are not stacked, or to make their victory doubly certain, resort to stratagems such as changing from a first class railway car, in which they have left Paris, to a third class car from which to alight in their districts, as wearing the poorest clothing and using the worst grammar in their speeches so as to affect the air of the common people, which would be comical if it were not serious.[32] This, together with a feeling that corruption has already decided the election, or, if not, will do so, has the effect of repelling the good people, the *élite,* who, as a consequence, lose interest in the whole affair.[33] Still another factor that makes

26 "Une campagne royaliste au 'Figaro,'" *Enquête sur la monarchie,* 485-486.

27 *Ibid.,* 484.

28 "Réponse à M. Louis Dimier," *Enquête sur la monarchie,* 242.

29 "Une campagne royaliste au 'Figaro,'" *Enquête sur la monarchie,* 484.

30 *Ibid.,* 529.

31 *Ibid.,* 530.

32 *Ibid.,* 529.

33 *Ibid.,* 531.

these people wash their hands of the whole sordid game is the vicious system of mendicancy that has been built up and is maintained by these alien oligarchs. The elector or voter begs favors of the deputy, who begs from the minister, who begs for the votes of the deputy, who, in turn, begs for the votes of the elector.[34] Vicious and corrupt it may be, but it keeps the " anti-national oligarchs in power.

Political parties also serve to keep the French divided and enslaved to this selfish minority. Each shouts to the electors, " Join us and we will divide the profits," [35] and the result is civil and military disorder. France is being torn to pieces by these rapacious party men.[36] " The politicians pillage the state. And the state pillages the nation." [37] That is the system. The cost of government has increased during the last twenty-five years of peace to the tune of nearly a billion francs; and men who are in a position to judge fear the worst. No, contrary to the preachments of these politicians, disinterestedness is a personal virtue. A disinterested corporation or party simply does not exist. So they proceed with their wholesale thievery for the good of the party without the slightest thought of the future [38] or of the nation. After all " France is not a party." [39] They seem, at times, it is true, to be as divided by these parties and party issues almost as effectively as they have succeeded in disuniting the French, their subjects. They really may be at loggerheads among themselves—for an instant; but, next day, this " anti-French *bloc* " will be more united than ever. " Their nature so inclines them." These foreigners, it must be remembered, are bound one to the other by ties of blood and of mutual interests which are ever foremost in their thought and action.[40]

34 *Ibid.*, 525.
35 *Ibid.*, 478.
36 *Ibid.*, 485.
37 *Ibid.*, 524.
38 *Ibid.*, 525.
39 *Ibid.*, 485.
40 " Comment faire la monarchie," *Enquête sur la monarchie*, 418.

The interests of the nation and of public safety, meanwhile, receive but scant attention. Aliens themselves and beneficiaries of the equally alien doctrine of individualism, they have, while remaining true to their own traditions, cut off thousands of Frenchmen from their own. They have not so much ignored the true French tradition as they have fought and opposed it both openly and underhandedly. They have even been prompted by passion to violate not only their own principles, but the law itself. For example, their doctrine holds that a man is not to be interfered with if he wishes to drink strong liquor to the point of extreme intoxication. Similarly, he is not to be hindered from cutting off his own nose or finger. He still remains a citizen and a sacred individual. But let him enter an order of Catholic teachers, or, to be more concrete, let him become a superior in such a congregation: his "quality as man and as citizen promptly disappears." He loses his place in society and in the state.[41] Moreover, property rights are just as insecure as are those of persons in the face of the "nefarious pettinesses" that are perpetrated by these villains for party advantage.[42] These measures are prompted by their anti-Clericalism, for they fear the power of the Roman Church. If the minister of finance were to climb up Eiffel Tower and were to throw from its top the accumulated gold reserves of the Bank of France into the Seine, both poor and rich alike would consider him a likely candidate for the mad-house. But when the minister of the interior does almost the same thing with the spiritual heritage of France, her "virtues, talents, and science," he is applauded.[43]

Some, who are not so completely carried away by passion, or who calculatingly hope to bring about the destruction of Catholicism by a flank attack, say that it is Catholicism's Roman connection that they object to, that they have no objection to a

41 "La Politique religieuse," *La Démocratie religieuse*, 311-312.

42 "Réponse à M. Eugène Ledrain," *Enquête sur la monarchie*, 273; "Une campagne royaliste au 'Figaro,'" *Enquête sur la monarchie*, 504.

43 *Ibid.*, 504.

French Catholic Church completely separated from Rome. They would complete the French nationality by giving it a national church. " Nationalist, it will tend to denationalize us. Framed in the interest of order, it courts revolution. I have cautioned the patriots and the men of order concerning this. The Roman attachment is precisely that which conserves for Catholicism in France its double character, ordered and French." [44] Just as happened in England and Germany, " the importance of the 'tradition' of which Rome is the guardian would diminish, while the importance of the Scriptures would increase." France would be " inundated with Bibles in the vulgar tongue." French art, poetry, thought, and language would be subjected to the influence of the " Semitic genius " as never before.[45] Since the traditional art of France is a priceless possession and Rome's influence helps to preserve it, the Roman connection is most important. It likewise prevents the democratic abbots from becoming too influential. Without Rome, they could no longer be kept in place. Priests would marry, as they do in other countries that have national churches, and France would have to contend with a new " abominable scourge "—that of being overrun by a tribe of Levites.[46]

What is the condition of France, now that she has been ruled several decades by these foreign thieves and villains? With her alien parliamentary system,[47] France has never been weaker or

44 " Une campagne royaliste au 'Figaro,' " *Enquête sur la monarchie*, 505.

45 *Ibid.*, 506.

46 *Ibid.*, 507-508.

47 Born in England, parliamentarism has remained English despite several unsuccessful transplantations. Crown and Lords simply serve as restraints upon the dominant House of Commons. " Voilà le parlementarisme à l'état pur, tel qu'il réussit en Angleterre pour des raisons qui tiennent au fond de l'histoire anglaise et tel qu'il échoue dans tous les autres lieux où le système anglais à été adopté." Germany has a parliament, but without the scourge of parliamentarism, because she has taken into account the special German situation (" Réponse à M. Eugène Ledrain," *Enquête sur la monarchie*, 271-272).

more conquered than she now is.[48] The decline, which set in when France ejected her kings, has been progressive.[49] Although the " four confederated states " have maintained a firm hold on the reins of the government, its personnel and policies have been marked by changeableness and instability. This necessarily weakens the state. Even the constitution is violated. In fact, the powers that be have the habit of violating it.[50] In one sense this is excusable, for its principles and provisions being contrary to nature's imperious rules, necessity demands that they be violated.[51] The chief fault of these alien rulers is that they violate it only in detail.[52] However, this vacillation and instability are in accord with the feminine character of the republican rule.[53] This is true, likewise, of its weakness. But how can a government be strong so long as the power to make war and peace resides in each individual or in the Lower Chamber, which is not in session when it is needed? [54] This system expressly rules out the three primary requisites of a successful diplomacy: rapidity, continuity, and secrecy. It also rejects the necessary requisites of a successful war. For this, promptitude and mystery are absolute necessities. Yet they are made impossible despite the fact that necessity is the " queen of the world." [55] Moreover, the government is so burdened by its many petty functions that the natural attributes of a sovereign state—politics, diplomacy, and the military—tend to disappear.[56] While it is measurably competent in petty details, it is woefully incompetent in big matters that concern the nation as a whole.[57]

48 " Une campagne royaliste au ' Figaro,' " *Enquête sur la monarchie,* 496-497.

49 *Ibid.,* 498.

50 *Ibid.,* 509.

51 *Ibid.,* 511.

52 *Ibid.,* 512.

53 *Ibid.,* 499.

54 *Ibid.,* 510.

55 *Ibid.,* 511-512.

56 *Ibid.,* 526.

57 *Ibid.,* 531.

Decentralization would free its hands so that it would be able to devote its talents and energies to the matters that relate to public safety, but the Republic cannot decentralize for the simple reason that those who rule must hold the elector, and, to hold the elector, it is necessary to have loyal servants. In order to have better elections, more and better civil servants are required.[58]

France, being a " work of art " and not the result of a fatality or of evolution, being the work of men, artists, and kings, with the happy collaboration of nature,[59] seems tired of the growing disorder.[60] Frenchmen are more and more evincing a desire to escape from the politicians [61] and to free themselves from the shackles of " administrative serfdom." [62] The republican disorder is, in fact, " conspiring to establish a superior order," [63] for there is a widespread impatience with the weakness and vacillation of the government, coupled with a fear of the spectre of socialism. If the state were strong, prudent, and independent, there would be little to fear from the latter, because of the numerous medium-sized or small estates; but, since the government is elective and is constrained to beg for votes by

58 " Un roi n'a besoin que de *l'assentiment* général, Mais il faut au pouvoir républicain une délégation expresse et constamment renouvelée de la *volonté* nationale. Il ne dure pas sans l'électeur. Ce pouvoir est donc obligé de tenir l'électeur. Pour tenir l'électeur, il faut tenir le fonctionnaire. Pas de bonnes élections sans le fonctionnaire et, quand on souhaite des élections meilleures, il faut des fonctionnaires plus nombreux et meilleurs! Vous savez ce que ça veut dire.

Qu'un Etat se démocratise, il se centralise aussitôt. L'élu et l'électeur, subsistant l'un de l'autre, se rapprochent, se soudent par la violence de leur appétit commun " [*ibid.*, 527; *cf.* " Réponse à M. Charles le Goffic," *Enquête sur la monarchie*, 197; also " Que la république ne peut pas décentraliser," J. Paul-Boncour and Charles Maurras, *La République et la décentralisation: un débat de 1903* (Paris, 1923), 65-124, *passim*].

59 " Une campagne royaliste au ' Figaro,' " *Enquête sur la monarchie*, 494-495.

60 " Comment faire la monarchie," *Enquête sur la monarchie*, 419.

61 " Une campagne royaliste au ' Figaro,' " *Enquête sur la monarchie*, 478.

62 *Ibid.*, 534.

63 *Ibid.*, 487.

making numerous concessions and promises, the collectivist danger is a very real one.[64]

Some, who share these sentiments, suggest that the Republic be retained, but reformed along nationalist lines by restricting the functions of parliament to controlling the tax levies and placing a dictator in the Elysée who would be the " organ of the general interest." [65] But they forget that the Republic has been the property of a party which has been able to withstand all assaults. This party is the Old Republican party. If it were in a position to accept the normal conditions of the functions of government, it might be acceptable; but this it is not, for it is in " contradiction with the normal life, the safety of the French Order." The latter demands a strong army and " respect for property, for acquired fortune "; it desires the " solid establishment of public peace," and economies; it is a friend of Catholicism; it prescribes war against what Auguste Comte denominated the " revolutionary dogmas." [66] The Old Republican Party, on the other hand, delivers the army over to parliament and to the press; while it normally condemns the pillaging of the state to subsidize the democracy, it welcomes the support of the subversive elements in times of trouble such as 1889 and 1899; it is anti-Catholic; it enforces a legal respect for the dogmas of the Revolution. " But," one is asked, " cannot this party be changed? Why may it not be changed in the direction of this French order? " The answer is that it cannot do so without losing or destroying the bone-structure that gives it its power. This osseous frame-work, as everyone knows, is made

64 *Ibid.*, 500. France has relatively few industrial workers proper. " J'ai donc bien le droit d'établir qu'en France le progrès actuel du socialisme ne saurait résulter des faits économiques, des faits naturels, des faits purs. Il résulte d'une impurité et d'un artifice. Il procède de l'intrusion d'un élément étranger dans l'ordre économique. C'est un scandale, vous disais-je: c'est un scandale politique, rien de plus . . . Le socialisme est rejeté par la nature du sol français, du peuple français. Un seul excitant du socialisme en France: le régime électif" (*ibid.*, 516-517).

65 *Ibid.*, 535.

66 *Ibid.*, 535-536.

up of two confessional minorities, the Jews and the Protestants, who, as we have seen, are bound together by mutual interests and blood in what Waldeck-Rousseau imprudently described as a "natural entente." "The party of Order has no choice. If it rejects anarchy, let it adopt the monarchy. If it rejects the monarchy, let it resign itself to anarchy." [67]

Since public safety and the national interests alike demand order and discipline, a government free from dependence upon elections, and the abolition of the enervating centralized administrative system, those who are conscious of the weakness of France under the Republic and who fear for the safety of the country are of necessity constrained to accept the solution offered by the monarchy. It alone can meet the demands of public safety. An authoritarian king would again make France great and strong. He would restore to France the grandeur that is justly hers.[68] He could do this because he would be free from electoral cares and unhampered by the administrative minutiae that now burden the government. He could act quickly and, at the same time, could pursue a policy faithfully and steadfastly over a long period of time. Strength without would result from the new order and discipline within. France would again be a work of art. The dictator-king would be the great

67 *Ibid.*, 536. "C'est l'étude de '*l'immense question de l'ordre*' (Auguste Comte) qui nous a rendus royalistes," he said (*ibid.*, 534).

68 "Réponse à M. Jacques Bainville," *Enquête sur la monarchie*, 213. "J'aurais beaucoup de questions à faire à M. Ledrain. D'abord, qu'entend-il par l'achèvement de la France. La France était-elle si achevée que cela en 1789? Est-elle achevée aujourd'hui? Je vois au delà notre frontière bien des populations de langue et de civilisation françaises qu'une politique suivie et sage, une politique d'audace et de temporisation capétienne, pourrait, au long des âges, annexer à notre domaine politique. J'aperçois même sur le Rhin, si nécessaire à notre défense militaire, plus d'une Marche germanique dont l'annexion progressive et la lente transformation en Marches françaises auraient aussi leur utilité . . . Personne ne sait ce qui serait arrivé si la forte Maison de France avait continué de veiller à la suite de nos changements historiques; mais il paraît assez probable que la même cause eût engendré les mêmes effets. Effets de grandeur et de gloire. Effets de sage et continu développement" ("Réponse à M. Eugène Ledrain," *Enquête sur la monarchie*, 279).

arbiter in labor disputes; and, although he would not give the workers all that they demanded, they would return to work from a sense of *noblesse oblige*.[69] Inasmuch as all strong and happy states have dynastic kings, France, too, could hope to be again happy and strong.[70]

This royalist solution of the question of the safety of France likewise has the advantage of being scientific and positivist. It is the truth discovered by reason. That it is in substantial agreement with tradition does not detract from its scientific character, for tradition, instinctive as it may be, is not always without profound reasons of its own.[71] Moreover, it is a Catholic as well as a positivist solution. " . . . Auguste Comte always considered Catholicism a necessary ally of science against anarchy and barbarism." [72] Divided in matters relating to the sky, positivism and Catholicism often agree on those having to do with the earth. They " tend to fortify the family. The Church and positivism tend to support the political authorities as coming from God or flowing from the best natural laws. The Church and positivism are friends of tradition, of order, of the fatherland, and of civilization. In a word, the Church and positivism have some enemies in common. Moreover, there is not a French positivist who forgets that, if the Capetians made France, the bishops and clerics were their first coöperators." [73]

69 " Une campagne royaliste au 'Figaro,' " *Enquête sur la monarchie*, 518.

70 *Ibid.*, 486.

71 *Ibid.*, 479-481.

72 "Il [Comte] répétait souvent:—Que ceux qui croient en Dieu se fassent catholiques, que ceux qui n'y croient pas se fassent positivistes . . . Il envoyait un de ses disciples au Gesù de Rome, pour traiter avec les Jésuites. Un malentendu fit échouer ce projet, mais, en quittant les Pères, le délégué de Comte prononça ces graves paroles: *Quand les orages politiques de l'avenir manifesteront toute l'intensité de la crise moderne, vous trouverez les jeunes positivistes prêts à se faire tuer pour vous, comme vous êtes prêts à vous faire massacre pour votre Dieu*" (*ibid.*, 481).

73 *Ibid.*, 481; *cf.* "La Politique religieuse," part two, and "'L' Action française' et la religion catholique," *La Démocratie religieuse*, 255-304, 413-551, *passim*.

Positivism not only points out the evils of the revolutionary doctrines and of the democratic political systems that are based upon them, it not only reveals the advantages that royalism or the monarchy would bring to the nation, but it also shows how this beneficient system may be brought into being. In short, it calls for action as well as for a theory based upon realities. First of all, it rules out despair. That is permitted him who is to die. But nations, compared with men, are immortal. " Broken and divided, they can revive indefinitely." As is well known, there was a French governor in Berlin when Fichte proclaimed in his famous addresses the " universal genius of the German blood and spirit. France can survive equal defeats." [74] Moreover, what one generation fails to accomplish, the next will be able to carry out. But the greatest justification of hope is force. The multitude always follows energetic minorities. It is these that really make history. Therefore, in order to restore the monarchy, the masses need not be converted to royalism. It is enough that the French of the twentieth century do not hate kings as did the Romans in the time of Brutus. Let the energetic minority institute the monarchy. The masses will accept the *fait accompli*. And let the monarchy be established by force, for the governments of this world have been so introduced since this world has been a world.[75] A few of the weaker spirits may object that this would be illegal. As a matter of fact the resort to force is entirely legitimate, for, as has been shown, an " hereditary and traditional, anti-parliamentary and decentralized monarchy " is necessary for France. Laws are sacred, it is true; but the most sacred law of all is that of public safety.[76] " He who said, ' France loves the fist,' uttered a great sentence." [77] If this energetic minority limited itself to legal means only, it would find that its opponent, the Old Republican Party, would violate all the laws it could to oppose it advantageously. Force,

74 " Comment faire la monarchie," *Enquête sur la monarchie*, 414-415.

75 *Ibid.*, 415-416.

76 " Une campagne royaliste au ' Figaro,' " *Enquête sur la monarchie*, 485.

77 " Comment faire la monarchie," *Enquête sur la monarchie*, 418.

it is true, has not always brought the desired results. MacMahon failed because he felt that considerations of personal honor forbade his opposing anarchy too drastically; Boulanger, because he lacked courage and audacity; Déroulède, because he had no reasonable idea. The military leaders, on principle, opposed the anarchism implicit in the plebiscitarian idea.

If the nationalist, Catholic, and conservative opposition desires the power to unseat the anti-French rulers of France, it must meet the following three conditions: first, it must unite; second, it must unite on an idea, for unity of end is the first condition of discipline; third, this idea must be true, otherwise there will be no chance even of immediate success.[78] This last is true, because no conservative revolution is possible without the aid of certain elements in the army and in the administration. To secure this aid the road that is mapped out must be certain and true. This was not true in 1899. This condition the monarchy meets. " By its theoretical truth, the Monarchy can therefore reunite in the name of the national interest men of every origin and every condition: this is the first point. And by its moral, active, and efficient truth, by its disciplining, ordaining, hierarchical value, the Monarchy is agreeable without debate to the military and civil chiefs who, at a given moment, will dispose of the means of an action against anarchy." [79] The immediate task, therefore, is to secure the unity of this opposition upon the political truth, " to establish the Monarchy in the thoughts in order to establish it in the facts." [80]

These conclusions, derived from his method of analysis, this " organizing empiricism," thus make the acceptance of the following program (1903) of the *Action Française* inevitable to all who are truly interested in and concerned about the safety and the grandeur of France:

78 *Ibid.*, 420-423.

79 *Ibid.*, 423.

80 *Ibid.*, 426; *cf.* Charles Maurras and H. Dutrait-Crozon, " Si le coup de force est possible," *Enquête sur la monarchie*, 541-600, *passim.*

The *Action Française* addresses itself to patriotism, when it is conscious, reflective, and rational.

Founded in 1899, in the midst of a political, military, and religious crisis, the *Action Française* is inspired by the nationalist sentiment; its distinctive work has been to submit this sentiment to a serious discipline.

A true nationalist, it has set up as a principle, places the fatherland above everything: he therefore conceives, therefore treats, he therefore resolves all pending political questions in their relation to the national interest.

To the national interest, and not to his caprices of sentiment.

To the national interest, and not to his likes or dislikes, his penchants or his repugnances.

To the national interest, and not to his sluggishness of intellect, or his private designs, or his personal interests.

In yielding to this rule, the *Action Française* was constrained to recognize the rigorous necessity of the monarchy in contemporary France.

Given the will to save France and to place this will to safety above all else, it is necessary to conclude for the Monarchy: the detailed examination of the situation demonstrates, in effect, that a French Renaissance can take place only on this condition.

If the restoration of the Monarchy appears difficult, that proves only one thing: the difficulty of a French renaissance.

If one wishes the latter, one must wish the former.

The *Action Française* desired the latter and the former, it therefore became royalist. Every one of its numbers has tended, since eighteen months, to make royalists.

The old royalists have had pleasure in seeing themselves confirmed, by reasons often new, in their tradition and in their faith. But the *Action Française* has aimed more particularly at the patriots who are all still enlisted in the old democratic, revolutionary, and republican prejudice; it is dissipating this anarchistic prejudice and, from patriotism being rendered more conscious, it is expressing and revealing the royalism which it had been found implicitly to contain. Many republicans have thus been brought back to royalty. Many others will come, if the *Action Française* is enabled to reach them and to teach them.

In the name of the results realized, in view of the possible results, the *Action Française* demands an ardent, devoted, and incessant coöperation of all royalists, old or new.[81]

81 "La Rêponse de M. Jules Lemaître," *Enquête sur la monarchie*, 384, note 2. It will be observed that by 1903 Maurras had won in regard to the disputed points of the program or declaration of 1899, discussed on pages 263 and 264 above. In the *Action Française* of Jan. 15, 1905, when the formation of the *Ligue d'Action Française* was announced, the above program was accompanied by the following "Declaration," which all members of the new League were asked to subscribe to:

"Français de naissance et de coeur, de raison et de volonté, je remplirai tous les devoirs d'un patriote conscient.

Je m'engage à combattre tout régime républicain. La République en France est le règne de l'étranger. L'esprit républicain désorganise la défense nationale et favorise des influences religieuses directement hostiles au catholicisme traditionnel. Il faut rendre à la France un régime qui soit Français.

Notre unique avenir est donc la Monarchie telle que la personnifie l'héritier des quarante rois qui, en mille ans, firent la France. Seule la Monarchie assure le salut public et, répondant de l'ordre, prévient les maux publics que l'anti-sémitisme et le nationalisme dénoncent. Organe nécessaire de tout intérêt général, la Monarchie relève l'autorité, les libertés, la prospérité et l'honneur.

Je m'associe à l'oeuvre de la Restauration monarchique.

Je m'engage à la servir par tous les moyens" (Coudekerque-Lambrecht, *op. cit.*, 122-123).

CHAPTER XIX

THE ACTION FRANCAISE: "A CONQUERING IDEA"[1]

"A TRUE nationalist . . . resolves all pending political questions in their relation to the national interest." This sentence, if one accept Maurras' definitions of the terms used, may well be regarded as not only a summary of his life in the years that followed, but also as an epitome of the history of the *Action Française*. It should be added that, inasmuch as the safety of France demanded, in his opinion, the monarchy as a "logical necessity," he conceived, treated, and resolved the political questions of the day from that angle, hoping to bring about the requisite unity among the opponents of the Republic against that propitious moment when force could be used to advantage in bringing down the Republic and its revolutionary doctrines. Another condition of success, it will be recalled, was that they not only unite, but also that they unite upon the political truth, for without it they could not hope for victory. Truth and necessity being one, the truth that they were to unite upon was royalism in the sense of a dictator-king.[2] To impress this truth upon the nationalist and conservative opponents of the Republic and to persuade them to rally around it with the enthusiasm that is inspired by certitude, Maurras worked indefatigably as a polemist and political critic, using the problems of the day and the, to him, unwise policies of the government to illustrate the truthfulness of his doctrine.

In this work he was aided powerfully by other factors. His colleagues of the *Action Française* were among these. Paul

1 During the "crisis" of 1910-1911, Maurras said, "Nous avons cessé d'être un parti subsistant de ses forces anciennes, ralliant un personnel une fois compté: nous sommes devenus *une idée conquérante*" [*L'Action Française*, October, 1910; Coudekerque-Lambrecht, *Léon de Montesquiou: sa vie politique, L'Action Française* (Paris, 1925), 503].

2 Vaugeois once referred to their campaign as one for a "dictatorial and Jacobin monarchy" (*ibid.*, 18-19).

Bourget once said that the *Action Française* was not a party, but a doctrine.[3] It was, to be precise, an organ of Maurras' doctrine of integral nationalism. In view of his passion to dominate the thoughts of others and the moral superiority which his doctrine gave him over his colleagues, one may even go so far as to say that the *Action Française* was virtually Charles Maurras himself. True to a considerable extent while Henri Vaugeois, its founder, was still alive, it was clearly apparent after Vaugeois' death in 1916.[4] However, no matter how aggressive, determined, and measurably efficient the campaign of Maurras and his colleagues was, it could never have achieved the success it did if the Dreyfusards had not pursued a vindictive policy of revenge after 1899, or if the international situation had not taken a turn favorable to it in 1905 and more particularly in 1911.

To purify the army of their political enemies the Dreyfusards gave the minister of war full power to classify the officers of the army as he saw fit. Hitherto the advancement of the officers had been determined by inspectors general. These were now suppressed by General de Gallifet. Having achieved this, he was replaced by General André with instructions to accelerate the work of purification. This naturally created a need for information of a special sort; hence the *fiches,* or secret information regarding the political and religious opinions of the men in question. If they were seen in a Catholic church, if their children were intrusted to the care of a Catholic educational institution, if their wives had friendly relations with known royalists, their chances of advancement were nil. Government officials high and low were asked to coöperate in assembling this information. An elaborate system of espionage resulted. But

3 *Ibid.*, 298.

4 Léon Daudet, speaking of the period when he became, with Maurras, a co-director of the *Action Française*, remarked, "Vaugeois donna l'impulsion à la propagande. Mais il n'y a aucune espèce de doubte: l'âme du mouvement, ce fut Maurras" [Léon Daudet, *Vers le roi* (Paris, 1921), 51; *cf.* Louis Dimier, *Vingt ans d'Action française* (Paris, 1926), 310-311, 337; Coudekerque-Lambrecht, *op. cit.*, 694].

more serious for the army was the retirement of many valuable officers and their replacement by untried and, frequently, less valuable men. This naturally gave rise to considerable commotion and brought the charge from the anti-Dreyfusards that this espionage was the work of Free Masonry. In 1902 Combes promised that these proceedings would cease. Two years later, however, when he was again reminded of these practices, he replied that he did not know about them. In the midst of an exciting debate upon this question in the Chamber of Deputies, November 4, 1904, Syveton, one of the nationalist members,[5] administered several resounding slaps on the face of the minister of war, André. This gave rise to a battle royal in the Chamber between the opposing deputies which was followed by a vote of censure and temporary expulsion from the Chamber of Syveton. Disregarding the president's order that he retire, he went only upon the arrival of soldiers who were called to usher him out. The government lost no time prosecuting him for premeditated outrages against a minister in the exercise of his duties. But the trial, which was set for December 9 was never held; Syveton was found dead the day before, apparently a suicide because of family troubles. This, at least, was the official version of his death. That of his friends was murder for political reasons. "Who was interested in Syveton's disappearance on that day and not another? The government, and the government only," the *Action Française* declared.[6] The thousands of patriots who attended the funeral several days later restrained themselves during the exercises; but, once they had separated at the Montparnasse cemetery, many of the younger ones began to shout, "*Vive la France! Vive la Liberté!*" Attacked by the police, some went so far as to add, "Down with the assassins!"

The violence with which the *Action Française* denounced the government during this affair brought it many adherents among

5 He, with Vaugeois and Dausset, had been one of the founders of the *Ligue de la Patrie Française*.

6 Jan. 15, 1905; Coudekerque-Lambrecht, *op. cit.*, 118-120.

the young people of Paris.[7] They came to the *Action Française* begging for direction and leadership; and this it was only too glad to give. The result was the formation of the *Ligue d'Action Française* which was formally announced in the review on January 15, 1905. Its announced purpose was to enable the *Action Française* to follow events more closely and perhaps to inject some new factors in them.[8] While this step was noted with pleasure by the friends of the review, some were shocked by the last promise in the Declaration which its members were asked to sign: " I promise to serve it [the monarchical restoration] by all possible means (*par tous les moyens*)." To this feeling of their " timorous friends," who argued that ultimate goals are not attained without transitions, Vaugeois replied that resolution was necessary to establish or bring about these very transitions for the hesitant throng. Moreover, he added, this appeal was directed at leaders, not followers.[9]

But, violent or not, the *Ligue* prospered. In the brief span of six months, more than twenty-five sections were founded in the provinces. New adherents were won in Paris also. Among these the Marquise de MacMahon should be mentioned, for she brought prestige, wealth, and an indefatigable energy, all of which were most useful to the *Action Française*.[10] Many public meetings were held under the auspices of the *Ligue* in which Maurras' doctrines were presented and explained. Inas-

7 Louis Dimier: " Désormais, l'Action Française fut seule à détenir l'espoir du pays " (*op. cit.*, 23); Coudekerque--Lambrecht, *op. cit.*, 120.

8 Coudekerque-Lambrecht, *op. cit.*, 122.

9 *Ibid.*, 123-124.

10 " Celle [i. e. adhésion] de la Marquise de MacMahon apportait à *l'Action Française* un concours précieux. La Marquise de MacMahon était fille du Marquis de Vogué, ancien ambassadeur à Vienne, membre de l'Académie Française, Président du Conseil d'administration du *Correspondant*. Présidente des Dames Royalistes, elle parcourait la France avec une énergie et un dévouement inlassables, organisent des groupements féminins, donnant des conférences que son talent d'orateur rendait fécondes. Sa situation et sa personnalité imposaient " (*ibid.*, 126). She later founded and directed the *Association des Jeunes Filles Royalistes* which was helpful to the movement in countless ways.

much as one of his basic doctrines and prejudices was anti-parliamentarism, the *Action Française* and its *Ligue,* while coöperating with the other royalist organizations which were striving for a parliamentary monarchy, remained separate and distinct, and largely independent.[11] As the *Ligue* spread from one end of France to the other, the need arose for an organization that would meet the spiritual and intellectual needs of the students in Paris more specifically. Hence the formation of another organization, the *Etudiants d'Action Française* in December, 1905.

The *fiches* affair and the death of Syvetón had thus played into the hands of the *Action Française.* It now had a nation-wide organization and a special organization for students in Paris, both of which were to be strengthened by the continued desire of the Dreyfusards for revenge. The act of separation of church and state was promulgated in December, 1905. The property of the church having been declared the property of the state, disputes, often accompanied by violence, arose in many parts of France between faithful Catholics and the civil officials who were ordered to make inventories of the property in question. Many *ligueurs* of the *Action Française* participated in these fracases and suffered imprisonment for their faith or for what they considered to be their patriotism.[12]

11 This was emphasized in May, 1905, when a monarchist press and propaganda congress met in Paris. Members of the *Action Française* attended, but refrained from voting. "... Ce Congrès marque une date important dans la vie de *l'Action Française*; car c'est à cette occasion qu'eut lieu la première divergence entre les royalistes qu'elle avait groupés sur la seule idée du salut public, et ceux qui restaient partisans des méthodes 'libérales' et parlementaires" (*ibid.,* 142-143). According to Dimier, the *Action Française* was not bound to be an organ of the Prince, because it was not royalist at its inception (*op. cit.,* 191-192).

12 The *Bulletin de la Ligue d'Action Française* of February 1, 1906, ended in these words: "Nous avons servi l'armée française; il faut servir l'Eglise de France, par devoir religieux si nous sommes croyants, et, si nous ne le sommes pas, par devoir patriotique. Nous contribuerons de la sorte à faire comprendre que les royalistes ne sont que des patriotes plus conscients et plus clairvoyants que les autres. N'est-ce pas en montrant ses chevrons et ses

While the government was being thus openly opposed, the directing committee of the *Action Française* met frequently with friends, among whom was Léon Daudet. Son of the famous Alphonse, he had given up the idea of becoming a physician after several years of study and had chosen to become a writer. He had joined Edouard Drumont's force at *La Libre parole* and had written several books. In 1904 he had had an interview with the Duke of Orleans in London and had been very favorably impressed. He had admired the attitude of the *Action Française* in regard to Syveton's death.[13] In 1906 he began to attend their meetings.[14] His good humor, his verve, his ability as an orator, his satirical powers, and his violence in word and deed made his adherence a valuable accession to the movement.[15] The subject that was discussed at these meetings which Daudet and other friends attended was whether or not they should establish an institute of higher instruction in royalism, or, to use Daudet's expression, a "royalist Sorbonne." [16] This they finally decided to do, upon the insistence of friends who had the means to make it a success financially.[17] It was opened February 14, 1906, and operated as a subsidiary of the *Ligue d'Action Française*.[18]

cicatrices qu'un soldat se fait écouter dans le conseil?" (Coudekerque-Lambrecht, *op. cit.*, 144).

13 *Ibid.*, 158.

14 Léon Daudet, *op. cit.*, 20.

15 Louis Dimier, *op. cit.*, 122-123; Coudekerque-Lambrecht, *op. cit.*, 157-158. Daudet's following remark about himself must be a sample of his humor: "D'autres assuraient que Daudet étant violent—j'ai toujours eu, *je ne sais pourquoi*, cette réputation..." (*op. cit.*, 44. The present writer's italics).

16 *Op. cit.*, 225.

17 "Inspirée surtout par la Comtesse de Courville et le Comte de Lur-Saluces..." (Coudekerque-Lambrecht, *op. cit.*, 158).

18 The nature of the "superior instruction" that was given here is indicated by the following list of the seven chairs that were created: "La chaire du *Syllabus* pour la politique catholique; la chaire *Auguste Comte* pour la philosophie positive; la chaire *Frédéric Amouretti* pour les relations internationales; la chaire *Rivarol* pour l'histoire des idées politiques; la chaire *Sainte-*

Meanwhile, as the *Institut d'Action Française* was being discussed and inaugurated, Jean Rivain busied himself with the establishment of a publishing house, the *Nouvelle Librairie Nationale,* to publish particularly the bulletins and pamphlets of the *ligueurs,* and books of the members of the *Action Française.* It was designed " to manufacture the implements of the war of the nationalist Independence." [19] This it did, first under Rivain, and later under Georges Valois, who placed the book propaganda of the *Action Française* on a par with its other forms of propaganda.

To the Dreyfusard annulment of the verdict of Rennes of 1899 against Dreyfus and to the promotion of Dreyfus and Picquart by special legislation, the *Action Française* replied by opening a subscription for a gold medal which was to be presented to General Mercier who had played so important a rôle in the original condemnation of Dreyfus. He was now hailed as the " true justiciar." And, not satisfied with this act of defiance, the *Action Française* began to commemorate all of the dates of the Dreyfus affair, launched a violent anti-Jewish campaign, and published excerpts from a severe indictment of Joseph Reinach written by Maurras and Frédéric Delebecque under the pseudonym, Henri Dutrait-Crozon.[20] This anti-Dreyfus campaign was continued with the old zeal and bitterness until 1912, when the *union sacré* of 1914 may already be seen upon the horizon. When, in 1908, at the ceremony accompanying the translation of Zola's remains to the Panthéon, Louis Grégori fired two shots at Dreyfus and wounded him, the *Action Française* stoutly defended Grégori.

Meanwhile, because the other journals gave but little or no publicity to the meetings of the *liguers,* the necessity of a daily

Beuve pour l'empirisme organisateur; la chaire *Maurice Barrès* pour le nationalisme française; la chaire *La-Tour-du-Pin* pour l'économie sociale" (*ibid.,* 163).

19 *Ibid.,* 192.

20 This was published in book form in 1905 as *Joseph Reinach historien: révision de l'histoire de l'affaire Dreyfus.*

organ of the movement obtruded. In 1907 an effort was made to purchase Drumont's *La Libre parole.* Drumont was not unwilling to give up the direction of the journal so long as he would be privileged to contribute his daily article. He was dissuaded, however, by Gaston Méry who preferred a republican dictatorship to a restoration of the monarchy. Having failed in this attempt to secure a journal that was already established, it was agreed that they would found one of their own. After assembling a working capital of 300,000 francs with considerable difficulty, the daily *Action Française* was launched on March 21, 1908. The review, which had been published on the first and fifteenth of every month since 1899, was now discontinued. Vaugeois continued as the director of the daily; Daudet and Maurras alternately supplied the leading article, except on Sunday, when Vaugeois furnished it; Jacques Bainville, who with Maurras now left the *Gazette de France,* commented upon the international situation daily; and Maurras reviewed the press. Friends of the *Action Française,* seeing how little capital they had to start with, expressed the fear that this venturesome undertaking would end as a dismal failure in less than six months, while three months was the time limit that was set by those who were less friendly. Both were to be deceived, as the event showed.[21]

An important aid to those who were struggling to keep the new journal going was the welcome adherence of Jules Lemaître to their movement. A quiet writer of note who disliked publicity and crowds, he was a distinguished and respected member of the Academy. In 1898 he had accepted the presidency of the *Ligue de la Patrie Française.* He was pronouncedly anti-Dreyfusard, but could not bring himself to accept the idea of a dictator-king until 1908, when he finally admitted there was no resisting Maurras' dialectics.[22] His " Letters to my Friend," in which he showed in his inimitable way why the monarchy alone

21 Léon Daudet, *op. cit.,* 26-35; Louis Dimier, *op. cit.,* 180-182; Coudekerque-Lambrecht, *op. cit.,* 309-327.

22 *Léon Daudet, op. cit.,* 190; Louis Dimier, *op. cit.,* 184.

would assure the public safety was published in a series of eleven articles in the *Action Française*.[23] His name, joined with that of Paul Bourget, gave the movement the support of two of the most distinguished writers of France. Both occasionally contributed to the journal and presided over meetings of the *Ligue*.

Lemaître declared his adherence to the *Action Française* early in November, 1908. A month later the excitement that accompanied the Thalamas episode likewise helped to increase the number of subscribers and readers of the journal. It ultimately did more, for from it arose the present annual festival in honor of the memory of Joan of Arc. Thalamas was selected by the authorities of the Sorbonne to give a free public course on the "Pedagogy of History" in the academic year of 1908-1909. This immediately aroused the ire of the *Action Française* and other nationalist groups, because Thalamas was the man who, several years before, had taken a student to task at the Lycée Condorcet for saying that Joan of Arc was a heroine inspired of God. Far from having been so inspired, the professor declared, the evidence adduced at her trial clearly established her servitude to the devil. Moreover, the trial had been regular and proper in every sense; and, in view of her immoral relations with the officers of the royal army, her condemnation was not undeserved. This Voltairean version of the life and death of the Maid of Orleans created so much indignation among his students that they felt impelled to make demonstrations at the different statues of the heroine in the city. Some four years later the man who had thus dishonored a memory that was held sacred by many Frenchmen was honored by the University even though he lacked the requisite standing in the academic world to give courses at the Sorbonne. That there would be opposition was to be expected. Upon his entry in the classroom to give the first lecture of the course, he was received with cat-calls, tumultuous shouting, and eggs thrown by the

23 Republished with comments of Maurras in the *Enquête sur la monarchie*, 365-411.

nationalist students who had come in force to break up the meeting. Having successfully dodged the first egg that came his way, Thalamas decided to leave in haste, after he had been hit by two in quick succession. But a stalwart member of the *Etudiants d'Action Française* threw himself in his path, grabbed the professor by the neck, and gave him a thorough face-slapping. This precipitated a free-for-all fight between the opposing factions of students in the classroom which ended with the admirers of Joan marching out with shouts of "Spit upon Thalamas!" Joined by other students who were attracted by the tumult and by this act of defiance against the authorities, they marched a thousand strong to the statue of Joan at the Pyramids Square and placed a bouquet of flowers on the pedestal of the statue. Then they marched on to the offices of the *Action Française* where they were received with praise and enthusiasm.[24] When, a week later, Thalamas again tried to begin his course under more favorable conditions— no one was to be admitted into the classroom unless he had a card of admission signed by the professor—the *Action Française* apprised its readers of the plan and invited its friends to be at the Sorbonne at the given time to show the disgust with which this " ignoble retreat " inspired them.[25]

Some three thousand patriots answered the call and assembled around the statue of Auguste Comte where they were hemmed in by a cordon of police who forbade them to enter the University grounds or the classroom in question. The rioters, however, decided to enter by force. They pushed on and forced the entrance of the classroom where they were resisted by Thalamas' auditors until armed municipal guardsmen came and drove them out. Reassembling in the street, the patriots, with shouts of " *Vive l'armée!* " paraded to the same statue of Joan, their numbers increasing as they proceeded. Here, as several leaders of the *Etudiants d'Action Française* placed a huge

24 Coudekerque-Lambrecht, *op. cit.*, 107, 388-389; Louis Dimier, *op. cit.*, 111-112.

25 Coudekerque-Lambrecht, *op. cit.*, 397.

bouquet at the feet of the heroine, they were vigorously attacked by the police. Some were wounded, and some were arrested. The cortege broke up with shouts of "Spit upon Thalamas! *Vive Jeanne d'Arc!*"[26]

Thalamas' course was continued, however. When the third Wednesday arrived, the Latin Quarter was in a veritable state of siege. Soldiers and police were everywhere. The nationalists nevertheless assembled under the windows of the classroom, shouting "Spit upon Thalamas!" Here they were charged and dispersed by the police. Reassembling, they marched with growing numbers to the offices of the *Action Française* where they arrived four or five thousand strong. Here they gave the *Action Française* a great ovation and dispersed. The day had not been a great success.

Maurice Pujo, one of the leaders of the *Action Française,* now worked out a plan of attack for the fourth Wednesday that was quite ingenious. The police were out again in full force. Some fifty *étudiants* joined the class of Professor Egger which was in session in the Guizot classroom from 3:15 to 4:15. They maintained the best deportment. When the lecture was over the regular members of the class departed. The *étudiants* remained. Students for the next class began to enter, when Pujo, seeing that his men were in control of the exits, ascended the platform and informed the students who had come for Professor Puech's class that they might retire if they wished, that he was obliged to take the professor's place and offer a free course on Joan of Arc. This announcement was greeted with wild applause. The students who had come to hear Professor Puech remained. As the news of this substitution spread outside the classroom, many other students came, until Pujo's audience numbered some three hundred. Announcing that they were at home here and that violence alone could eject them, he sat in the professor's chair and began his first lecture on Joan. He had hardly begun, however, when the beadle interrupted with the request that Pujo leave his place. The inter-

26 *Ibid.,* 397-398.

rupter was forcibly ushered out and Pujo was at the point of resuming his discourse, when Professor Puech entered the room. Although he had been warned two days earlier, he now asked Pujo what he was doing. Dissatisfied with the reply, he reiterated the beadle's request that Pujo leave. He, too, was ushered out by a strong *ligueur*. As Pujo was at the point of bringing his lecture to a close, officers of the law, followed by a band of armed soldiers, came bearing an order from the dean of the faculty, Croiset. Pujo pronounced the lecture finished and asked the students not to resist the soldiers. They retired quietly and peaceably.[27]

The explosion of a bomb disrupted Thalamas' class of January 6, 1909. Five days later, Pujo undertook to substitute his course for that of Dean Croiset. Speaking to the students who had come to hear him and those who had come to hear the dean, he denounced both Thalamas and Croiset. There was some heckling from Croiset's students, but they refused to comply with the request of their opponents that they retire. Croiset then entered. Pujo, after introducing himself as politely as the circumstances permitted, repeated what he had said. Croiset ordered him to leave. Pujo refused. A battle ensued which ended upon the arrival of an officer of the law. Several arrests followed. Thalamas' course was continued and week after week the *Action Française* invited the *étudiants* to show their displeasure. The seventh demonstration brought 107 arrests alone. Pujo was sentenced to three months' imprisonment and to the payment of a fine of a hundred francs.[28]

On the evening of the day this judgment was handed down the *Action Française* honored the *Camelots du roi* with an artistic festival for the part they had played in the Thalamas

27 On the following day the *Action Française* published this notice: "Au cours de l'incident provoqué par l'expulsion de l'appariteur, son trousseau de clefs—les clefs de la Sorbonne—est resté entre les mains de l'un de nos amis. Il a déposé ce trousseau dans nos bureaux. M. Croiset, Doyen de la Faculté, pourra l'y faire prendre. Nous le tenons à sa disposition" (Coudekerque-Lambrecht, *op. cit.*, 404).

28 *Ibid.*, 419-422.

affair. This group had arisen from the need of hawking the new journal in the streets of Paris. Having been referred to as *camelots* (peddlers) in their license from the police, they were so designated by the management of the *Action Française* until the need arose of describing them to foreigners, when someone hit upon the name, "Peddlers of the King." [29] It quickly became popular. Pujo, their leader, now under sentence of imprisonment and fine, was naturally cited with the highest praise and the new song of the *camelots, La France bouge,* was sung with zest and enthusiasm. An adaptation of *Le Midi bouge* of Paul Arène, it had come into being during the anti-Thalamas demonstrations. Pujo, Maurras, and others contributed to its eleven stanzas, the sentiment of which was that France was "seeing red" because of the dominance of the Jews in French public life.[30]

Several weeks later the last scheduled lecture of Thalamas was broken up by some fifty *étudiants* who entered the classroom by deception. As Thalamas began his lecture, Pujo raised his voice and shouted, "Be silent, M. Thalamas, you have no right to speak in the Sorbonne!" Thalamas arose from his chair, picked up his papers, and started to leave. But his way was barred. He was caught by one of the *étudiants* and was given a first-class flogging amidst the applause of the witnesses. This, however, promptly came to an end as the police arrived and arrested forty-five persons. The others, after rejoining their friends outside, decided to end the day with a fitting anti-Dreyfusard flourish. They paraded to the Denfert-Rochereau Square where they tore down and broke up the statue of a defender of Dreyfus, Ludovic Trarieux.

The Sorbonne had refused to be intimidated, but the *Action Française* had gained a considerable following among the students of Paris. While it could not claim credit for the promulgation at Rome of the beatification of Joan of Arc on April 18, 1909, it and allied nationalist groups were gratified by the

29 Louis Dimier, *op. cit.*, 119-120.

30 They may all be found in Coudekerque-Lambrecht, *op. cit.*, 425-429.

event. A considerable number of *camelots* went to Rome to witness the ceremony, while *étudiants* and *camelots* who remained in Paris honored the heroine by taking crowns to her four statues in the city. Resisted by the police on the ground that they had no authorization from the custodian of public monuments to decorate statues, they insisted on carrying out their project. Riots resulted and arrests followed. The *Action Française* was, however, making progress in its campaign to establish the cult of the blessed heroine of France.

Early in the following year the *Jeunesse d'Action Française* was organized. It comprised the *étudiants,* the *camelots,* and other students who now joined the movement. The anti-Thalamas demonstrations were bearing fruit. Other crusades followed. The Jew, Schrameck, director of the penitentiary services, was prevented from giving a lecture on these services at the *Ecole des Hautes Etudes* by the newly liberated Pujo and a band of *camelots.* More important was the success of the *jeunesse* in forcing another Jew, Lyon-Caen, to resign his deanship of the law faculty of the University against the wishes of Doumergue, the minister of public instruction. The flood of 1910 in Paris was also turned to account by the *Action Française.* It raised money by subscription, distributed free soup to the needy, and sent the *camelots* out to help the police discourage brigandage in the abandoned homes and to rebuild homes that were wrecked. The *Action Française* thus won friends and, with the exception of a few incidents in the districts where the police were ordered not to let the *camelots* coöperate with them, the police in general welcomed its assistance and seemed to be inclined to look upon it with greater indulgence.[31]

Meanwhile, as Paris was recovering from the devastation wrought by the flood, what has been called the "crisis" in the history of the *Action Française* began to make its appearance. It had its inception in an article dealing with a supposed interview which its author had with the Duke of Orleans in the

31 *Ibid.,* 471-476.

Gaulois of March 20, 1910. The Prince was said to have formally disavowed the politics of the *Action Française*. Appearing in a royalist journal, as it did, this looked bad. When Roger Lambelin, chief of the Prince's office in Paris, was consulted, he said his bureau had not been consulted and that, therefore, the writer had made the statement solely upon his own responsibility. This did not satisfy the leaders of the *Action Française*. To them, it appeared that the government had won an important victory over the *Action Française* through the aid of the Jewish director of the *Gaulois,* Arthur Meyer. Maurras and several other leaders were sent to Seville to interview the Pretender. While the trip was not a complete success,[32] the Duke of Orleans did say in a declaration that was drawn up in their presence that his words regarding the *Action Française* had been misinterpreted, that he had not criticized its policies in regard to current problems, and that its ideas were in complete agreement with his. While much was made of this statement both in the journal and in meetings of the *Ligue,* the *Action Française* continued to vilify Arthur Meyer as the agent of the government and of the Jews. But, shortly after the minister of the interior had announced a policy of appeasement toward the extremists of the Right and of the Left, a new situation was created by Lucien Lacour's slapping of Briand, the prime minister, at the dedication of the monument of Jules Ferry at the Tuileries. Lacour, who was vice-president of the *camelots,* had suffered imprisonment; as a Catholic, he hated both Ferry and Briand; and, as a former soldier, he disliked the appointment to the ministry of war of Lafferre, one of the ring-leaders in the *fiches* affair. Grievances he therefore had. As the opposition thundered imprecations upon the *Action Française,* the latter invited more by launching an appeal to the country to raise a sum to defray the cost of a gold medal that was to be given Lacour in prison.

This was too much for the moderates in the official entourage of the Prince. A note of "confidential instructions" was sent

32 Louis Dimier, *op. cit.,* 196.

to the *Action Française* from the Paris office of the Duke, demanding control of all its acts, the right to revise all of its articles, etc. These demands were summarily rejected by the directors of the journal on the ground that the aim was to hinder and destroy it. " We then had only to choose," Montesquiou said later, " either, if we yielded, to die of a slow consumption, or to break the windows in order to have air. We have broken the windows, and now, I assure you, we are breathing more freely." [33] This had all come about, he added, because the Prince had been misled by false counsellors. To this refusal to accept the dictation of the Paris office, the Prince replied by condemning the leadership of the *Action Française* and denouncing the use of violence in the effort to advance his cause. The schism could scarcely have been more complete. The *Action Française,* while fervently protesting its loyalty to the Prince, replied to these strictures by reiterating in the journal and on the platform that he was the victim of a Jewish intrigue.[34]

As the crisis continued, the *Action Française* conducted a bitter campaign against the Jews, one that culminated in a brilliant victory for the *camelots* and the journal. Henry Bernstein, a prominent Jewish playwright who had deserted from the army after seven months of service and had boasted of his desertion, had written a play, *Après moi,* which was to be produced at the Comédie-Française, beginning February 20, 1911. Unable to prevent its presentation on the first evening, although they had substituted " Jewish deserter " for " *Après moi* " on the signs advertising the play, the *camelots,* with Pujo leading, interrupted the performance of the second evening with cat-calls and a speech by Pujo. Although the police force at the theatre was augmented the third evening, comments about the deserter were ingeniously intercalated in the lines by the *camelots,* frequently to the amusement of the audience. This continued. For example, when, during the performance of the fifth evening, one of the characters asked, " What is the irre-

33 Coudekerque-Lambrecht, *op. cit.*, 513; *cf.* Louis Dimier, *op. cit.*, 197.

34 Coudekerque-Lambrecht, *op. cit.*, 528.

parable thing?" a *camelot* replied in a loud voice, "It is to be circumcised."[35] The play ended amidst derisive laughter and cries of "Deserter!" The police were active, but the demonstrations continued even though the actors had changed the lines to discourage interruptions from the audience. On the eighth night the audience was made up almost wholly of police and *camelots*. When the inevitable interruptions began, the police acted swiftly and brutally. The *camelots* protested noisily; then gradually left the theatre. Outside some six or seven thousand patriots milled about, shouting against the deserter. Pujo, at the head of a column of *camelots*, charged the entrance, but was arrested inside. The play and the campaign against it continued until the last performance was given on March 2. The government had intervened to suppress the play. On this occasion more than ten thousand patriots participated in the riot which the protestants staged.

Finally, on May 19, 1911, the *Action Française* published a letter which the directing committee had received from the Prince in which he declared himself enlightened concerning the intrigues that had given rise to the crisis, accepted the vows of the directors, and applauded the efforts and the generous spirit of those who were making sacrifices for his cause.[36] Less than a month later the Prince's Paris office announced the temporary suspension of the *Correspondance nationale* and the Prince's acceptance of the resignation of the head of the office.[37]

This retreat of the Duke was doubtless dictated by the fear of losing the support of the legitimist royalists who were not enthusiastic admirers of the Orleanists and who, for the most part, supported the *Action Française* during the crisis.[38] The Prince thereafter not only asked the *Action Française* for advice on how to restore the monarchy, but also gave it a free hand. However, according to Dimier, who it must be recalled

35 *Ibid.*, 543.

36 *Ibid.*, 571.

37 *Ibid.*, 575.

38 Louis Dimier, *op. cit.*, 198-199.

was writing after he had severed relations with the *Action Française,* the victory of the latter brought no political results whatsoever. "It did not create the monarchy; from the credit which it acquired with the Prince, it drew no important action. After, as before this decisive step, the rôle which it played was no other than that of a nationalist party to which it mattered little that Monsieur the Duke of Orleans had given it its freedom." [39] Despite the statement of Vaugeois that Maurras was in "constant communication" with the Prince, it remained only an abstract desire. The Prince, who had lost several important friends because of his retreat, was now, except for rare and brief references, abandoned by the *Action Française.* He had the solitude which is usually associated with exile.[40]

This quasi-abandonment of the Pretender may be explained in part by the emergence of questions that were more immediately related to the question of public safety than that of the restoration—questions that brought a change in the policy of the government and were, in turn, emphasized by this change. This last is illustrated by the following statement of Maurras, penned in 1916. After referring to the Thalamas affair which we have discussed above and to the election of Thalamas to the Chamber of Deputies in 1910—after he had recanted and publicly retracted his earlier statements concerning Joan of Arc—Maurras continued, "However, up to 1911, there were policemen to arrest and judges to punish by fine or imprisonment youths who were guilty of carrying flowers to the Saint of the fatherland. It is only since 1912 that the cult of the good Lorrainer can be celebrated by immense corteges in the streets of Paris." [41] On May 28, 1911, the police interfered with the celebration. Some *ligueurs* and *camelots* were injured and a considerable number were arrested.[42] But, on the eve of her day

39 *Ibid.,* 201.

40 *Ibid.,* 203.

41 "Préface de 1916," *Quand les Français ne s'aimaient pas* (Paris, 1926), xi.

42 Coudekerque-Lambrecht, *op. cit.,* 568-571.

in 1912, Pujo was summoned to the prefecture of the police and was informed that the government would not oppose the demonstration that had been planned, that the police had been instructed to arrive at an agreement with the *Action Française* regarding the dispositions to be made. The presence of the police and soldiers, useless as it was in the interest of order, made the procession the more impressive. On the following day almost all the press demanded that this festival be given official sanction and be made a national fête. A commission was named to bring this about.[43]

This reversal of policy on the part of the government in regard to the cult of Joan is but symptomatic of the new spirit that came to dominate in France after the Agadir crisis of 1911. After the fall of the Caillaux ministry in January, 1912, which, according to the *Action Française,* brought to an end the "great republican period" that had begun in 1899,[44] the "Poincaré experience" created a situation that prompted Etienne Rey to write in 1912 that the old prejudice against the army was disappearing, that there was a widespread desire for a government that could and would govern, and that patriotism was definitely becoming more popular throughout the country. "The best of the nationalist doctrine," he concluded, "is now in the hands of the republican party."[45] Already in 1912 the policy of the republican government was substantially what it was in the "last year" before the war, when it was frequently referred to as that of the "*Action Française* without the king."[46] The leaders of the *Action Française* would have been superhuman not to have been affected by this flattering acceptance of their doctrine by the ruling forces of France.

Perhaps more satisfying than the change of policy of the government was the response of the people to this change. "The renaissance of French pride" was not simply a political pheno-

43 *Ibid.*, 617.

44 Joseph Caillaux, *Mes prisons* (Paris, 1921), 17.

45 Etienne Rey, *La Renaissance de l'orgueil français* (Paris, 1912), 137.

46 *Kiel et Tanger* (Paris, 1921), 231.

menon: it was moral, spiritual, and popular. Happy in their new-found pride, erstwhile Dreyfusards did not mind admitting that the *Action Française* was in large part responsible for this "renaissance." Already before the Agadir crisis Jules Lemaître had noticed that the young republican followers of Briand were showing a propensity to adopt all or part of the program of the *Action Française*. This, however, was kept under cover until the Agadir awakening permitted them to come out into the open with the ideas they shared with the *Action Française*. Patriotism again became fashionable, and people no longer blushed for showing it.

Poincaré, less circumspect than Briand and his followers, threw all considerations of prudence aside in applying the doctrines of the *Action Française*. He even violated republican principles by calling upon the regional and municipal fatherlands to come to the aid of the common French fatherland.[47] Maurras had criticized Delcassé, after his resignation in 1905, for not having kept the French public informed.[48] This lesson was now carefully observed by Delcassé himself in 1911 and by Millerand and Poincaré in 1912. Poincaré had a reception room for the Parisian press at the Quai d'Orsay, while Millerand, as minister of war, had the soldiers parade in the streets at frequent intervals so that the people might see them and salute the flag. People learned to look upon the generals, the admirals, and the "military politicians" with confidence and gratitude. The latter were enthusiastically applauded, when, borrowing the phraseology of the *Action Française,* they announced that they were upholding the national interest over against that of the party.[49] "Believing success assured, some republican optimists lost all restraint: without discretion, they confessed whence the example and the lesson came." [50]

47 *Kiel et Tanger*, 230-231.

48 As Ernest Dimnet expressed it, while everyone was talking peace, "Delcassé was preparing war, and he knew it; and he knew that Germany knew it" [*France Herself Again* (New York and London, 1914), 145].

49 *Kiel et Tanger*, 228-229.

50 *Ibid.*, 229. Etienne Rey, for example, said, "Il est certain qu'il y a

Except for its extreme chauvinism, the *Action Française* was apparently more considerate of the government. This was true even during the Franco-German negotiations of 1911 over the Congo region. According to Maurras, revelations were brought to the *Action Française* by misguided patriots which could have been used to embarrass seriously the Caillaux government, but that it refused to do so because it could do nothing that would weaken France's external position.[51] Similarly, after the "great republican period" had given way to the "Poincaré experience" in January, 1912, when the *Action Française* saw many of its own doctrines given nation-wide publicity by the powerful propaganda machine of the government and made the basis of the latter's policy, there was a tendency not to want to jeopardize the application of these doctrines. Except for a few minor accidents or clashes with the police, such as that at Versailles on December 1, 1912, when the *ligueurs,* after a hearty banquet, placed flowers at the feet of the Louis XIV statue,[52] the relations between the *Action Française* and the republican government were more friendly than they had been at any time before. In fact, the government's policies were, for the most part, vigorously supported. Maurras' enlarged *Kiel et Tanger* and Daudet's *Avant-guerre* were published in 1913 to heighten the widespread fear of Germany which the government was stirring

quelques années le sentiment de la patrie avait fléchi dans tout le pays; en lui donnant une forme vigoureuse et combative, *l'Action Française* a préparé son réveil, et pris une part des plus actives au mouvement actuel de renaissance française" (*op. cit.,* 132-133).

51 Although this fits perfectly with considerations of public interest, one is left wondering if this was the sole reason, if the recent crisis may not have cooled its ardor for the restoration of the monarchy.

52 The clash seems to have been less the fault of the *ligueurs* than of the police. Maurras, who figured in this affair and tried to avoid trouble, was arrested and condemned to eight months' imprisonment for having administered "blows and wounds." Impartial witnesses claimed he was innocent of the charge. The case was appealed; but, before it appeared in the court of appeal the government had had an amnesty law passed that suppressed the effects of the condemnation. He was not permitted to seek acquittal (Coudekerque-Lambrecht, *op. cit.,* 652-653).

up to justify its new aggressive policy. The government was criticized only when it showed weakness in pursuing this policy. And Barthou's ministry was defended as had been Poincaré's. Its three-year military law was supported with ardent zeal in the journal and in special public meetings which the *Action Française* convened and sponsored; and the *camelots,* now, curiously enough, allies of the government, disrupted protest meetings against the law.[53]

It further aided the government by bitterly denouncing opponents of this forward policy—especially Caillaux and Jaurès. When, in December, 1913, Barthou was forced out of office by a combination of votes controlled by Caillaux, the newly chosen leader of the Radical Socialist Party, the violence of the nationalists was extreme.[54] In the campaign of vilifying abuse that was launched against the person and activities of Caillaux, now minister of finance, by the nationalist journals, Gaston Calmette, the director of the *Figaro,* dealt the lowest and apparently the most painful blows, for it was he who was murdered by the enraged wife of Caillaux on March 16, 1914. The nationalists, furious before this act of violence, were now fanatically so.[55]

53 *Ibid.*, 661; *Pour en sortir* (Paris, 1926), 33.

54 That this was not liked by Poincaré, the President of the Republic since January, 1913, may well be imagined. Baron Guillaume, the Belgian minister to France and an eye-witness of these developments, described Poincaré's predicament to his home government in the following manner in a report of March 10, 1914: "L'obligation où M. Poincaré s'est trouvé . . . de confier le pouvoir à M. Caillaux, tout en l'attribuant nominalement à M. Doumergue, l'a profondément indisposé. *La personnalité du ministre des Finances, dont il connaît les qualités et aussi toutes les faiblesses, lui est profondément antipathique. Il y a vu un échec pour la politique militaire et nationaliste qu'il poursuit depuis le jour déjà où il avait été placé à la tête du gouvernement comme président du Conseil . . .*" [Joseph Caillaux, *op. cit.*, 23, note (1). The italics are Caillaux's].

55 Louis Dimier: "Une colère égale à celle qu'avaient soulevée les premières manoeuvres pour Dreyfus s'alluma du haut en bas de l'échelle sociale, dans tous les coeurs. La rue respirait la vengeance, les grands intérêts souhaitaient la dictature, la réflexion philosophique augurait la fin du régime. Les comparaisons historiques, toujours puissantes en pareil cas, inspiraient des idées semblables; on rappelait qu'à la chute du second empire le meurtre

On the day after the shooting, when it appeared that Caillaux was determined not to give up his position in the government, the *Action Française* characteristically announced, "If today Joseph Caillaux is still minister of finance, we invite our friends and all good Frenchmen to meet this evening, at nine o'clock, between the Opera and Drouot Street, in order to go and dislodge from his palace the assassin who has dishonored France." [56] However, Caillaux, who was now loudly denounced in the streets and in the nationalist press as "assassin," "bandit," and the "lacerator of the Congo," was spared this indignity by a timely resignation. Two days later the *Action Française* announced that the obsequies of Calmette would be celebrated on the following day, and invited its friends and the Parisian populace to be present.[57] Six thousand *ligueurs* responded to the appeal and helped to swell the total of some twenty thousand Parisians who attended the exercises.[58] Out of respect for the expressed desire of the Calmette family, "the most religious silence was observed" during the ceremony, though "cries of indignation and of vengeance" arose in every breast. As the *ligueurs* were marching home, however, trouble

de Victor Noir commis par Pierre Bonaparte avait servi d'avant-coureur. Quel moment pour l'Action Française, si son aptitude au coup de force, annoncée depuis quinze ans, eût été réelle!" (*op. cit.*, 242).

56 *L'Action Française*, March 17, 1914; Coudekerque-Lambrecht (*op. cit.*, 721).

57 "Si nos amis et la population parisienne se sont rendus en foule aux funérailles de Déroulède [he had died January 30, 1914, and had been buried February 3; the column of the *Action Française* was said to have numbered at least 3,000 persons], ce sera pour eux un devoir plus impérieux encore de suivre le cercueil de ce bon Français que l'on a tué parce qu'il voulait révéler à la France les crimes des bandits au pouvoir. C'est pour nous tous, Français, que Calmette est mort! les balles qui l'ont frappé lâchement par la main d'une femme ont été le dernieur moyen employé par des misérables aux abois pour empêcher de paraître la vérité où nous pouvions trouver le salut. Elles étaient aussi un essai audacieux pour intimider et faire taire à jamais ceux qui refusent de se résigner au règne des voleurs et des assassins" (Maurice Pujo, *l'Action Française*, Mar. 19 1914; Coudekerque-Lambrecht, *op. cit.*, 729).

58 *Ibid.*, 730.

arose. Someone shouted, "*Vive Caillaux!*" To this the column, responding to a signal from Pujo, replied with deafening shouts of "Down with Caillaux! down with the Assassins!" The "aggressor" was promptly seized and manhandled by the *ligueurs*. As the latter were leaving, their victim drew a revolver from his pocket and fired—apparently in the air, for no one was injured. The angry *ligueurs* now proceeded to punish him thoroughly until he was rescued by the police.[59]

Although the *Action Française* and the other nationalist groups were in an angry mood over the defeat of the Barthou ministry in December, 1913, and the assassination of Calmette, there was little in the political developments up to the outbreak of the World War that assuaged their wrath. It is true, the Doumergue ministry had come to power with the promise to "apply loyally" the three-year law, even though some of its members were outspoken opponents of it. The nationalists, therefore, had a promise that could not be broken if the government continued to pursue the program of compromise with which it came to power. The Leftist victory in the legislative elections from April 26 to May 10, 1914, which was won despite the hue and cry about the "assassin Caillaux," the formation

59 The events of this day provoked the following remarks in the *Vorwaerts* of Berlin which the *Action Française* republished with pride in its own columns, April 14, 1914: "*L'Action Française* est aujourd'hui indiscutablement l'organisation de combat la mieux conduite en France, sans excepter, hélas! la classe ouvrière elle-même. Les deux mille [Coudekerque-Lambrecht said six] adhérents qui se déployaient là (aux obsèques de Calmette) avec une discipline admirable ne paraissent pas être d'une intelligence supérieure, mais ils sont énergiques, brutaux, fanatiques. La partie intellectuelle du mouvement jeune royaliste est concentrée dans son journal, intitulé également *l'Action Française* qui, depuis six ans qu'il existe, a acquis un nombre importants de lecteurs. *L'Action Française* est incontestablement, parmi les journaux non socialistes de France, le plus intéressant. Il offre le plus bizarre mélange d'intelligence et de vulgarité, de science et de stupidité. En égard à la platitude du triste républicanisme bourgeois décadent qui, radical aussi bien que modéré, est rivé à l'insipide pacotille du profit politique quotidien, la critique de Maurras, Bainville, etc., avec leurs larges perspectives, offre incontestablement beaucoup d'attrait. Une grande partie des étudiants est maintenant sous leur influence" (Coudekerque-Lambrecht, *op. cit.*, 749).

of the *Fédération des Gauches* by Millerand, Barthou, and others in January, 1914, and the new interpretation which the *Action Française* now placed upon its *par tous les moyens* by adding "even legal"—i. e. by participating in the electoral campaign to secure votes for the men it favored [60]—was really a more serious political defeat for those who were interested in continuing the militaristic and nationalistic policy that Poincaré had inaugurated in 1912. The Leftists not only won a decisive majority of the deputies, but Caillaux himself was reëlected with a thumping majority. As Caillaux remarked later, "Everyone perceived that the will of the country pointed to a Caillaux-Jaurès ministry, or, at least, to a government placed under the aegis of these two men." [61] However, the "will of the country" had to bow to the determination of the patriots and nationalists who were interested in continuing Poincaré's aggressive policy; for, when, on June 2, Doumergue was forced out, a cabinet crisis ensued that culminated almost two weeks later in the formation of the Viviani Radical Socialist and Socialist Republican ministry on a platform calling for an income tax and the organization of the reserves—i. e. the retention of the three-year law. The law was again saved, though most of the ministers were opposed to it. It was in this precarious position when the World War began.[62]

The nationalists were both alarmed and angry. The *Action Française,* which had set aside party considerations in its appeal

60 Louis Dimier, *op. cit.*, 240-241.

61 *Op. cit.*, 25.

62 Charles Seignobos, "L'Evolution de la 3e République," in Ernest Lavisse, *Histoire de France contemporain*, VIII, 287-288; Coudekerque-Lambrecht, *op. cit.*, 768-771. On May 31 *Le Temps* published an interview of General Joffre in which he declared he would resign his position as chief of staff of the army if the new Chamber tampered with the three-year law. Explaining the program of the ministry, Viviani said, "Si, en octobre 1915, je suis encore au pouvoir, je ne libérerai pas les classes qui seront sous les drapeau" (Coudekerque-Lambrecht, *op. cit.*, 769). Count Albert de Mun, seeing that the law was again saved, remarked that it was curious and instructive to note that though the radicals had denounced the law in their constituencies, none dared to take a position against it in this crisis.

to the " entire patriotic population " to enter into the celebration of Joan of Arc's day in May and to which more than 50,000 people had responded,[63] was violently partisan in its reaction to these developments and others that followed. The debate of July 13 in the Senate on military expenses brought forth the statement of Messimy, the secretary of war, that he had received an " imperative demand " from the minister of finance to reduce expenses.[64] This, coupled with the acquittal of Mme. Caillaux three days later, inspired more diatribes against Caillaux, who, though not finance minister, was held to be so unofficially. These developments and the widely heralded reports of German espionage were assumed to justify the statement that Germany was actually ruling France.[65] But Caillaux was not the only influential French politician in German pay, according to the *Action Française*. In his article of July 18, 1914, Maurras declared, " Everyone knows that M. Jaurès is Germany. . . . It is known that our politics is not one of words. The seriousness of acts corresponds to the realism of the ideas." [66] Thirteen days later, amidst the excitement created by the approach of war and the mobilization of the French army, Jaurès died at the hand of the assassin, Villain.[67] The day of *revanche,* so long sought by Barrès and Maurras, had come: it was to bring down the " enemy within " as well as the one without.

Lack of space and the limits imposed by our topic, " The *Rise* of Integral Nationalism in France," forbid our following

63 Coudekerque-Lambrecht, *op. cit.*, 752-753.

64 *Ibid.*, 794.

65 *Ibid.*, 806.

66 Joseph Caillaux, *op. cit.*, 27.

67 Already a year before, July 24, 1913, Jaurès, after referring to the repeated demand of certain journals that he be assassinated, had said, "Après des colonnes de calomnies, vos journaux ajoutent en parlant de moi, de nous, de nos amis: à cette exécution s'ajoutera au jour de la mobilisation une exécution plus complète" (*ibid.*, 28). According to Caillaux, Villain carried out only half of his task, that he had looked for him (Caillaux) in vain two whole days (*ibid.*, 28).

the growth of Maurras' movement further. Suffice it to say, Maurras and the *Action Française* gained added credit and prestige in the eyes of many Frenchmen during the war. It joined heartily in the *union sacrée* that was proclaimed at the outset of the war; it applauded the adjournment of parliament and the establishment of a virtual military dictatorship; and it played an important rôle in exposing and fighting the defeatism of Caillaux and Malvy, a crisis that resulted in the establishment of Clemenceau's dictatorship. According to Caillaux, this dictatorship was less Clemenceau's than that of the *Action Française* and the allied nationalist groups that supported and controlled him.[68] Long before the war was over it joined the other nationalist journals in demanding that Germany pay the entire cost of the war; and, in order not be outdone by the others, it added the demand that the Rhineland be seized and parceled out to the French soldiers as remuneration for their services during the war.[69] It warned the French public not to be taken in by Woodrow Wilson's idealism [70] and insisted that public safety demanded not only that France have the Rhineland, but also that Germany be reduced to the morcelated state it was in after the Treaty of Westphalia.[71] Since the Treaty of Versailles failed to realize these objectives, it was bitterly denounced as "the bad treaty." [72] For these aims the *Action Française* continued to fight as stubbornly as it did for a restoration of the monarchy, though there is reason to believe that public safety, even under the Republic, was more important to it than the desired restoration.[73]

68 *Op.* cit., 62.

69 *La Part du combattant* (Paris, 1917), 42.

70 In *Les Trois aspects du président Wilson* (Paris, 1920), Maurras described Wilson as the "Puritan pope of Peace and Justice" (195), the "president of adversity" (204), whose Fourteen Points were a sort of "Chinese medicine" (130).

71 *Le Mauvais traité* (Paris, 1928), I, 26, 34-35; II, 159-304.

72 *Ibid.*, I, 71-157.

73 *Cf.* Louis Dimier, *op. cit.*, 314-329.

CHAPTER XX

CONCLUSION

Diogenes Laertius, in his letter to Pythocles, said of Epicurus, " He holds that the Sage will be reverent in time and place to his Prince, and that he will cherish whatsoever will solicit his good graces. He will not be troubled by visions in sleep any more than by the things that pass before his eyes while awake." Similarly, in another letter, to Herodotus, he said, " . . . It is not meet that the life of a happy person be embarrassed by affairs which could trouble his repose and his felicity, as from being anxious about something, and from getting into an angry passion, or from rejoicing over his success, because such passions would be capable of rebuking him . . . with fear, indigence, and infirmity. Again, we must not think that every time we see lightning in the sky and hear thunder that it is the Gods who are wreaking their anger upon the earth: because Divinity is not accustomed to harboring such feelings. I always find it well to speak of these things with words chosen with such skill that they offend no one, and at the same time are not repugnant to what is right: because, otherwise, our souls would never be exempt from the passions which the difference of opinions on this dispute could produce for them." [1]

That Maurras has been reverent toward the Prince of his choice and that he has cherished a goal dear to the Prince few will gainsay. But how different his life has been from the peaceful life of Epicurus, living with his disciples in a quiet garden near the Dipylon! Despite his vaunted *musique intérieure* Maurras' fierce polemics and sharp invective have been too genuine to be characterized as simple mechanical operations that left his inner being unmoved. Instead of seeking words that would not offend, he has chosen words that would; instead

1 *Les Six livres de Lucrèce de la nature des choses,* translated by Michel Marolles, Abbé de Villeloin (Paris, 1659), 375, 351.

of striving to avoid disputes in the hope of attaining and preserving the perfect serenity and tranquility of soul characteristic of the gods of Epicurus, he has sought them. True to his principle, *par tous les moyens,* he has usually forced the issue and refused the enemy quarter, undeterred by generally accepted moral considerations.

To have asked whether this was moral would not have made sense to him, for " supreme happiness," the " sovereign good," engendered by beauty and preserved by public safety, justified any measures whatsoever, provided they brought the desired results. Hence his desire to free men from moral and metaphysical concepts such as God, Liberty, Justice, Duty, and the like, which might hinder the attainment of the desired objective. Once these moral and metaphysical " clouds " were brushed aside and swept away, beauty, and its repository, a great and powerful France, would stand resplendent and grow unhindered toward perfection in the bright, clear sunlight of naturalism and " Traditionalism." Before streamlining was conceived by our modern airplane and automobile designers, Maurras devised a " streamlined " system of ideas which was likewise designed to attain the given objective more speedily and more surely.

As an artisan of beauty, Maurras was especially concerned with form—enduring form. He was, in fact, a sort of Phidias, a worker in stone.[2] As a political sculptor, he was interested in the frontiers of his country. To touch them was to disfigure it as one mutilates a beautiful work of art. Hence his desire that the army, the navy, and the diplomatic service be directly under the dictator-king, unrestrained by an uncertain and unwieldy parliament. Hence, likewise, his *politique d'abord:* the monarchy was necessary to realize the political work of art, the orderly state he envisaged. While institutions such as the family,

2 Pierre Moreau: " Il est, en vrai fils de l'Hellade, plus enclin à saisir les formes et les mouvements que les couleurs. Il est moins peintre que sculpteur" [*Le Victorieux XXe siècle* (Paris, 1925), 58. *Cf.* Abbé C. Mauriés, *Maurras et l'ordre chrètien* (Lyon, 1933?), *passim*].

the corporation, the commune, the province, and the nation were to the state what principles were to art,[3] they were also, in a sense, political " stones " with which the political sculptor worked. They were " real," but not so the individual who was but an " abstraction." He, therefore, was rejected, but not solely on theoretical grounds. There was also the practical consideration that he was not sufficiently stone-like: he was unreliable because he was too often motivated by sentiment or caprice and because his life-span was too short. He had no place in any order of things conceived to endure: his was but to do—even die—as the principles of this aesthetic political science demanded. However, though a cipher politically, he was called upon to accept the religion of the state, to worship the State-God, than which, according to Brunetière who deplored its growth, " there is nothing more ' pagan ' nor more specifically Greek." [4] So complete would be the moral power of this State-God, and so loyal its devotees that they would " conceive," " treat," and " resolve all pending political questions in their relation to the national interest."

That Maurras has devised, or revived an almost compelling system of thought, especially for the youth of France, hampered by conventions, impatient with a system of government largely dominated by middle-aged and old men, and champing at the bit for action, is readily conceded. They are not the sort to analyze a system of ideas critically: their desire for action, even if it bring broken heads, leaves little or no room for so prosaic a pastime. There are, however, questions that Maurras' youthful countrymen might well ponder over before throwing in their lot with any or several of the subsidiary organizations of the *Action Française*. Will, for example, political science

3 Abbé C. Mauriés, *op. cit.*, 24.

4 Ferdinand Brunetière, " La Renaissance du paganisme dans la morale contemporaine " (1903), *Discours de combat* (Paris, 1914), III, 124. He thought the " dechristianizers " were not aware of what they were doing, that they were not taking into account what humanity would lose and were not considering what would replace Christianity once it were destroyed as they so heartily desired.

ever be a complete and perfect science? [5] Is there not something wrong with an "organizing empiricism" that produces the following equation: individualism = Protestantism = Hebrewism = Germanism? Is it not more "organizing," more *a priori* than empirical, especially when it be considered that Taine and Renan, who taught Maurras' generation to stress the influence of customs and traditions, learned to do so themselves from the romantic school of Savigny where it was emphasized as a reaction against the rationalism of the eighteenth century? [6] Is not organizing data for a purpose such as proving a given point a metaphysical operation? What, for example, gives this purpose the authority of a categorical imperative or of an absolute idea—absolute, though not so described? Is not one who rebels against the generally accepted *mores* of his time and place supremely individualistic and romantic? [7] Is not one who shares and propagates an alarmist psychology approaching the "effeminacy" of romanticism? [8] Should not an empirical student avoid the generalization that all men are essentially bad as well as that of Rousseau that they are good? Would not the tremendous social and economic changes of the nineteenth century require a different art and different government from that of Louis XIV's time?

Having carefully considered questions of this nature, our young Frenchmen should try to picture themselves, their rights and obligations, in a political system established *par tous les moyens* and which, once so established, would presumably retain this principle of action. If they have been brought up in Catholic homes, as happens so often in France, they should give due regard to the rôle Maurras has marked out for the Church, for to use it for political ends would doubtless, as Mauriès

5 Abbé C. Mauriès, *op. cit.*, 35.

6 Georges Guy-Grand, *Le Procès de la démocratie* (Paris, 1911), 79.

7 Alphonse V. Roche, *Les Idées traditionalistes en France de Rivarol à Charles Maurras* (Urbana, Illinois, 1937), 211.

8 Pierre Lasserre, *Mise au point* (Paris, 1931), 53.

suggests, "create confusions which would alter its nature." [9] If they have been reared in Protestant or Jewish homes, their decision will doubtless be less difficult. However, unless their interests clearly dictate it, few will engage in this sort of mental prophylaxis: it is less romantic than parading the streets of Paris and chasing opponents from them.

National defeat accompanied by the loss of territory and prestige, both of which serve as constant reminders of national disgrace, creates, it seems, a fertile soil for the growth of a peculiarly robust type of nationalism. The experience of the French people after 1871 and that of the Germans after 1919 are in this respect somewhat analogous. And the lessons that may be gleaned from the history of France from 1871 to 1914 bode ill for the peace of the world in the years before us. They presage a frightful end or the maiming of not only millions of men in the flower of youth (who may be beautiful in death, as Maurras insists, but who would be more useful to society alive), but also for countless men and women, old and young, not only in France and Germany, but the world over. One need only cite the wide compass of the last war and the present complexity of the relations between peoples to show that this Franco-German feud is not merely an academic question to men and women of other nationalities—even to Americans. Their interest in its development and in its implications would, therefore, appear to be, not meddlesomeness, as some French writers have chosen to regard it, but a wholly justifiable measure in the light of what the future may hold in store for them because of the existence of this vendetta.

They owe it to themselves, if not to mankind, not to be misled by the thinly veiled sophistry of such men as Fortunat Strowski, who has described France as being entirely innocent of nationalism. Patriotism, which is simply love of the national soil and not an abstract sort of thing, Frenchmen have, he says. Indeed, France is the "country of pure patriotism," the

9 Abbé C. Mauriès, *op. cit.*, 50.

example, *par excellence,* of " pure patriotism," because she has natural limits, her unity is old, and her patriots feel at ease.[10] It is only in countries without natural boundaries that patriotism " evaporates, dilutes itself, loses itself—in order to transform itself into nationalism. The soil is replaced by a mysticism." [11] It is the mysterious forces that seem to radiate from the material forces or things into the atmosphere that constitute nationalism.[12] Now the French have no acquaintance with these mysterious forces. " Instinctively the French consider a possession which they might add to the national territory badly acquired, if outside the natural boundaries." [13] France, for example, evacuated Mainz without any mental reservations whatsoever. Her patriotism " excludes the follies of Imperialism and of Nationalism." [14] " We obviously do not wish," he continues, " to use this word (i. e., nationalism) in the political sense that it has assumed in some countries. To us ' integral nationalism ' connotes the program of a party of constructive opposition; and it has no relation with that which the foreigners call the nationalism of France. Integral nationalism is solely a plan of internal politics and a precise doctrine. The nationalism of which we speak is more instinctive than intellectual. Its power often comes from its confused obscurity. It has as its substance the idea that a people sets up for itself of its place and of its mission among other peoples." [15] And this, according to Strowski, is totally foreign to France—even to the *Action Française!*

We willingly grant to M. Strowski his definition of patriotism; but his definition of nationalism leaves his reader with the impression of a " confused obscurity " which, he says, often explains nationalism's power. To say in almost the same breath

10 Fortunat Strowski, *Nationalisme ou patriotisme* (Paris, 1933), 12, 14, 47.

11 *Ibid.*, 12.

12 *Ibid.*, 23-25.

13 *Ibid.*, 21.

14 *Ibid.*, 22.

15 *Ibid.*, 25-26.

that nationalism is essentially instinctive, rather than intellectual, and then to about-face and say that it "has as its substance the *idea* that a people sets up for itself . . .," is confusing indeed. Serious students of nationalism are in general agreement that nationalism is a spiritual and historical force that is based upon patriotism and a consciousness of nationality, which, in turn, is essentially a linguistic and cultural phenomenon.[16] The nationalism of Barrès and Maurras, in view of the foregoing pages, may not, therefore, be written off as being simply patriotism. Moreover, to say that "integral nationalism is solely a plan of internal politics" is simply contrary to fact, as the above pages demonstrate. If, however, some doubt remains in the mind of the reader regarding this point, the following statement of Maurras should wholly dispel it: "The maximum of our internal power having been attained by the establishment of the hereditary, traditional, anti-parliamentary, and decentralized Monarchy, we will have obtained by the formation of the robust alliance of our friendships, the maximum of our external power. Assured of power, power ordered and which endures, it will be possible to come to action: action, be it immediate, be it over a long period, for the recovery of our possessions and action with a view to a European and planetary peace which, putting an end to the barbarous anarchy of our dominant races, will finally deserve to be called the *French peace,* alone worthy of the human race.".[17] What a dream! and what an example of Strowski's

16 Carlton J. H. Hayes, *Essays on Nationalism* (New York, 1926), 1-29; G. P. Gooch, *Nationalism* (New York, 1920), 5-7, 125.

17 *Kiel et Tanger,* 171. He continues, "Il n'est pas permis de marchander à l'oeuvre de Bismarck, nationaliste prussien, ou de Disraeli, nationaliste anglais, l'admiration qu'elle comporte. Mais enfin, il y a quelque chose audessus, c'est l'oeuvre d'un Metternich: son Europe, qui est celle de Richelieu, de Lionne, de Choiseul et de Vergennes, apparaît bien supérieure aux nationalités de Cavour et de Canovas. Cette Europe elle-même était inférieure à la chrétienté d'Urbain II et d'Innocent III. La chrétienté unie n'existant plus depuis la Réforme, il n'en subsiste pas moins une civilisation commune à sauvegarder. La France peut en être le soldat et le gendarme, comme le Siège catholique romain peut en redevenir le docteur et le pro-

"idea" of a people's place and mission among other peoples! Nevertheless, we are told that integral nationalism is "solely a plan of internal politics."

Lord Cecil once distinguished patriotism from nationalism in the following manner: "The patriot," he said, "loves his own country. The nationalist hates all countries but his own." In view of Maurras' advocacy of "Latinism" which, of course, should redound to France's benefit,[18] and his numerous expressions of gratitude for the aid of her allies during the war, this definition of the nationalist applies to him only to a degree, as is true of Hitler and Mussolini. When; for example, the foreign policies of the former Entente and Associated Powers were in fundamental disagreement, Maurras' former thankfulness quickly turned to hatred. Soon after the French soldiers had marched into the Ruhr, he suggested that a French army in Berlin would best solve the problem created by the pro-Prussianism of England and the United States.[19] Short of that, he argued, France should at least stay in the Ruhr, for its coal rightfully belonged to her.[20] In short, when other countries were helpful to France in the attainment or the protection of her national interests, he appreciated their aid; when, however, they opposed her, his expressions of gratitude promptly turned to those of hatred.

moteur. Le monde jaune organisé par le Japon, le monde sémitique ressuscitant, ici dans l'Internationale juive et ailleurs dans l'Islam, nous menacent de furieuses secousses, et tout le monde ne méprise pas l'apport intarissable des continents noirs: que de croisades pacifiques ou guerrières à organiser! Et, si l'on est tenté de se croire isolé, qu'on se rappelle tout ce qui parle encore français et latin dans le monde, l'immense Canada et cette carrière infinie que nous ouvrent les Amériques du Centre et du Sud! Ce n'est pas la matière qui se refusera à l'audace française. L'esprit français trouve à choisir entre innombrables objets" (*ibid.*, 171-172). *Cf. Décernez-moi le prix Nobel de la paix* (Paris, 1931), *passim.*

18 *Action Française*, July 10, 1922; also *Promenade italienne* (Paris, 1929), 61-72.

19 *Action Française*, Feb. 16, 1923.

20 *Action Française*, Mar. 13 and 16, 1923.

In the February issue of the *Contemporary Review* of 1935, H. Powys Greenwood, to whom we are indebted for the definitions of Lord Cecil, just quoted, discussed the newly formed International of Nationalists, the meetings of which he had attended in Berlin. This, the general world outlook, and the tentative moves toward a rapprochement of French and German war veterans and industrialists prompted him to find fault with the above definition of a nationalist and to venture the following definition of nationalism: " Nationalism . . . with its exaggerations, its flag-waving, its patriotic songs, its marching and the like, is the banner under which the middle classes of Europe are successfully resisting the assaults of the 'proletariat.' " [21] Hence the intense interest of S. A. and S. S. students of Germany in Fascist or nationalist movements elsewhere, he argued. Although this definition mistakenly implies that nationalism is not used by the proletariat when and where it is in the saddle politically, there is doubtless much truth in it. For example, its central point was not overlooked by Maurras even before Mussolini's " march on Rome." In the *Action Française* of March 15, 1922, Maurras said, " This well founded past gives us the right to recall the numerous occasions when we have also added that a strong and well organized national doctrine, should be, coöperating with the religious sentiment, a factor of social understanding. Labor and capital can find in the necessities of the fatherland a motive to collaborate and agree. This phenomenon, undeniably established, of the spontaneous absence of any strikes 'in the Stinnes, Thyssen, and Krupp establishments' because of the German national spirit, presents an experimental confirmation of our abstract view. . . . A popular education oriented in the national sense has become more and more indispensable."

Mr. Greenwood, an able and experienced observer of the European political scene, after the proceedings of the conference of the International of Nationalists had ended with the singing of all the national anthems of the countries participat-

21 No. 830, 151.

ing, which required him and the other participants to stand at attention more than twenty minutes, went to Paris. Here he had an experience which he described as follows: "When I arrived in Paris, I went to see one of the leading men on a newspaper which is at the moment strongly advocating a conciliatory foreign policy, even towards Germany. As soon as this subject came up, he stiffened. 'Yes,' he said, 'That is the policy of my paper. But I am going to give you my personal views. Reconciliation with Germany is impossible. The only thing the Germans understand is force. We did not crush them properly in 1918. We ought to have gone back to the traditional policy of Richelieu, to have divided them and kept them divided. [How like Maurras!] Failing that, we ought to have seized our opportunity of making a preventive war when Hitler came to power. The Germans are not really a nation—it is merely that periodically somebody comes along and tries to convince them that they are.'" This provoked the following comment from Greenwood: "During many years' residence in Germany, I never remember hearing the wildest nationalist or Nazi speak thus of the French. Here is a classic example of the nationalism attacked by Lord Cecil—unbeatable for suspicion and bitterness. Although here in Paris there are neither bands nor flags, and uniforms are rarely to be seen, it would be difficult for decades of Nazi mumbo-jumbo to turn out more ardent nationalists than can be met on any street-corner or field of France to-day. Germany is trying, amidst the execration of the world, to create a religion of race; for generations France, or at any rate French civilization, has been the real religion of France. Just as there is no more nationalistic people than the French, so there is none more intensely bourgeois. France affords the clearest possible demonstration of the connection between nationalism and middle-class civilisation." [22] Mr. Greenwood was doubtless irritated by the interview and may, therefore, have drawn an exaggerated picture of the nationalism of France; but we offer this statement as a corrective to those of

22 *Ibid.*, 153-154. *Cf.* E. R. Curtius and A. Bergsträsser, *Frankreich* (Berlin, 1931), I (Curtius, "Die französische Kultur"), 195.

Strowski and as a tribute to the achievement of Maurras, Barrès, and Péguy.[23]

It is not our purpose to belabor Professor Strowski. The statements to which he gave utterance are, however, so widely accepted and the evidence disproving them is so profuse and plentiful that we are constrained to illustrate their falsity further by considering Maurras' attitude toward Mussolini and Fascist Italy, which Strowski agrees is nationalistic.[24] In the *Action Française* of July 18, 1923, Maurras discussed Mussolini at some length. Mussolini, he said, followed no ideological doctrine.[25] Experience was his guide. Nevertheless, despite the floating appearance of his design, it had a " continuity and an order " that made sense. He had restored the state, honored

23 After the Dreyfus crisis, except for his unwillingness to accept the monarchy as a "logical necessity," Maurice Barrès continued to work for the "renaissance of French pride" much as did Maurras; and, after the long-sought revenge had finally been attained, until his death in 1923, he advocated a policy of almost equally uncompromising sternness towards Germany. Among his later works in the interest of this campaign are, *Les Amitiés françaises* (1903); *Les Bastions de l'Est: Au service de l'Allemagne* (1906), *Colette Baudoche* (1909), *Le Génie du Rhin* (1921); *La Colline inspirée* (1913); *La Grande pitié des églises de France* (1914); *Les Traits éternels de la France* (1918); *Un jardin sur l'Oronte* (1922). His regular contributions to the *Echo de Paris* and his presence in the Chamber of Deputies from 1906 to 1923, likewise proved useful to the cause. For example, on June 24, 1920, he secured the passage of the bill which made Joan of Arc's day a national holiday [Mme. Adrienne Blanc-Péridier, *Maurice Barrès* (Paris, 1929), 33].

Charles Péguy, who fell at Villeroy, Sept. 5, 1914, at the age of forty-one, was profoundly moved by what Strowski called the "mysterious forces" that emanate from statues, historic buildings, the whole of Paris, etc. [Charles Péguy, *Notre patrie* (Paris, 1915, first published in 1905), 37-39]. A mystic of the first order, he was not as selective in regard to the French tradition as was Maurras: he disdained nothing. He accepted his wounded fatherland and encouraged it by love, faith, and hope [Daniel Halévy, *Charles Péguy et les cahiers de la Quinzaine* (Paris, 1918), 146-148]. *Cf. Oeuvres complètes de Charles Péguy* (Paris, 1920?), 3 vols., *passim.*

24 *Op. cit.*, 32.

25 This is corroborated by Gustav W. Eberlein in *Der Faschismus als Bewegung: Enstehungsgeschichte der faschistischen Revolution* (Würzburg, 1929), 13-15; also by Herman Finer in *Mussolini's Italy* (New York, 1935), 14-20, 38-39.

Catholicism, enforced the law, denied the right of free association, and had restored to the family the freedom of testation. He had proclaimed in parliament that there was no such thing as liberty, that liberties alone existed. And these remarks had been received with wild applause! Noting these developments and commenting upon the extraordinary power of truth when it is simply and clearly stated, Maurras said, " We have no embarrassment in recognizing the great value of the formulas of Mussolini, inasmuch as they are first cousins and even twin sisters of those which the *Action Française* has not tired of sending forth into the world during what is now almost a quarter of a century. There is, I confess, some pleasure in saluting them in passing. Whatever mediocrity the Republic and Democracy have imposed upon the politics of France, even when perchance distinguished men are in power, in spite of our retrograde humanitarians and our lagging pacifists, Paris has not ceased to advance ideas capable of rendering service to sister cities and to sister nations. Those who believe that a reactionary France would have nothing to teach men have been given the lie by the event. We have not made the fatherland lose its rank. We have even made it reconquer it." It is true, the *Action Française* had no " great contact " with Fascism; but Corradini and other members of the Italian nationalist group had long been their comrades. In the review, *Il Regno,* which they founded in 1905, they frequently cited and commented upon Maurras' writings. The movement prospered and through its newspaper, the *Idea Nazionale,* which soon replaced the review, gained considerable power over public opinion. " When the group of the *Idea Nazionale* finally joined the army of Mussolini, it brought, besides a moral influence and a political authority of the first order, a vocabulary, a method, a general point of view regarding the political life of the fatherland, and it placed them at the disposal of the Dictator, who borrowed from them heavily." To appreciate fully the source of his ideas and policies, all one needed to do was to follow the course of his actions in a general way.

While the brilliant success of his "dearest truths" beyond the mountains filled him with "admiration, joy, and a little pride," it also inspired him with a certain uneasiness and a profound regret. Uneasiness, because a European power that increased its strength and prestige usually did it at the expense of its neighbors. Not that he was jealous, for the Italians were their companions in arms and their mother-city was also that of the French. No success and progress could be more agreeable to him than theirs. "All the same, if, in place of the baneful Waldeck, the ideas of the *Enquête sur la Monarchie,* the ideas of *Dictateur et Roi* had been taken and secretly favored in France by a national government! What security, from the outset! What development, later! . . . No bitterness, but what regret! I say: what regret for France, that there was not at this distant epoch a group of statesmen to take over our principles, our program, to work from that time on to effect them." [26]

We shall not chide M. Strowski further. That there is a "nationalism of France" and that the integral nationalism of Maurras and his colleagues was and is its spearhead, is unquestionable.

We must now close this account of the rise of this integral nationalism by considering a question which the above statement of Maurras naturally provokes: "Why was not Maurras equally successful in applying his doctrine in France as Mussolini was in Italy?" To raise this question is not to belittle Maurras' achievements which, as the foregoing pages demonstrate, were very real and considerable—particularly his influence upon the policies of the French government after 1911. But, up until the Daladier "experience," inaugurated in 1938, the outcome of which is still in the future, France, with the exception of her temporary war-time dictatorships, continued to have a parliamentary régime and had no dictator-king. Inasmuch as Maurras himself felt the need of answering this question, we should, in all fairness, give his reply. "The Italian

26 *Action Française,* July 18, 1923; D. P. and C., III, 125-126.

nationalists," he said in the *Action Française* of August 2, 1932, "dominated after 1912, the Fascists after 1922, and the first had their beginning seven years *after* us. But neither one nor the other had to deal, as we, with a wholly pure republican democracy. In 1922, as in 1912, Italy had a monarchy: her State was capable, by parliamentary accident, of being an anarch*ic* State, it was not at all anarch*istic*. From Federzoni up to Mussolini, all who worked for order and authority met, from the outset, with high favors, with powerful assistance, energetic support, open or concealed, and that in the environs of the highest authorities of the State! In France, our operations were difficult after another manner! We have had everything against us, and first of all the State, and in the most politically centralized country of the world!"[27] This, he added, had not prevented them from gaining considerable ground and would not prevent their ultimate success.

There are, of course, other reasons which Maurras could not present without enlarging upon his own limitations or making admissions such as a man in politics cannot afford to make. A powerful polemist and a brilliant writer, Maurras was better equipped to point the way to revolution than to play the active rôle of leader in it. Benito Mussolini, the "man of action," was, of course, fashioned in a different mold. Maurras, the theorist, was constrained to look to a statesman-Monk or a general-Monk to carry out his program, for much of which, as we have seen, he found the former, at different intervals, in Poincaré, Clemenceau, and Millerand. Although he clearly dominated the *Action Française* and somewhat jealously guarded his mastery

27 D. P. and C., III, 135. Maurras thought state intervention was being carried too far in Italy, though he admitted there was some justification for it there. "Dans un pays aussi anciennement unifié que la France, les dangers de l'étatisme sont, à la lettre, mortels. Dans un pays aussi divers que l'Italie une certaine dose d'étatisme peut être excellente" (*Promenade italienne*, 73). To Mussolini's "Outside the State, nothing that is human or spiritual has any value," Maurras objected, holding that the individual being exists, but that he should be subordinated to the state, not excluded from it. "Pourquoi parler de 'force morale,'" he asked, "et détruire en principe le facteur moral?" (*Action Française*, June 12, 1932; D. P. and C., III, 133).

over it,[28] he was the first to recognize his limitations in the broader realms of action; hence his regret that there was no group of statesmen in France, at the turn of the century, to accept and apply his doctrines. He could only hope to rule through others. Another reason that Maurras could not well advance is the fact that most of his countrymen favored the "pure republican democracy" because their love for the principles of the Revolution was doubtless more deep-seated than was that of the Italians. The tradition of the Revolution, which Maurras not only excluded from the "Tradition" of France, but also combated unremittingly, was dearer to them than he was willing to admit.

Nevertheless, Maurras, the great anti-Rousseau of nineteenth and twentieth-century France, was and is not only tolerated, but also appreciated and admired by thousands, if not millions, of his countrymen, not of the extreme Left, as one who did much to restore the old canons of French taste and beauty and one who was for his generation the watchdog of the public safety of France. To his friends and to countless others, his election, in 1938, his seventieth year, to the French Academy was a belated recognition of and reward for these services.

28 Louis Dimier, *op. cit.*, 317, 335-337, 348; Georges Valois (Georges Gressent), *Contre le mensonge et la calomnie* (Paris, 1926), xviii-xxii. Both characterized him as being a master, but not a chief.

BIBLIOGRAPHY

Acker, Paul, *Petites confessions: visites et portraits*, vol. i, 3rd edition (Paris, 1903).

L'Action française, *Almanach de l'Action française* of 1927 and 1935.

L'Action française, *Les Pièces d'un procès: l' "Action française" et le Vatican,* preface by Charles Maurras and Léon Daudet (Paris, 1927).

Adam, George, *The Tiger: Georges Clemenceau, 1841-1929* (New York, 1930).

Adam, Mme. Juliette, *Nos amitiés politiques avant l'abandon de la revanche* (Paris, 1908).

Agathon (Henri Massis and Alfred de Tarde), *Les Jeunes gens d'aujour d'hui*, 12th edition (Paris, 1919).

Améras, Henri d', *Avant la gloire: leurs débuts* (Paris, 1903).

Amouretti, Frédéric, "La Faiblesse républicaine," *Le Soleil*, Apr. 17, 1896.

Armbruster, Paul, *Maurras und das Christentum: die Antwort auf eine Lügenkampagne* (Strasbourg, 1926).

Aulard, A., *Taine, historien de la Révolution française*, 2nd edition (Paris, 1908).

Auriac, Jules d', *La Nationalité française: sa formation* (Paris, 1903).

Bainville, Jacques, *Bismarck et la France, d'après les Mémoires du Prince de Hohenlohe . . .* (Paris, 1918).

——, *Histoire de deux peuples* (Paris, 1915).

——, *Histoire de trois générations* (Paris, 1918).

——, *La Presse et la guerre: l'Action française* (Paris, 1915).

Barenton, Hilaire, *L'Action française et l'oeuvre de Charles Maurras* (Paris, 1916).

Barrès, Maurice, *Les Amitiés françaises* (Paris, 1903).

——, *Amori et dolori sacrum* (Paris, 1921).

——, *Les Bastions de l'Est:*

Au service de l'Allemagne (Paris, 1906);

Colette Baudoche: histoire d'une jeune fille de Metz (Paris, 1909);

Le Génie du Rhin (Paris, 1921).

——, *La Colline inspirée* (Paris, 1913).

——, *La Culte du moi:*

Le Jardin de Bérénice (Paris, 1910);

Sous l'oeil des barbares (Paris, 1911);

Un homme libre (Paris, 1912).

——, *Du sang, de la volupté et de la mort* (Paris, 1914).

——, "L'Effort d'un semestre," *La Cocarde*, Mar. 7, 1895.

——, *L'Ennemi des lois* (Paris, 1910).

——, *La Grande pitié des églises de France* (Paris, 1914).

——, *Huit jours chez M. Renan* (Paris, 1913).

——, *Un jardin sur l'Oronte* (Paris, 1922).

——, *Une journée parlementaire: comédie des moeurs en trois actes* (Paris, 1894).

——, *Mes cahiers*, vols. i-iv, Jan., 1896 – Sept., 1906 (Paris, 1929-1931).
——, "Le Point de vue historique," *La Cocarde*, Feb. 16, 1895.
——, "Le Premier mot de l'année," *La Cocarde*, Jan. 1, 1895.
——, "La Querelle des nationalistes et des cosmopolites," *Le Figaro*, July 4, 1892.
——, *Le Roman de l'énérgie nationale:*
L'Appel au soldat (Paris, 1911);
Les Déracinés, 2 vols. (Paris, 1920);
Leurs figure (Paris, 1911).
——, *Scènes et doctrines du nationalisme*, 2 vols. (Paris, 1925).
——, "Le Sentiment nationaliste," *La Cocarde*, Nov. 18, 1894.
——, *Taine et Renan*, edited, with comments, by Victor Giraud (Paris, 1922).
——, *Les traits éternels de la France* (New Haven, 1918).
——, *Vingt-cinq années de vie littéraire* (Paris, 1912).
——, "Violence! Violence!," *La Cocarde*, Jan. 8, 1895.
——, *Le Voyage de Sparte* (Paris, 1906).
Beauclair, Henri, *Une heure avec M. Barrès par un faux Renan* (Paris, 1890).
Bellesort, André, *Sainte-Beuve et le XIXe siècle* (Paris, 1927).
Benjamin, René, *Charles Maurras, ce fils de la mer* (Paris, 1932).
——, *Grandes figures: Barrès, Joffre* (Paris, 1931).
Benoit, Charles, *La Monarchie française*, 2 vols. (Paris, 1935).
Bérenger, J., *Charles Maurras et Frédéric Amouretti* (Cannes, 1913).
Bever, Ad. van, *Anthologie littéraire de l'Alsace et de la Lorraine* (Paris, 1920).
Bidou, Henri, "Maurice Barrès," *Revue de Paris*, Dec. 15, 1923, vol. vi, 926-928.
Blanc-Péridier, Mme. Adrienne, *Maurice Barrès* (Paris, 1929).
——, *La Route ascendante de Maurice Barrès*, preface by Charles Maurras (Paris, 1925).
Blei, Franz, "Maurice Barrès," *Oesterreichische Rundschau*, Nov. 15, 1906, vol. ix, 129-133.
Bodley, J. E. C., *Cardinal Manning, The Decay of Idealism in France, The Institute of France* (London, 1912).
Boheman, Mauritz, *Précis de l'histoire de la littérature des félibres*, translated from the Swedish by Christian Lange (Avignon, 1906).
Bonald, L. G. A. vicomte de, *Oeuvres de M. de Bonald*, 15 vols. (Paris, 1836-1843).
Bordeaux, Henri, *Les Ecrivains et les moeurs*, vol. i (Paris, 1900).
——, "Le Retour de Barrès à sa terre et ses morts," *Revue de deux mondes*, Jan., 1924, 7 Pér. xix, 118-141.
——, *Voyageurs d'Orient*, 2 vols. (Paris, 1929).
Bourget, Paul, *Le Disciple* (Paris, 1926).
——, *Essais de psychologie contemporaine*, 2 vols. (Paris, 1926).
——, "Maurice Barrès," *Revue des deux mondes*, Dec. 15, 1923, 7. Pér. xviii, 946-948.

——, *Nouvelles pages de critique et de doctrine*, vol. ii (Paris, 1922).
——, *Outre-mer* (notes sur l'Amérique), vol. ii (Paris, 1895).
Brémond, Henri, *Pour la romantisme* (Paris, 1924).
Brousse, Paul, *Frédéric Mistral: ses oeuvres, le Félibrige* (Perigueux, 1903).
Brownell, W. C., *French Traits* (New York, 1896).
Brunetière, F., *Discours de combat*, 3 vols. (Paris, 1914).
——, *Histoire de la littérature française classique, 1515-1830*, 4 vols. (Paris, 1927).
Chamson, André, *L'Homme contre l'histoire: essai sur la puissance de l'uchronie* (Paris, 1927).
Charensol, G., *L'Affaire Dreyfus et la troisième république* (Paris, 1930).
Charles-Brun, Jean, *L'Evolution felibréenne* (Lyon, 1896).
——, *Le Régionalisme* (Paris, 1911).
Charpentier, Armand, *Historique de l'affaire Dreyfus* (Paris, 1933).
Chenu, M. le Bâtonnier, *La Ligue des patriotes* (Paris, 1916).
Clemenceau, Georges, *L'Iniquité*, 2nd edition (Paris, 1899).
——, *Vers la réparation*, 2nd edition (Paris, 1899).
Clerc, Michel, *Les Métèques athéniens* (Paris, 1893).
Clouard, Henri, "Charles Maurras et la critique des lettres," *La Revue critique des idées et des livres*, 1911, vol. xiii, 47-72; 133-157.
——, "La 'Cocarde' de Barrès," *La Revue critique des idées et des livres*, Feb. 10 and 25, 1910, vol. viii, 205-230; 332-358; 397-419.
——, *Les Disciplines: nécessité littéraire et sociale d'une renaissance classique* (Paris, 1913).
Cochin, Augustin, "Le Patriotisme humanitaire," *La Revue universelle*, Apr. 1, 1920.
Comité permanent de l'union des sociétés de gymnastique de France, *Mémoire ... sur la création d'une école gymnastique à Reims* (Reims, 1882).
Comte, Auguste, *Cours du philosophie positive*, 4th edition, vols. iv-v (Paris, 1877).
——, *Discours sur l'ensemble du positivisme* (Paris, 1848).
——, *Système de politique positive*, vol. ii (Paris, 1852).
Les Contemporains, *Charles Maurras* (Paris, 1925).
Coudekerque-Lambrecht, *Léon de Montesquiou: sa vie politique—l'Action française* (Paris, 1925).
Croquez, Albert, *Edouard Drumont* (Paris, 1909).
Curtius, E. R., *Maurice Barrès und die geistigen Grundlagen der französischen Nationalismus* (Bonn, 1921).
Curtius, E. R., and Bergsträsser, A., *Frankreich*, 2 vols. (Stuttgart and Berlin, 1931).
Daudet, Léon, *L'Agonie du régime* (Paris, 1925).
——, *Une campagne d'Action française* (Paris, 1910).
——, *La Chambre nationale du 16 novembre* (Paris, 1923).
——, *Charles Maurras et son temps* (Paris, 1927).
——, *Études et milieux littéraires*, 9th edition (Paris, 1927).
——, *La Guerre totale* (Paris, 1918).
——, *L'Hécatombe: récits et souvenirs politiques, 1914-1918* (Paris, 1923).

——, *Hors du joug allemand: mesures d'après guerre* (Paris, 1915).

——, *Oeuvre philosophique: l'Hérédo, le monde des images* (Paris, 1925).

——, *Le Poignard dans le dos: notes sur l'affaire Malvy* (Paris, 1918).

——, *Le Rêve éveillé*, 14th edition (Paris, 1926).

——, *Souvenirs des milieux littéraires, politiques, artistiques et médicaux: Fantômes et vivantes, Devant le douleur, L'Entre-deux-guerres, Salons et journaux* (Paris, 1920);
Au temps de Judas, Vers le roi, Alphonse Daudet (Paris, 1926).

Davin, E., *Istres: histoire locale et notes*, preface by Charles Maurras (Marseilles, 1923).

Déroulède, Paul, *Chants du soldat, 1870-1882* (Paris, 1888).

Descoqs, Pedro, *A travers l'oeuvre de M. Charles Maurras* (Paris, 1913).

——, "Monomorphisme et action française," *Annales de philosophie chrétienne*, vol. clx, 225-251.

Descaves, Lucien, *Sous-offs* (Paris, 1892).

Dietz, Jean, *Maurice Barrès* (Paris, 1927).

Dimier, Louis, *Les Maîtres de la contre-révolution* (Paris, 1907).

——, *Vingt ans d'Action française et autres souvenirs* (Paris, 1926).

Dimnet, Ernest, *France Herself Again* (New York and London, 1914).

Drumont, Edouard, *La Dernière bataille* (Paris, 1890).

——, *La France juive*, 2 vols., 43rd edition (Paris, 1886).

——, *De l'or, de la boue, du sang* (Paris, 1896).

——, *Sur la chemin de la vie* (Paris, 1914).

——, *La Tyrannie maçonnique* (Paris, 1899).

Dublaix, Commandant, *Le Duc d'Orléans: sa doctrine, son programme* (Paris, 1925).

Durkheim, Emile, *Sociologie et philosophie*, preface by C. Bouglé (Paris, 1924).

Dutrait-Crozon, Henri, *Joseph Reinach historien: révision de l'histoire de l'affaire Dreyfus*, preface by Charles Maurras, 2 vols. in one (Paris, 1905).

——, *Précis de l'affaire Dreyfus* (Paris, 1909).

Eberlein, Gustav W., *De Faschismus als Bewegung: Einstehungsgeschichte der faschistischen Revolution* (Würzburg, 1929).

Elliott, W. Y., *The Pragmatic Revolt in Politics: Syndicalism, Fascism and the Constitutional State* (New York, 1928).

Faguet, Emile, "L'Avenir de l'intelligence," *Les Annales politiques et littéraires*, Sept. 24, 1905, 23rd year, vol. ii.

——, *En lisant Nietzsche* (Paris, 1904).

——, *Le Pacifisme* (Paris, 1908).

——, *Politiques et moralistes du dix-neuvième siècle*, 3 vols. (Paris, 1891).

——, *Les Préjugés nécessaires* (Paris, 1911).

Faÿ, Bernard, *Since Victor Hugo: French Literature of To-day*, translated by Paul Doolin (Boston, 1927).

Feuillerat, Albert, *French Life and Ideals* (New Haven, 1925).

Fichte, Johann Gottlieb, *Reden an die deutsche Nation* (Leipzig, Kröners Taschenausgabe).

Finot, Jean, *Race Prejudice*, translated by Florence Wade (New York, 1906).

Flandreysy, Jeanne de, *La Maison de Baroncelli en Italie du Xe au XVe siècle*, preface by Charles Maurras (Avignon, 1924).

Fournière, Eugène, "Le Nationalisme: lettre à M. J. Soury," *La Revue socialiste*, July and Dec., 1902, vol. xxxvi, 1-30; 385-414.

France, Anatole, "À Charles Maurras," *La Revue critique des idées et des livres*, Apr. 25, 1911, vol. xiii, 129-131.

——, *La Vie littéraire*, vol. iv (Paris, 1892).

Franck, Henri, *La Danse devant l'arche*, 5th edition (Paris, 1921).

Fustel de Coulanges, Numa-Denis, *Questions historiques*, edited by Camille Jullian (Paris, 1893).

——, *Recherches sur quelques problèmes d'histoire* (Paris, 1885).

Galli, Henri, *Gambetta et l'Alsace-Lorraine* (Paris, 1911).

Gennep, Arnold van, *Traité comparatif des nationalités*, vol. i: *Les Élements extérieures de la nationalité* (Paris, 1922).

Gérin-Ricard, Lazare de, *Les Idées politiques de Joseph de Maistre et la doctrine de Maurras* (La Rochelle, 1929).

Gilbert, Louis, *Du catholicisme romain au protestantisme français: jalons de route d'un disciple de Maurras* (Paris, 1932).

Gillouin, René, *Esquisses littéraires et morales* (Paris, 1926).

——, *Essais de critique littéraire et philosophe* (Paris, 1913).

——, *Idées et figures d'aujourd'hui* (Paris, 1919).

——, *Maurice Barrès* (Paris, 1907).

Girard, Georges, "Essai de bibliographie de l'oeuvre de Charles Maurras," *Bulletin de la Maison du livre française*, 4th year (1923), 558-561.

Giraud, Victor, *Les Maîtres de l'heure: Maurice Barrès* (Paris, 1918).

Gobineau, Joseph-Arthur comte de, *Essai sur l'inégalité des races humaines*, 2nd edition, 2 vols. (Paris, 1884).

Gohier, Urbain, *Les Gens du roi: Sidi Maurras ben Ma'aras, ou le maure pion* (Paris, 1926).

Goldenweiser, Alexander, *Early Civilization* (New York, 1922).

Guérard, Albert L., *Five Masters of French Romance* (London, 1916).

——, "Maurice Barrès and the Doctrine of Nationalism," *The Texas Review*, Apr., 1916, vol. i, 275-290.

Guignier, Francis, *L'Homme que se cite: contribution à la biographie de M. Maurras* (Paris, 1912).

Gurian, Waldemar, *Der integrale Nationalismus in Frankreich* (Frankfurt am Main, 1931).

Guy-Grand, Georges, *L'Avenir de la démocratie* (Paris, 1928).

——, *Le Conflit des idées dans la France d'aujourd'hui: trois visages de la France* (Paris, 1921).

——, *La Philosophie nationaliste* (Paris, 1911).

——, *La Philosophie syndicaliste* (Paris, 1911).

——, *Le Procès de la démocratie* (Paris, 1911).

H., J. M., "Charles Maurras," *Dublin Magazine*, Dec., 1913, vol. i, 414-417.

Hadzsits, George D., *Lucretius and his Influence* (New York, 1935).

Halévy, Daniel, *Charles Péguy et les Cahiers de la quinzaine* (Paris, 1918).

——, *Visites au paysans du centre* (Paris, 1921).

Hanotaux, Gabriel, *Contemporary France*, translated by J. C. Tarver, 4 vols. (London, 1903).

Hartmann, Eduard von, *Philosophie des Unbewusten*, 4th edition (Berlin, 1872).

Hauser, Henri, *Le Principe des nationalités: ses origines historiques* (Paris, 1916).

——, *Le Problème du régionalisme* (Paris, 1924).

Hayes, Carlton J. H., *Essays on Nationalism* (New York, 1926).

——, *France, a Nation of Patriots* (New York, 1930).

——, *The Historical Evolution of Modern Nationalism* (New York, 1931).

Henriot, Emile, *À quoi rêvent les jeunes gens* (Paris, 1913).

Herluison, Jean, "Maurice Barrès et le problème de l'ordre," *La Revue critique des idées et des livres*, Feb. 10, 1911, vol. xii, 257-272.

Hermant, Abel, *Le Cavalier Miserey* (Paris, 1887).

Herzog, Wilhelm, *Der Kampf einer Republik: die Affäre Dreyfus* (Zürich, 1932).

Hitler, Adolf, *Mein Kampf*, 2 vols. (Munich, 1934).

Hons, Gabriel des, *Anatole France et Jean Racine, ou le clé de l'art francien*, preface by Charles Maurras (Paris, 1927).

Jacquet, René, *Nôtre maître Maurice Barrès* (Paris, 1900).

Johannet, René, *Le Principe des nationalités* (Paris, 1923).

Kessel, J., "Une déjeuner avec M. Charles Maurras," in George Surez, *Peu d'hommes, trop d'idées*, 29-48 (Paris, 1928).

Kühn, Joachim, *Der Nationalismus im Leben der dritten Republik* (Berlin, 1920).

Laberthonnière, L., *Autour de "l'Action française,"* (Paris, 1911).

Laërce, Diogène de, "Vie d'Epicure," in *Les Six livres de Lucrèce De la nature des choses*, translated by Michel de Marolles, abbé de Villeloin, 2nd edition (Paris, 1659).

Lalou, René, *Contemporary French Literature*, translated by W. A. Bradley (London, 1924).

Lamartine, Alain de, *Un ennemi de la civilisation chrétienne: Charles Maurras dans le "Chemin de Paradis"* (Paris, 1920).

Lamy, Etienne, "'L'Action française' et 'Le Correspondant,'" *Le Correspondant*, Dec. 10, 1907, vol. cxciii, 984-1005.

La Rochefoucauld, François duc de, *Oeuvres complètes* (Paris, 1825).

Larpent, G., *L'Affaire Phillippe Daudet* (Paris, 1925).

——, *Pour connaître Charles Maurras: réponse à des diffamateurs* (Paris, 1926).

Laski, Harold J., *Authority in the Modern State* (New Haven, 1927).

——, *The Dangers of Obedience and other Essays* (London, 1930).

——, *Liberty in the Modern State* (London, 1930).

Lasserre, Pierre, *Charles Maurras et la renaissance classique* (Paris, 1902).

——, *Frédéric Mistral: poète, moraliste, citoyen* (Paris, 1918).

——, *Georges Sorel, théoricien de l'impérialisme* (Paris, 1928).

——, *Mise au point* (Paris, 1931).

——, *La Morale de Nietzsche* (Paris, 1902).

——, *Portraits et discussions* (Paris, 1914).
——, *Renan et nous* (Paris, 1923).
——, *Le Romantisme française* (Paris, 1907).
——, *Trente années de vie littéraire: pages choisies* (Paris, 1919).
La Tour du Pin Chambly de la Charce, René, marquis de, *La Monarchie française* (Paris, 1908).
——, *La Représentation professionnelle* (Paris, 1905).
——, *Vers un ordre social chrétien: jalons de route, 1882-1907* (Paris, 1907).
Launay, Robert, "Maurice Barrès à 'L'Action française,'" *Mercure de France*, Feb. 1, 1924, vol. clxix, 668-678.
Lavelle, Louis, "La Situation du moi dans le monde," *Le Temps*, Apr. 7, 1935.
Lazare, Bernard, *L'Antisémitisme: son histoire et ses causes* (Paris, 1894).
Lefèvre, Frédéric, *Une heure avec . . .*, vol. ii (Paris, 1924).
Lemaître, Jules, *Literary Impressions*, translated by A. W. Evans (London, 1921).
Lesourd, Paul, *La Terre et les morts de Maurice Barrès* (Paris, *c.* 1925).
Levine, Louis (Lewis Levitzki Lorwin), *The Labor Movement in France: a Study in Revolutionary Syndicalism* (New York, 1912).
Lièvre, Pierre, *Maurras* (Paris, 1925).
Lugan, A., *Horizons d'âmes* (Paris, 1926).
Macard, Kurt, *Taines Milieutheorie in Zusammenhang mit ihren erkenntnistheoretischen Grundlagen* (Kiel, 1910).
Maistre, Joseph de, *Considérations sur la France*, followed by *Fragments sur la France* (Lyon and Paris, 1924).
——, *Du pape* (Paris, Garnier Frères, date ?).
——, *Soirées de Saint-Pétersbourg* (Paris, Garnier Frères, date ?).
Maréchal, Christian, "La Philosophie de Bonald," *Annales de philosophie chrétienne*, Oct., 1910, vol. xi.
Maritain, Jacques, *Une opinion sur Charles Maurras et le devoir des catholiques* (Paris, 1926).
Massis, Henri, *Jugements*, vol. ii (Paris, 1923).
——, *La Pensée de Maurice Barrès* (Paris, 1909).
Maurel, André, *Les Écrivains de la guerre* (Paris, 1918).
Mauriès, C. abbé, *Maurras et l'ordre chrétien* (Lyon, 1933 ?).
Maurras, Charles, "Académie française," *La Gazette de France*, Mar. 26, 1898.
—— (and Lucien Moreau), "L'Action française," *Le Correspondant*, June 10, 1908, 959-981.
——, "À Florence," *La Gazette de France*, Mar. 15, and 22, 1897.
——, "À la Ligue de la 'Patrie française,'" *La Gazette de France*, Mar. 12, 1899.
——, *L'Allée des philosophes*, 16th edition (Paris, 1925).
——, "Les Alliances," *La Gazette de France*, Oct. 10, 1901.
——, *Les Amants de Venise: George Sand et Musset* (Paris, 1926); also in *La Gazette de France*, Sept. and Oct., 1901.
——, *Anatole France: politique et poète* (Paris, 1924).

——, *L'Anglais qui a connu la France* (Paris, 1928); also in *Minerva*, Apr. 15, 1902, as "Deux temoins de la France."

——, *Anthinéa: d'Athènes à Florence* (Paris, 1926).

——, "Anthologie: Jules Tellier, Lionel des Rieux, Gabriel d'Annunzio," *Revue encyclopédique*, Nov. 15, 1895, 419-423.

——, "L'Anthologie impériale," *Revue encyclopédique*, 1896, 734-736.

——, *L'Anthropophage* (Paris, 1930).

——, *Après dix ans*, preface (published separately) to the new edition of *Quand les français ne s'aimaient pas* (Paris, 1927).

——, *Au signe de Flore: la fondation de l'Action française, 1898-1900* (Paris, 1931).

——, "L'Auteur de 'Leurs figures,'" *La Contemporaine*, Jan., 1902, Nos. 15-22, 73-89.

——, "Autour de l'affaire Dreyfus," *La Gazette de France*, Jan. 9, 1898.

——, "Autour d'une représentation: Émile Pouvillon et Gabriel Monod," *La Gazette de France*, Jan. 31 and Feb. 1, 1899.

——, *L'Avenir de l'intelligence* (Paris, 1927).

——, "L'Avenir de l'ordre," *La Revue universelle*, Apr. 1, 1920.

——, *La Bagarre de Fustel ou les débuts de la Ligue d'Action française*, in *Les Cahiers d'Occident*, vol. II, i, 1-108 (Paris, 1926).

——, "Balzac royaliste," *La Gazette de France*, Aug. 19 and 23, 1900.

——, "Le Baptème de Jésus: un nouvel évangéliste," *Revue bleue*, Aug. 6, 1892, vol. i.

——, *Barbarie et poésie*, vol. i, of *Vers un art intellectuelle* (Paris, 1925).

——, "Le Beaumarchais de la rue des Tournelles," *La Gazette de France*, June 16, 1897.

——, *Le Bibliophile Barthou*, including René de Planhol's *L'Oeuvre de Charles Maurras* (Paris, 1929).

——, *La Bonne mort: conte* (Paris, 1926).

——, "Jean Carrère, ou les étapes d'une conversion," *La Gazette de France*, Feb. 26, 1895.

——, *Casier judiciaire d'Aristide Briand* (Paris, 1931).

——, *Charles Maurras et la critique des lettres*, introduction by Henri Clouard (Paris, 1914 ?).

——, *Les Chefs socialistes pendant la guerre* (Paris, 1918).

——, *Le Chemin de Paradis: contes philosophiques*, 8th edition (Paris, 1920).

——, "Chez nos exilés: enquête sur la monarchie," *La Gazette de France*, July 29, 30; Aug. 1, 2, 3, 4, 5, 11, 22; Sept. 5, 6, 7, 27; Nov. 9, 15, 1900.

——, "Le Ciment romain: à Charles Vincent," *La Gazette de France*, Mar. 9, 1899.

——, "Les Circonscriptions naturelles," *La Cocarde*, Jan. 11, 13; Feb. 1, 1895.

——, "Comment l'étranger nous espionne," *L'Action française*, Apr. 27, 1926.

——, "Comment Mussolini parle aux Allemandes," *L'Action française*, Feb. 8, 1926.

——, "Comment on nous dénationalise," *La Gazette de France*, Jan. 26, 1899.

——, *Les Conditions de la victoire:*
La Blessure intérieure, 1916, vol. iv (Paris, 1918);
La France se sauve elle-même, 1914, vol. i (Paris, 1916);
Ministère et parlement, 1915, vol. iii (Paris, 1916);
Le Parlement se réunit, 1914-1915, vol. ii (Paris, 1917).

——, *Le Conseil de Dante, 1321-1921* (Paris, 1920).

——, *Contes philosophiques:*
La Consolation de Trophime, vol. i (Paris, 1928);
Eucher de l'Ile, ou la naissance de la sensibilité, vol. ii (Paris, 1928);
Les Serviteurs, vol. iii (Paris, 1928).

——, "La Contre-partie militaire," *L'Action française*, Dec. 14, 1926.

——, *Corps glorieux, ou la vertue de la perfection* (Paris, 1929).

——, *Corse et Provence* (Paris, 1930).

—— (and Raymonde de la Tailhède), *Un débat sur le romantisme*, preface and appendix by Pierre Constance (Paris, 1898).

——, *De démos à césar*, 2 vols. (Paris, 1930).

——, "De la soumission à l'objet," *Revue encyclopédique*, 1895, 239-243.

——, *La Démocratie religieuse*, containing *Le Dilemme de Marc Sangnier, La Politique religieuse*, and *L'Action française et le religion catholique* (Paris, 1921).

——, *Dictionnaire politique et critique*, articles of Maurras selected and assembled by Pierre Chardon, 5 vols. (Paris, 1932-1933).

——, "Le Divin capital," *L'Action française*, Feb. 15, 1926.

——, "D'une ingrate patrie, ou d'une ingrate république," *L'Action française*, Apr. 15, 1935.

——, "Encore la démocratie: A X, à Y et à Z," *La Gazette de France*, Feb. 23, 1902.

——, "Encore la latin," *La Gazette de France*, Jan. 5, 1902.

——, *Enquête sur la monarchie*, including *Une campagne royaliste au 'Figaro,'* and *Si le coup de force est possible* (Paris, 1925).

——, *Entre le Louvre et la Bastille* (Paris, 1931).

——, "Essai sur la critique," *Revue encyclopédique*, 1896, 969-974, republished and amplified as *Prologue d'un essai sur la critique* (Paris, 1932).

——, *L'Étang de Berre* (Paris, 1924).

——, "Étude biographique: Arthur Rimbaud," *Revue encyclopédique*, 1892, 7-13.

——, "Les Faits," *La Gazette de France*, Nov. 17, 1901.

——, "Fascisme et nationalisme contre étatisme," *L'Action française*, Apr. 9, 1923.

——, "Fédéral-National . . . ," *La Cocarde*, Dec. 21, 1894.

——, "La Fin de la seconde expérience Poincaré," *L'Action française*, May 15, 1924.

——, "Une France fédérative: promenade au congrès," *La Cocarde*, Jan. 30, 1895.

——, *Gaulois, Germains, Latins*; in *Les Cahiers d'Occident*, vol. I, i (Paris, 1926).

——, "La Guerre et la vertue," *L'Action française*, Apr. 4, 1927.

——, "La Guerre ou la paix," *La Gazette de France*, Apr. 17, 1902.

——, "Le Guerre religieuse," *La Gazette de France*, Mar. 23, 1898.

——, "L'Hérédité et l'élection," *La Gazette de France*, Feb. 25, 1899.

——, *Heures immortales, 1914-1919* (Paris, 1932).

——, *L'Idée de la décentralisation* (Paris, 1898).

——, "L'Idée nationale," *L'Action française*, Apr. 6 and 19, 1935.

——, "Les Idées positives," *La Gazette de France*, May 2, 1898.

——, *Les Idées royalistes sur les partis, l'état, la nation* (Paris, 1919).

——, "Il n'y a plus d'affaires Dreyfus," *La Gazette de France*, Jan. 19, 1899.

——, "Imposture et tenacité," *La Gazette de France*, Apr. 22, 1899.

——, "L'Institution de la Russie," *La Cocarde*, Nov. 5, 1894.

——, "Intermède philosophique:
La Cité juive: d'après le marquis de La Tour du Pin," *La Gazette de France*, Jan. 4, 1899;
Les Solutions: d'après le marquis de La Tour du Pin," *La Gazette de France*, Jan. 7, 1899.

——, *Ironie et poésie* (Paris, 1923).

——, "L'Italie et nous," *L'Action française*, Nov. 4, 1926.

——, "Le Jour des morts: Bossuet, Hugo, Musset et Taine," *Revue encyclopédique*, 1896, 760-763.

——, *Une jubilé* (Liège, 1926).

——, "Une justification économique de la charité," *La Reforme sociale*, 1886, 592-598.

——, *Kiel et Tanger, 1895-1905: la République française devant l'Europe, 1905-1913-1921* (Paris, 1921).

——, "Kiel et Tanger: la trahison constitutionelle," *La Revue critique des idées et des livres*, July, 1910, vol. x, 5-27.

——, *La Lettre à Schrameck* (Paris, 1925).

——, "Lettre d'Arles: jeux pour la patrie provençale," *La Gazette de France*, May 28, 1899.

——, *Lettre de Charles Maurras à sa Sainteté le Pape Pie XI, suivi de l'histoire d'un document* (Versailles, 1927).

——, "Une lettre de Mme. Juliette Adam," *La Gazette de France*, Oct. 27, 1901.

——, "Lettre de Provence: le faux printemps," *La Gazette de France*, Feb. 16, 1897.

——, "'Leurs figures' par Maurice Barrès:
L'Oeuvre d'art," *La Gazette de France*, Feb. 13, 1902;
Leur sens politique—et Barrès?," *La Gazette de France*, Feb. 16, 1902.

——, *Libéralisme et libertés: démocratie et peuple* (Paris, 1927).

——, "Linguistique: les patois de France," *Revue encyclopédique*, 1894, 272-273.

——, "Les Loisirs d'une ancien ministre," *La Gazette de France*, Apr. 6, 1902.

——, *Lorsque Hugo eut cent ans: indications* (Paris, 1927).

——, "Machiavel," *La Gazette de France*, Apr. 13, 1902.

——, *Mar e lono* (Paris, 1930).
——, *Le Mauvais traité: de la victoire à Locarno—chronique d'une décadence*, 2 vols. (Paris, 1928).
——, *Méditations sur la politique de Jeanne d'Arc* (Paris, 1931).
——, "Les Menées royalistes à la 'Patrie française,'" *La Gazette de France*, Mar. 21, 1899.
——, "Les Métèques," *La Cocarde*, Dec. 28, 1894.
——, "Mistral et Montenard: paysages des Provence," *La Revue universelle*, Dec. 1, 1923.
——, "Le 'Moi' dans la littérature," *Revue encyclopédique*, 1895, 218-220.
——, "Le Monodisme: psychologie d'une quiproquo," *La Gazette de France*, Apr. 26, 1899.
——, "Les Murailles d'Antibes," *La Cocarde*, Jan. 25, 1895.
——, "La Musée des passions humains," *Le Figaro*, Aug. 9, 1897.
——, *La Musique intérieure* (Paris, 1925) .
——, *Napoléon avec la France, ou contre la France?* (Paris, 1932).
——, "Nationalisme," *L'Action française*, Oct. 21, 1926.
——, "Nationalisme et catholicisme," *L'Action française*, Oct. 5, 1925.
——, "Nationalisme et impérialisme," *L'Action française*, Aug. 23, 1927.
——, "Le Nationalisme et la paix sociale," *L'Action française*, Mar. 15, 1922.
——, "Le Nationalisme intégral," *Le Soleil*, Mar. 2, 1900.
——, "La Nihilisme russe et la philosophie allemande," *La Reforme sociale*, Sept. 1, 1887.
——, "Notes de critique (in the *Gazette de France*):
Antiphysis: à propos d'un article de M. Emile Faguet," Aug. 11, 1901;
À propos d'un républicain," Oct. 25, 1901;
Le Génie allemande," July 7, 1901;
La Mathématique," Aug. 1, 1901;
Question sur les femmes nouvelles," July 14, 1901;
La Retrait de Barrès," Sept. 15, 1901.
——, "Notes de Provence: d'un paysan étatiste et d'un matelot anarchiste," *La Cocarde*, Sept. 20, 1894.
——, "Notre mandat syrien," *L'Action française*, Nov. 17, 1926.
—— (and Léon Daudet), *Notre Provence*, part ii, *À Martigues*, by Maurras (Paris, 1933).
——, *Les Nuits d'épreuve et la mémoire de l'état* (Paris, 1924).
——, "Organisme et démocratie," *La Gazette de France*, May 1, 4, 6, and 10, 1899.
——, "L'Origine du mal en Orient," *L'Action française*, Feb. 6, 1923.
——, *Pages littéraires choisies*, 6th edition (Paris, 1922).
——, "Pape et dictateur," *L'Action française*, Jan. 20, 1926.
——, *La Pape, la guerre et la paix* (Paris, 1917).
——, "Paroles d'un alsacien," *L'Action française*, Mar. 15, 1926.
——, *La Part du combattant* (Paris, 1917).
——, "La Part du combattant," *L'Action française*, May 12, 1921; Nov. 4, 1922; Jan. 11, 1926.

——, *La Patrie sacrifiée* (Rouen, 1928).
——, "Le Patriotisme honteux," *L'Action française*, Mar. 13, 1935.
——, "Le Paysage maître de l'âme," *Revue encyclopédique*, 1895, 199-205.
—— (and Joanny Drevet), *Paysages et cités de Provence* (Grenoble, 1932).
——, *Petite manuel de l'enquête sur la monarchie* (Versailles, 1928).
——, *Les Plus belles pages de Maurras* (Paris, 1931).
——, *La Politique de Charles Maurras*, vol. i: *1926-1927* (Paris, 1928).
——, "La Politique des Monod," *La Gazette de France*, June 27, 1897.
—— (and Maurice Pujo), *La Politique du Vatican* (Paris, 1928).
——, "La Politique et l'art nouveau," *La Gazette de France*, Dec. 12, 1901.
——, *Pour en sortir: ce qu'il faut à la France* (Paris, 1926).
——, *Pour la défense nationale:*
Décernez-moi le prix Nobel de la paix, vol. ii (Paris, 1931);
Les Lumières de la patrie, vol. iii (Paris, 1931);
Sur la cendre de nos foyers, vol. i (Paris, 1931).
——, *Les Princes des nuées* (Paris, 1928).
——, *Principes* (Paris, 1931).
——, *Prologue d'un essai sur la critique* (Paris, 1932).
——, *Promenade italienne* (Paris, 1929).
——, *Le Quadrilatère* (Paris, 1931).
——, *Quand les français ne s'aimaient pas: chronique d'une renaissance, 1895-1905* (Paris, 1926).
——, *Quatre nuits de Provence* (Paris, 1930).
——, "Quelle France?," *La Cocarde*, Jan. 3, 1895.
——, "Le Rattachement de l'Autriche," *L'Action française*, Jan. 26, 1926.
——, *Réflexions sur l'ordre en France, 1916-1917* (Paris, 1927).
——, "Joseph Reinach et M. Charavay," *La Gazette de France*, Feb. 5, 1899.
——, "M. Joseph Reinach: professeur d'impudence," *La Gazette de France*, Apr. 30, 1899.
——, "La Renaissance d'une nation: sur un page de Fustel," *La Gazette de France*, Jan., 23, 1902.
——, *La République de Martigues* (Paris, 1931).
—— (and J. Paul-Boncour), *La République et la décentralisation: un débat de 1903* (Paris, 1923).
——, "Révolutionnaire comme l'Evangile!," *La Gazette de France*, Apr. 19, 1899.
——, *Romantisme et révolution*, including *L'Avenir de l'intelligence; Auguste Comte; Le Romantisme féminin; Mademoiselle Monk; L'Invocation à Minerve; Trois idées politiques: Chateaubriand, Michelet, Sainte-Beuve* (Paris, 1925).
——, "Les Royalistes et la démocratie," *La Gazette de France*, May 16, 1899.
——, *La Sagesse de Mistral* (Paris, 1926).
——, "Sagesse! Sagesse!," *La Gazette de France*, Feb. 9, 1899.
——, "Scènes et doctrines du nationalisme: à Maurice Barrès," *La Gazette de France*, May 29, 1902.

——, "Le Secret du ministère, ou la raison de l'amnestie," *La Gazette de France*, Dec. 20, 1900.

——, *Les Secrets du soleil* (Paris, 1929).

——, "Société d'éthnographie nationale," *La Gazette de France*, Mar. 26, 1895.

——, *Sous la terreur ... 20e septembre à 15e novembre, 1927*, epilogue by Charles Maurras (Paris, 1927).

——, *Sous l'étoile du mage* (Paris, 1931).

——, "Le Suicide d'une nation: sur un page de Fustel," *La Gazette de France*, Jan. 19, 1902.

——, "Sur le conformisme à la mode," *L'Action française*, July 23, 1921.

——, "Sur le Rhin," *L'Action française*, July 24, 1927.

——, *Sur les étangs de Marthe entre Berre et Caronte* (Paris, 1927).

——, "Sur un mot de Barrès," *L'Action française*, Apr. 19, 1935.

——, "Le Système fédératif," *La Quinzaine*, Sept. and Oct., 1896, vol. xii, 51-73; 296-317.

——, "Taine et les monarchistes," *La Gazette de France*, Nov. 20, 1900.

——, *Théodore Aubanel* (Paris, 1927).

——, *Tombeaux* (Paris, 1921).

——, *Le Tombeau du prince* (Versailles, 1927).

——, *Triptique de Paul Bourget* (Paris, 1931).

——, *Les Trois aspects du Président Wilson* (Paris, 1920).

——, "Les Trois mensonges du 'Pensiero,'" *La Cocarde*, Jan. 2, 1895.

——, "Trois romantiques: M. Gustav Kahn, M. Émile Verhaeren, M. Georges Rodenbach," *Revue encylopédique*, 1896, 216-219.

——, "Universités régionales," *Le Soleil*, Jan. 3, 1896.

——, "Le Vatican contre le réarmement britannique," *L'Action française*, Mar. 13, 1935.

——, "La Vie nouvelle de Dante," *Revue encyclopédique*, Mar. 5, 1898, 205-209.

——, "La Vision de moi de Maurice Barrès," *La Revue indépendante*, Apr., 1891, vol. xix, 43-53.

——, *Le Voyage d'Athènes* (Paris, 1929); published originally in *La Gazette de France*, Apr. 15, 17, 18, 19, 20, 22, May 29, 1896; and republished as part of *Anthinéa* in 1901.

Mazel, Henri, *Histoire et psychologie de l'affaire Dreyfus* (Paris, 1934).

Le Mercure de France, Apr., 1895, vol. xiv, 1-65, "Une enquête franco-allemande."

Meyer, Eduard, *Der Freiheitsgedanke in seiner ethischen Bedeutung bei Nietzsche* (Cologne, 1921).

Millet, Raymond, and Simon Arbellot, "Les Ligues et groupements," *Le Temps*, Jan. 24, 27, 28, 29; Feb. 3, 4, 9, 10, 11, 17, 18, 19, 21; Mar. 3, 14, 24; Apr. 23, 24, 26, 1935.

Mistral, Frédéric and Marie, *Excursion en Italie*, with translation into the French by Charles Maurras (Paris, 1930).

Mistral, Frédéric, *Mes origines: mémoires et récits*, translation (Paris, 1906).

——, *Miréo: pouemo provençau*, with French translation (Paris, 1921).

——, *Oeuvres de Frédéric Mistral,* text and translation, 4 vols. (Paris, 1886-1889).

——, *Proso d'armana,* with French translation (Paris, 1926).

Mitscherlich, Waldemar, *Der Nationalismus Westeuropas* (Leipzig, 1920).

Montesquiou, Léon, comte de, *Le Réalisme de Bonald* (Paris, 1911).

Moon, Parker T., *The Labor Problem and the Social Catholic Movement in France* (New York, 1921).

Moreau, Lucien, "Autour du Nietzschéisme," *L'Action française,* June 1, 1905, vol. xviii.

Moreau, Pierre, *Le Victorieux XXe siècle* (Paris, 1925).

Morland, Jacques, *Enquête sur l'influence allemande* (Paris, 1903).

Muret, Charlotte Touzalin, *French Royalist Doctrines since the Revolution* (New York, 1933).

La Muse française: revue de la poésie, June 10, 1927, vol. vi, no. vi, " Charles Maurras: poète et critique de la poésie," the entire number.

Mussolini, Benito, *Edition définitive des oeuvres et discours,* vol. i (Paris, 1935).

——, *Le Fascisme: doctrine, institutions* (Paris, 1933).

Nietzsche, Friedrich, *Der Wille zur Macht: Versuch einer Umwerthung aller Werthe* (Leipzig, 1901).

——, *Ecce homo* (Leipzig, 1911).

——, *Thus Spake Zarathustra,* translated by Thomas Common (The Modern Library, New York, date ?).

Oakesmith, John, *Race and Nationality: an Inquiry into the Origin and Growth of Patriotism* (New York, 1919).

Paris, Henri, comte de (*The editorial*), *Courier royal,* May 10, 1935, 1st year, no. vi.

Parmentier, Florian, *Histoire de la littérature française de 1885 à nos jours* (Paris, 1914).

Parodi, D., *Traditionalism et démocratie* (Paris, 1909).

Péguy, Charles, *Notre patrie* (Paris, 1915).

Péladin, Josephin, *Curieuse,* vol. ii of *La Décadence latine* (Paris, 1886).

Pierre, Jules, abbé, *Avec Nietzsche à l'assaut du christianisme* (Limoges, 1910).

——, *La " Gageure folle," ou l'apologétique et l'orthodoxie de M. Charles Maurras jugées par des théologiens antimodernes et antidémocrates et lettre au R. P. Pègues, O.P.* (Paris, 1926).

——, *L'Immoralisme de M. Charles Maurras, ou trente années de guerre contre la morale chrétienne* (Paris, 1927).

Planhol, René, *L'Oeuvre de Charles Maurras,* in Charles Maurras' *Le Bibliophile Barthou* (Paris, 1929).

Platz, Hermann, *Geistige Kämpfe im modernen Frankreich* (Munich, 1922).

——, " Der Nationalismus im französischen Denken der Vorkriegszeit," *Deutsche Rundschau,* Jan. and Feb., 1919, vol. clxxiii, 12-33; also in Joachim Kühn's *Der Nationalismus im Leben der dritten Republik* (Berlin, 1920).

Poincaré, Raymond, *Au service de la France:neuf années de souvenirs*, vol. i (Paris, 1926).

Prévost-Paradol, Lucien A., *La France nouvelle*, 14th edition (Paris, 1868).

Proudhon, P.-J., *Du principe fédératif* (Paris, 1868).

——, *La Guerre et la paix*, introduction and notes by H. Moysset (Paris, 1927).

——, *Jésus et les origines du christianisme*, arranged and edited by Clement Rochel (Paris, 1896).

Rageot, Gaston, "Deux faces de l'esprit contemporain: Anatole France, Maurice Barrès," *Causeries françaises*, May 16, 1924.

Reinach, Joseph, *Histoire de l'affaire Dreyfus*, 7 vols. (Paris, 1904).

——, *Les Petites catilinaires:*
Bruno-Le-Fileur, vol. iii (Paris, 1889);
Le Cheval noir, vol. ii (Paris, 1889);
La Foire boulangiste, vol. i (Paris, 1889).

Renan, Ernest, *Essais de morale et de critique*, 4th edition (Paris, 1889).

——, *Qu'est-ce qu'une nation?*, in *Discourses et conférences*, 2nd edition, 276-310 (Paris, 1887).

——, *La reforme intellectuelle et morale* (Paris, 1872).

La Revue critique des idées et des livres, May 10, 1911, vol. xiii, 257-272, "Discourses prononcé au diner de la 'Revue critique,'" the occasion being the 25th anniversary of Charles Maurras' literary life.

Rey, Etienne, *La Renaissance de l'orgueil français* (Paris, 1912).

Roche, Alphonse V., *Les Idées tradionalistes en France de Rivarol à Charles Maurras* (Urbana, Ill., 1937).

Rose, John Holland, *Nationality in Modern History* (London, 1916).

Roux, Marie de, *Charles Maurras et le nationalisme de l'Action française*, 26th edition (Paris, 1926).

——, "Un critique du nationalisme: M. Georges Guy-Grand," *La Revue critique des idées et des livres*, Feb. 10, 1912, vol. xvi, 257-266.

Séailles, Gabriel, *Ernest Renan: essai de biographie psychologique* (Paris, 1895).

Segard, Achille, *Charles Maurras et les idées royalistes* (Paris, 1919).

Seignobos, Charles, in Ernest Lavisse's *Histoire de France contemporaine*:
Le Déclin de l'empire et l'établissement de la 3e république, 1859-1875, vol. vii (Paris, 1921);
L'Évolution de la 3e république, 1875-1914, vol. viii (Paris, 1921).

Sorel, Georges, *Les Illusions du progrès*, 4th edition (Paris, 1927).

——, *Réflexions sur la violence*, 7th edition (Paris, 1930).

Souday, Paul, *Les Livres du temps*, 3 vols. (Paris, 1929).

Soury, Jules, *Campagne nationaliste, 1899-1901* (Paris, 1902).

——, *Les Fonctions du cerveau* (Paris, 1891).

——, *Lettre à Charles Maurras* (Paris, 1899).

Spronk, Maurice, "Le Nationalisme," *L'Action française*, Aug. 1, 1899, vol. i, 15-26.

Stannard, Harold, *Gambetta and the Foundation of the Third Republic* (London, 1921).

Stendhal (Henri Beyle), *Rome, Naples et Florence*, preface by Charles Maurras, 2 vols. (Paris, 1919).
Strowski, Fortunat, *Nationalisme ou patriotisme* (Paris, 1933).
Taine, H. A., *History of English Literature*, translated by H. van Laun, vol. i (Philadelphia, 1896).
——, *Les Origines de la France contemporaine*, 23rd edition, 12 vols. (Paris, 1901).
Taitinger, Pierre, *Les Cahiers de la jeune France* (Paris, 1926).
Talvart, Hector, *Fiche de Charles Maurras* (La Rochelle, 1930).
——, *Maurras religieux et suscitateur de foi* (La Rochelle, 1930).
——, *Louis Veuillot et la monarchie* (La Rochelle, 1927).
——, *Veuillot, Maurras et les éternels libéraux* (La Rochelle, 1927).
Tharaud, Jérôme and Jean, *Mes années chez Barrès* (Paris, 1928).
——, *La Vie et la mort de Déroulède* (Paris, 1914).
Thibaudet, Albert, *Les Idées de Charles Maurras*, 7th edition (Paris, 1920).
——, *Mistral, ou la république du soleil* (Paris, 1930).
——, *Les Princes lorrains*, 13th edition (Paris, 1924).
——, *La Vie de Maurice Barrès*, 2nd edition (Paris, 1921).
Tocqueville, Alexis de, *L'Ancien régime et la révolution*, 7th edition (Paris, 1866).
Truc, Gonzague, *Apologie pour l'Action française* (Paris, 1927).
——, *Charles Maurras et son temps* (Paris, 1917).
Valois, Henri, *Contre le mensonge et la calomnie* (Paris, 1926).
Vaugeois, Henri, *La Fin de l'erreur française* (Paris, 1928).
——, *Notre pays: figures de France, voyages d'Action française, le temps de la guerre* (Paris, 1916).
——, "Réaction d'abord," *L'Action française*, Aug. 1, 1899, vol. i, 1-15.
Vaussard, Maurice, *Enquête sur le nationalisme* (Paris, 1923).
Vettard, Camille, "Maurice Barrès et Jules Soury," *Mercure de France*, vol. clxx, 685-695.
Vialatoux, J., *La Doctrine catholique et l'école de Maurras* (Lyon, 1927).
Vizetelly, E. A., *Republican France, 1870-1912* (Boston, 1912).
Voguë, E. M. de, *Les Morts qui parlent* (Paris, 1922).
Watson, John B., *Behavior* (New York, 1914).
——, *Psychology from the Standpoint of a Behaviorist* (Philadelphia, 1919).
Weil, Bruno, *L'Affaire Dreyfus*, translated from the German (Paris, 1930).
——, *Grandeur et décadence du général Boulanger*, translated by L. C. Herbert (Paris, 1931).
——, *Panama*, translated by Albert Lehman (Paris, 1934).
Wissler, Clark, *Man and Culture* (New York, 1923).
Zévaès, Alexandre, *L'Affaire Dreyfus* (Paris, 1930).
——, *Au temps du Boulangisme* (Paris, 1930).
——, *Histoire de la troisième république, 1870-1926* (Paris, 1926).
——, *Le Scandale du Panama* (Paris, 1931).

INDEX